Frontispiece   Aldobrandino of Siena, *Livres pour la santé garder* (*Régime du corps*), late thirteenth century. British Library, Sloane MS 2435, f. 10ᵛ.

Music as Medicine

The History of Music Therapy since Antiquity

Edited by

PEREGRINE HORDEN

Aldershot • Brookfield USA • Singapore • Sydney

Published by
Ashgate Publishing Limited
Gower House
Croft Road
Aldershot
Hants GU11 3HR
England

Ashgate Publishing Company
Old Post Road
Brookfield
Vermont 05036–9704
USA

Ashgate website: http://www.ashgate.com

British Library Cataloguing in Publication Data

Music as Medicine: The History of Music Therapy since
   Antiquity.
   1. Music therapy—History.
   I. Horden, Peregrine.
   615.8'5154

Library of Congress Catalog Card Number: 99–68871

ISBN 1 84014 299 5

This book is printed on acid free paper

Printed and bound in Great Britain by
MPG Books Ltd, Bodmin, Cornwall

Contents

List of Figures   vii
List of Contributors   ix
Acknowledgements   xi

Introduction   1
   Peregrine Horden

1   Musical Solutions: Past and Present in Music Therapy   4
   Peregrine Horden

PART I: ANCIENT LITERATE TRADITIONS
Commentary on Part I, with a Note on China   43
   Peregrine Horden

2   Music Therapy in Antiquity   51
   Martin West

3   Jewish and Muslim Traditions of Music Therapy   69
   Amnon Shiloah

4   Music Therapy: Some Possibilities in the Indian Tradition   84
   J. B. Katz

PART II: MEDIEVAL EUROPE
Commentary on Part II, with a Note on the Early Middle Ages   103
   Peregrine Horden

5   Music and Medicine in the Thirteenth Century   109
   Christopher Page

6   Music Therapy in the Later Middle Ages:
   The Case of Hugo van der Goes   120
   Peter Murray Jones

PART III: RENAISSANCE AND EARLY MODERN EUROPE
Commentary on Part III, with a Note on Paracelsus   147
   Peregrine Horden

7   Marsilio Ficino, the Second Orpheus   154
   Angela Voss

8 Music, Melancholy, and Medical Spirits in Early
   Modern Thought   173
   Penelope Gouk

9 Curing Man and the Cosmos: The Power of Music in
   French Renaissance Poetry   195
   Noel Heather

10 Musical Treatments for Lovesickness:
    The Early Modern Heritage   213
    Linda Phyllis Austern

PART IV: TARANTISM
Commentary on Part IV, with a Note on the Origins
   of Tarantism   249
   Peregrine Horden

11 Ritualized Illness and Music Therapy: Views of Tarantism
    in the Kingdom of Naples   255
    David Gentilcore

12 Medical Theories of Tarantism in Eighteenth-Century Spain   273
    Pilar León Sanz

13 Tarantism in Contemporary Italy: The Tarantula's Dance
    Reviewed and Revived   293
    Karen Lüdtke

PART V: MODERN CURRENTS
Commentary on Part V, with Notes on Nineteenth-Century
   America and on Mesmerism and Theosophy   315
   Peregrine Horden

14 Music as Cause and Cure of Illness in Nineteenth-
    Century Europe   338
    Cheryce Kramer

15 Shamanism, Music, and the Soul Train   353
    Keith Howard

16 The Music Therapy Profession in Modern Britain   375
    Helen M. Tyler

Index   395

List of Figures

Frontispiece   Aldobrandino of Siena, *Livres pour la santé garder* (*Régime du corps*), late thirteenth century. British Library, Sloane MS 2435, f. 10^v. By permission of the British Library, London.   ii

6.1   Queen Mary Psalter, early fourteenth century. British Library Royal MS 2.B.VII, f. 51^v. By permission of the British Library, London.   125

6.2   Bible of Duke Borso d'Este, mid-fifteenth century. Biblioteca Estense Universitaria, Modena, MS V.G.12, f. 119^v. By permission of the Ministero per i Beni e le Attività Culturali.   126

8.1   The divine monochord, from Robert Fludd, *Utriusque cosmi historia*, vol. 1 (1617), p. 90. Wellcome Trust Medical Photographic Library, London.   176

8.2   Man the microcosm, from Robert Fludd, *Utriusque cosmi historia*, vol. 2 (1619), p. 275. Wellcome Trust Medical Photographic Library, London.   177

9.1   The universe according to Nicolas Lefèvre de la Boderie, from the opening to 'Introduction sur l'harmonie du monde', in Guy Lefèvre de la Boderie (trans.), *L'harmonie du monde* (Paris, 1578).   199

10.1   Philip Ayres, *Emblemata amatoria* (London, 1683), sigs. E3^v–E4. By permission of the Folger Shakespeare Library.   214

10.2   Jacob Cats, *Proteus ofte Minnebeelden* (Amsterdam, 1627), p. 254. National Gallery of Art Library, Washington DC.   224

10.3   P. C. Hoofts, *Minnezinnebeelden*, in *Werken*
        (Amsterdam, 1671), sig. Een. National Gallery of
        Art Library, Washington DC.   229

10.4   Jean 1er Le Blond after Pieter van Mol, *Omnia
        vincit amor nec mucica vincit amorem* ([Paris]
        n.d.). By permission of the Bibliothèque Nationale
        de France, Paris.   233

10.5   Interior lid of Giovanni Francesco Antegnati[a],
        pentagonal virginal, 1537. Victoria and Albert
        Museum, London, keyboard catalogue no. 2.   236

10.6   Gabriel Metsu, *Cello Player*. Buckingham Palace,
        London. The Royal Collection © Her Majesty The
        Queen.   238

11.1   Athanasius Kircher, *Magnes sive de arte magnetica*
        (Rome, 1641), facing p. 874. Wellcome Trust
        Photographic Medical Library, London.   258

12.1   Geographical distribution of cases of tarantism
        discussed by eighteenth-century Spanish authors.   276

12.2   Representation of the biological cycle of the
        tarantula by F. X. Cid, *Tarantismo observado en
        España* (Madrid, 1787), p. 19. By permission of the
        Biblioteca Nacional, Madrid.   279

12.3   Music in F. X. Cid, *Tarantismo observado en
        España* (Madrid, 1787). By permission of the
        Biblioteca Nacional, Madrid.   285

List of Contributors

Linda Phyllis Austern, *Northwestern University*

David Gentilcore, *University of Leicester*

Penelope Gouk, *Wellcome Unit for the History of Medicine,
University of Manchester*

Noel Heather, *Royal Holloway College, University of London*

Peregrine Horden, *Royal Holloway College, University of London*

Keith Howard, *School of Oriental and African Studies,
University of London*

Peter Murray Jones, *King's College, Cambridge*

J. B. Katz, *Westminster School, London*

Cheryce Kramer, *University College, London*

Pilar León Sanz, *University of Navarra, Pamplona*

Karen Lüdtke, *Linacre College, Oxford*

Christopher Page, *Sidney Sussex College, Cambridge*

Amnon Shiloah, *Hebrew University, Jerusalem*

Helen M. Tyler, *Nordoff–Robbins Music Therapy Centre, London*

Angela Voss, *University of Kent*

Martin West, *All Souls College, Oxford*

Acknowledgements

This volume originated in a conference, which I proposed as long ago as 1994, and which was finally held at Royal Holloway College, University of London, in April 1997. I am immensely grateful for the enthusiasm of the participants, and for the financial support extended to the conference by the Wellcome Trust, the Society for the Social History of Medicine, the History Department of Royal Holloway, and the Warden and Fellows of All Souls College, Oxford. Publication of the proceedings has been greatly facilitated by a grant from the bequest of the late Miss Isobel Thornley to the University of London. At Ashgate, Rachel Lynch and Caroline Cornish were tireless in support of the volume's progress. Humaira Erfan Ahmed prepared camera-ready copy with extraordinary skill and care. Also deserving the warmest acknowledgement are the patient contributors, both those who revised their original conference presentations and those who responded keenly and efficiently to my commissioning of new essays. For advice and references bearing on the Commentaries and Chapter 1, I am grateful to Gary Ansdell, Margaret Bent, Christopher Cullen, Robert Darnton, Ruth Davis, Sarah Hibberd, Jane Lightfoot, Grant Olwage, Derek Parfit, David Parkin, Paul Robertson, Emilie Savage-Smith, Grant Scott, and Tony Wang, as well as to several contributors. In particular, the Commentary on Part III could not have been written without the expert assistance of Ian Maclean and Charles Webster.

Introduction

Peregrine Horden

At various times and in various cultures over the past two and a half millennia – and probably still further back in time – music has been medicine. Performing or listening to music have variously been thought to achieve something more than arousal or entertainment; something different from, though often related to, enhanced spiritual awareness; something that beneficially outlasts the performance – that maintains or restores the health of mind and, even, body.

How exactly has this therapeutic power of music been conceptualized and explained? Who has done that – why, and in what social or intellectual setting? Who has actually used music as or in therapy? What were their techniques and purposes? How important has music therapy been within the broad medical and musical culture of any given place and time – central or marginal, occasional or enduring?

These historical questions and others arising from them are the focus of the present volume. They are addressed (perhaps for the first time in English) in a systematic, scholarly, and sceptical manner. The volume's aim is to provide a history of music therapy since antiquity that is as comprehensive as the available space, expertise and evidence permit. The primary focus is the European intellectual and medical tradition, from its classical roots to the development of a music therapy profession in the decades since the Second World War. At least some comment is ventured on every major period in between, and, specifically, on every century since the end of the Middle Ages. In addition, there are chapters on the Judaic and Islamic traditions, so important to medieval European developments; on India; and on South-East Asia. There is thus broad geographical scope as well as chronological depth with respect to one area. Editorial commentaries on the five parts into which the book is divided outline the themes of each chapter, some connections between chapters, and topics that the ideal volume might have embraced.

With such broad coverage, questions of definition obviously arise. What is to count as music, what as medicine? How should the relationship between theory and practice be understood? On what yardstick can musical cures be measured? No editorial stipulation will be made here, other than that the term 'music therapy' is to be understood in a very large sense, as a convenient label, rather than in the narrower terms to which modern professionals might adhere. Some aspects of the problem of definition are touched on in Chapter 1. But ultimately it must be for each contributor to wrestle with the task of refining our notions of music and medicine so that they can be sensitively applied to possibly very alien therapeutic cultures. A comparative volume such as this must steer an uneasy course between Enlightenment universalism and Romantic relativism: between crassly imposing our own categories on the past and merely rehearsing, without analysis, whatever categories arise from the evidence. Indigenous conceptions of health and healing, of music and cosmology, are part of the problem, not the solution.

In a field of such difficulty, comparatively little explored, all findings are necessarily provisional. The aim is to synthesize what can already be known, to search neglected sources, to offer some original perspectives, and to suggest where more research may be fruitful. We can do no more than establish the contours of the subject. Further enquiry and, in particular, more sophisticated exploration of the changing cultural environment of music therapy, must be delegated to other volumes.[1]

It is hoped that the present collection of essays will interest audiences as diverse as its contents. Three of the contributors are anthropologists, two are musicologists, one is a practising music therapist; the majority are historians. Most, therefore, are investigating the past, sometimes the very distant past, with no more thought for the present than is inevitable in historiography. They write without reference to modern professional practice; their history is not teleological. That is, they are not trying to find the historical roots of modern music therapy. Indeed, we shall see that the force of the classical tradition, within which much of their subject matter must be located, means that they are more often looking backwards than forwards. Something similar is even true of the two ethnographic contributions below. The shaman (Chapter 15), a figure often invoked by historians, presents himself to the ethnographer as burdened with a history – or, better, a historical interpretation – that reaches back into a 'traditional' past of considerable antiquity. And clearly the attenuated world of contemporary tarantism (Chapter 13) can also only be understood in historical terms. Alone amongst our contributors, the music therapist (Chapter 16) is explicitly seeking out the origins of her own current practice. In that sense hers is – quite legitimately – a 'present-minded' contribution. All the others are 'past-minded'.

Overall, then, the past is not set out in this volume simply to help us to understand the present, an expanded version of the historical backdrop that might be included in a professional manual. The present may, however, be used to understand the past: to enliven our sense of its possibilities. If we are asking what has been done and said about music therapy in history, it will at least be useful, as a preliminary, to gain some idea of what such therapy can do today. Accordingly, Chapter 1 begins in the present and works its way, across the domains of music therapy and ethnomusicology, back into the past. In the process it broaches the question of continuity, which will loom large over subsequent contributions. After that editorial opening, the historical sequence of chapters that makes up most of the collection begins in the remotest past and works its way forward to the present. In our beginning is our end, therefore. And we begin under the auspices of that strange figure of German Romanticism, Novalis: 'every illness is a musical problem – its cure a musical solution'.

Notes

1.   See the companion to this one, P. Gouk (ed.), *Musical Healing in Cultural Contexts* (Aldershot, 2000).

CHAPTER ONE

Musical Solutions:[1] Past and Present in Music Therapy

Peregrine Horden

I

'The present age is one of overproduction ... never has there been so much music-making and so little musical experience of a vital order.' Thus Constant Lambert, the composer. He was writing in 1934, in the classic *Music Ho! A Study of Music in Decline*.[2] The chapter is entitled 'The appalling popularity of music'. It goes on to complain that, thanks to the 'gramophone', the 'wireless' and the loudspeaker, 'music of a sort is everywhere and at every time'. The result: total anaesthesia. If the BBC broadcast the Last Trump, Lambert expostulates, 'it is doubtful if it would interfere with the cry of "No Trumps" from the card table'.

> We have at present no idea of what havoc may be wrought in a few years' time by the combined effect of the noise of city life and the noise of city music – an actual atrophy of the aural nerves would seem to be indicated ... We live in an age of tonal debauch where the blunting of the finer edge of pleasure leads only to a more hysterical and frenetic attempt to recapture it. It is obvious that second-rate mechanical music is the most suitable fare for those to whom musical experience is no more than a mere aural tickling, just as the prostitute provides the most suitable outlet for those to whom sexual experience is no more than the periodic removal of a recurring itch. The loud speaker is the street walker of music.[3]

Were he writing today, Lambert's metaphors would doubtless be even more florid. Music is omnipresent, and – worse – mechanized to an extent that he could scarcely have envisaged. Only within certain fundamentalist Muslim states is there any escaping its dictatorship over the acoustic environment, its unvarying and literally inhuman rhythm. The agents of infiltration now include the 'mini-system' and the Walkman. Much of their output is, however, ignored, left as background. The responses evoked by that which really is listened to, however 'profound' they may be, are fleeting. In a relatively tiny market for recorded classical music, 'crossovers', tenor megastars, or concert warhorses predominate, while for the minority there is huge variety that encourages a detached promiscuity among collectors, a pseudo-culture of far vaster proportions than Malraux's 'museum without walls'.[4] To quote George Steiner, a more measured, but no less disheartened, critic of aural culture than Lambert:

> If we choose, we can put on Opus 131 while eating the breakfast cereal. We can play the *St. Matthew Passion* any hour of the day or week ... the effects are ambiguous: there can be an unprecedented intimacy, but also a devaluation ... A Muzak of the sublime envelops us.[5]

And with the mechanical beat and harmonic banality of most popular music, profundity, even of the fleeting kind furnished by the latest technology, is seldom in question. Not only can music be so readily meaningless, an addiction to decibels and metrical bass; it can be positively damaging, to the ear when brought too close to loudspeakers, to society when the sound falls directly on the inner ear from the headphone, perhaps to the whole intellect.[6]

Some recent experiments can be adduced which seem to illustrate that potential for damage, at a very basic, cellular level. But they also point towards an alternative, and less bleak way of summing up our aural culture. Despite all the evidence that a greater quantity of music is more utterly ephemeral and trivialized in our time than ever before, attention can, increasingly, also be called to havens of serious and profound response that relieve the global landscape of rock and its offspring.

It is not just a question of a minority for whom listening to classical music is life itself. Picture the following. Six human cell cultures are aligned *in vitro*. Five are of tumour cells – malignant glioma, breast adenocarcinoma, colon adenocarcinoma, skin malignant melanoma and lung carcinoma; the remaining one is of normal dermal fibroblasts. The cultures are placed in separate humidified incubators. One incubator contains a water-resistant hi-fi speaker connected to a portable stereo system. The control incubator has no such musical attachment. Each culture is tested in triplicate for an average of four experiments. Music plays from cassette tapes from 5.00 p.m. to 9.00 a.m. continuously for ten days at a constant volume. One type of music consists of 'primordial sounds' – Sama Veda from the 'Maharishi Ayur-Veda system of natural health care'; the other is 'Back in Black' by the rock band AC/DC. Compared with no music at all, primordial sound significantly decreases the average growth across cell lines. In the presence of hard rock, however, growth of cells, though inconsistent, tends significantly to increase. 'We conclude,' write the authors of the research paper just summarized, 'that sound has an effect on the growth of neoplastic and normal human cells in vitro'.[7] But the possible newspaper headlines can be imagined: hard rock gives you cancer; Ayurvedic sound cures cancer. How can this happen?

Cells and intracellular structures apparently vibrate dynamically. These vibrations may play a role in the cell's self-regulation, affecting its shape, motility, and signal transduction. They can be changed by both growth factors and carcinogenesis. Incoming vibrations, such as sound waves, are perhaps transferred from the peripheral membrane to the nucleus and DNA. Sama Veda has a preponderance of low frequency tones and a regular slow rhythm, which may, by some means yet to be determined, restore the DNA to its own normal low-frequency vibrations. 'Back in Black', on the other hand, includes more high-frequency tones than the 'primordial sound' and its tempo and rhythm are alike irregular. It literally sets up the wrong vibrations.

The experiments and hypotheses I have been reporting are those of three members of the Department of Pathology, College of Medicine, Ohio State University. Their work was supported by the Lancaster Foundation, Bethesda, Maryland, and also by the Maharishi Ayur-Veda Foundation of America. There are three reasons for selecting their paper as an opening example in this collaborative historical enquiry into music's healing potential.[8]

First, it can stand as an extreme instance of how seriously the powers of music are nowadays being taken – a *ne plus ultra* of musical therapy to set against the provocatively glum panorama with which I prefaced it. For cancer, along with AIDS, is the most terrifying modern disease. And in this example we are being told that music – without benefit of psychosomatic mechanism, cultural expectation, placebo effect and so on – is apparently capable of retarding the growth of cancer cells, at least *in vitro*.

Second, the paper represents the ambiguous status of musical therapeutics today. The research project could hardly be described as mainstream. It comes from the world of complementary medicine. It appears in the relatively new journal *Alternative Therapies in Clinical Practice*. And its purpose, one senses, is more to endorse than to test the 'system of natural health care known as Maharishi Ayur-Veda, which ... utilizes "primordial" sounds as one of its techniques for restoring health'.[9] On the other hand, the authors can reasonably assert that they are not alone in their finding that sound or music can have a significant and positive impact on living organisms:[10]

> A study conducted in India showed that experimental plants exposed to sound waves in the form of Nadeshwaram music showed more vigorous growth ... In the US, Hicks demonstrated that corn receiving broadcast of a continuous low note had an increased yield ... Retallack conducted a study in which plants showed a positive reaction when exposed to Ravi Shankar or Bach, growing toward the speaker, while a second group of plants exhibited a negative reaction to acid rock, growing away from the speaker and showing a random growth pattern.[11]

As such research comes to seem less marginal, the finding that plants or cell cultures have better musical taste than people will presumably lose its shock value. Meanwhile, its proponents can point to others involved in music therapy whose standing is less ambiguous than their own: professional music therapists and those researching music's psycho-physiological effects (see further below, and Tyler, Chapter 16).

A third reason for using this paper is that it opens up a historical perspective. Besides a sweeping appeal to congenial research by others, it looks to the past for legitimation. It looks to the non-European past above all, to Ayurvedic healing in ancient India; but also to the medical antiquity of the Persians and Hebrews; and additionally to the classical tradition in Europe, a tradition which runs from the Greeks to the Renaissance and on into the nineteenth century (and is the main subject of this volume).[12] Present-day enquiry is presented as continuous with the efforts of these much earlier cultures. The relationship of music to medicine is portrayed as almost always having been close. An analogy is implicitly drawn with traditional ways in which the regularity of music (harmonic or rhythmic) has been thought to alleviate irregularity or imbalance (dissonance) in the mind or body. To such traditions there has been only one interruption: 'the technological explosion of allopathic medicine in the 20th century'.[13]

To sum up so far: the findings of the research paper which I have been relaying are of ambiguous stature as normal science; they occupy an extreme position on the spectrum of musical possibilities, at the opposite end from the trivializing of so much contemporary music. None the less, they open up a surprising range of therapeutic territories. These territories can be labelled – not altogether objectively – the 'heterodox', the 'professional', and the 'historical'. The professional is mainstream music therapy in Europe and America; the heterodox represents a variety of non-mainstream currents; history is the domain to which they both variously appeal for precedent or legitimacy. I shall spend the rest of this chapter looking at each in turn, to sketch what continuities and discontinuities have been discerned within and between them – and with how much justification. I shall thus, as intimated in the preceding Introduction, be moving from the present back into the past, in order to open the ground for subsequent chapters, which follow a reverse course, from antiquity back to the present.

II

The heterodox shows itself in a variety of forms and has been given a variety of more or less pejorative labels: New Age, para-scientific, esoteric, and so on. Animating many of these is an appeal to some non- (or perhaps omni-) denominational spirituality. Certainly there is a common aspiration to proclaim musical response as something more than a passing pleasure, a temporary psychological and somatic reconfiguration. 'While I'm singing my soul is beautiful', muses Luciano Pavarotti, drawing on the analogy between personal and cosmic order which we shall encounter many more times in what follows.

It's not ego, like some think. It's therapy – for me and the audience. People who listen to music want to be happy in this stupid
life today when everyone has taken to drugs … There have been
periods in life when religion was important … The god of today
is negative gossip.[14]

Until the tenor megastar changes all that, presumably. There are
rock equivalents, equally ready to substitute their health-restoring art
for contemporary negativity. In the companion volume to this one,
Linda Austern places The Smashing Pumpkins' album, *Mellon Collie
and the Infinite Sadness*, in a tradition of musical auto-therapy that
descends from Robert Burton.[15] Those seeking a less muscular
therapy than Messrs Pumpkins' or Pavarotti's find ready encouragement in CD catalogues and web sites. 'David Naegele creates [in his
CD *Temple in the Forest*] a tranquil meditative environment …
evoking an overwhelming feeling of renewal and well-being'. One
disc of music by Stephen Rhodes, based on 'mesmerising patterns of
hypnotic harmony', is simply entitled *Music for Healing*. Another,
Inner Peace, is confidently promoted as 'stress-busting'.

In this musical cauldron, Gregorian chant can meet New Age,
pseudo-orientalism or earth magic to promote spiritual journeying, or,
more accurately, its sales rhetoric.[16] Debussy, Schubert, Aretha
Franklin and Crosby, Stills, Nash and Young, are all recommended
impartially as vehicles of healing.[17] Played while in your bath, a track
entitled 'Echoes of Ages', on a CD called *Bliss*, will induce perfect
relaxation.[18] The appeal to the past may be a little more specific. Sung
narratives of miraculous healing in the *Cantigas de Santa Maria* compiled for the thirteenth-century King Alfonso the Wise are recommended on a CD cover (SK 62263) as a cure for the evils of moder-
nity.[19] The School of Music Thanatology at the 'Chalice of Repose
Project' within the St Patrick Hospital, Missoula, Missouri, advertises
a 'clinical practice that prescribes music [live voice and harp] to tend
to the needs of the dying. The school draws its inspiration from 11th-
century French monastic medicine'.[20] This is doubtless a serious and
professional form of palliative medicine. Its historical sense is a little
weaker, though: in medieval monastic ritual for the dying it was the
anointing of the sick which was quasi-medicinal; the accompanying
liturgy was directed to God.[21] In dealing with this whole topic, it can

be hard to know what to take seriously. During 1998, BBC Radio 3 broadcast the assertion of an organist that we each have a special tone which resonates with the whole being and promotes health if sung or hummed for a long time – an old idea that 'goes back to the walls of Jericho'. Only the date of the broadcast – 1st April – distinguished this from many a programme extolling the mantra, or for that matter from another Radio 3 talk, this time about the monochord, a strung healing table of a kind that doubtless has equally venerable antecedents.

For all the apparent indifference generated by the mechanization of music in the second half of the twentieth century, there is clearly widespread heterodox interest in music's healing capacity, whether the music is part of complementary or New Age therapies, the vehicle of auto-therapy in the private world of the headphones, or something more mainstream. Here are two examples of that interest.

The first has been remarked with surprising infrequency in discussions of music therapy. It is the response to *Awakenings*. This was Oliver Sacks's famous account of the 'semi-survivors' of the sleeping sickness epidemic of the 1920s, patients very often immobilized into post-encephalitic Parkinsonism until revivified in various ways over four decades later by the 'miracle drug' L-DOPA. Fascination with their history is such that the book has run through several editions and its contents have inspired plays, documentaries and a feature film.[22] In the book, as in some of its reincarnations, 'music has been the profoundest non-chemical medication for our patients'.[23] Music roused the akinetic to normal movement and calmed the excited – for the duration of its playing.[24] A musician patient, who knew all Chopin by heart, had merely to be told an opus number to play the music over to herself in her mind.[25] Most, of course, needed mechanical assistance:

> One minute would see Miss D. compressed, clenched, and blocked, or jerking, ticcing, and jabbering – like a sort of human bomb; the next, with the sound of music from a wireless or gramophone, the complete disappearance of all these ... and their replacement by a blissful ease and flow of movement ... It was necessary that the music be *legato*; *staccato* music (and especially percussion bands) sometimes had a bizarre effect ... [26]

A more recent sign of popular preoccupation with such phenomena were the thousands of letters received by Paul Robertson,[27] the presenter of a Channel 4 series broadcast in May 1996, 'Music and the Mind', which was accompanied by a booklet of the same title. The resonances with a broader culture of musical therapy were unmistakable. After the opening exploration of the neurology of musical response, the second programme was called 'Healing and Harmony'. Not merely was the familiar equation of bodily and musical order repeated; the brain in particular was seen as 'musicalized'. To quote the booklet of the series: 'we use beautifully tuned systems of the brain to integrate a whole mass of complex information … So durable is the musical system that it often survives when other systems fail'.[28] (Hence music as, if nothing else, a therapy of last resort.) The human being is even presented as 'a kind of symphonic composition'. The similarity urged by philosophers of antiquity (see West, below), and which is likely in more recent times to be taken as metaphorical, becomes literal once again.

> The ancient belief that a 'harmonious' condition generates health and happiness, whilst a discordant state of mind and body encourages sickness and unease, has become part of the language of healers … heart-disease patients when making music are less able to co-ordinate and empathise with the rhythms of other music makers. But what is cause and what is effect? *Is disease damaging musicality, or is damaged musicality – being 'out of tune' – making people ill?*[29]

That recalls one of Oliver Sacks's informants, who referred to herself as being 'unmusicked' by Parkinsonism.[30] The larger point, however, is this: although Sacks and Robertson between them can sum up a widespread lay concern with music's healing properties, the reception of their work also illustrates how interest extends to more professional, clinical endeavours. Sacks is, after all, a professor of neurology in New York. And Robertson's programme and booklet introduce us to the projects of two other specialists, both at work in Germany: Ralph Spintge, who runs a pain clinic and has compiled a database of the effects of music on 90,000 or more patients; and David Aldridge, Professor for Clinical Research Methods at the Institute for Music Therapy at the University of Witten Herdecke,

whose research involves devising ways to analyse and assess what is
actually going on in successful music therapy. It is Aldridge who
wants us to see human life as a composition. 'Music is ... isomorphic
with the process of living'.[31] At Spintge's clinic, music of their choice
is available to all patients, not just to distract them but, Spintge is
convinced, to speed their recovery. Specially composed music is also
played before, after, and even during operations:

> Fifteen minutes of soothing music lulls the patient into such a
> state of well-being that only 50 per cent of recommended doses
> of sedatives and anaesthetic drugs are needed to perform other-
> wise very painful operations. Indeed some procedures are now
> undertaken without any anaesthetic ... More invigorating music
> then alerts the patients' systems so they can actively respond to
> the surgeon. Once this is complete the music then takes the
> patient back into a relaxed state for recovery.[32]

III

As with cell cultures in the laboratory (with which we began), so with
entire human beings; and as for the heterodox, the first of my three
categories, so for the second, the professional: rhythm seems to be the
key. 'Pieces [of music] composed to create specific physiological
change ... are designed to lock into the innate neurophysiological and
biological rhythms that underlie the vital functions of the body.'[33]

Chronic pain and perioperative stress are but two of the areas presumably susceptible to this sort of analysis and in which music is
today used as therapy. The full range defies brief summary, least of all
by a non-specialist.[34] Suffice it to say that it embraces music played *to*
patients (or clients); music both live and recorded, composed or
improvised, conducted, sung or played *by* patients. The patients come
individually or in groups, and on occasion their families are involved.
They may be mentally or physically ill or disabled. Their ages span
the prenatal (in some tentative experiments) at one extreme, and the
comatose, the very elderly and terminally ill at the other. The music is
sometimes ancillary, as in the operating theatre; sometimes it com-
plements other therapies; sometimes it is the primary form of therapy.
So it may be associated with every kind of technique from the most
invasive to the mildest palliative. The physical settings in which

music is used vary from the operating theatre and hospital ward to the specialized clinic or school, the day-centre, the charity, the home – or the prison.[35] A sonic spectrum might be envisaged running from the highest tinkling metallic percussion to the vibro-acoustic bed or chair, the speakers set into which play tones with a frequency of 40 Hz.[36]

Problems for which the low tones of vibro-acoustic therapy have been found efficacious include severe physical disability, rheumatoid conditions, muscle spasm, pulmonary disorders, and cerebral palsy. The list of problems or clinical contexts for which music therapy more generally has been pronounced helpful would of course be much longer. To offer no more than an alphabetical sample: asthma, AIDS, aphasia, autism, bereavement, cancer, deafness, dental problems, depression, dementia, eating disorders, emotional disturbance, epilepsy, inflammatory bowel disease, kidney failure, schizophrenia, multiple sclerosis, sexual abuse.

The profession whose work has brought all this to increasing public attention is now substantial in scale and nearly global in scope. There are over 300 music therapists in Britain, proportionately many more in the United States. The World Federation of Music Therapy draws members from some twenty-eight countries, including China, Poland, Israel and South Africa. (Only the Russian Federation and the Muslim Middle East seem unrepresented.) 126 training courses are known to be available, over 70 of them in the USA. There is clearly massive investment in the future of this profession. Meanwhile, the quantity of germane research papers increases ever more rapidly, to an extent that must simultaneously exhilarate and depress those therapists trying to keep abreast of it. The merest surfing of web databases such as the USA National Library of Medicine's 'PubMed' yields the following among recent titles in biomedical journals: '"Brain music" in the treatment of patients with insomnia'; 'Enhancement of spatio-temporal reasoning after a Mozart listening condition in Alzheimer's disease' (a variation on the educational use of background music which has become known as 'the Mozart effect');[37] 'The effect of constant baroque music on premature infants'; 'Music therapy: facilitating behavioural and psychological change in people with stroke'.[38] Success everywhere: few seem willing – or are allowed – to report that music made little or no difference in their particular cases, or worse, that it was positively damaging,[39] a music-therapeutic version of iatrogenic disease.[40]

The alluring article titles and their triumphalist tone prompt, then, the general question of what music therapists actually do with all this training and research. Their discipline's nature and purpose have proved remarkably hard to specify. The music produced (or reproduced) may decrease hormone levels, diminish stress, enhance immune functions, and reduce muscle tension, heart rate and blood pressure; but it may also be directed at less measurable goals such as self-expression or bolder socialization. The World Federation of Music Therapy's official definition is correspondingly open-ended:

> Music Therapy is the use of music and/or musical elements (sound, rhythm, melody, and harmony) by a qualified music therapist, with a client or group, in a process designed to facilitate and promote *communication, relationships, learning, mobilisation, expression, organisation and other relevant therapeutic objectives*, in order to meet physical, emotional, mental, social and cognitive needs. Music Therapy aims to develop potentials and/or restore functions of the individual so that he or she can achieve better intra- and interpersonal integration and, consequently, a better quality of life through prevention, rehabilitation, or treatment.[41]

Reference to curing is noticeably missing; the italicized aims are broad and increasingly vague; treatment comes last and is, it seems, connected only indirectly to the music. The therapy may be no more (though also no less) than an objectification of the problem, a form of diagnosis.[42] Criteria of success will be as elusive as definitions. The children with learning disabilities who might be taken as the emblematic clients of music therapists in the Anglo-American world are not so much being treated as communicated with. The music is both symbol and vehicle of the wider transaction between therapist and client, a transaction that seems to embrace both disease and cure, and indeed frustrates any attempt to separate them.

By way of illustration, consider Sophie.[43] At four months of age she was found to have difficulties with her fine and coarse motor control (she could not crawl or pull herself up to stand). Although her hearing was normal, she also failed to speak. She played alone, seemingly immune to distraction. No organic causes could be traced for any of this. In her first session with a music therapist she was very anxious and played a small bell and chime bar almost inaudibly. By the fifth session, however, she was playing a drum in rhythms loosely related to those of the therapist's improvisation. Her parents began to find her freer and more sociable in daily life: she spoke in a babble but could remember words and was keen to communicate. In the remaining therapy sessions her improvisational skills developed considerably. Concurrently, her awareness of her surroundings and her independence of action increased in proportion.

When there are case histories like that to reckon with, it is entirely comprehensible that Leslie Bunt, an eminent and experienced music therapist, should write: 'we are at the stage when the "Does it work?" question seems rather meaningless given the complex interaction of so many variables involved in any piece of therapeutic work'.[44] How can the personal contribution of the therapist be distinguished from that of the music, or indeed from other kinds of 'treatment' which the musical one may complement, such as art therapy? Recall Yeats's 'how can we know the dancer from the dance?' ('Among schoolchildren'). Is such a distinction appropriate? How can the outcomes of therapy be categorized and assessed in ways that give weight to parental instincts as much as to clinical calibrations, to the psychosomatic as much as to the organic – above all, to the evolving *meaning*, for both therapist and client, of the problems being addressed?

It is easy to see why therapists resort to metaphor when trying to capture the elusive essence of their art: to the notion, for instance, that life is a musical composition, to which the actual music of the therapist is 'entrained' (attuned) so that subsequent adjustments of the music can bring with them analogous changes in the patient.[45] It is also easy to see why the aesthetics of Susanne Langer, for whom music was *par excellence* a symbolic analogue of the inner life, survive in the writings of music therapists when they have been rejected by most philosophers of art (for their Cartesian separation of the inner world from outward behaviour, their unanalysable concept of an emotion's logical structure, and the circularity implied in asserting that emotions can be described in musical terms).[46]

IV

'Each music therapy group becomes a miniature society.'[47] And yet it
is precisely the social dimension that seems to be relatively neglected
in the case histories of professional music therapists. Which is surprising, because it is from the wider social arena that some of the ailments and disabilities encountered by music therapists derive their
significance, and it is in the wider social arena that all the outcomes of
treatment must eventually be manifest. One body of writing which
might assist and even inspire the music therapists – and put some perspective on their difficulties with definition and evaluation – is thus
the social anthropology of music and healing, to which, still under my
'professional' heading, I shall devote the present section of the
chapter. From this discipline, in reports mainly from sub-Saharan
Africa but also, notably, from Sri Lanka and South-East Asia,[48] can be
found examples of healing practice, 'professionalism' of a very different kind, that is stimulatingly alien. None of the usual distinctions
seems to apply. In northern Malawi for instance:

> *Vimbuza* – a multivocal term, a complex of meanings and refer-
> ences – encompasses a class of spirits, the illnesses they cause,
> and the music and dance used to treat the illnesses. As spirit,
> *vimbuza* is the numinous energy of foreign peoples and wild
> animals; as illness, it is both a spirit affliction and an initiatory
> sickness; as musical experience, it is a mode of trance. For
> patients possessed by *vimbuza* spirits, trance dancing is a cooling
> therapy; for adepts, it is the means for transforming a disease into
> a vocation; and for healers, it is the source of an energizing heat
> that fuels the divination trance.[49]

In such a world, sufferers become healers; both, at certain specified
moments, become part of more complex transactions involving larger
groups; singing, drumming and instrumental melody, words, dancing
and imagery alike contribute to some all-encompassing ritual. The
living and the ancestors, the human world and that of spirits may all
be involved. As in some American or European music therapy, the
music can be the diagnosis as well as the therapy; it can also be the
disease itself.[50]

The afflictions addressed by rituals of this kind would not necessarily count as illnesses in Western biomedical terms. A classic exam-

ple comes from the healing cult of the Congo basin made famous by John Janzen in *Lemba, 1650–1930: A Drum of Affliction in Africa and the New World*. As in other such cults, *Lemba* showed itself in the individual in physical symptoms such as abdominal pain and difficulty with breathing. It was, however, distinguished from those cults by its social exclusivity. It struck the elite households of the north bank of the Congo: chiefs, judges, traders. What the affliction was – what the *Lemba* drum and its associated magical medicines and bracelets were being deployed against – remained unclear. Janzen could not tell until (to quote one of his commentators),

> casually, he superimposed a map of the provenance of *Lemba* texts and artefacts on to one of the long-distance trade routes. They matched … the *Lemba* cult provided a way of calming conflicts of interest between the naturally competitive and divisive activity of trade and the social order of lower Zaire … *Lemba* protected their health from the disease of capitalism.[51]

Here, 'socio-somatic' seems a more appropriate category than psychosomatic. 'What is recognized as illness … is a model of the disorder rather than the disorder itself', a model constructed in and on the body.[52] Even so, some of the ways in which spirit-caused afflictions are resolved by indigenous healers, African or Asian, show points of contact with Western therapy. The music is highly personal – improvised and variable – personal to both the patient and the healer.[53] Whether spirits are invoked or not, the objective may well be the entrainment (metaphorically) of sick body and healing sound.

> Melodies rise, fall, cut straight across, or wind sinuously … What Temiars [of the Malaysian rain forest] describe as the disorientation of illness is counterbalanced by the sense of being 'located' on paths inscribed in song … vocalizations embody sonic action: 'blowing' cools the patient; 'sucking' helps extract the illness agent, bringing it to the patient's body surface, so it can be drawn out into the medium's hand, or swept away with a leaf whisk.[54]

The pity is all the greater, then, that music therapists and social anthropologists have, in recent decades, been writing largely in ignorance of one another. It was not always thus, as we shall see in a moment. And among current music therapists, it is of course possible to find occasional reference to John Blacking, one of the pioneers of ethnomusicology, or to generalized notions of shamanism.[55] Yet there are no obvious signs that the major detailed ethnographies of healing cults – such as Janzen's *Ngoma*, Roseman's *Healing Sounds from the Malaysian Rainforest*, or Friedson's *Dancing Prophets* – are having any impact on the ways in which music therapists conceive their role.[56] In fairness, it should be added that those works are all quite recent, and that sustained ethnographic interest of their type is hardly much older. Evans-Pritchard's classic account of Azande magic, first published as long ago as 1937, embraced the witch doctors' seance during which divinatory 'medicines' (magical trees and herbs) were activated by drumming, singing and dancing.[57] Yet his was an isolated example. Even Victor Turner's highly influential discussions of Ndembu healing rituals published in the 1960s, notably his *The Drums of Affliction*, actually had little detail to offer about drumming, or indeed about the healing functions of music generally.[58] Not that anthropologists now have reason to feel superior when knowledge of cognate disciplines is in question. In 1996 Friedson could still write of the place of music in biomedicine in terms of muzak piped into doctors' waiting rooms – as if music therapy did not exist.[59]

The worlds of 'western' music therapy and 'traditional' musical healing are hardly far removed from one another in geographical terms. In Greek Macedonia, illness-generating social conflicts are both expressed and healed in the songs that accompany the fire-walking of possessed Anastenarides.[60] Spirit cults involving music can be found among expatriate communities in northern Europe, for example the Creole migrants from Surinam in an Amsterdam suburb.[61] Music therapy is already well represented in South Africa and will presumably spread to other parts of the continent, where its practitioners will find that biomedicine and indigenous therapies have already established a division of labour in the treatment of local ills. It will be fascinating to see how the two traditions of musical therapeutics interpenetrate.

No more need be said here about the ethnography of musical healing. The topic deserves much more sustained treatment, but it starts to receive that in contributions to Penelope Gouk's volume, *Musical Healing in Cultural Contexts* (by several authors discussed here, among others). It will also reappear in the present collection, briefly in

Amnon Shiloah's survey of the Islamic tradition and more fully in the chapters by Karen Lüdtke and Keith Howard. One feature common to music therapists and musical healers is, however, worth noting now: the invocation of history. Both esteem ancestors more than contemporaries.

V

To views of the past, then; the last of the three headings that I proposed above.

> In the time of the Prophet Adam, Eve was sick ... Adam looked for medicine; he looked and looked but couldn't find any ... he asked the *bomoh* [Malay healer], 'Do you have any medicine to treat Eve?' This is what ... the *bomoh* said: 'I have medicine for everything!' He brought over a *gebana* (hand drum); he had a *rehab* (spike fiddle). Adam asked what those things were. 'This is a bowl for medicine,' he said, pointing to the *gebana*. 'This is a medicinal herb', he said, pointing to the *rehab*. Then he treated his patient – he played. After he played, Eve was cured of her sickness.[62]

The shaman informant even went on to say that the original act of musical healing was Gabriel's reintegration, at God's behest, of Adam, after the infusion of divine breath had broken his body into little pieces. Music therapists and those engaged in related research may not look quite so far back for antecedents; sometimes a nineteenth-century precursor is venerable enough. But they do, as we have already seen, advert to early civilizations of the Mediterranean, the Middle East and India. Having mentioned ancient Greeks, Egyptians and Hebrews in the opening chapter of his account of contemporary music therapy, Leslie Bunt concludes by offering us, as the discipline's 'emblem', no less a figure than Orpheus.[63] In this he is to some extent following the example of Juliette Alvin (on whom see further Tyler, Chapter 16). In what remains the classic short introduction to music therapy, Alvin too connects Orpheus with present-day concerns and ways of talking about musical performance, and, conversely, she relates the effects of a music box on an autistic child to something deep in mankind's biological past.[64] In a chapter which functions as a general survey of music in healing, she embeds, within

a *tour de force* of potted medical history, a narrative of music in
therapy that runs from 'primitive man' through Pythagoras,
Cassiodorus, Bernard of Clairvaux and Robert Burton,[65] to the physicians of the early modern age who were the first to write specific
treatises on music's healing power.

Throughout, there is a presumption of continuity. It is made explicit
at a later stage of Alvin's book: she prefaces her survey of the modern
practice of music therapy – which occupies only the last sixty-three
pages of a 163-page text – with a brief account of tarantism, the healing cult which we shall revisit in later chapters.[66] The account is entitled 'The continuous thread'.[67] Elsewhere the presumption is implicit,
but hardly less obvious. The figures named or quoted are (for her)
more than remote precursors – they are colleagues, doing the same
thing with essentially the same means, as today's therapists. An
account by Richard Brocklesby, Dr Johnson's physician, of the slow
recovery of a pathologically grief-stricken Scottish patient is presented virtually as a case history in the modern clinical sense.[68] More
tellingly, the substantial historical part of Alvin's book culminates in
paired accounts of the biblical David and Saul (see Shiloah and Jones,
below) and the castrato Farinelli (subject of a feature film) and the
Spanish Philip V. These not only suggest that comparisons between
the two kings' cases can be made across the intervening millennia;
they place as much emphasis on the evolving personal relationship
between the two depressives and their singing therapists as on the uses
of music in their respective treatments. 'Each of the approaches we
have described is valid today; every music therapist uses them more
or less consciously.' That is Alvin's general conclusion to her retro-
spect.[69]

The past is called upon to validate the present, to show that apparently novel approaches have in fact been tried for centuries. Alvin was
one of the pioneers of the modern music therapy profession in
Britain.[70] She gave so much space to history in her introduction to the
subject presumably because music therapy was then still young and
vulnerable to criticism: it needed an impressive pedigree.[71] Newer
textbooks, such as Leslie Bunt's, can be correspondingly briefer and
more selective in their historical backgrounds because their profession
is more securely established.[72] None the less, authors of such works

continue to rely on what, until postmodernity corroded it, could be felt as the cohesion and durability of the Hellenic- and Judaeo-Christian tradition. These authors take it as axiomatic that the past can be interpreted in much the same light as can the present – that David, or Pythagoras, can be seen as more or less a founding father of music therapy. If there has been any great interruption, any break in the continuity of musical thought and practice across the ages, then it would (for them) be quite a recent one. As those who treated cancer cells with Ayurveda put it, 'the technological explosion of allopathic medicine in the 20th century obscured the traditionally close relationship between music and medicine'.[73] Biomedicine – technologically triumphalist, dehumanizing, viewing the patient as a machine with broken parts rather than as a person for whom illness has meaning – was almost bound to undervalue the psychological or interpersonal dimension of healing.[74] Now, however, a more sensitive, holistic conception of medicine is firmly back in fashion – no longer simply the preserve of 'alternative' practitioners.[75] Music therapy can (it is implicitly contended) return from the margins to the centre and reclaim its inheritance.

VI

Grant for the moment that such an inheritance really exists. How are music therapists to feel its invigorating touch? The footnotes to the historical backdrops painted, on differing scales, by Alvin and Bunt inevitably refer mostly to a few secondary works, and their re-presentation of them is more a series of detached vignettes than connected historical writing. Bunt leans on Alvin, and both derive most of their evidence from an anthology of reprinted articles published in New York as long ago as 1948. *Music and Medicine*, edited by Dorothy M. Schullian and Max Schoen, has endured as the major resource in English for those wanting something more than scattered anecdotes. Their collection, comprising articles already published as chapters in books or papers in musicological or medical journals, remains therefore in some ways the best available model for the present collection. In it, the findings of musicologists and medical historians march with those of social anthropologists and therapists, in a way that they have seldom, if ever, done since. The chapters essay a history of music therapy from the earliest times to the twentieth century (including a discussion of tarantism by one of the fathers of modern medical history, Henry Sigerist).[76] And they show everywhere a familiarity with the primary sources that is still unusual in this particular field.

The context in which that project was conceived was the wartime use of music as a palliative in military hospitals and factories, the rapid expansion of the universities, and the first steps towards the establishment of professional training in music therapy. It is a context analysed by Penelope Gouk in the companion volume to this one and needs no elaboration here. What diminishes the value of the Schullian–Schoen collection over fifty years on, and suggests the need for its replacement, is precisely the depth to which it bears the stamp of its time. An opening discussion of 'Music and medicine among primitive peoples' appears very much as a foil to that 'civilized' tradition, while a later contribution, by the composer Howard Hanson, pronounces the novelty of Boogie Woogie to be a harmful aural drug.[77] Such preconceptions distort the history presented. And that history has many gaps in it (most obviously the Middle Ages and the nineteenth century). None the less the overall message is, predictably, one of continuity – from Pythagoras right through to the first professional music therapists, for whose calling the book was evidently to serve as manifesto. It is a continuity which is grounded in the achievements of 'dead European males' (or their texts) and which depends on Western 'art music' as the main therapeutic vehicle – both of which manifestations of 'elitism' make it automatically unpalatable in many quarters today.

In some ways the most solidly valuable part of the Schullian and Schoen anthology was the bibliography that Schullian contributed, including historical discussions reaching back to seventeenth- and eighteenth-century evidence.[78] Since 1948 a certain amount has been written on the topic in English, though none of it widely influential or combining breadth and scholarship.[79] Musicologists have had little of a historical kind to add; medical historians have done no better. It is perhaps symptomatic that the brief entry for 'music therapy' in *The New Grove Dictionary of Music and Musicians* confines itself to modern practices and omits Schullian and Schoen from its bibliography (although it does include a few historical texts). And no discussion of the topic is to be found in that otherwise authoritative and up-to-date conspectus, *The Companion Encyclopedia of the History of Medicine*.[80]

Meanwhile, however, the question of continuity seemed to have been settled elsewhere – on a scale, and at a scholarly level, that admitted no further doubt. In 1977, W. F. Kümmel published a revised version of his Habilitationsschrift, *Musik und Medizin: Ihre Wechselbeziehungen in Theorie und Praxis von 800 bis 1800*.[81] A densely learned text of over 400 pages written in German and difficult to obtain could not be expected to have much impact on Anglophone historians of medicine, still less on music therapists. The book is seldom cited and, one suspects, more often cited than read. Its sheer density has probably deterred proper evaluation. For that reason, and because it makes the strongest case yet for the continuity and significance of musical healing in the pre-modern past, I shall devote my final two sections to it.

VII

Kümmel quotes or paraphrases texts from right across the period indicated by his subtitle, in a profusion which attests massive reading in Latin and a range of vernaculars, among tomes of music theory, medicine, philosophy, theology and literature. Music, as it emerges here, was of profound importance in the Western medical tradition – and in the Middle Ages too, not just in antiquity and modern times as Foucault among others had argued ('since the Renaissance, music had regained all those therapeutic virtues antiquity had attributed to it.').[82] Theorists and practitioners of all kinds, from all the major European countries, and in almost every century, recommended listening or performing as a means of preventing or alleviating ill health.

'Every healing', as Novalis would say, 'is a musical solution'. 'Music heals the sick' had been the still more succinct conclusion of the music theorist Tinctoris, writing at the end of the Middle Ages but looking back to their dawn, and to the great encyclopaedist of that time, Isidore of Seville.[83] 'Throughout Spain', the physician Rodericus a Castro wrote in 1614, 'whenever anyone falls seriously ill, it is usual to summon musicians'.[84] No mere collection of general assertions, the book's thematic chapters expound the history of music as a perceived remedy for: phrenitis, mania, melancholia,[85] fever, pain, insomnia, plague, that mysterious virus 'the English Sweat',[86] lethargy, apoplexy, catalepsy, consumption, and epilepsy. To take a fairly extreme example that can be set beside our opening one of cancer cells: in the early sixteenth century the German religious reformer Ulrich von Hutten urged listening to singers and instrumentalists for those undergoing treatment (with a decoction of guaiac wood) for syphilis, a disease with which he was himself terminally afflicted.[87] The complete list of conditions thought to be musically treatable resembles the scope of modern music therapy in its diversity, embracing both mental and physical ailments, chronic conditions and rapidly lethal epidemics. To it, moreover, we must add, first, those places or occasions in which music was thought to be helpful in an auxiliary capacity – in the bath and the hospital, and after having been bled; second, the capacities of music as preventive medicine: in pregnancy, early childhood, and old age, and as a factor in generally beneficial self-regulation.

The sheer volume and thoroughness of Kümmel's documentation seems to brook no contrary argument. Nor need such arguments be searched out in the present chapter. It is for the contributors writing below to review his findings in detail, whether implicitly or explicitly, and to show how far his extremely positive assessment of the role of music in therapy applies to their respective areas and periods. The task preliminary to all that, which should, however, be undertaken here, is to gain some overall perspective on the hundreds of citations that Kümmel adduces in favour of the ubiquity and continuity of music in pre-modern therapeutics. Just how widespread and significant were the practices reported? What sort of continuity is being represented?

First, it is important to register that Kümmel has a far broader purview than music therapy. His title is 'music and medicine' and he is concerned with the whole spectrum of ways in which they may have interacted.[88] So he includes discussions of the 'music' of the pulse – a means of description and diagnosis which becomes a therapeutic technique in itself only towards the end of the long period surveyed in his book, when it was proposed that the pulse's rhythm might be altered by an actual musical counterpart.[89] Kümmel also pays considerable attention to the idea of music as a model of the human frame [*musica humana*], which, as we shall see, animates much discussion of music therapy, but for the sake of completeness is again pursued in his book as a subject in its own right. And he makes space for sections on music in child care, which often seems to have involved no more than the philosophy of lullabies; on *Tafelmusik*, to accompany eating and improve digestion; and on the recreational uses of music at spas – none of which topics is indisputably central to the history of musical healing. Subtract some of this material from the evidence submitted and its mass seems a little less daunting and incontrovertible.

A second feature to note is that the range of sources pressed into service can undermine the author's thesis about the importance of musical medicine. Literature, philosophy, and music theory play at least as great a part in sustaining the case for ubiquity and continuity as do medical texts. While all equally part of the European intellectual tradition, they do not necessarily show that music was important in medicine. Indeed, the very abundance of non-medical evidence hints at an alternative argument which recurs in several chapters below (for example West, Chapter 2; Page, Chapter 5; and Gouk, Chapter 8): that music therapy has often been more theorized than practised, has been of greater interest to philosophers than to physicians. Certainly Kümmel has comparatively little evidence of a practical kind to present. Case books or other detailed medical records are admittedly hard to come by until we have reached some way into the modern period. And Kümmel does include some extracts from *consilia* (letters of advice published by eminent physicians) and some individual case histories, mostly royal.[90] None the less, it has to be said that there is far less evidence of music's actual use in therapy than might be expected. The medical sources make up only a part of the whole; and they are overwhelmingly prescriptive in character: they tell us more about ideals than about actuality.

The impression of ubiquity and continuity in musical healing is initially strengthened but then, on closer reading, called into question by Kümmel's manner of presenting his material. He organizes it thematically, which enhances our sense of the enormous range of medical tasks to which music has been applied. But that organization also has its disadvantages. Quotations as it were flash past, so that we can be moved from antiquity to the early nineteenth century within a matter of paragraphs. Evidence of all kinds jostles together without its authors being fully identified, their writings being characterized, or the immediate contexts of their assertions about therapy being set out. Disagreements about musical healing – its capacities and its limitations – get relatively little attention. Instances of music as a first resort are 'lumped' together with instances of it as a last one.[91] Moreover, evidence must be repeated under each of the disease headings to which it pertains, which can create the suspicion that the single march past of a huge army is actually the effect of a smaller number of soldiers coming round again and again.

VIII

The soldiers proclaim, essentially, a composite of some fundamentals of ancient medicine and one fundamental of ancient musical theory.[92] Let us step back from reviewing Kümmel and examine these a little further. The musical idea is that each mode or rhythm or type of music has its specific ethos, which can induce a specific response in the hearer (see West, Chapter 2; Katz, Chapter 4; and Part III). The medical ideas are threefold. First, there is in a sense only one disorder or disease: an imbalance of the four humours (blood, phlegm, yellow bile, black bile) that are the basic ingredients of the body.[93] Second, therefore, 'mental illness' as modern medicine conceives it is somatic in origin. On the other hand, third, the mind can hinder or generate ill health. This medicine is not entirely physicalist: the psychosomatic traffic is two-way. These various strands of thought remained distinct, and expressions of them often fragmented, in ancient writers such as Galen, the great physician of Roman imperial times and, like Hippocrates, one of the presiding geniuses of the European medical tradition. It was the Arab scholars of the Islamic Middle East from the ninth century onward – the heirs of ancient Greek medical learning by way of translations – who synthesized the strands and thereby provided the framework within which the uses of music in therapy could be conceptualized.

The briefest exposition can be found in the work known to Western medicine as the *Isagoge* [*Introduction*] of Johannitius (Hunain ibn Ishaq), an Arabic synopsis so convenient that, in Latin translation, it was widely diffused across medieval Europe (see Jones, Chapter 6). This text distinguishes between the 'naturals' (chiefly the four elements, qualities such as hot or moist, and the four humours), the 'contra-naturals' (disease, its causes and 'sequels'), and the 'non-naturals'. The last are the pertinent ones here; they are the determinants of health. They include air and the environment, eating and drinking, exercise and baths, sleep, coitus, and the 'passions of the soul'.[94] Johannitius writes:

> Sundry affections of the mind produce an effect within the body, such as those which bring the natural heat from the interior of the body to the outer parts or the surface of the skin. Sometimes this happens suddenly, as with anger; sometimes gently and slowly, as with delight and joy ... some affections disturb the natural energy both internal and external, as, for instance, with grief.[95]

Those sentences represent the conceptual gateway through which music comes into medicine – under the heading of 'delight and joy'. Music – of the appropriate ethos – can manipulate the accidents of the soul, mitigating those which cause disease, strengthening those which prevent it. That is why Gentile da Foligno, lecturer in the medical faculty at Perugia, advised all at risk of catching the Black Death of 1348 to avoid sadness, rage and solitude because these upset the bodily complexion and encouraged disease. In the same vein, he counselled seeking joy and delight by means of 'melodies, songs, stories, and other similar pleasures'.[96] In the chapters that follow, as to some extent in earlier examples here, we encounter other grander formulations of how music 'works' medically – notably that which sees *musica instrumentalis* (actually including vocal music) as literally harmonizing *musica humana*, the disordered (that is, unhealthy) human frame, with the musical order of the cosmos, *musica mundana* (see West, Chapter 2; and Part III). But the application of the non-naturals is an underlying constant of learned medicine so long as that medicine continues to subscribe to the tenets of ancient, and medieval Arab, thought.

Take the example of melancholy (compare Gouk, Chapter 8; and Austern, Chapter 10). Its treatment across the two and a half millennia that separate Hippocrates and modern times has usefully been chronicled by Stanley W. Jackson (in a book written seemingly in ignorance of Kümmel's). 'Much in the way of therapeutic advice', Jackson concludes, 'was based on classical concerns with *the regimen* ... It often seemed as though the prescriber had run down a checklist of the six non-naturals.'[97] To that extent, it might be mere personal predisposition that an individual physician explicitly recommended music rather than one of the other possible ways of cheering the patient. And yet, with respect to melancholy at any rate, some changes of fashion are detectable across the centuries. Most of the ancient Roman authorities – Celsus, Soranus, Aretaeus of Cappadocia, Galen, Galen's late antique epigones – include no discussion of music in their recommendations for treatment.[98] Predictably, it is the Arab scholars, notably Ishaq ibn Imran, who first consider it, and whose advice passed to the West in Latin translation.

> The physician must counteract melancholics' suspicions, mitigate their anger and grant them what they used to like ... they should use reasoned and pleasant discourse ... with diverse music and sweet-smelling, clear and delicate wine.[99]

Similarly mixed remedies reappear in some, but not all, of the major medieval texts. Following Constantine the African, translator of Ishaq, the medieval authority Bartholomaeus Anglicus (Bartholomew the Englishman) wrote that melancholics must be 'gladded with instruments of music and some deal be occupied'; in the 1530s Thomas Elyot counselled avoidance of anger, study or solitude, 'and rejoice thee with melody, or else be alway in such company, as best may content thee'.[100] The repetitions continue through the writing of Robert Burton (considered by Gouk below) and into the eighteenth century – and then music is apparently dropped. None of the major eighteenth- and nineteenth-century figures reviewed by Jackson specifically recommends it.[101]

If, with these examples in mind, we now return to the many other instances of musical therapeutics assembled by Kümmel, it becomes apparent that 'song' was frequently prescribed in the same breath as wine or women (the doctors are all male, their implied patients mainly so). That is, the physicians Kümmel cites are suggesting not music therapy so much as a more general 'soul' therapy, protecting health by lifting spirits. Music is only one of several obvious resources, a possibility always in the background but not inevitably the technique of choice, its explicit recommendation perhaps sometimes being arbitrary. A jolly story might serve equally well.[102] Most educated physicians did, however, know at least a little music theory, which might have inclined them to single it out. Music has never in its own right been a part of formal medical curricula in schools or universities. But it did enter the armoury of the learned because the study of the liberal arts was, until the eighteenth century if not later, nearly always a prerequisite of reading for a medical degree. And the primary arts text on music, as we shall see, was Boethius's treatise with its anecdotes of marvellous musical healings.[103]

The intellectual tradition just described lasts, as Kümmel's title shows, for a millennium, from the Arab synthesis of ingredients bequeathed by classical antiquity to the demise of humoral pathology in the early nineteenth century.[104] Within that long span, the beliefs anciently established remained valid, a few sceptical pronouncements apart. As an explanatory framework and a justification of music and other 'non-natural' diversions, they endured changing conceptions of human physiology (chemical, mechanistic, vitalist, neurological, and so on). That is why we shall find in subsequent chapters – and can already detect in both Kümmel's pages and recent music therapy textbooks – a limited number of anecdotes being endlessly recycled: of David or Pythagoras, or Farinelli. That is why Tinctoris writing in the fifteenth century leans on Isidore writing in the seventh, who in his turn professes to have found instruction in still older vignettes.[105] The old nostrums remained for the most part unquestioned. Yet by the time the famous music critic Eduard Hanslick, scourge of Wagner and perfect Brahmsian, came to publish his tract *Vom Musikalisch-Schönen* [*On the Musically Beautiful*] in 1854, the tradition had dissolved. Hanslick can presume a certain ignorance in his readers in a way that would have been hazardous even half a century earlier.

It may not be known to many music lovers [he writes] that we possess an extensive literature concerning the bodily effects of music and their medical applications. Rich in interesting curiosities but untrustworthy in observation and unscientific in explanation, most of these musico-medical writings seek to raise up some very complex and incidental property of music to the status of sovereign remedy.[106]

Hanslick quotes with obvious contempt the physician Peter Lichtenthal, whose *Der Musikalische Arzt* (1807) lists gout, sciatica, epilepsy, catalepsy, pestilence, delirium, convulsions, the jitters, nymphomania and stupidity as among the disorders amenable to musical treatment. 'It is a bit of a problem', he concludes, 'that up to now no doctor has ever been known to send his typhus patients to Meyerbeer's [opera] *The Prophet* or to reach for a horn instead of a lancet.'[107] Perhaps Hanslick was himself more of a prophet than he knew. And the later nineteenth century was certainly not lacking in music therapy (see Part V, below). But the framework was different by then; the non-naturals and the medical system that they represented had been left behind. Lichtenthal was among their last European advocates.

Kümmel's mass of evidence on this tradition that ends in the 1800s need not therefore be quite as overwhelming as it may first appear. To summarize: it includes some subjects not obviously central to the topic of musical therapeutics, and numerous texts that do not bear directly on medical practice. Many of the discussions of music mentioned are tralatician in nature: they repeat ancient commonplaces. The evidence is homogenized a little by being treated thematically and without sufficient respect for context. Above all, the medical tradition of the non-naturals – which does indeed last for the millennium embraced by the book's title – puts forward music as just one remedy among a range of useful diversions: it announces music's broad potential, but not always much more than that.

How far was that potential actually realized? Kümmel's work offers one answer – which may be too sanguine. Other studies that traverse some of his territory yield a very different picture. An authoritative history of epilepsy, for example, does not seem to find it worthwhile to mention any of the authors Kümmel musters in his pages on the musical treatment of the condition, and reveals no refer-

ence to music among the dietary recommendations it does adduce.[108]
New studies of the history of gout and syphilis, similarly, have
nothing of substance on musical treatment.[109] With the relatively few
exceptions footnoted in the following pages, it seems that recent historical scholarship, whether consciously or not, has declined to
endorse Kümmel's optimistic gloss on the evidence.

Clearly the matter requires further investigation. Some of that is
undertaken in subsequent chapters. Other aspects must be left to later
occasions: we cannot match Kümmel's breadth of scope. The role of
music in magic is one topic, perhaps peripheral to music therapy, that
would repay more than the sporadic notice it gets below. In magical
incantations is it *prima la musica, dopo le parole* – or the other way
round?[110] Which aspect of the magician's performance has been
thought primarily efficacious? A related question might be asked of
religious liturgy, on which we have already touched in the context of
rites for the dying.[111] How, for example, should the singing of a mass
explicitly for the relief of fever, sung in honour of that ailment's
patron saint, be understood to benefit sufferers? Is the saint's health-
bringing intercession with the Deity thought to be in any sense
dependent on the music of the mass?[112] A slightly different example:
at the graveside, is the singing of a ritual lament in any sense therapeutic?[113] These and like questions take us out from music therapy
conceived as a part of learned medicine into a wider cultural world
that seems to require a historical equivalent of the ethnography quoted
earlier.

As part of such wider investigations, some attention should also be
paid to the areas or the evidence in which we might expect to find
music therapy but do not: the writings of that great composer–physician of the twelfth century, Abbess Hildegard of Bingen, for instance;
of those Renaissance polymaths Girolamo Cardano, who discoursed
on both music and medicine but not simultaneously, and Michael
Maier, whose emblem book *Atalanta fugiens* (1617) keeps separate its
fugues and its images of healing; or of Richard Napier, the English
cleric and astrological physician, who in the early decades of the
seventeenth century treated over 2,000 patients with mental disorders
and whose casebooks are priceless evidence of early modern medicine.[114] Loud silences of that kind must alter our notion of the 'con-

tours' of musical healing in the past. Not every cure is a musical solution.

Kümmel's work stimulates considerations such as these. Above all, it raises yet again the task of weighing continuity against discontinuity. Kümmel is careful to exclude the phrase 'music therapy' from his title and to distance the activities of the physicians he describes from those of modern music therapists.[115] For him the decline of humoral pathology marks a caesura in musical therapeutics. Before that, he contends, musical medicine was different – but it was continuous. Other writers, as we have seen several times now, are less scrupulous in the way they divide up the past, but are no less ready to accept a vision of continuity. For them, the past can readily be reclaimed by the present. There may be an intervening obstacle: usually the era of biomedicine's unquestioned dominance. Once that obstacle is conceptually vaulted over, however, the rest of history becomes available, *en bloc*, to endorse the claims and practices of today.

For such easy recourse, the present collection hopes to substitute a less anachronistic historical panorama – one marked by change and disagreement as much as by smooth traditionalism, in which the absences figure alongside the presences. Some of the cultures discussed here have no concept of music that corresponds to ours; and their ideas of medicine and its capacity to heal rest on alien principles. The improvisations of today's music therapists – children of John Cage and Karlheinz Stockhausen, as Tyler notes in her chapter – would have been shunned as cacophony only a few decades ago. Medieval physicians, trained to run through the non-naturals as part of preventive medicine, needed only to recommend music: they did not have to perform it themselves, and their involvement would usually have been extremely shallow by comparison with the intense interaction between patient and client that characterizes today's music therapy sessions.[116]

Modern music therapy needs a history from which it may derive a sense of its own particularity. That history must not, however, be written in Whiggish, teleological spirit. Medical history, for its part, needs music therapy – needs, that is, to include it in its master narrative of the past – but in just measure, a golden mean between excess and deficiency that should be the hallmark of scholarship as well as the ideal state of the body. The historical essays which follow mark a first step in that direction.

Notes

1. 'Jede Kranckheit ist ein musicalisches Problem – die Heilung eine *musicalische Auflösung*': Novalis, *Schriften*, vol. 3, ed. R. Samuel et al. (Stuttgart, 1960), p. 310, no. 386.

2. London, 1934; 3rd edn 1966, p. 200.

3. Lambert, *Music Ho!*, pp. 201, 204–5.

4. A. Malraux, *Museum without Walls*, English trans. (London, 1967).

5. G. Steiner, *In Bluebeard's Castle: Some Notes Towards the Redefinition of Culture* (London, 1971), p. 90.

6. R. Scruton, *The Aesthetics of Music* (Oxford, 1997), pp. 496 ff.

7. H. M. Sharma, E. M. Kauffman and R. E. Stephens, 'Effect of Different Sounds on Growth of Human Cancer Cell Lines In Vitro', *Alternative Therapies in Clinical Practice*, 3.4 (1996), pp. 25–32 at 25.

8. P. Gouk (ed.), *Musical Healing in Cultural Contexts* (Aldershot, 2000), should be seen as complementary to the present volume, being mainly anthropological in approach, in contrast to our historical thrust.

9. Sharma et al., 'Effect', p. 26.

10. Sharma et al., 'Effect', p. 25.

11. Sharma et al., 'Effect', cite: T. C. N. Singh and A. Gnanam, 'Studies on the Effect of Sound Waves of Nadeshwaram on the Growth and Yield of Paddy', *Journal of Annamalai University*, 16 (1975), pp. 78–99; C. B. Hicks, 'Growing Corn to Music', *Popular Mechanics*, 119 (1963), pp. 118–21; D. Retallack, *The Sound of Music and Plants* (Santa Monica, CA, 1973), pp. 20–33. See also P. Tompkins and C. Bird, *The Secret Life of Plants* (New York, 1973), pp. 145–62.

12. Sharma et al., 'Effect', pp. 25, 29–30.

13. Sharma et al., 'Effect', p. 29.

14. *Radio Times*, 11–17 July 1998.

15. '"No Pill's Gonna Cure My Ill": Gender, Erotic Melancholy, and Traditions of Musical Healing in the Modern West', in Gouk, *Musical Healing*, pp. 113–36. See also her chapter below.

16. See Lüdtke, Chapter 13, for New Age versions of tarantism.

17. E. Miles, *Tune your Brain: Using Music to Manage your Mind, Body and Mood* (http://www.tuneyourbrain.com.13).

18. Britannia Music Company Catalogues, 1998–99. Compare 'New Spirit', a CD and book club that offers titles such as *The Tao of Music: Using Music to Change your Life*.

19. SK 62263. The compiler, Aegidius of Zamora, accepted in ch. 2 of his *Ars musica* the standard ancient *topoi* about musical healing; but that is another matter.

20. See http://www.stpatrick-hospital.org/chalice/musicthan.html.

21. See F. Paxton, *Christianizing Death: The Creation of a Ritual Process in Early Medieval Europe* (Ithaca and London, 1990), included in the 'Chalice of Repose' list of books for sale.

22. First published 1973, 4th edn, 1990: references are to the Picador paperback. See pp. xxi–xxiii for the textual history, 367–86 for the *Nachleben* of stage and screen.

23. Sacks, *Awakenings*, p. xiii.

24. Sacks, *Awakenings*, pp. 17, 125, 160, 270.

25. Sacks, *Awakenings*, p. 330.

26. Sacks, *Awakenings*, p. 60.

27. Paul Robertson, personal information.

28. P. Robertson, *Music and the Mind* (London, 1996), p. 24.

29. Robertson, *Music and the Mind*, p. 25, italics added.

30. Sacks, *Awakenings*, p. 60 n. 45.

31. *Music Therapy Research and Practice in Medicine: From out of the Silence* (London and Bristol, PA, 1996), p. 51.

32. Robertson, *Music and the Mind*, p. 27.

33. Robertson, *Music and the Mind*, p. 27.

34. Among a large literature, I have leaned most heavily on two monographs: L. Bunt, *Music Therapy: An Art Beyond Words* (London and New York, 1994); D. Aldridge, *Music Therapy Research and Practice in Medicine: From Out of the Silence* (London and Bristol, PA, 1996). Among collections of articles, the most useful have proved to be: R. Spintge and R. Droh (eds) *MusicMedicine*, International Society for Music in Medicine, IV. International MusicMedicine Symposium … 1989 (Saint Louis, 1992); M. Heal and T. Wigram (eds), *Music Therapy in Health and Education* (London and Philadelphia, 1993); T. Wigram, B. Saperston and R. West (eds), *The Art and Science of Music Therapy: A Handbook* (Chur, Switzerland, 1995); D. Aldridge (ed.), *Music Therapy in Palliative Care* (London and Philadelphia, 1999).

35. Bunt, *Music Therapy*, p. 9.

36. Bunt, *Music Therapy*, p. 55.

37. C. F. Chabris et al., 'Prelude or Requiem for the "Mozart Effect"', *Nature*, 400 (26 Aug. 1999), pp. 826–8. Compare the journal *Psychology of Music*, 26 (1998), or *Musica Research Notes*, via http://www.musica.uci.edu/.

38. http://www.ncbi.nlm.nih.gov/PubMed/.

39. Though compare L. Marchette et al., 'Pain Reduction during Neonatal Circumcision', in Spintge and Droh, *MusicMedicine*, pp. 131–6.

40. Bunt, *Music Therapy*, p. 30.

41. World Federation of Music Therapy, *Bulletin*, 1 (July 1997), italics added.

42. Aldridge, *Music Therapy Research*, pp. 181, 259.

43. I summarize Aldridge, *Music Therapy Research*, pp. 265–7. Bunt, *Music Therapy*, includes many other case histories: see p. 162.

44. Bunt, *Music Therapy*, p. 179.

45. C. D. Maranto, 'Applications of Music in Medicine', in Heal and Wigram, *Music Therapy in Health and Education*, p. 159.

46. See Bunt, *Music Therapy*, p. 73; Aldridge, *Music Therapy Research*, pp. 161–2; J. Alvin, *Music Therapy*, first published 1966 (revised paperback, London, 1983), p. 92. S. Langer, *Philosophy in a New Key* (Cambridge, MA, 1942); *Feeling and Form: A Theory of Art* (London, 1953). Scruton, *The Aesthetics of Music*, pp. 147, 166–7. Langer's theories are discussed more fully in *The Philosophy of Music Education Review*, 1.1 (1993).

47. B. Hesser, 'The Power of Sound and Music in Therapy and Healing', in C. B. Kenny (ed.), *Listening, Playing, Creating: Essays on the Power of Sound* (Albany, NY, 1995), pp. 43–50 at 47.

48. J. M. Janzen, *Ngoma: Discourses of Healing in Central and Southern Africa* (Berkeley, Los Angeles and Oxford, 1992); M. Roseman, *Healing Sounds from the Malaysian Rainforest: Temiar Music and Medicine* (Berkeley and Los Angeles, 1991); B. Kapferer, *The Feast of the Sorcerer: Practices of Consciousness and Power* (Chicago and London, 1997), esp. pp. 115–20; R. Devisch, *Weaving the Threads of Life: The Khita Gyn-Eco-Logical Healing Cult among the Yaka* (Chicago and London, 1993). For older bibliography see S. M. Friedson, *Dancing Prophets: Musical Experience in Tumbuka Healing* (Chicago and London, 1996), pp. xii, 186 n. 3, but especially R. Katz, *Boiling Energy: Community Healing among the Kalahari Kung* (Cambridge, MA and London, 1982). Note also F. Hurter, *Heilung und Musik in Afrika* (Frankfurt am Main, Bern and New York, 1986).

49. Friedson, *Dancing Prophets*, p. 12. See also Janzen, *Ngoma*, ch. 1, for example p. 12.

50. Friedson, 'Dancing the Disease: Diagnostics and Therapeutics in Timbuka Healing', in Gouk, *Musical Healing*, pp. 67–84.

51. G. Prins, 'But What was the Disease? The Present State of Health and Healing in African Studies', *Past and Present*, no. 124 (1989), pp. 176–7. Compare Janzen, *Ngoma*, pp. 35–7.

52. M. Herzfeld, 'Closure as Cure: Tropes in the Exploration of Bodily and Social Disorder', *Current Anthropology*, 27 (1986), pp. 107–20.

53. For example Janzen, *Ngoma*, p. 143. See also Janzen, 'Theories of Music in African Ngoma Healing', in Gouk, *Musical Healing*, pp. 46–66, esp. p. 59.

54. M. Roseman, '"Pure Products Go Crazy": Rainforest Healing in a Nation-State', in C. Laderman and M. Roseman (eds), *The Perform-*

ance of Healing (New York and London, 1996), p. 252. See also Roseman, *Healing Sounds*, ch. 4. Janzen, *Ngoma*, pp. 176–7, compares healing 'cults of affliction' to institutions such as Alcoholics Anonymous.

55. Bunt, *Music Therapy*, pp. 72–3, 185. Compare Alvin, *Music Therapy*, pp. 9–10, 19, 23. For shamanism, see Howard, Chapter 15.

56. See M. Pavlicevic, *Music Therapy in Context: Music, Meaning and Relationship* (London and Chicago, 1998), a book by a therapist working in South Africa which, despite its title, largely ignores a promising ethnographic context.

57. E. E. Evans-Pritchard, *Witchcraft, Oracles, and Magic among the Azande*, abridged edition (Oxford, 1976), pp. 72–7.

58. Friedson, *Dancing Prophets*, pp. xiii–xiv; Turner, *The Drums of Affliction: A Study of Religious Processes among the Ndembu of Zambia* (Oxford, 1968). See also Turner, *The Forest of Symbols: Aspects of Ndembu Ritual*, first published 1967 (Ithaca and London, 1970), ch. 10: 'A Ndembu Doctor in Practice', pp. 385, 389.

59. Friedson, *Dancing Prophets*, p. xi. Gouk, *Musical Healing*, to which Friedson contributes (pp. 57–84), represents a conference at which music therapists and medical anthropologists were at last able to communicate.

60. L. M. Danforth, *Firewalking and Religious Healing: The Anastenaria of Greece and the American Firewalking Movement* (Princeton, NJ, 1989), pp. 103–22. See also n. 56.

61. I. van Wetering, 'Women as *Winti* Healers: Rationality and Contradiction in the Preservation of a Suriname Healing Tradition', in M. Gijswijt-Hofstra, H. Marland and H. de Waardt (eds), *Illness and Healing Alternatives in Western Europe* (London and New York, 1997), pp. 243–61.

62. Laderman, 'The Poetics of Healing in Malay Shamanistic Performances', in Laderman and Roseman, *The Performance of Healing*, p. 116.

63. Bunt, *Music Therapy*, p. 187.

64. Alvin, *Music Therapy*, pp. 12, 16.

65. On whom see Gouk, below.

66. Gentilcore, León, Lüdtke, below.

67. Alvin, *Music Therapy*, ch. 4.

68. Alvin, *Music Therapy*, p. 46, quoting R. Brocklesby, *Reflections on Ancient and Modern Musick, with the Application to the Cure of Diseases* (London, 1749), pp. 34–5. On Brocklesby and his context see Gouk, below.

69. Alvin, *Music Therapy*, p. 58, drawing on I Samuel chs 16, 18–19, 24. On Farinelli see now P. Barbier, *Farinelli: le castrat des Lumières* (Paris, 1994), pp. 111 ff. For David see Shiloah, Chapter 3; and Jones, Chapter 6. Contrast J. Godwin, *Harmonies of Heaven and Earth: The Spiritual Dimension of Music from Antiquity to the Avant-Garde*

(London, 1987), p. 36, on how such anecdotes may be 'more a burden than an asset to the profession today': they exaggerate expectations.

70. Tyler, Chapter 16.

71. For a taste of the criticism see again Tyler.

72. Bunt, *Music Therapy*, pp. 10–11. Compare W. B. Davis, K. E. Gfeller and M. H. Thaut, *An Introduction to Music Therapy: Theory and Practice* (Dubuque, IA, 1992), pp. 16–37 ('Music Therapy: An Historical Perspective').

73. Sharma et al., 'Effect', p. 29.

74. M. Foucault, *The Birth of the Clinic* (London, 1973), is the classic narration of the disappearance, in the late-eighteenth to nineteenth centuries, of the sick person from the clinician's gaze, to be replaced by a body with lesions. On the more recent, reactive, 'patient as person' movement see briefly R. Porter, *The Greatest Benefit to Mankind* (London, 1997), p. 682.

75. Though compare B. J. Good, *Medicine, Rationality, and Experience: An Anthropological Perspective* (Cambridge, 1994), ch. 3: 'How Medicine Constructs its Objects'.

76. See Part IV below.

77. 'Emotional Expression in Music', in Schullian and Schoen, *Music and Medicine*, pp. 244–65. Compare the opinion quite widespread in 1920s and '30s America that jazz was evil and corrupting: A. P. Merriam, *The Anthropology of Music* (Evanston, IL, 1964), pp. 241–4. For full discussion, see P. Gouk, 'Sister Disciplines? *Music and Medicine* in Historical Perspective', in Gouk, *Musical Healing*, pp. 171–96.

78. *Music and Medicine*, pp. 407–71.

79. Carl Gregor, Herzog zu Mecklenburg, *Bibliographie einiger Grenzgebiete der Musikwissenschaft* (Baden-Baden, 1962), adds over a decade's worth of material.

80. W. F. Bynum and R. Porter (eds), 2 vols. (London, 1993). See also I. G. Berrios and R. Porter (eds), *A History of Clinical Psychiatry* (London, 1995), which mentions music with reference only to David and Saul (p. 414).

81. *Freiburger Beiträge zur Wissenschafts- und Universitätsgeschichte*, vol. 2, Munich.

82. *Madness and Civilization: A History of Insanity in the Age of Reason*, paperback edn, abbreviated translation (London, 1971), p. 178.

83. Kümmel, *Musik und Medizin*, p. 223. New edn and trans. R. Strohm and J. D. Cullington, *On the Dignity and Effects of Music ... Two Fifteenth-Century Treatises*, Institute of Advanced Musical Studies, King's College London, Study Texts no. 2 (1996), ch. 14 (112), pp. 57, 73, with 64 n. 49. Compare, in the same volume, Egidius Carlerius, 'Treatise on ... Church Music', 87, pp. 28, 44: 'euphonious music has sometimes even cured severe illnesses'.

84. Kümmel, *Musik und Medizin*, p. 227, citing Rodericus a Castro, *Medicus Politicus, sive de Officiis Medico-Politicus Tractatus* (Hamburg, 1662), p. 276.

85. Jones, Chapter 6.

86. M. Taviner, G. Thwaites and V. Gant, 'The English Sweating Sickness, 1485–1551: A Viral Pulmonary Disease?', *Medical History*, 42 (1998), pp. 96–8.

87. Kümmel, *Musik und Medizin*, pp. 334–5; U. von Hutten, *De Guaiaci Medicina et Morbo Gallico Liber Unus* (Mainz, 1519). For context see now J. Arrizabalaga, J. Henderson and R. French, *The Great Pox: The French Disease in Renaissance Europe* (New Haven and London, 1997), pp. 100–103.

88. Kümmel, *Musik und Medizin*, p. 13.

89. See C. R. S. Harris, *The Heart and the Vascular System in Ancient Greek Medicine* (Oxford, 1973), ch. 7. N. Siraisi, 'The Music of the Pulse in the Writings of Italian Academic Physicians (Fourteenth and Fifteenth Centuries)', *Speculum*, 50 (1975), pp. 689–710; S. Hafenreffer, *Monochordon symbolico-biomanticum ...* (Ulm, 1640), an eccentric early modern treatise on pulse.

90. On *consilia*, see Siraisi, *Taddeo Alderotti and His Pupils: Two Generations of Italian Medical Learning* (Princeton NJ, 1981), ch. 9; J. Agrimi and C. Crisciani, *Les 'Consilia' médicaux*, Typologie des Sources du Moyen Age, no. 69 (Turnhout, 1994).

91. For example Kümmel, *Musik und Medizin*, pp. 236, 301, 319, 360.

92. Kümmel, *Musik und Medizin*, ch. 4.

93. See Siraisi, *Medieval and Renaissance Medicine* (Chicago and London, 1990), pp. 101–106, for this and what follows.

94. For the non-naturals, see G. Olson, *Literature as Recreation in the Later Middle Ages* (Ithaca and London, 1982), pp. 40–44; L. García-Ballester, 'On the Origin of the "Six Non-Natural Things" in Galen', in G. Harig and J. Harig-Kollesch (eds), *Galen und die Hellenistische Erbe* (Wiesbaden, 1993), pp. 105–115. Further, Shiloah, Jones, and Gouk, below.

95. Trans. E. Grant, *Sourcebook of Medieval Science* (Cambridge, MA, 1974), pp. 708–9.

96. J. Arrizabalaga, 'Facing the Black Death: Perceptions and Reactions of University Medical Practitioners', in L. García-Ballester et al. (eds), *Practical Medicine from Salerno to the Black Death* (Cambridge, 1994), p. 280. See also A. Wear, 'Fear, Anxiety and the Plague in Early Modern England', in J. R. Hinnells and R. Porter (eds), *Religion, Health and Suffering* (London and New York, 1999), p. 355, for a seventeenth-century parallel; more generally Olson, *Literature as Recreation*, ch. 5.

97. Jackson, *Melancholia and Depression: From Hippocratic Times to Modern Times* (New Haven and London, 1986), pp. 392–3.

98. Jackson, ch. II.2; compare Kümmel, *Musik und Medizin*, pp. 290–91.

99. Trans. in R. Klibansky, E. Panofsky and F. Saxl, *Saturn and Melancholy* (London, 1964), p. 85, with Jackson, *Melancholia*, p. 59.

100. Jackson, *Melancholia*, pp. 64, 82. Further, Jones, Gouk, Austern, below.

101. Although he can produce a few references to it in writings of lesser figures: Jackson, *Melancholia*, pp. 300–304.

102. Olson, *Literature as Recreation*, ch. 2, esp. pp. 55–64.

103. Siraisi, *Medieval and Early Renaissance Medicine*, pp. 65–8; Kümmel, *Musik und Medizin*, pp. 70–71. See further Commentary on Part II, and Austern, below.

104. See L. J. Rather, 'Systematic Medical Treatises from the Ninth to the Nineteenth Century: The Unchanging Scope and Structure of Academic Medicine in the West', *Clio Medica*, 11 (1976), pp. 289–305.

105. Isidore, *Etymologiae*, IV.13.

106. Hanslick, *On the Musically Beautiful*, trans. G. Payzant (Indianapolis, 1986), p. 51. Contrast C. Burney, *A General History of Music*, 2nd edn (London, 1789, repr. New York, 1957): the opening 'Dissertation on the Music of the Ancients', section 10, dutifully, if sceptically, repeats the usual anecdotes.

107. Hanslick, *On the Musically Beautiful*, pp. 52–3. On Lichtenthal see further Kramer, below.

108. O. Temkin, *The Falling Sickness: A History of Epilepsy from the Greeks to the Beginnings of Modern Neurology*, 2nd edn (Baltimore and London, 1971), pp. 66 ff., 102 ff., 232 ff., 291 ff. Compare Kümmel, *Musik und Medizin*, pp. 376–7 (not citing this work).

109. R. Porter and G. S. Rousseau, *Gout: the Patrician Malady* (New Haven and London, 1998); Arrizabalaga et al., *The Great Pox*.

110. As in Richard Strauss's opera *Capriccio*. See West, this volume, and his *Ancient Greek Music* (Oxford, 1992), p. 32. Contrast J. Combarieu, *La musique et la magie* (Paris, 1909), an attempt, in the grand manner, to derive the whole of music from magical incantation.

111. See C. Rawcliffe, 'Medicine for the Soul: The Medieval English Hospital and the Quest for Spiritual Health', in Hinnells and Porter, *Religion, Health and Suffering*, pp. 316–38.

112. F. S. Paxton, 'Liturgy and Healing in an Early Medieval Saint's Cult: The Mass *in honore Sancti Sigismundi* for the Cure of Fevers', *Traditio*, 49 (1994), pp. 23–43. Compare H. Sigerist, 'The Story of Tarantism', in Schullian and Schoen, *Music and Medicine*, pp. 96–8.

113. G. Holst-Warhaft, *Dangerous Voices: Women's Laments and Greek Literature* (London, 1992), p. 73.

114. B. Newman (ed.), *Voice of the Living Light: Hildegard of Bingen and her World* (Berkeley, Los Angeles and London, 1998); N. G. Siraisi, *The Clock and the Mirror: Girolamo Cardano and Renaissance Medicine* (Princeton, NJ, 1997), esp. p. 122; H. de Jong, *Michael Maier's Atalanta Fugiens*, Janus supplement 8 (Leiden, 1969), with F. Yates, *The Rosicrucian Enlightenment* (London, 1972), pp. 70–91; M.

MacDonald, *Mystical Bedlam: Madness, Anxiety, and Healing in Seventeenth-Century England* (Cambridge, 1981).

115. Kümmel, *Musik und Medizin*, p. 412.

116. H. Tyler, 'Music Therapy', in T. Ford (ed.), *The Musician's Handbook*, 3rd edn (London, 1996), p. 92.

PART I

Ancient Literate Traditions

Commentary on Part I,
with a Note on China

Peregrine Horden

I

There have been four major traditions of literate, learned medicine in world history. One is that of the Greeks and Romans, another (which descended from the first)[1] that of the Arabs, a third that of the Indian subcontinent, the fourth that of the Chinese.[2] All are focused on classical texts of considerable, though of course varying, antiquity. The first part of our collection ranges principally across three of these traditions, as well as touching on Judaic texts, especially biblical ones. In two cases (Shiloah, Chapter 3; and Katz, Chapter 4) the authors heroically embrace both distant origins and more recent evidence. By contrast, West's discussion of the Mediterranean world can stop on the threshold of the Middle Ages because this volume's primary focus is the European classical tradition and other chapters, in Part II, will pick up the story.

Why begin like this? First, because these various traditions provide the earliest hard evidence of the extent and nature of musical therapeutics. There is simply no point in starting earlier. Synopses of the subject included in music therapy manuals occasionally try to take us further back – to the pre-classical civilizations of Mesopotamia or Egypt for example.[3] Yet specific and pertinent references are never forthcoming. There may well have been magical uses for healing music in proto-historic times. And these, if they were documented, could perhaps be part of our subject matter here, just as they will be when we come to the Renaissance (see Part III). Perhaps music once derived from magic; yet, as West points out, the singing of an incantation is by no means clearly an essential or even an important part of a magical operation: the words matter far more.[4] In default of specific evidence that is older than classical antiquity, we can only speculate; and in Chapter 2 we shall see West speculating about the very ancient – even palaeolithic – beliefs that might underlie traces in early Greek

literature of the use of musical instruments to manipulate the spirits –
spirits of the very animals from whose bodies the instruments were
made. Here the figure of the shaman makes his first appearance. He
will hover in the background later on, as well as come to the fore in
the penultimate chapter as a representative of non-European musical
healers of the present day (see also Chapter 1). Apart from him and
his presumed antecedents, enfolded by the mists of time in the
Siberian tundra, there are, however, no very early musical healers of
whom we have even indirect information. So, West's speculation
apart, we must begin where we do, with the literate medical cultures.

A second reason for putting them at the start of this collection is
that we need, as early in the proceedings as possible, to gain some
idea of the place of music therapy in traditions which have often, from
the end of antiquity onwards, been upheld as the practice's golden
age. In the last section of Chapter 1, it was suggested that claims for
the centrality of music in the European classical tradition of medicine
have perhaps been exaggerated. The case for the defence now has to
be reviewed in more detail, culture by culture, period by period. What
will emerge from that review may be dispiriting for those who hope to
find historical justification for the modern standing of the professional
music therapist. That does not make the results any the less interesting
or valuable as history.

Music was not in the regular armoury of the educated physician in
ancient Greece, Rome, India or China. Whether we look at the corpus
of writings ascribed in Hellenistic times to Hippocrates, at the still
more voluminous canon of Galen's works, the fundamental treatises
of Ayurveda, or the Chinese *Inner Canon* or the *Canon of Problems*,
therapy involving music is scarcely described or recommended. It is
philosophy and religion that make conceptual room for music therapy.
Indeed, within those currents of writing, as within literature more
widely, music therapy may be of absorbing conceptual interest. But it
seems to have been only marginal to learned medical authorities.
Indeed, several of the late antique medical writers mentioned by West
thought music therapy was useless in many cases – which is, of
course, testimony to its probable availability, but availability outside
the best medical circles as these writers defined them.

We start, then, on a strong note of caution. After his initial discussions of shamanism, magic and early Greek religion, West introduces us to the figure who has so often been taken as a founding father of music therapy, Pythagoras. But Pythagoras is not a reassuring figure. He remains elusive because there is no reliable evidence about him and precious little about his followers – although we can say with some confidence that they are the first groups that we know to have used music systematically as a vehicle of therapy, for bodily as well as psychological ailments. The cosmological ideas of the Pythagoreans are also important because they become entwined with the development of the notion that each musical mode has a specific ethos, a notion touched on in Chapter 1 and, in West's contribution, given a fuller explanation and historical context.[5]

All this seems at least promising; yet it is not a promise that Roman medicine – heir to Greek learning in this as in so much else – was to fulfil. West documents a phenomenon that has dogged the historiography of music therapy: the semblance of activity created by the recycling of anecdote. There are occasional instances of music's being recommended for ills of the psyche, but very much in a 'low-key' manner that anticipates the manipulation of the non-naturals in medieval thought (see Horden and Jones), with music put on the same medicinal level as pleasant wine and conversation. 'Music therapy [West concludes] was fringe medicine, even if one or two doctors are recorded as having made some use of it.' Interest in its potential was sustained – and transmitted to later centuries in Europe – by philosophical and musicological literature, especially those currents associated with the names of Pythagoras and, still more, Plato – to whom is owed the most influential formulation of the theory that music therapy works by effecting an attunement of soul to cosmos.

If music therapy in classical antiquity can be summed up as mainstream philosophy but marginal medicine, the medieval Arab medical world was far more generous. This literate culture owed much, via translations from Greek or Syriac, to the learning of Greece. In medical terms, though, it was dominated by the voluminous outpourings of Galen, who had virtually nothing to say about music therapy. None the less, medieval Islamic medicine seems to have given music therapy a relative prominence in both theory and practice, in the consulting room and the hospital, which had no clear precedent, and which it was not to enjoy again until quite modern times. The efflorescence should not be exaggerated. The largest corpus of surviving clinical case histories in medieval Islamic medicine, that of al-Razi (865–925), for example seems not to mention musical treatment.[6] Scholars such as Ibn Hindu (of whom more in Chapter 3) regarded genuine musical healing as belonging to the remote past, a technique almost lost even by Hippocratic times, the stuff of anecdote from very early on:

> The science of music also belongs to the medical art in some way or other. Relying on Hippocrates, Theon of Alexandria tells that the previous philosophers [sc. Pythagoreans?] would cure the sick by melodies and by playing the instrument called *lyra*, and the shawm. However ... that kind of therapy has decayed and vanished. Even Hippocrates, with all his greatness, did not know it any longer ...[7]

At least it can be said that music therapy appears to have been more widely discussed and respected in early Islam than it had been in the ancient Mediterranean world. Why this should have been so is very difficult to establish, not least because of the extremity of the orthodox suspicion of music in Islamic culture. Ancient example is certainly not enough, even though the Arabs were influenced by some ancient medical writers more favourable than Galen to musical healing (notably Rufus of Ephesus). Persian or other 'oriental' influences should perhaps also be envisaged, although very little can be said about them.[8] Such unsolved problems apart, music therapy in the medieval and Ottoman Islamic Middle East has been the subject of several illuminating essays.[9] Only now, however, in the writings of Shiloah, of which we have here an example, is it receiving fully rounded treatment.[10] Deliberately omitting the use of incantations in the 'Medicine of the Prophet' (pieces of medical advice attributed to Muhammed, later systematized),[11] Shiloah's chapter otherwise ranges widely, from ancient Israel to the modern Middle East. Its focus is, however, Arab learning in medieval and Ottoman times, and the significant development during that period of classical ideas about the attunement of individual and environment through music, and about the associated concept of 'ethos'. This development supplies the theoretical dimension that could be found in ancient philosophy but hardly at all in ancient medicine. As for the practice, Shiloah finds it in the major hospitals of the Caliphate – few in number admittedly, but large and lavish, and, unlike contemporary Western foundations, secular in character. Descriptions of them, often by travellers from abroad, leave no doubt as to the regularity and status of music in the therapy of some of the grander hospitals, whose patients were primarily the insane.[12]

As we turn towards India, the contrast with classical Greek conceptions becomes less striking than the similarities. In the Hindu traditions expounded by Katz, theory seems more abundant than evidence of practice, as it was in the time of Plato. There are many texts that bear on therapy in a very broad sense, a conceptual 'space' in which musical therapeutics might have been expected. There is an equivalent to the Greek notion of ethos, and – yet again – an abundance of anecdotes, about the power of music to alter nature. There is also some evidence of musical incantation and, as with the Greeks, of the use of music to counteract snakebite. Yet when the central texts of classical Ayurvedic medicine are interrogated, they yield only some general comments on the way in which music can be part of a beneficial environment, comments vaguely akin to the European theory of the non-naturals. Beyond that, nothing. In keeping with that absence of evidence (which, in this case, really does seem to be evidence of absence), Katz ends his account by referring to a manuscript tantalizingly (and perhaps uniquely) recorded as concerning rāga therapeutics – a manuscript now lost.

II

This collection is comparative in scope and (it is hoped) sceptical in outlook. Part of its point is to show where music therapy has not been significant as well as where it has. There seemed, however, to be no need to carry the principle to its extreme and include a chapter on the last of the great traditions of learned medicine, the Chinese. In one sense the whole of Chinese culture, including music, is therapeutic. That is because the Chinese word for culture can be roughly translated as 'drawing out in order to dispel' (*wen* for 'drawing lines', *hwa* for 'dissolve').[13] The ingredients of music therapy in the more usual, narrower sense also seem to be present. The individual body is viewed as a microcosm, which is, superficially, close to the Platonic–Pythagorean conception. But there is also, perhaps unexpectedly, a second mirror of the universe: the state. Along with ritual, music thus has a social-cum-ethical role which is analogous to the governance of the individual body in the Pythagorean tradition.

> Music serves to unite. Ritual serves to differentiate. Through union the people come to be friendly toward one another, and through differentiation the people come to learn respect for one another. When music gains the upper hand there is reckless abandon ...[14]

Thus the earliest fully developed treatise on music to survive, the *Yue Ji*. In appropriate quantities, music is calming, satisfaction-inducing; it can 'level out' likes and dislikes. It counteracts the social disharmony which is pathogenic to the extent that it can hinder recovery from sickness. Most resoundingly – and gnomically: 'only through music can no falsehood be done'. From such conceptual beginnings, music takes its place in a system of correspondences as complex as anything that we shall find in medieval Islamic thought. The Five Phases, *wu xing* (for which 'elements' would be a misleading translation), are aligned with specific colours, flavours, emotions, visceral systems, etc. – and with the five musical modes.[15] Emotions for which music might have been seen as palliative, such as pent-up anger, fear and melancholy, are, as in the European tradition, considered to be potentially pathogenic (at least in women and children).[16] But, as with both Hippocratic and Ayurvedic medicine, there is (so far as I can establish) nothing in the canonical texts of Chinese medicine to suggest that music, though an image of cosmos, body politic, and individual body, was much used to transfer order – that is, health – from the cosmos to individuals. Like those of the Indian tradition, anecdotes about the quasi-magical transformative power of music concern its effects on nature, not on disease.[17]

Hence the ancient Mediterranean, the Islamic Middle East, and India are all represented in what follows; China is omitted. With this particular subject, ancient learned medicine, returns seemingly diminish as one moves across Eurasia.

Notes

1.   D. Gutas, *Greek Thought, Arabic Culture: The Graeco-Arabic Translation Movement in Baghdad and Early 'Abbasid Society* (London, 1998). Further Shiloah, below.

2.   For general background see L. Conrad, M. Neve, V. Nutton, R. Porter and A. Wear, *The Western Medical Tradition 800 B.C. to A.D. 1800* (Cambridge, 1995), and, for the oriental traditions, W. Bynum and R. Porter (eds), *Companion Encyclopedia of the History of Medicine*, 2 vols (London, 1993), vol. 1.

3.   W. B. Davis, K. E. Gfeller and M. H. Traut, *An Introduction to Music Therapy: Theory and Practice* (Dubuque, IA, 1992), p. 18; C. W. Hughes, 'Rhythm and Health', in D. M. Schullian and M. Schoen (eds), *Music and Medicine* (New York, 1948), pp. 171–2.

4.   See, for example, *The Greek Magical Papyri in Translation*, vol. 1: *Texts*, ed. H. D. Betz (Chicago and London, 1992). Compare P. Lain Entralgo, *The Therapy of the Word in Classical Antiquity* (New Haven and London, 1970); F. C. R. Thee, *Julius Africanus and the Early Christian View of Magic* (Tübingen, 1984).

5.   See also West, *Ancient Greek Music* (Oxford, 1992), pp. 246–53.

6.   C. Álvarez Millán, 'Practice versus Theory: Tenth-Century Case Histories from the Islamic Middle East', in P. Horden and E. Savage-Smith (eds), *The Year 1000: Practical Medicine at the End of the First Millennium*, special issue of *Social History of Medicine* (forthcoming, 2000).

7.   Trans. J. C. Bürgel, *The Feather of Simurgh: The 'Licit Magic' of the Arts in Medieval Islam* (New York and London, 1988), pp. 98–9.

8.   For Rufus, see C. Burnett, '"Spiritual Medicine": Music and Healing in Islam and its Influence in Western Medicine', in P. Gouk (ed.), *Musical Healing in Cultural Contexts* (Aldershot, 2000), pp. 85–91 at 85–6. For 'oriental' influence, E. Neubauer, 'Arabische Anleitungen zur Musiktherapie', *Zeitschrift für Geschichte der arabisch-islamischen Wissenschaften*, 6 (1990), pp. 229, 260.

9.   Neubauer, 'Arabische Anleitungen'; J. C. Bürgel, 'Musicotherapy in the Islamic Middle Ages as Reflected in Medical and Other Sources', *Studies in the History of Medicine*, 4 (1980), pp. 23–8; Bürgel, *The Feather of Simurgh*, ch. 4.

10.   Shiloah, *Music in the World of Islam: A Socio-Cultural Study* (Aldershot, 1995), pp. 49 ff.

11.   For example, Ibn Qayyim al-Jawziyya, *Medicine of the Prophet*, trans. P. Johnstone (Cambridge, 1998), ch. 31, with M. W. Dols, *Majnūn: The Madman in Medieval Islamic Society* (Oxford, 1992), ch. 8 (c).

12.   Dols, *Majnūn*, ch. 6 (a), (c).

13.   Tony Wang, personal communication.

14. Trans. S. Cook, '*Yue Ji* – Record of Music', *Asian Music*, 26.2 (1995), 1–96; quotation at II.1 (p. 42). For what follows see I.6,7; II.5; VI.4.

15. N. Sivin, *Traditional Medicine in Contemporary China* (Ann Arbor, 1987), pp. 54–7. F. Bray, 'Chinese Medicine', in Bynum and Porter, *Companion Encyclopedia*, pp. 728–54 at 734–6.

16. Bray, 'Chinese Medicine', p. 738.

17. L. Picken, 'The Music of Far Eastern Asia: 1. China', in E. Wellesz (ed.), *Ancient and Oriental Music* (London, New York and Toronto, 1957), pp. 87–8.

CHAPTER TWO

Music Therapy in Antiquity

Martin West

The connection between music and medicine is very ancient. In all probability (though there is no direct proof) it goes back to palaeolithic times. It certainly has its roots in a primitive world-view, and before I consider music therapy in the Graeco-Roman world, I want to say something about these primitive roots.

Ever since the beginning of human society, men and women have had to contend with sicknesses and ailments, both physical and psychological. What did they see as the source of these ailments? In the case of a physical injury caused by a knife or an arrow or a falling stone, the answer was obvious. But for many kinds of ailment the answer was not obvious. Pre-scientific man had no conception of viruses or bacteria or the degeneration of cells. Illness was something of supernatural origin, caused probably by an enemy's evil magic, or by the angry spirits of the dead. The only way to counter it, therefore, was by using magical techniques of one's own. In most primitive societies this meant engaging the services of the specialist, the witchdoctor or shaman, the man who alone knew the requisite techniques and possessed the necessary equipment with which to deploy them. This was a man able to contact and command the spirits, able if need be to travel to the other world and negotiate with the spirits or actually to fight and overpower them.

The most primitive musical instruments had the potential to be used for magical purposes, and specifically for the purposes of conjuring spirits from the other world. The particular instruments I have in mind, which seem to be the most primitive at any rate in Europe and Asia, are the drum, the bow, the flute, and the horn. They go back into remote antiquity; a bone flute has recently been reported from a Neanderthal context in Slovenia dated between 43,000 and 67,000 years ago.[1]

The drum, made of skin stretched over a frame, produced a boom-
ing sound. The hunter's bow, when one end of it was put in the mouth
to provide a resonator, became a musical bow, which made a twang-
ing sound; it was from this that the harp eventually developed. The
flute, made by drilling holes in a hollow bone, gave out a series of
high whistling notes. And the horn of a cow made a simple sort of
trumpet.

But where did these sounds come from? *We* know that all these
instruments work by setting up vibrations and amplifying them, and
that the pitch of the note depends on the frequency of the vibrations.
But for the pre-scientific mind, the only attainable explanation is that
the mysterious sonorities are voices inherent in the things that produce
them. If you bang a gong, what you hear is the voice of the metal, or
of a spirit lodged in the metal.

Now consider the instruments I mentioned. They are all made from
parts of dead animals: the skin of the drum, the bowstring of gut or
sinew, the flute of bone, the cow-horn. Is it not an easy conclusion
that the unearthly sounds they produce come direct from the other
world? The drum is the shaman's typical instrument, which enables
him to summon and captivate the spirits, or to fly to the centre of the
world, where he can gain access to other worlds. There stands the
World Tree, from a branch of which (according to some Altai
shamans) the shell of their drum is fashioned.[2] When the drum is
animated by being anointed with blood – or beer, another life-giving
liquid – it comes alive and tells its story through the shaman's voice.
The wooden shell tells how it grew as a tree and was cut; the animal
from whose skin the drum has been made 'tells of its birth, its parents,
its childhood, and its whole life to the moment when it was brought
down by the hunter. It ends by promising the shaman that it will perform many services for him.'[3]

We can find traces of this idea, that the dead creature can speak
through the musical instrument made from its body, in Greek and later
literature, no longer as a serious doctrine, but in the realm of the
riddle, the metaphor, and the folk-tale. The Homeric *Hymn to Hermes*
tells the amusing story of how the infant god Hermes, on the very first
day of his life, slipped out of his cradle and stole Apollo's cattle. On
the way he found a tortoise, and told it, 'when you die, you will sing

sweetly'.[4] Then he killed it and made its shell into a lyre, thus inventing the instrument. The same story was treated by Sophocles in his
satyr-play *The Trackers*, which Tony Harrison adapted with some
success a few years ago at the National Theatre. A satyr-play is
nothing to do with satire; it is a kind of comedy with a mythological
setting and a chorus of satyrs, who are semi-human creatures who live
in the wild and have rather childlike characteristics, being cowardly,
innocent, and inquisitive. On hearing the novel sound of the lyre, they
question Hermes' mother, the nymph Cyllene, about it. She has told
them that it comes from a dead animal. 'But how am I to believe',
asks their spokesman, 'that the dead one's utterance can make such a
noise?' 'You must believe it,' she replies, 'for the creature acquired a
voice when it died, though it had none while it was alive.'[5] We have
an early elegiac couplet in which a symposiast explains to his fellows
that it is time for him to leave:

> For I'm called home now by a carcass of the sea,
> that e'en in death speaks through a living mouth.

Evidently he lives nearby, and his wife, or is it his father, is
summoning him by means of a conch, a shell trumpet; this is the
'carcass of the sea that e'en in death speaks through a living mouth'.[6]
Another verse riddle goes like this:

> A dead ass hits my ear with his horned leg.

The solution is a Phrygian pipe or hornpipe, made from an ass's shin-
bone with a cow's horn attached to the end.[7] Let me further recall the
medieval folk-tale motif of the musician who comes across the bone
of a murdered man and makes a flute out of it: the bone, thus rendered
vocal, is able to sing and denounce its owner's murderer. Lovers of
Mahler will be familiar with this theme from *Das klagende Lied*.

Here, then, is one potential source of the notion that music can be
harnessed for the purpose of healing. By means of music the expert
may conjure and control spirits, make them speak their secrets, com-
pel them to do his will. They can speak not only in the notes of the
instrument but also through the voice of the shaman: when he vocifer-
ates in strange tones, his audience recognizes that these are the voices
of the spirits speaking through him.

When we come to archaic Greece, we are in a different world from that of the Siberian shaman. And yet sometimes we seem to be only a step away from it. There are legends of singers whose music gave them power over nature. Amphion with his lyre conjures the stones together to build the walls of Thebes. Orpheus by his song exercises control over the natural world, the birds and the animals; he travels to the other world to recover the soul of Eurydice, and it is by virtue of his music that he is able to prevail over the powers of the underworld and induce them to release her. He has often been seen as a shamanistic figure.[8]

There are no stories of his acting as a healer of the sick. There are, however, references in fifth-century Athens to incantations of which Orpheus was the author and which (so the contexts imply) might include some of a therapeutic nature.[9] We hear of healing incantations already in the *Odyssey* (though not there in association with Orpheus). When the story is told of how Odysseus acquired the scar on his thigh which becomes one of the proofs of his identity, we learn that he was on a hunting expedition in his youth and was gored by a wild boar even as he thrust it through with his spear. His companions bound up his wound and stopped his bleeding with an incantation.[10] There are several other references in classical Greek writers to the use of incantations in healing and to assist childbirth, as well as for various other purposes.[11] It is clear that they did not form any part of mainstream medical practice but were resorted to by the superstitious.

It is doubtful whether incantations really deserve to be included under the heading of musical therapy, because – although the word means literally a 'singing over' someone; *incantare* = ἐπαείδειν – they depend for their efficacy on their wording rather than on any musical qualities. They are basically magic spells, and for all we know they may have been intoned or muttered rather than sung. A more definitely musical measure against sickness was the paean. This was a form of communal holy song performed in various circumstances, but especially associated with the idea of purification from injurious elements. One situation in which it was appropriate was plague. It is said that in the seventh century BC, when Sparta was suffering from a plague, an oracle recommended summoning Thaletas, who was a noted composer of paeans from Gortyn in Crete. This was done, and Thaletas successfully delivered the city from the pestilence by means of his music.[12] On a later occasion, in the fourth century, the women of Locri and Rhegium in south Italy were afflicted by a strange madness: they would suddenly jump up in the middle of dinner, hearing the call of a voice, and rush off into the country. The two cities consulted the oracle and were advised to sing twelve paeans a day (probably one every hour, on the hour) for sixty days. This called for a total of 720 paeans, and led to a great increase in the number of paean-writers in the area.[13]

We are not yet quite in the sphere of musical therapy as we would ordinarily understand the term, because these paeans are not supposed to exercise a direct effect on the sufferers: they work by appeasing the god who is causing the affliction. But there is one context in which we do hear of paeans (indeed, paeans of Thaletas) being sung in order to put people in a calm state of mind. It is alleged that Pythagoras used to sing them to his disciples, accompanying himself on the lyre, so as to bring them into a serene mood, or that they all sang them together.[14]

Now Pythagoras is a figure of particular importance for this whole matter. Let me first say something about who and what he was. Many people perhaps think of him as a mathematician on account of the so-called Pythagoras' Theorem, the one about the square on the hypotenuse, which was in fact known to the Babylonians centuries before Pythagoras; there is no evidence that Pythagoras knew it or was in a position to prove it.[15] Actually, we know very little that is definite about Pythagoras, because he left no writings, and his followers in later centuries were in the habit of ascribing all sorts of their own ideas to him. But we can say that he lived in the latter part of the sixth century BC, and that he seems to have been a sort of guru who beguiled his followers with exotic doctrines about the transmigration of the soul through a succession of animal bodies, punishment and purification, and a paradise in the sun and moon. He, or at any rate some of his early associates, had an interest in number which was probably more mystical than truly mathematical in character: number came to seem to them to be the key to the universe. They discovered that the basic musical concords, the octave, the fifth, and the fourth, corresponded to numerical ratios, 1:2, 2:3, and 3:4 respectively, and this inaugurated a long tradition of calculating ratios for the various intervals in each type of scale. It seemed to provide a new basis for theorizing about the effects of music on the soul. On the other hand, the early Pythagoreans maintained a series of primitive-looking taboos and superstitions governing the conduct of daily life.

Several threads come together at this point. There are some shamanistic features about Pythagoras – stories of his associating with gods and spirits, of his having a special relationship with animals, of his performing typical shaman's feats such as visiting and returning from the underworld, or being seen in two places at once.[16] He was interested in Orpheus, and he – or at any rate early Pythagoreans – put out poems under Orpheus' name. We hear of one 'Orphic' poem, evidently of Pythagorean origin (though probably not early Pythagorean) called 'The Lyre', which was about the use of lyre music to assist the soul to pass between this world and the other: a late version of a primitive shamanistic theme.[17] Among the cryptic sayings which Aristotle attributes to the early Pythagoreans, there is one that is worth quoting here. They said that the sound made when a bronze gong is struck was the voice of one of the demons imprisoned in the bronze.[18] This supplies another link with the primitive sphere of belief that I spoke of earlier.

Now, it is precisely in Pythagorean circles that we hear of a systematic use of music for therapeutic purposes. Aristoxenus wrote that the Pythagoreans 'used medicine for purifying the body, music for purifying the soul'. Other authors tell us that it was the Pythagoreans' custom to use song and lyre music when they got up in the morning to make them bright and alert, and when they went to bed to purge them of all the day's cares and to prepare them for agreeable and prophetic dreams. Iamblichus says that they had particular melodies that were most helpful in countering despondency and vexation, others appropriate to passion and rage, and others again to subdue lust; they also made use of dancing for such purposes. He notes that in addition to songs they made some use of wordless melodies, that is, tunes played on the lyre.[19]

When ancient writers talk about 'the Pythagoreans', it is important to ask, though often difficult to discover, which Pythagoreans the information relates to, or to what period. As I have said, everything in

Pythagorean tradition, early or late, tended to be projected back onto Pythagoras himself. In the case of this musical psychotherapy, there is no reliable basis for attributing it to Pythagoras. The earliest source is Aristoxenus in the fourth century BC. He had personal connections with Pythagoreans of his own time, and his information no doubt relates to them. There is in fact one named Pythagorean of about 400 BC, Kleinias of Tarentum, who is associated with this sort of practice. It is reported of him that whenever he found himself angry, he would play the lyre, and if anyone asked what he was doing, he would say 'I am calming myself'.[20]

The effect of different kinds of music on the emotions and on the character of the listener was much discussed by theorists from the second half of the fifth century on. The first we know of who wrote about this was Damon, an associate of Pericles and Socrates, considered the greatest Athenian intellect of his time. He published an essay (which does not survive, unfortunately) in which he argued that the various different modes and rhythms used in Greek music were intimately connected with different ethical qualities. He held that songs and dances set up particular commotions in the soul and laid down patterns in it which reflected their own qualities. These patterns would shape a boy's unformed character; or in the case of a grown man, they might bring out latent traits. It was therefore important for the state to regulate music and education (in which music played a major part), to ensure that the young received the right sort of influences. They should be taught to sing and play such melodies as were characterized by manliness, restraint, and even-handedness. Damon went into technical detail, describing six different modal scales, specifying the notes and intervals in each and pronouncing on their ethical qualities. He did the same with rhythms and tempi, commending some and condemning others on the ground that they expressed aggression, frenzy, or other undesirable qualities. Damon addressed his essay to the Council of the Areopagus, a high body which had (nominally) a responsibility for supervising public morality. It sounds as if he was seriously proposing some sort of state control over music as a public health measure.[21]

This is the sort of totalitarianism that we associate with Plato, and in fact Plato was much influenced by Damon's theories about music.

In several of his dialogues he puts forward very similar views. He has much the same conception of modal scales and rhythms becoming imprinted on the souls of the young and, if they are of an orderly nature themselves, instilling order in those souls. He explains why it is that scales, rhythms, and dance movements have ethical qualities: it is because they are patterned on the voices and movements of people who have those qualities. So qualities already present in humanity get encoded in music and dance and are then transmitted through music and dance into the younger generation. Hence it is important, especially in education, to make sure that only the right kinds of music are used. In the *Republic* and again in the *Laws*, he discusses the qualities of individual modes. Of Damon's six, he gives his approval to only two, the Dorian and the Phrygian.

In one passage, in the *Timaeus*, Plato brings the theory into a more distinctly therapeutic context:

> Attunement (ἁρμονία), having motions akin to the circuits in our soul, has been given by the Muses to the intelligent user of the arts not for mindless pleasure, as it is fashionable to assume, but as an aid to bringing our soul-circuit, when it has got out of tune, into order and harmony with itself. And rhythm likewise, in view of the unmeasured and graceless condition that comes about in most of us, was bestowed by them for the same purpose.[22]

Here, then, it is not just a matter of generally bringing people up in the right sort of musical environment for the sake of their characters, but of the intelligent man using music to heal himself when he recognizes that his soul-circuits are out of kilter. This corresponds very closely to the story about Kleinias the Pythagorean playing the lyre to calm himself when he was angry.

The modes which Plato approved, the Dorian and the Phrygian, were generally agreed to be markedly distinct in character. The Dorian was considered steady and dignified, stern, manly, and without frills; everyone speaks well of it. The Phrygian, on the other hand, was regarded as exciting and emotional. It is a little surprising that Plato accepted it in his ideal city-state, but he seems to have been impressed by its religious associations.

The idea that a person's mood might be directly affected by the mode of the music he was hearing finds its clearest expression in an anecdote about an intellectual – significantly, it is Pythagoras in some versions, Damon in others – who is out one evening and comes upon a drunken hooligan or hooligans indulging in wild behaviour and attended by a piper who is playing in the Phrygian mode. The sage persuades the piper to change to the Dorian mode – or according to others the Spondaic, which was even more solemn in character – and the disorderly conduct at once ceases.[23]

One at least of Plato's pupils is said to have practised musical therapy: Xenocrates of Chalcedon, who was head of the Academy from 339 to 314. According to Martianus Capella, *Xenocrates organicis modulis lymphaticos liberabat*: that is, he used instrumental music to cure hysterics.[24] The specific reference to instrumental music is of interest, because it confirms that the effect was ascribed to the music itself, with the modes and rhythms intrinsic to it, independently of any words. When Hesiod remarked on the power of epic song to make a grieving man forget his sorrows, he was no doubt referring to the absorbing narrative rather than the musical aspects of the performance.[25] It remained a matter of debate in antiquity whether music does in fact exercise any effect on the emotions apart from the words with which it is associated. The common view, following Damon and Plato, was that it does: the modes and rhythms were potent in themselves. But Damon's view was contested by a sophist of the early fourth century (perhaps Alcidamas), and later Epicurus, Philodemus, and Sextus Empiricus were to deny that music devoid of words was capable of exercising any moral effect on the hearer, though it could certainly give him pleasure.

The principal Greek musical instruments were the lyre and the aulos. The aulos was not a flute, as it is constantly mistranslated, but a reed instrument of the oboe type; it was almost always played in pairs, that is, the player had two of them in his mouth at once and played one with each hand. In terms of their psychological or therapeutic effects, the lyre and the aulos were sharply differentiated. The Dorian mode was more associated with the lyre, the Phrygian with the aulos. In the Pythagorean tradition it is the lyre that plays the major role. It is the lyre that Kleinias and other Pythagoreans are said to use in their freshening-up and calming exercises. Later writers say that Pythagoras considered the aulos loutish [ὑβριστικόν] and vulgar, and even recommended his disciples to wash their ears out after hearing it, whereas the lyre was suitable for purifying their souls of irrational passions.[26] In the neo-Pythagorean poem which I mentioned earlier, 'The Lyre', it was this instrument that was supposed to assist the soul in its ascent from the lower to the upper world.

If the lyre is a power for good, the aulos is more ambivalent. It is notorious for inflaming the passions, which the Pythagoreans were against. The verb κατ-αυλέω, literally 'play the aulos over' someone, meant metaphorically to bewitch or put a spell on him. In some circumstances it was held to produce positively good effects. Plato refers to orgiastic frenzy being cured by means of religious dancing to the aulos. He compares the process to that by which a restless child is put to sleep by rocking and lullabies: the regular movement imposed from without by the rocking or the dancing overcomes the wild internal jerkings of the soul and creates order and calm.[27] Aristoxenus himself used the aulos to cure a man who could not stand the sound of a trumpet and would scream and become frantic if he heard one. He cured him by accustoming him to listen to the aulos, which he gradually played louder until the man could tolerate the trumpet.[28]

I have spoken so far mainly about the use of music in treating psychic disorders, but there was some belief in its applicability to physical ailments too. I quoted Aristoxenus' statement that the Pythagoreans 'used medicine for purifying the body, music for purifying the soul'. But later writers mention Pythagorean musical therapy applied to bodily ills. 'With rhythms, melodies, and incantations', says Porphyry in his *Life of Pythagoras*, 'he charmed away psychic and somatic afflictions ... He had healing songs also for illnesses of the body, which he would sing over the sick and cure them.' Iamblichus writes in similar terms in his book on *The Pythagorean Life*: 'Sometimes they also cured certain afflictions and ailments, it is said, by "incantation" in the true sense [i.e. singing over the patient]; something like this is probably the source of the general use of this word "incantation".'[29]

Otherwise we hear little of incantations after the fifth century BC, but we do hear something of the use of aulos music. Ismenias, one of the many noted aulos-players who came from Thebes, around 400 BC, is reputed to have applied his music successfully to the cure of sciatica.[30] According to Theophrastus, sufferers from sciatica could be kept free of the complaint if someone played the aulos over the affected part in the Phrygian mode. He also mentioned fainting, panic, and epilepsy as conditions that could be alleviated by means of the aulos. Bolus of Mendes, in a book that went falsely under the name of Democritus, also listed a number of ailments that could be cured by aulos-playing, including snakebites.[31] Another apparently Hellenistic medical writer described how an aulos-player had brought relief to what are vaguely called 'painful places': the performance had made them palpitate, as if dancing in response to the music, and then the pain had gone away.[32]

When we turn to Rome, we find that the evidence is largely just a reflection of Greek theory and Greek anecdote. There was a native tradition of incantations against injury or disease; Cato quotes a couple – which look like complete gibberish – to be used in a magical ritual for curing dislocations, and Varro, with a patronizing smile, quotes a more intelligible one for pain in the feet. It had to be chanted twenty-seven times [ter noviens], and the sufferer had also to touch the earth, spit, and fast. Clearly this belongs in the realm of magic ritual and not music therapy. One or two more of these popular incantations are recorded in the works of Pelagonius and Marcellus.[33]

The greatest scholar Rome ever produced was M. Terentius Varro, an older contemporary of Cicero. The seventh book of Varro's lost Disciplinae, a survey of the liberal arts, was devoted to music. It drew largely on Greek sources, and reproduced most of the stock stories about Thaletas overcoming the plague in Sparta with his paeans, about the Pythagoreans and Damon, about Xenocrates, and about those who cured sciatica by means of the aulos. From Varro all these items became commonplaces of the Latin tradition down to Martianus Capella and Boethius.

For the rest, there is little in the way of new developments to record. Further reports of practical therapy by music remain largely within existing parameters. Cicero mentions that his old friend, the blind Stoic Diodotus, made use of lyre music in the Pythagorean manner to relax his mind.[34] Another friend of Cicero's, the physician Asclepiades of Bithynia, is said to have often cured phrenetics by means of symphonia, which probably means instrumental music, and to have treated deafness with trumpet-blasts, which sounds a dubious procedure.[35] Cicero tells us that he had himself availed himself of Asclepiades' medical expertise, though he does not admit to those particular complaints or mention musical treatment. Maecenas had soft music played outside his bedroom to banish the cares of the day from his mind and lull him to sleep.[36]

The picture is extended a little by the one reference to musical therapy in Celsus' eight books on medicine, written in the time of Tiberius. Among the varieties of mental illness he mentions those who suffer from *tristes cogitationes*, which sounds like depression. In treating this, he says, *symphoniae et cymbala strepitusque* are beneficial.[37] The reference to cymbals and loud noise recalls the Bacchic and Corybantic cults known from Plato, in which the initiates danced themselves into a frenzy and out again to the accompaniment of drums, cymbals, and Phrygian aulos music. I mentioned earlier Plato's reference to the curing of orgiastic frenzy by dancing. But Celsus does not seem to have that kind of scene in mind, but rather the special provision of violent auditory stimuli for the benefit of the depressive patient.

A later instance of the use of instrumental music to calm a phrenetic is recorded by the sixth-century Syriac ecclesiastical historian John of Ephesus. The patient was the Emperor Justin II (565–78). According to John, he would rush about in a suicidal frenzy, scream and jabber, bite those who approached him, or hide under his bed. What soothed him most was being run about on a trolley as fast as possible, but his chamberlains also succeeded in keeping him quiet for long periods by playing an organ in an adjacent room.[38]

Medical writers of the imperial period occasionally acknowledge the power of music and song to calm the soul or raise the spirits. Rufus of Ephesus (*c*. 100 AD) recommended music, together with other pleasant stimuli such as diluted wine, friendly converse, listening to poetry, and walking in gardens, for the relief of lovesickness. He cited a claim attributed to Orpheus, that he could turn men's spirits in whatever direction he chose by his music.[39] Galen notes that people's ethos, and thus their health, may be corrupted by a bad environment, including the words and music that they listen to, and that the healer must understand these effects: Asclepius himself often prescribed the composition of songs or mimes to calm the soul and thus cool the overheated mixture of humours in the body; nurses soothe infants by means of vocal melody.[40] Soranus of Ephesus referred to the effects of Phrygian or Dorian aulos music on the mood.[41]

With regard to the treatment of physical afflictions, on the other hand, the picture is somewhat different. The occasional references to the use of musical therapy by practising physicians should not mislead us into thinking that it was a regular and accepted recourse of ancient medicine. There was, after all, a powerful tradition of scientific medicine in antiquity, represented by a voluminous body of technical literature, from the Hippocratic corpus onwards. In all this literature music therapy of physical ills is almost wholly ignored, or it is mentioned only to be dismissed. The author of the Hippocratic treatise *On the Sacred Disease* (that is, epilepsy), whose view is that this ailment is in fact no more sacred or supernatural than any other, pours scorn on the charlatans who claim to treat it with incantations and ritual purifications.[42] He does not seem to know of more distinctly musical forms of therapy being applied to this disease. The great Alexandrian physician Herophilus worked out a theory of the pulse according to which the relation between the diastole and the systole was analysed in terms of musical or poetic rhythms, changing over the course of a lifetime from pyrrhic to trochaic, then to spondaic and finally iambic. Varro and others refer to the theory in the context of music therapy, but Herophilus had apparently said nothing about using rhythmic sounds to control the pulse. Soranus rejected as folly the belief that music and song could reduce the strength of a physical affliction.[43] Quintus Serenus (or Serenius), the author of a medical textbook in Latin hexameters, dismisses as an old wives' tale the idea that fever can be dispelled by modulated singing [*uario carmine*].[44] Mainstream medicine relied on diet, exercise, baths, drugs, or, if necessary, surgery. Music therapy was fringe medicine, even if one or two regular doctors are recorded as having made some use of it.

Interest in the idea was sustained not so much by medical literature as by philosophical and musicological literature; more specifically, by those traditions of philosophical and musicological literature which reflected the influence of Pythagoreanism. The Pythagorean discovery of the mathematical basis of musical intervals led, as I have said, to the conviction that number and number ratios were at the heart of everything. Sometime before Aristotle a Pythagorean cosmogony was invented (perhaps by Philolaus of Croton), according to which the world developed by the generation of numbers from an initial One, which 'breathed in' a piece of infinity and so divided itself into two. Things were understood to be numbers, and their relationships – justice, for example – could be expressed as mathematical relationships. In Plato's *Phaedo* the theory is discussed that the soul is a ἁρμονία, a tuning, the body being the physical instrument like the lyre which is tuned and put into order. There is no mention of music therapy here, but it is obvious that the upholders of the theory must have been very close to the idea that any disorder in the tuning of the soul might respond to the music of a correctly tuned instrument: the well-tempered lyre would produce the well-tempered man. Aristotle echoes this line of thought in his *Politics*:

> It is clear that music is capable of conferring a particular quality on the soul's character ... And there seems to be (in the soul) some sort of kinship with the ἁρμονίαι and the rhythms, so that many of the sages say, some of them that the soul is a ἁρμονία, others that it possesses ἁρμονία.[45]

The Socrates of the *Phaedo* refutes the theory that the soul is a ἁρμονία, which had the undesirable consequence that it could not exist without the body. But Plato went on in other works to portray the universe as permeated by mathematical formulae and harmonic relationships. In the *Republic*, for example, there is the doctrine of the Harmony of the Spheres, according to which the planetary and stellar spheres make up a vast musical instrument, tuned to the notes of the diatonic octave. I have already quoted one of various passages where Plato speaks in terms of the soul having circuits or revolutions [περίοδοι], analogous to those of the heavenly bodies. Against such a theoretical background, the obvious fact that we do respond to music and that it can affect our moods could easily be given a rational explanation. Music, the soul, and the whole universe were governed by the same principles of mathematical order and proportion. The musical scale, above all, provided the paradigm of an ordered set of proportional relationships, matched at the cosmic level by the ordered set of seven planetary spheres and the stellar firmament beyond them, corresponding to the eight notes of the octave.

The influence of Platonic theory is conspicuous in the two major Greek writers on music in the Roman period, Ptolemy and Aristides Quintilianus. For Ptolemy the whole order of nature is characterized by proportional arrangements similar to those of musical tunings. He gives a detailed analysis of the soul into three parts, which correspond to the musical concords of octave, fifth, and fourth. Just as these concords, considered as scales or scale segments, have respectively seven, five, and four different possible species or modal structures, so the three parts of the soul have respectively seven, five, and four faculties or virtues. The tuning of the parts governs the condition of the soul. Hence, he writes,

> our souls are quite plainly affected in sympathy with the actual activities of a melody, recognising the kinship, as it were, of the ratios belonging to its particular kind of constitution, and being moulded by the movements specific to the idiosyncrasies of the melodies, so that they are led sometimes into pleasures and relaxations, sometimes into griefs and contractions; they are sometimes stupefied and lulled to sleep, sometimes invigorated and aroused; and they are sometimes turned towards peacefulness and restraint, sometimes towards frenzy and ecstasy, as the melody itself modulates in different ways at different times, and draws our souls towards the conditions constituted from the likenesses of the ratios.[46]

Aristides Quintilianus has an even more elaborate theory of cosmic harmony. He holds that everything is based on number and proportion, and that our earthly music is but an imperfect imitation of the music of the spheres, the celestial attunement manifested in the revolutions of the heavens. The soul too is an attunement, based on the same set of ratios as a musical scale. It is because of this kinship that the soul is moved by music. Alternatively, it is moved because, in entering the body, it has become enmeshed in a structure of sinews and breath, and these, like the strings of a lyre or the air in an aulos, vibrate in sympathy when a stringed or wind instrument is sounded. Aristides holds that the effects produced by music on the soul are basically of three types: depressant, stimulant, and calming. Because of its power, music is of importance both for educational and for therapeutic purposes.[47]

Such lofty theories as these, developed in a straight line from Plato and pre-Platonic Pythagoreanism, could be held to give philosophical respectability to the concept of music therapy, though they did not have an obvious bearing on such practices as treating sciatica or snakebites with oboe music, and they do not appear to have inspired much therapeutic practice.

It is appropriate to end this survey by returning to Boethius, whose *De institutione musica*, written in the early years of the sixth century, became the main channel by which knowledge of ancient musical theory was perpetuated in the Middle Ages in the West. Imbued with the Platonist theory of the cosmic harmony to which we respond with our kindred organs, he retails the familiar stories and examples that demonstrate the power of music over mind and body: Pythagoras' calming of the drunken hooligan, Terpander's delivery of Lesbos from a plague (a variant of the tradition about Thaletas), Ismenias' treatment of sciatica, the Pythagoreans' morning and evening songs, the connection between musical rhythm and the human pulse, the soothing of babies with lullabies.[48] All this served to emphasize the profound importance of music for human life and education. The case was persuasive, and the authority of the writer made it influential.

Notes

1. *The Times*, 5 April 1997.

2. M. Eliade, *Shamanism: Archaic Techniques of Ecstasy* (Princeton, 1972), pp. 168–9.

3. Eliade, *Shamanism*, p. 170. For a different approach to the significance of the shaman's drumming see R. Needham, 'Percussion and Transition', *Man*, 2 (1967), pp. 606–13.

4. *Hymn to Hermes*, 38; compare 443, where Apollo describes the sound of the lyre as 'this wonderful voice of one newly slain'. References to classical works that can be read in any edition (or translation, if available) include only title and section or line number. Where necessary, the editor's name is added in parentheses at the end of the reference.

5. Sophocles, *Ichneutai*, 299–300.

6. Theognidea 1229–30.

7. 'Cleobulina' fragment 3 (West).

8. M. L. West, *The Orphic Poems* (Oxford, 1983), pp. 4–5 with literature.

9. Euripides, *Alcestis*, 967; *Cyclops*, 646.

10. *Odyssey*, XIX.456–7. Contrast the more thoroughly scientific treatment of Menelaus' thigh-wound by Machaon at *Iliad*, IV.213 ff.: he removes the arrow, loosens the patient's armour, sucks blood from the wound, and applies healing drugs.

11. M. L. West, *Ancient Greek Music* (Oxford, 1992), p. 32.

12. Pratinas (*Poetae Melici Graeci*, 713 (iii)) in pseudo-Plutarch, *De musica*, 1146bc.

13. Aristoxenus fragment 117 (Wehrli); see M. L. West, 'Ringing Welkins', *Classical Quarterly*, 40 (1990), pp. 286–7.

14. Antonius Diogenes in Porphyry, *Vita Pythagorae*, 32; Iamblichus, *De vita Pythagorea*, 110.

15. W. Burkert, *Lore and Science in Ancient Pythagoreanism* (Cambridge, MA, 1972), pp. 428–9.

16. Burkert, *Lore and Science*, pp. 141–3, 155–9, 162–3.

17. West, *The Orphic Poems*, pp. 29–30.

18. Aristotle fragment 196 (Rose) in Porphyry, *Vita Pythagorae*, 41.

19. References listed in West, *Ancient Greek Music*, p. 31 n. 90; add Iamblichus, *De vita Pythagorea*, 114.

20. Chamaileon fragment 4 (Wehrli) = fragment 6 (Giordano).

21. For Damon see West, *Ancient Greek Music*, pp. 246–7.

22. Plato, *Timaeus*, 47d

23. West, *Ancient Greek Music*, p. 31, with references.

24. Martianus Capella IX.926. G. Wille, *Musica Romana: Die Bedeutung der Musik im Leben der Römer* (Amsterdam, 1967), pp. 415 and 643, oddly renders *organicis modulis* as 'durch Orgelmusik'. The organ had not yet been invented in Xenocrates' time.

25. Hesiod, *Theogony*, 98–103, see 55 with my note ad loc.: West (ed.), *Hesiod, Theogony* (Oxford, 1966), p. 175.

26. Iamblichus, *De vita Pythagorea*, 111; Aristides Quintilianus II.19, p. 91.27 (Winnington-Ingram).

27. Plato, *Laws*, 790d–1a.

28. Theophrastus fragment 726A (Fortenbaugh).

29. Porphyry, *Vita Pythagorae*, 30, 33; Iamblichus, *De vita Pythagorea*, 114; compare 164, 244.

30. Boethius, *Institutio musica*, I.1, p. 185.20 (Friedlein).

31. Theophrastus fragment 726A–C (Fortenbaugh); pseudo-Democritus (Bolus) B 300.7 (Diels–Kranz).

32. 'The brother of Philistion' in Caelius Aurelianus, *Chronicae passiones*, V.1.23 (from Soranus). Philistion was a famous doctor of the fourth century BC, but nothing is known of his 'brother'.

68 MARTIN WEST

33. Cato, *De agricultura*, 160; Varro, *De re rustica*, I.2.27; Pelagonius, p. 121.58 (Ihm); Marcellus, *De medicamentis*, VIII.191; XXI.3; W. Morel, *Fragmenta Poetarum Latinorum* (Stuttgart, 1963), p. 31.

34. Cicero, *Tusculans*, V.113.

35. Censorinus, *De die natali*, XII.4; Martianus Capella IX.926.

36. Seneca, *De Providentia*, III.10; perhaps reflected by his protégé Horace, *Odes*, III.1.20.

37. Celsus, *De medicina*, III.18.10.

38. John of Ephesus, *Historia Ecclesiastica*, III.2–3.

39. Quoted by the Arabic physician Abu Ja'far ibn al-Jazzar; see C. Burnett, 'European Knowledge of Arabic Texts referring to Music', *Early Music History* 12 (1993), pp. 2–4.

40. Galen, *De tuenda sanitate*, I.8.14, 20, 29 (*Corpus Medicorum Graecorum*, V.4(2).19 ff).

41. Caelius Aurelianus, *Chronicae passiones*, I.5.175.

42. 'Hippocrates', *De morbo sacro*, I.4, 12, 39.

43. Caelius Aurelianus, *Chronicae passiones*, V.1.23.

44. Q. Serenus, *Liber medicinalis*, 930 ff. (Baehrens, *Poetae Latini Minores*, 3.150).

45. Plato, *Phaedo*, 85e ff.; Aristotle, *Politics*, 1340b11–19.

46. Ptolemy, *Harmonics*, III.4–7; translation from A. Barker, *Greek Musical Writings*, vol. 2 (Cambridge, 1989), p. 379.

47. Aristides Quintilianus II.3–6, 17–18; III.7, 9 ff. Translations may be found in Barker, *Greek Musical Writings*, vol. 2, pp. 459 ff.

48. Boethius, *De institutione musica*, I.1, pp. 184–6 (Friedlein); Wille, *Musica Romana*, pp. 659–60.

CHAPTER THREE

Jewish and Muslim Traditions
of Music Therapy

Amnon Shiloah

I

'Studying the literature of past civilizations', writes the music therapist Chava Sekeles, 'and ... the healing rituals of traditional societies reveal that certain musical principles do in fact repeat themselves in quite surprising ways in differing cultures.'

> For example a change of the organism's equilibrium by auditory overstimulation has always been a characteristic of traditional societies which indulge in ecstatic ceremonies. This, even today can be employed in music therapy.[1]

Sekeles adds that therapy can usually be achieved either by excitation or by relaxation; that is to say, either by means of an ecstatic state provoked by a strong rhythmic stimulus believed to drive away evil forces, or by an hypnotic state usually produced by repetitive music of an incantatory nature through which harmony can be restored to the patient's body and soul. Both methods are universally known and can be traced to a remote past. Indeed, from antiquity until this very day, when, as we shall see (Tyler, Chapter 16), the medical profession increasingly accepts the efficacy of music therapy, music has been widely recognized among both primitive and sophisticated societies as a medium possessing curative powers. Among the various psychological and spiritual aspects of this medium Sekeles mentions the major therapeutically potent factor of imagination:

> Imaging, visions, dreams transport the patient through experiences which differ from his day-to-day existence ... In some cases this could be described as rebirth.[2]

Such a 'rebirth' is exactly what is alluded to in the First Book of
Samuel: 'And the spirit of the Lord will come mightily upon thee, and
thou shalt prophesy with them [a band of prophets playing on timbrel,
pipe and two types of lyre] and shalt be turned into *another man*' (I
Samuel 10.6). This biblical evidence of the power of music, evidence
that has been quoted time and again in both Jewish and non-Jewish
literature, concerns Saul, the first King of Israel (*c.* 1020–1000 BC),
and describes the role of music in inspiring ecstasy and prophetic
vision. Even more telling for our purpose is the evidence in the same
Book of Samuel, which is also connected with King Saul. It refers to
the skilful playing on the *kinnor* [lyre] which was said to have had a
therapeutic effect on the king, who was afflicted with an 'evil spirit' (I
Samuel 16.16–18) (compare Jones, Chapter 6). In this case, however,
David's intimate, meditative playing seems rather to have cast a hypnotic spell that exorcized the evil spirit.[3]

The ecstatic procedure to which Sekeles refers is quite frequently
found in the magico-religious healing rituals of certain Muslim confraternities like the Moroccan 'Isawiyya, or 'Isawa, the Hamadisha – a
society more aptly described as a community of exorcists – and the
Gnawa – a group of black descendants of slaves who may have been
brought to North Africa from the coast of Guinea. The special therapeutic ritual used by them is called *hadra*, the name usually given to
the North African Sufi rite which assists adepts in attaining mystical
union with God. It should be noted that the North African term *hadra*
is intimately linked to the concept of *sama* [listening or audition] and
this refers in classical Sufism to the ritual said to intensify the adepts'
love of God and sensation of ecstasy; its application in the healing
ritual performed by those communities has been rejected by Sufi
authorities and considered as marginal. 'The chief aim of their *hadra*',
states Fritz Meier, is 'to induce trances or fits in themselves and in the
sick in order to clear a path for certain spirits to pass through the soul
and depart from it, that is to release psychic blockages.'[4]

A more positive evaluation of the claimed affinity with classical
mysticism is found in a recent enlightening study on the Moroccan
Gnawa – a brotherhood who have placed themselves under the patronage of Bilal, the prophet's black muezzin.[5] According to Viviana
Pâques, for the Gnawa words are far from being the only sources of

uplift for the initiate; they rather consider music as essential to the revelation of the universe, and as a prominent factor in their system of faith. Indeed, songs, instrumental music and dances are signs and symbols of a whole web of knowledge and ideas, and dictate a series of mystical techniques which make the adept not only knowledgeable but, particularly, an actor, a participant. Hence, dance steps, music tempi and the like are loaded with signification. It is said that listening attentively to the melody of the *gumbri* [a long-necked three-stringed lute] is the best way for the adept's soul to be caught in a lake of allusions. The effect of the music is tremendously increased when a subtle game of perfumes (incenses) is used at a precise moment in the ritual to reinforce the totality of codes to which the adepts are committed. For the Gnawa, rituals usually mark and enhance all their proper feasts; they can also be performed in private on the demand of an adept, or of a sick person wishing to receive the *baraka* [benediction, grace] or a healing service.

The group of musicians who ensure the unfolding of all ceremonies comprises first a player on *gumbri* considered as knowledgeable, who assumes the role of master of the ritual; he also beats the *ganga* [a big side-drum]. The other musicians of the group are four or six *qeraqeb* players. The *qeraqeb* is a pair of iron clappers or castanets tied to the players' palms. The musicians also take part in the dancing and can beat small drums. To the metallic beat, the dancers display their skills in a sequence of acrobatic figures performed with impressive rapidity. A little before midnight (all ceremonies are held at night, hence the general name given to them: *Lila*, meaning 'night'), the lute is purified with incense before the last phase in which, along with the *ganga*, it accompanies the ecstatic dance of exorcism. The patient in need of a cure becomes agitated, stands up and makes frenetic gestures, dancing himself into a trance. He finally reaches a state of exhaustion which supposedly indicates his release from the spirit that has possessed him.

II

Let us now turn back to the classical tradition. Evidence concerning the use of music as an agent which activates body and soul is to be found in some writings of Maimonides, the famous Rabbinic codifier, philosopher and physician (d. 1204). In his article 'Ethics and Meta-Ethics, Aesthetics and Meta-Aesthetics in Maimonides', W. Z. Harvey writes about the aesthetics which emerge from Maimonides' intellectual theology. Man, as Maimonides explains, 'has a psychological need for beauty, and psychological needs are no less real than biological ones; and so if one is to be healthy and fit to pursue intellectual knowledge, he must fulfil his psychological needs even as he fulfils his biological ones'. Harvey quotes in this regard the following statement in Maimonides' *Eight Chapters*, 5:

> If the humor of black bile agitates him [i.e. if he suffers from melancholy], he should make it cease by listening to songs and various kinds of melodies, by walking in gardens and fine buildings, by sitting before beautiful forms and by things like this which delight the soul and make the disturbance of black bile disappear from it. In all this he should aim at making his body healthy, the goal of his body's health being that he attain knowledge ... [see also Jones, Chapter 6; Gouk, Chapter 8][6]

This approach is emphasized and extended in Maimonides' medical writings, particularly in the *Epistles* to al-Afdal (d. 1225), the eldest son of Saladin who suffered from bouts of melancholia. The very detailed regimen he gave to his patient included dietary and fitness recommendations, as well as instructions of a psychological nature. Wine and music are among the things proposed. Wine is a good soporific, helps purify the blood, eliminates the vapours caused by the black bile and ensures a pleasant sleep. Maimonides further urges that sleep in the afternoon and at night should be induced by singing and music. The performance should be given by a singer to the accompaniment of a stringed instrument. The singer should decrease gradually the volume of his voice and attenuate the sound of the strings so that it becomes mere whispering; both should cease completely when the patient falls asleep. On waking, the patient should spend the remaining part of the day reading books of his preference, or, what is far more desirable, conversing with an interlocutor endowed with pleasant and eloquent speech. The musical performance in the evening is longer, because the musician should also entertain the patient during the two hours that follow dinner. Maimonides concludes: 'all this is enjoyable for the heart and helps in dissipating gloomy thoughts'.[7]

Maimonides' disciple Ibn 'Aqnin (d. 1226) was a physician, philosopher and commentator on his great teacher. He stated in his commentary of the Mishna tractate *Avot* that the human being is expected to devote all his deeds to heaven; for that purpose he has to keep himself fit, both physically and mentally. As in his famous work *Tibb al-Nufus* [*Hygiene of Souls*], Ibn 'Aqnin uses in this commentary his skill as a physician, attributing to music the power of remedy for mental illness. He writes:

> in the case of melancholy ... [when the sick person] cannot see things as they are and he is afraid of things of which he has no reason to be afraid, this is a bad disease. He can cure it by listening to the performance of instrumentalists and to the singing of poems accompanied by these five instruments: *kinnorim* and *nevalim* [lyres], *man'ammim* [perhaps *mena'ne'im*, rattles], *mezalzelim* [cymbals], and *'uggavim* [wind instruments].[8]

A famous blind doctor of the sixteenth century, Da'ud al-Antaki, wrote a medical encyclopaedia called *al-Tadhkira* [*Memorial for Wise Men*][9] in which he drew extensively from the *Epistle on Music* of the Brethren of Purity, to whom I shall return in a moment.[10] In the concluding part of the chapter on music of this encyclopaedia, which was held in great esteem in North Africa, al-Antaki introduced medical applications for the eight rhythmic modes (the number in vogue at that time), providing them with appellations which suggest their major effects. In musical tracts written at about the same time, one also finds precise medical properties attributed to the specific musical modes practised in 'art music': for instance, *rast* is good for hemiplegy; *'iraq* helps to cure acute conditions of the humours such as brain diseases, vertigo, pleurisy, and suffocation.

As for hospital treatments, some evidence is included in the treatise of the Brethren of Purity (tenth century) who identified themselves with mystical doctrine. Though they basically adhered to the philosophic and metaphoric approach to music therapy, as we shall see later, the following statement might be a hint of real practice. In enumerating the effects that the different musical modes produced, they said about one of them: 'it was used in the hospitals, at the break of day, and it had the virtue of solacing the pains due to the infirmities and ills suffered by the patients, alleviating their violence and even curing certain sicknesses and infirmities'.[11]

According to Michael W. Dols, 'the relationship between music, one's temperament and hospitals is emphasized, unexpectedly in an early exposition of Sufism'. In his *Kashf al-mahjub*, al-Hujwiri (d. between 1072 and 1077) discusses the overwhelming influence of music on the neophyte, an influence which might cause him to loose his senses and even die. He mentions in this context that in the hospitals of Rum (Byzantium) they invented a wonderful instrument, the *anghalyun*, which resembled a stringed instrument.

> The sick are brought to it two days a week and are forced to listen, while it is being played on, for a length of time proportionate to the malady for which they suffer; then they are taken away. If it is desired to kill anyone, he is kept there for a longer period, until he dies ... Physicians and others may listen continually to the *anghalyun* without being affected in any way, because it is consistent with their temperament.[12]

It is noteworthy that variations of this same story are to be found in several Arabic sources, including two which are earlier than al-Hujwiri's time. In the framework of a discussion on concordant and discordant sounds and their various effects, the Brethren of Purity say:

> Deafening, terrifying and incoherent sounds ... alter the humors, break the equilibrium and cause sudden death. There is an instrument which produces this kind of sound, called *al-urghun* [organ], which the Greeks employed in war to terrify the souls of their enemies.[13]

In a similar context, a discussion of the properties of diverse pitches, the great philosopher and theorist of music al-Farabi (d. 950), refers to extra-high, unnatural and deafening sounds, as well as to the instruments which produce them, as being employed in special cases wherein their effect is either curative or poisonous. He mentions as an example the instruments used in battle which produce such sounds, adding that instruments of this sort were invented by a king of ancient Egypt and a king of Byzantium.[14]

Concerning the use of music in hospitals, it is hard to improve on what Dols has written:

Musical performances were often given at the Mansuri Hospital in Cairo; one of the designated expenditures was for troupes of musicians to come each day and entertain the patients. During the Ottoman period, the older hospitals continued to employ music ... Evliya Chelebi visited Nur ad-Din Hospital in AD 1648, and he reported that concerts were given three times a day ... Similarly, the French traveller Jean Baptiste Tavernier visited the imperial capital in AD 1668 and later wrote an account of the Seraglio. On the right-hand side of the first court of the palace was a large structure that housed the infirmary for the whole complex ... Tavernier avers that many came there, under various pretences, in order to enjoy the greater freedom. 'They continue there for the space of ten or twelve daies, and are diverted, according to their mode, with a wretched kind of vocal and instrumental Musick' ...

In the Mansuri Hospital in Cairo, the patients suffering from insomnia were placed in a separate hall; they listened to harmonious music, and skilled story-tellers recited their tales to them. When the patients began to recover their sanity, they were isolated from the others, and dancing and various sorts of comedies were staged for their benefit ...

Evidence of these various aspects of the Islamic asylum is found in Evliya Chelebi's description of the mental hospital that was founded in Edirne (Adrianople) by Bayezid II (AD 1481– 1512); Evliya visited it in AD 1651 ... According to [him], there was a provision in the endowment of Bayezid's hospital in Edirne for three singers, and seven musicians (a flutist, a violinist, a flageolet-player, a cymbalist, a harpist, a harp-cymbal-player, and a lutenist) who were to visit the hospital three times a week. They played six different melodies, and many of the insane were reported to have been relieved by this 'nourishment of the soul'...[15]

That asylum remained active until the beginning of the twentieth century.

Among numerous other instances of hospital music, I would like to mention the following, which brings us back to the healing rituals discussed earlier. In 1831–32, the Moroccan 'Alawite and orthodox Sultan Mulay 'Abd al-Rahman built at Salé a *bimaristan*[16] attached to the sanctuary of the Sufi leader Sidi bin 'Ashir. This hospital which has also been in use until recently, dispensed with doctors; instead the sick relied for their cure upon the *baraka* of the saint and the *hadra* performed by the confraternities.[17]

It should be noted that some of the foregoing instances of ecstatic
and hypnotic healing are to a large extent tinged with strong belief in
magical and supernatural forces that otherwise find expression in
special formulas, selected scriptural verses, certain words and prayers,
rites, amulets, or a list of names of God and angels, presumably
endowed with exceptional virtues. A striking instance is the recourse
to the Book of Psalms by both Jews and medieval Christians, with
specific properties attributed to quite a number of individual psalms.
An example is Psalm 91 that all Jewish communities recite at burial
services and other appropriate occasions, because of its magical
power to drive away evil forces. Other psalms have been used as
prayers during a drought, prayers for and by the sick, and the like. As
time passed, the magical function was essentially relegated, and
played only a partial role in the theoretical approaches that increasingly found expression in writings on both music and medicine. It is
to these approaches that I turn next.

III

The period extending from the second half of the ninth to the end of
the tenth century, a period usually known as the golden age of Muslim
civilization, was marked by a remarkable intellectual effervescence
and animated by an eagerness for learning and for the pleasures of
philosophical contemplation. Numerous circles of scholars emerged,
each focused on a renowned spiritual master with whom they met
regularly to discuss and elaborate philosophical ideas, as well subjects
related to other areas of knowledge including music and medicine.[18]
The intense activity manifested in those circles was undoubtedly due
to their recent introduction to the Greek scientific and intellectual
heritage which had become available in Arabic translation. Under the
sponsorship and encouragement of the enlightened Caliph al-Mamun
(813–33), a vast enterprise had been undertaken: the translation of
philosophical and scientific works from Greek into Arabic and Syriac.
The work had been done in the *Bayt al-Hikma* (Institute of Science),
created by the caliph, and situated in the huge government-supported
library in Baghdad.

It was thanks to this important enterprise and the resulting close contact with Greek culture that both medicine and music developed as scientific areas and became subject to investigation and systematization that affected both their theoretical and their practical elements. Hence, in addition to the previous link between music and medicine that had characterized traditional healing, a new and more complex type of theoretical association between music and medicine emerged. It relied mainly on the humanistic and metaphoric approach that crystallized during this early period of Muslim civilization.

As one can infer from the writings of the epoch, an interesting fundamental aspect of this approach lay in the claim that wisdom is eternal and universal. Therefore, it does not belong to any particular group or people; it is rather the property of man in general, of mankind. This means that the peaks of thought reached by former generations should be considered not as the last word, but rather as potentially perfectible. Arguing in the same vein, the thinkers of that period came to the conclusion that the sciences of the ancients are in effect the joint patrimony of all men endowed with the faculty of reasoning which serves as their common denominator, regardless of religious or ethnic affiliation.

An Arab concept in vogue during that epoch – *insaniyya*, which means 'humanity' – can be attributed to this approach, which stands in the background of the blossoming of the first scientific writings on music, and medicine, as well as of other areas of knowledge. This approach was also definitive for the establishment of a mode of thought imbued with metaphoric and philosophical reasoning. Indeed, the association of the medical dimension with music was intimately integrated into a wide philosophical, ethical, psychological, astrological and cosmological conception that envisaged music as the knowledge of the order of all things and as the science of the harmonic relationships of the universe; at the same time, music was viewed as a power capable of exerting marvellous effects on the body as well as the soul of man.

The treatment of man's body and soul as an indivisible unity was a fundamental concept in the medicine of that epoch. The physician considered it his chief target not only to restore his patient's harmonious equilibrium but to help man to live in harmony with the whole of his surroundings. As with the science of music, the development of Arab medicine was to a large extent indebted to the impetus it received as a result of becoming acquainted with the translations of classical Greek medical works. It is true that in the case of medicine, before this period, some of the Greek heritage was already known, either in the original language or in Syriac translations, to the galaxy of Christian physicians who served in the famous medical schools.

The introduction to the Arab and Muslim world of Hippocratic and Galenic medical texts and Arabicized medicine was begun by the second half of the ninth century by two contemporary physicians: Yuhanna ibn Masawa (d. 857), known in the West as Jean Mesue,[19] and 'Ali ibn Sahl al-Tabari (d. 864). In the works of these scholars, as well as in the curriculum of the contemporary schools of medicine, some secular disciplines, primarily the study of philosophy, were invariably included. In his book, *The Paradise of Wisdom*, which has seven treatises, al-Tabari deals not only with medicine and pharmacy but also with philosophy, psychology, climatology and astrology. The work of Ibn Masawa, which constitutes one of the first texts written in Arabic, both covers the different medical branches, and also, as in his *Books of Times*, provides information concerning the twelve months of the year, touching upon astrology, meteorology, agronomy and hygiene. Another book of his, dedicated to aphorisms on medicine, was modelled after Hippocrates' aphorisms.

It should be noted that Ibn Masawa wrote his aphorisms on medicine at the request of his pupil Hunain ibn Ishaq (808–73), one of the most important participants in the huge enterprise of translating Greek and Syriac writings into Arabic. Hunain belonged to a famous Nestorian family of physicians that included his own son Ishaq. Hunain wrote hundreds of treatises of which only forty have come down to us. Among them is a text of a philosophical nature entitled *Book of the Aphorisms of the Philosophers*, a collection of stories, letters, and sayings ascribed to the ancient Greek philosophers. The book includes three chapters introduced as: 'Rare remarks [*nawadir*] of the philosophers on music'.[20] According to the author, the occasion leading to the composition of the *nawadir* was a wedding feast given by King Heraclius. A similar work is ascribed to a certain Bulos (Paul) and translated by Hunain's son Ishaq;[21] about half its text repeats sayings in the *nawadir* almost word by word. The aphorisms describe concisely the moral and therapeutic effects of music, its spiritual meaning as opposed to its intoxicating influence, and draws a comparison between the four strings of the *'ud* [lute] and the humours, elements, seasons, and so on. Interestingly, these same short aphorisms, which express the metaphoric viewpoints of two important physician-philosophers, recur in (among others) the writings of the great Arab philosopher and theorist of music, al-Kindi (d. after 810); of the geographer Ibn Khurradadhbih (825–911); of the historian and geographer al-Masudi (d. 956); of the Jewish religious authority and philosopher Sa'adya Gaon (882–942); of the anonymous authors known as the Brethren of Purity (mid-tenth century); of the Jewish Spanish poet and philosopher Moshe ibn Ezra (1085–1135); and of the Jewish Spanish poet and philosopher Yehuda al-Harizi (1170–1235) who translated Hunain's work into Hebrew. This broad distribution in time and place is an eloquent indication of the wide adoption of the approach described above and expressed in a miniaturist way in the aphorisms.

Another important aspect of the medical dimension is the theory dealing with 'the natural things' according to which the human body, like all substances in the sublunary world, derives from the mixture of the four cosmic elements (earth, air, fire and water) and the four qualities attributed to them by pairs of opposites, that is to say: dryness and cold for the earth; heat and dryness for fire; heat and moisture for the air; cold and moisture for water (see also Horden, Chapter 1; Jones, Chapter 6; and Gouk, Chapter 8). While the elements are not present in their primal state in the human body, they are represented by their analogous four humours – blood, yellow bile, black bile and phlegm; these are described by al-Majusi 'Ali ibn 'Abbas (d. *c.* 977) as 'the daughters of the elements', and can thus be placed in relation to them. All material existence was then ascribed to various combinations of the four elements and qualities. This doctrine, therefore, could account for climate and temperature as well as for different personal temperaments: sanguine, choleric, melancholy and phlegmatic (caused by a mixture of the four humours that comprise the body and the four qualities that comprise the climate). Each individual is characterized by the balanced mixture of prime qualities which determine his temperament. A perfect equilibrium of the four qualities is an ideal attainable only by exceptional individuals. Maintaining health or healing a disease, therefore, consists essentially in having the proper combinations for the interaction of the human body with those substances coming into contact with it.

In addition to this, some physicians, although not all, attributed great importance to the theory of astral influence according to which the planets exert their forces on the development of the foetus as well as on all phases of human life. It was therefore recommended that the physician take into consideration not only the horoscope of the sick individual, but also the disease's crisis cycles and the time needed for the administration of each type of treatment. In a treatise on the usefulness of astrology to the physician, the Egyptian Abu Nasr 'Adnan ibn 'Aynzarbi refers to Hippocrates, who said that astrology does the musician a great service. He adds that this service is indispensable for a medical prognosis, because just as the positions of the planets in the zodiac and the relations between them can determine the causes of many diseases, they also influence the period favourable for each treatment.

The full expansion of the approach, including the ideas encountered in the aforementioned medical theories, found appropriate expression and attained pre-eminence with the philosopher and music theorist Ya'qub ibn Ishaq al-Kindi (d. 870) and the Brethren of Purity. The figure of al-Kindi, who was also a physician, towers over the threshold of Islamic science and philosophy. He wrote thirteen treatises on the science of music. Only six of them have come down to us, but they are fairly representative of his emphasis on the ethical, cosmological and therapeutic approach the guiding spirit of which is the concept of harmony in its broadest sense. This concept is indeed central for understanding the complex network linking music to all attributes of the universe; and it dominates even the technical aspects and the parameters of a musical system. The network of correspondences is explained by reference to the four strings of the 'ud, called by al-Kindi the 'instrument of philosophers'. By this he meant the Greek philosophers who allegedly conceived the instrument and its parts as the image of the perfect harmony ruling the universe (see West, above). Hence the 'ud serves to demonstrate the affiliations of its four strings with elliptic arcs, the position and conjunction of the stars, seasons, days, ages, elements, humours, colours, and faculties of the soul. Al-Kindi states that the musician should develop diagnostic skills parallel to those of the physician in order, like him, to prescribe suitable treatment.

In their *Epistle on Music*, the Brethren of Purity state at the outset that their intention is not to teach of the practice of music but to make known the science of proportions and the modality of harmony, the knowledge of which presides over the mastery of all arts and contributes to the understanding of 'all the secrets of created things'. Hence, the musical harmony that explains the order and beauty of nature is a decisive factor in the spiritual and philosophical equilibrium of man; and, in the same way, the correct use of music at an appropriate time has a healing influence on the body.[22] This influence is especially expressed in changing the composition of the humours by strengthening or weakening one or more of them. The Brethren conclude that this phenomenon is common to all men on earth, and therefore the basic principles of music, which are universal, are also common to all men.[23]

Referring to astral influence, the Brethren claim that one of the reasons that led the philosophers (the Greeks) to establish the laws of music was the need to determine good and bad auguries from the positions and conjunctions of the stars. The stratagem they used consisted of prayer, fasting, hymns of praise and cantillation; invoking the grace of God would save them from whatever they feared. The mode or melody they used to this effect was called the 'saddening'.[24]

Both al-Kindi and the Brethren of Purity refer to music therapy as one aspect of the broad philosophical–metaphoric approach that considers harmony in its widest sense as a power involved in mastery of all arts. Originally conceived as such by the (Greek) philosophers, its proper manipulation for purposes of therapy implies a keen knowledge of the laws of universal harmony as well as their reflection in the music made by man. Therefore, this capacity belongs first and foremost to the musician-philosopher, because, as the Brethren say, the science of music is the principal wisdom leading to philosophical thought, and because harmony, wherever it is found in nature, cannot be described without being subordinated to the ideal laws of music.

It can be inferred from the foregoing remark made by al-Kindi that the musician should also have some knowledge of medicine. What about the physician? Abu'l Faraj ibn Hindu (d. 1019) was a man of letters and government official who was well trained and deeply steeped in Greek philosophy. Franz Rosenthal wrote about him: 'in the eyes of his contemporaries, this made him well qualified to write on medicine'.[25] In Ibn Hindu's sizeable medical encyclopaedia called *Miftah al-tibb* [*The Key to Medicine*], the eighth chapter is entitled 'The enumeration of those aspects of the sciences the physician must know in order to be perfect in his profession'. The sciences referred to in this chapter are philosophy, physics, astrology, arithmetic, music, theology and logic. Concerning the science of music, Ibn Hindu acknowledges that in treating certain diseases physicians often have recourse to musical modes which correspond to the condition of the patients and thereby contribute to healing. However, as he says, this does not imply that the physician himself is expected to blow a trumpet or reed-pipe or get up and dance; rather he should use the services of an expert musician, just as he uses the services of other experts, assistants and practitioners.[26]

Of course, in subsequent periods one finds a variety of additional opinions regarding the nature and scope of music therapy. The brevity of this presentation, however, has compelled me to focus only on some prevailing approaches and concepts.

Notes

1. C. Sekeles, *Music: Motion and Emotion – The Developmental-Integrative Model in Music Therapy* (Saint-Louis, 1996), p. viii. Compare Howard, Chapter 15.

2. Sekeles, *Music*, p. 22.

3. For an extensive comment on these instances see M. W. Dols, *Majnūn: The Madman in Medieval Islamic Society* (Oxford, 1992), pp. 174–9.

4. F. Meier, 'The Mystic Path', in B. Lewis (ed.), *The World of Islam* (London, 1976), p. 126.

5. V. Pâques, *La religion des esclaves: recherches sur la confrérie marocaine des Gnawa* (Bergamo, 1991).

6. W. Z. Harvey, 'Ethics and Meta-Ethics, Aesthetics and Meta-Aesthetics in Maimonides', in S. Pines and Y. Yovel (eds), *Maimonides and Philosophy* (Dordecht, Boston and Lancaster, 1986), pp. 134–5.

7.   *Teshuvot refuiyot [Medical Responsa]*, Medical Works, vol. 5, ed. S. Muntner (Jerusalem, 1969), pp. 148–50.

8.   M. Ben-Sasson, 'Originalité et plagiat dans l'oeuvre musicale d'Ibn Aqnin', in M. Abitbol (ed.), *Relations Judéo-musulmanes au Maroc* (Paris, 1997), pp. 309–10. See Gouk, Chapter 8; and Kramer, Chapter 14.

9.   *Tadhkirat uli'l-albab ... [Memorial for Wise Men ...]* (Cairo, 1937 edn), pp. 36–9.

10. 'The Epistle on Music of the Ikhwan al-Safa', in A. Shiloah, *The Dimension of Music in Islamic and Jewish Culture* (London, 1993), III, pp. 5–73.

11. 'The Epistle on Music', pp. 16–17.

12. Dols, *Majnūn*, p. 170.

13. 'The Epistle on Music', p. 25.

14. Al-Farabi, French trans. by R. d'Erlanger of *Kitab al-musiqi al-kabir*, *La musique arabe*, vol. 1 (Paris, 1930), p. 21.

15. Dols, *Majnūn*, pp. 171–3.

16. *Bimaristan* is a word of Persian origin; it means 'house of ills'. In some cases it has a more restricted sense: an insane asylum. See M. W. Dols, 'The Origins of the Islamic Hospital: Myth and Reality', *Bulletin of the History of Medicine*, 61 (1987), pp. 367–90.

17. For the last two pieces of information, see *The Encyclopaedia of Islam*, 2nd edn, s.v. 'Bimaristan'.

18. J. L. Kraemer, *Humanism in the Renaissance of Islam* (Leiden, 1986), introduction.

19. Yuhanna ibn Masawa was appointed head of the first hospital in Baghdad by the Caliph Harun al-Rashid.

20. A. Shiloah, *The Theory of Music in Arabic Writings* (Munich, 1979), pp. 134–5.

21. Shiloah, *The Theory of Music*, pp. 75–6

22. 'The Epistle on Music', pp. 12–13

23. 'The Epistle on Music', pp. 25–6.

24. 'The Epistle on Music', pp. 15–16

25. F. Rosenthal, 'The Defense of Medicine', *Bulletin of the History of Medicine*, 43 (1969), pp. 520–21.

26. Shiloah, *The Dimension of Music*, V, pp. 456–7.

CHAPTER FOUR

Music Therapy: Some Possibilities in the Indian Tradition

J. B. Katz

The underlying assumption of music therapy – that music has the power, and may be used, to 'cure, alleviate or stimulate'[1] – must carry particular resonance for any practitioner or scholar of South Asian music; in some of the earliest Indian sources of music theory and criticism we find strong links drawn between music and medicine or physiology, especially regarding the genesis of musical sound. The developed aesthetic of Indian music, as I and others have tried to extract it from the Indian musicological tradition,[2] shows a great interest in psychology as well as in music-structural matters. In the processes by which an Indian musician involves and inspires a listener we may certainly see possibilities for the relieving of affliction, for 'therapy' in a wide sense.

There are practitioners of music therapy in present-day India and among Indian communities outside the subcontinent. I am not aware that these practitioners commonly link their therapeutic theory or methods with classical Indian tradition. A recent source book[3] of Indian medicine funded by the Indian University Grants Commission refers to musical therapy as a 'young discipline being well cultivated in some modern countries, e.g. the United States and France', and merely recommends investigation of the principles of Indian music as a promising extension of the field. When I wrote to a learned friend in Mysore – a distinguished musicologist as well as professional scientist – to ask if he knew of textual sources for music therapy, he quickly wrote back: '… I have found no references in Sanskrit or vernacular musicological texts or other literature to music therapy'.

It may indeed seem surprising that both the literature of traditional Indian musicology [*saṅgītaśāstra*][4] and that of the indigenous Indian medical system of Āyurveda[5] should have little to say on the matter. The latter is, however, not completely silent. First of all, though there is admittedly no detailed account of the subject, there is clear enough recognition in the classical Indian medical treatises of the ritual and therapeutic importance of magico-religious utterances and incantations – *mantras* – as an essential both in the collection and preparation of medicines and in the treatments of certain conditions.[6] The influential medical compendium known as the *Carakasaṃhitā* contains an important chapter on *cikitsā* [therapeutics], most of which is firmly grounded in the study of symptomatology and of an elaborate materia medica; but in the list it offers of twenty-four remedies against curable poisoning the first item is mantra. There is the suggestion here and elsewhere in the text that incantation was at times a crucial accompaniment to pharmacological treatment. The magico-religious tradition of the Vedas (especially the *Ṛgveda* and the *Atharvaveda*)[7] represents an earlier phase of medical thinking and healing practice in India than the empirically and rationally based system found in the classical treatises of the early Christian era, such as the *Carakasaṃhitā*. It has been argued that these treatises imported, and incorporated into the mainstream tradition, material from an originally more marginalized realm of heterodox religious movements and travelling ascetics and healers, whose practices and associations would at first have kept them separate, on grounds of ritual purity, from orthodox and priestly society.[8] The treatises did, however, as we see in occasional hints such as those in the *cikitsā* chapter, continue to acknowledge the Atharvavedic tradition with its methods involving the use of charms, incantations, and the ritual telling of myths and stories at specifically prescribed times of day, month and year. The recognition of Vedic authority lent the later tradition an important notional element of sacred origin and validity, in much the same way that other learned disciplines, including the theory of drama, dance and music in their respective treatises took pains to trace their origins to other Vedas.[9] The introductory chapter – *Sūtrasthāna* ['Section on Fundamentals'] of the *Carakasaṃhitā* recognizes three distinct types of therapy – the *daivavyapāśraya*, 'resting on the spiritual', the *yuktivyapāśraya*, 'resting on the rational' (consisting of the rational administration of diet, drugs, and so on), and the *sattvāvajaya*, 'subjugation of the mental disposition' (summarily glossed in the text as the 'restraint of the mind from noxious matters').[10]

The first category, according to traditional commentators, uses the term *daiva* to mean 'that which is unseen' – the invisible fate which needs remedies such as incantation or appeasement to alleviate disorders, or possibly as a synonym for *devāḥ* (the gods themselves). The approach seems, to use a modern Western concept, holistic in realistically recognising the importance of a patient's mental disposition alongside the physiological considerations in symptomatology.[11] The physician, according to the classical medical *saṃhitā*s, is to be responsible for protecting a newborn child and its mother both with medicines and with apotropaic actions, while the room in which they rest should be 'enlivened with songs and music' and other environmental aids.[12] Specifically for the counteracting of snake poisoning, alongside the application of drugs and unguents there is a therapeutic prescription of the sounding of the musical instruments (drums) *bherī*, *mṛdaṅga* and *paṭaha*.[13] The whole of cultivated life was conceived in terms of the 'sixty-four arts'; vocal and instrumental music and dance were placed by Vātsyāyana (in his *Kāmasūtra*) and other writers on erotics and the life of courtesans at the head of a comprehensive list which embraces training in sciences, languages, culinary arts, and so on.[14] It was possibly from such a list that vocal and instrumental music were picked out to stand for general cultivation and education among the requisite qualities in those fit to attend the sick; here again, music figures as part of a general statement on physical and psychological health.[15] The best-known medical classic of Āyurveda, the *Suśrutasaṃhitā*, states in its *Sūtrasthāna* that a person should, after eating, 'enjoy soft sounds, pleasant sights and tastes ... in short anything that ravishes the soul and enwraps the mind with raptures of joy, since such pleasurable sensations greatly help the process of digestion. Sounds which are harsh and grating, sights which are abominable etc. ... or a loud side-splitting laugh after a meal [are] followed by vomiting'.[16] The greatest of the medieval Indian music theorists was Śārṅgadeva, a thirteenth-century scholar from a Kashmiri family who worked at the southern Indian Yādava court of Devagiri in the Deccan (near Aurangabad). His father appears to have been a distinguished physician, and the Āyurvedic connection may help to explain the particularly detailed account of human anatomy and the 'physiological' (in this case indebted to Yogic and Tantric concepts) genesis of sound which his music treatise, the *Saṅgītaratnākara*, offers in its introductory section; at all events, anatomical and medical models were commonly used in the theoretical explanation of musical sound. Furthermore, the classical theory of aesthetics made use of a detailed typology of emotions and their bodily and psychological manifestations.

Mention should also be made of the enduring traditions of *mantraśāstra* [science of mantra] originating in the Tantric heterodox religious practices and the medical practices which borrowed from them, both in India and beyond in Nepal and Tibet.[17] Among other things, mantras are used to repel possession by demons and adverse forces, and may be seen as one of a large class of apotropaic techniques which include ritual and devotional acts (aimed at 'appeasement' [*śānti*] of harmful influences), the recitation of poems, and the performance of songs.[18]

A common object of *śānti* is found in the influence of certain astrological phenomena. It is a well-known story that a cycle of song compositions by the south Indian (Karnatic) musician Muttusvāmi Dīkṣitar (1775–1835) was conceived for therapeutic purposes. To be precise, this is a sequence of *kṛtis*, structured songs in classical rāgas which form the core of the Karnatic concert repertory. In this case each one of the songs is addressed to one of the *navagraha*, the nine 'planets' (i.e. the seven observable heavenly bodies – sun, moon, Mars, Mercury, Jupiter, Venus, Saturn, and the ascending and descending nodes of the moon known under the names of Rāhu and Ketu). The planets, individually and as a group, are believed to exert immense influence on people's lives, and particularly in times of danger or crisis it is customary in Hindu society to appease them with prayers and rituals. The Sanskrit term *graha* [planet] means 'seizer', and perhaps originates in the notion that each of them 'seizes' or entraps or influences the lives and destinies of men. The last three of them, Saturn, Rāhu and Ketu are often associated with inauspiciousness and can be bringers of disaster, especially illness. Dīkṣitar's *navagrahakṛtis* are art-music versions of such appeasing or apotropaic hymns. The story attending their original conception is that Dīkṣitar's

pupil Tambiappan or Śuddhamṛdaṅgam Tambi, a *śuddhamaddala*
[drum] player in the Tyāgarāja temple of Tiruvārur, suffered from a
severe and chronic stomach complaint due to a bad constellation in his
horoscope. Dīkṣitar's nicely integrated suite of *kṛtis*, in an arrangement that uses and extends a standard sequential form in the Karnatic
tradition of compositional structures,[19] aimed to appease the contrary
forces in the constellation and therefore cure Tambi's ailment. A
problem here is that it may not have been the music in itself that was
expected to bring relief, but rather the poetic text which was set to the
music; nevertheless, the traditional view is that it was the function of
the composite art, the *kṛti*. It should be remembered that in the
Karnatic or south Indian classical repertoire instruments can perform
the *kṛtis*, that is, without the text but with a rendering of the melody
that notionally recalls the ethos of the text; indeed the standard view
among musicians is that for true validity the force of the text must
remain implicit in such a rendering.

This somewhat stray example is not, however, so eccentric in
Indian terms. The appeasement and settling of disorder and opposition, the establishment or reaffirmation of order, and the raising of
something conventional to the level of art, are identifiable as aims in
many Indian artistic activities. Music, when properly performed, is
efficacious and beneficial. When badly performed or wrongly used, it
can bring pain and disaster. This is a theme that we can find exemplified often enough. A popular folk-tale, which has been identified in
several languages in widely separate parts of the subcontinent, concerns the relationship between a demon and a poor Brahman who
enters into a contract with him. In a Tamil version the Brahman sees
the demon perched in a tree, and the demon tells his story:

> In my previous life I was born into a Brahman family and was a
> great expert in the art of music. I spent my whole life hoarding
> my knowledge and never shared it or taught it to anyone. That's
> why I've become a demon. That's God's punishment. If you turn
> around, you'll see a little temple. In that temple, a piper plays all
> day in the most atrocious manner, always out of tune. It's torture
> to me; it's like pouring hot molten lead in my ears. I cannot bear
> it. Every wrong note goes through me like an arrow. My whole
> body is sore; it feels like a sieve full of holes drilled by that
> dreadful noise. If this goes on any longer, I'll go stark mad and

do terrible things. Being a demon, I can't even kill myself. I'm bound to this tree. O good Brahman, I beg of you, please transport me somehow to the next grove where I can enjoy some peace. You will also release some of my own powers. You'll earn great merit if you help a poor demon who was once a Brahman like yourself.[20]

There are many stories from older and more recent oral tradition about the evocative power of well-performed music, not only to calm the savage breast but to influence nature itself.

> We are told, for instance, that the famous singer Naik Gopal, who lived during the sixteenth century at the court of Akbar the Great, was ordered by his monarch to sing rāga *Dīpak*. There are still some Indian musicians who insist that *Dīpak* creates fire if correctly performed. Naik Gopal begged his emperor to release him from this dangerous task, but Akbar remained adamant. The despairing singer, so the story goes, placed himself in the river Jumna in such a manner that the water reached up to his chin; then he began to sing. We are told that the water became increasingly hot and that suddenly flames burst from the artist's head and he perished ... Some musicians relate smilingly that *Kedār* melodies were taught by prison wardens and their assistants to those prisoners who were able to pay an adequate remuneration to their music teacher. If, by chance, the singing of *Kedār* did not melt the stones of the prison walls, the teacher would say that the rendition of the rāga was not absolutely correct.[21]

And conversely, Walter Kaufmann tells of how a traditional north Indian musician predicted the outbreak of the Second World War as the outcome of the inappropriate performance of Hindustani rāgas.

> The old man said, 'Do you know that you people in the West will soon experience a most terrible disaster? And do you know why? ... Because you people in the West abuse music and perform it at wrong times and occasions!'[22]

The idea that music influences order is an ancient one within the Indian tradition, and I believe we may find its early form already in the world of the Vedic chant, where the music of religious chant accompanied the sacrificial ritual. The Sāmavedic hymn had something like the status of a mantra, and was equally unchangeable in theory; every element in the sacrifice related to the functioning of the world, with men and gods entering into a contractual and reciprocal

relationship. 'Every part of the *yajña* ritual had a cosmic correspon-
dent which often also provided its *raison d'être*.'[23] The relationship is
expressed symbolically in the ancillary Vedic texts, where the various
parts of the *sāma-stotra*, the 'hymn suite', for instance, are linked to
cosmic elements, cardinal directions, seasons, times of day, colours
and so on. The balanced order of the cosmos, *ṛta*, was maintained
through due performance of ritual, including the *sāman* [hymn], and
the constituent parts of a *sāman* played their part in this maintenance.
Through *sāman* one could therefore participate in *ṛta*. A later Sāma–
vedic ancillary text states explicitly that *sāman* is itself the object of
worship.[24] Now admittedly such a source is bound to be dedicated to
the glorification of the Sāmaveda (and there with the musical) form
and treatment of the Vedic hymns, but the least we can say is that
there was a current view in some traditions that music was a means to
realization. We know this from statements of musicians that music is
a *sādhanā*, a means of worship, propitiation and spiritual empower-
ment, and also by inference from the kind of Vedic sources I have
mentioned. There is reasonable evidence that the Sāmavedic view
concerned specifically the power of the music itself, and not merely
the melody as a vehicle for an effective text.[25] Among their other
magical powers, the *sāmans* are linked with medical remedies
[*bheṣaja*] in the Atharvaveda, and specific *sāmans* are apparently
accorded particular curative properties.[26] There was a very strong
traditional belief held in Hindu India that all art music has its origins
in the Sāmaveda. This view will not stand up to close scrutiny, since it
is to be assumed that there was already in early times music of other
genres in existence – there is indeed even in Vedic primary sources
evidence of secular and dance music – and that there have been multiple factors and influences shaping music before and after the
Sāmaveda. But it is worth noting this belief in the sacred origins of art
music, because it relates to notions of sanctity and the necessity of
integrity in the performance of music.

Non-Vedic and post-Vedic theistic traditions appear to have contributed to the growth of the sophisticated *tāla* – rhythmic and
metrical – systems that became the principle of time organization in
Indian music. There is a long and, in its regional divisions, highly
complex history of devotional practice in which music has often been

used as an *upāsana*, that is worship, homage, and meditation. Some of the roots are in the early *śramaṇic* religions of Buddhism and Jainism, where we also have to accept a certain ambivalence in attitudes to music, since the overriding spiritual aim of liberation, *mokṣa*, excluded things sensual such as the allurement of music. Nevertheless, music and dance were accepted as parts of *sādhanā* in many traditions, and we might compare the coexistence of a strict rule against music in orthodox Islam with the rich traditions of its use in Sufi practice. In the case of Hindu devotional religions, the *bhakti* tradition fostered music and song as a principal means of worship.

The main body of traditional Indian musical lore has its origins in a field of technical discourse called *saṅgītāśāstra*, the first substantial surviving record of which is a Sanskrit text called the *Nāṭyaśāstra*, almost certainly a compilation of sources made in the early centuries AD. Some of the sources are of much greater antiquity.[27] Here music is one of the constituents of the ancient Indian drama, and the early aesthetic that was developed for music was in a sense subservient to the needs of the composite art form, where music, dialogue, lyric poetry and dance were of equal weight.

The Indian aesthetic theory is of a strongly psychological character. The *Nāṭyaśāstra* contains a detailed scheme of human emotional states called *bhāvas*. The drama is described as an 'imitative rendering of the emotions of all the people in the universe. In other words, emotion, emotional experience or emotive reactions to an experience, form the subject or content of dramatic and literary art.'[28] The mechanism involved is the arousal of a curiously mercurial entity called *rasa*, The word is a technical term in Sanskrit poetics indicating 'mood', 'sentiment', or 'flavour'. The word had already earlier carried non-technical meanings such as 'juice' and 'sap', and 'sauce', or the taste that food might contain.[29] The word has come into modern Indian vernacular languages – in Bombay you may ask for *usācā ras* and be given sugar-cane juice, and in southern India you may have a spicy liquid dish called *rasam*. In aesthetic theory the word *rasa* was elevated to a new category – not only something that resided in a dramatic work, but something which the observer of the drama could aspire to experience in himself. The idea of 'tasting' or 'savouring' the *rasa* was maintained. Essentially the doctrine was that mood –

bhāva – was portrayed, or suggested, on stage and, if successful, linked with a corresponding personal *bhāva* of the appreciative observer. The dominant *bhāvas* that make up the psyche are of fixed number – passion, humour, anger, and so on – and as a whole they were considered to cover the range of emotional experience. The precise mechanism of interaction between what happened on stage and what happened in the observers was variously explained by different post-*Nāṭyaśāstra* theoreticians, but a stable notion was that if the receiver was susceptible his *bhāva* would be transformed into, or would lead to, one of a corresponding number of *rasas*, the tasting of which was the essence of aesthetic experience. The word *rasika* – this susceptible receiver of art – is still used in Indian languages and means one who appreciates beauty. It can also be used negatively for a 'libertine'. A play or a poem, in this tradition, in addition to engendering various *rasas*, would be considered to lead to the tasting of a dominant *rasa*, and some theorists pursued the idea that there was an overall dominant *rasa*, into which all others led, and the savouring of which was the ultimate aim or achievement of the experience of art.

The *Nāṭyaśāstra* was a powerful influence on poetics and on aesthetic theory in other arts. Consequently, aesthetic discourse tended to be 'poetically correct'. Even now there are musicians and theoreticians who are preoccupied with identifying, even testing, the particular *rasa* of a *rāg*[30] – perhaps needlessly since there is in the Indian tradition itself a respectable model for bringing the diverse *rasas* into one overriding one.[31] The 'tasting' itself, *tout court*, is the essence of this version of the theory. One of the beauties of the *rasa* theory is the interrelatedness it presents of artistic creation and receiver. It is eminently illuminating in those Indian arts in which a structure or paradigm or 'type' is perceived behind, or beneath, or inside, the work of art. And in this tradition drama, poetry, even representational art, are means by which the aesthetic experience is achieved – not by an objective looking at an entity outside oneself, but by internalising and transforming its ethos in oneself.

Now an 'enculturated' Indian musician or listener has internalized, and made his own, a whole matrix of musical structures, melodic and rhythmic, which are only potential until realised in a particular performance. The melodic structures or 'types' are called rāgas, and some of us who write about the Indian art-music systems have likened them to visual icons, in that a good deal of detail is prescribed and understood in a 'pre-discursive' mode; it may be that you have a particular image of a saint or deity in mind, but there is also a more general notion of the iconic idea which enables you to identify a new, hitherto unexperienced, exemplar, as a representative of that icon. So it is with the rāgas. In a performance, you quickly identify the particular one, by a kind of differential diagnosis; the process has been neatly described for the Hindustani musical system by Harold S. Powers,[32] and another musicologist has depicted Indian musical creation and creativity as a process of transformation akin to that in other traditional art forms – that is to say, the transformation and transcendence of an already known archetype.[33]

As a melody progresses, the listener comes to know which rāga it represents. In practice the initial recognition can come quickly, because a short fragment of melody is sufficient to establish the rāga. A rāga is thus highly specific, at least within a single tradition. Indeed, so specific are the individual rāgas that there have even been traditions of representing their individuality by extra-musical images – pictures, and verses describing their 'personalities'. But such extra-musical depictions of ethos show the kind of variation and inconsistency which may be expected. The rāga is not only specific; it is also highly potential, since an infinite number of melodies can be composed out of it, or, as is commonly said, 'in' it – infinite not only in the variety of composed songs, but in the extension and elaboration of any one of them, in which musicians bring into play material they have absorbed in the course of their training performing careers. A song composition is strong in the value system of Hindustani music if, in addition to being in other ways inventive, well balanced, and internally consistent, it gives a clear and powerful and characterful representation of its rāga.

I have concentrated here on the melodic concept of rāga, but I would say that this is just the most sophisticated of a number of ingredients in Indian art music which represent the same principle; a collection of learned but 'pre-discursive' structures – melodic, rhythmic, metrical and compositional – comes into play in any new performance. The music is not a repertoire of pieces but an open-ended potential field based on these structures. Importantly for the listener, the experience of a good and strong performance is a 'validation' of conventionally accepted structures.

There is a strong tradition, in the technical literature, of accounting for the genesis of sound and musical material. While the Indian classical medical literature takes little detailed account of music, the classical Sanskrit music-theoretical texts draw from medical theory (Āyurveda), Yoga, and linguistic philosophy to explain how the human body and mind produce and apprehend music. The fullest expression is found in the great thirteenth-century classic already mentioned, the *Saṅgītaratnākara* of Śārṅgadeva, where the extensive introductory section of the text is devoted to the structure of the human body.[34] The body is a composite of the five *mahabhūtas*, gross elements, each one being the origin of certain physical and psycho-physical functions:

ākāśa (ether) – gives sound, faculty of hearing etc.

vāyu (air) – gives touch and movement etc.

agni (fire) – gives the body sight, colour and form etc.

jala (water) – gives sense of taste, relish etc.

pṛthivī (earth) – gives sense of smell, as well as qualities like fortitude, weight etc.

This is the physical composite in which musical activity takes place – a holistic view of the body and the person, from the Āyurvedic standpoint.

The contribution of Yogic philosophy comes in the use of the *cakras*, or psycho-physical centres of the body as in the *Haṭhayoga* system; arranged from the genital region to the head, these are depicted as the seats of various emotions. Correct meditation on certain of the *cakras* is related to the cultivation of music, for it is in the production and passage of air through the body, striking at various locations, that leads to articulate sound.[35]

From linguistic philosophy the music theory of the *Saṅgītaratnākara* borrowed and adapted some categories of phonetics and language analysis, and equated with them those of musical structures. The *Saṅgītaratnākara* tells us that music, like speech, starts with the soul [*ātman*] experiencing a 'desire to speak'; whereas speech arises when the soul comes together with the intelligent and reasoning mind and moves the air in the body through various places of articulation to produce different sounds, in the case of music the soul activates the 'body-harp' [śarīravīṇā] – a metaphorical harp placed within the human frame. This idea, seemingly older in origin than the Saṅgīta-ratnākara, involves the image of strings [nāḍīs] stretched across the various sthānas (positions corresponding roughly to the places of articulation in phonetic theory, though of course differently located); the air strikes the strings and produces musical notes of different pitches.[36]

Now all of this is to some extent fanciful and analogical, and a critic can find problems and internal inconsistencies in the system even if the premises are taken as established. But the scheme does indicate the traditional view of the origin of sound – something that pre-exists as potential and is realized in a concretizing process in the body. There has always been a notion of the need to preserve the integrity of music, not to distort and not to misrepresent. Stories in both music-theoretical and non-technical sources relate how the flawless singing of a rāga can actually bring it to life in a visual form – that is, perfectly represent the pre-discursive idea. Furthermore the texts I have referred to relate the integrity of music to physiological as well as aesthetic considerations.

I have mentioned three main ingredients in what I believe would be a synoptic 'classical Indian view' of musical experience. First, the ritual importance and power of music to preserve order and avert disaster, a notion which clearly figured in Vedic ritual and is, I believe, one of the underlying ideas in the traditional concept of the occult powers of music. Continuity may be seen in the ascription of specifically appropriate times and situations to the performance of rāgas, in both ancient and medieval texts (where the considerations of drama-turgical needs are prominent) and more recently in the notions of Hindustani musical practice. Secondly, the aesthetic model of the drama, rasa as extended to other art forms; the experience of art in this model leads to a supra-mundane flight of realization and enlightenment, where the entity, the rāga especially, is really seen and apprehended for what it is. Some of the post-Nāṭyaśāstra dramatic and poetic theorists speak of sādhāraṇīkaraṇa, a moment of 'generalization' in which individuality of experience is lost and the universal is sensed. The theory makes for an interesting comparison with the Aristotelian notion of *katharsis*, especially if we remain open to different possible interpretations of this theory.[37] Thirdly, the physiological model found in some of the music-theoretical treatises, with music as a bodily representation of a spiritual necessity, serves to stress the notion of integrity and 'health' which music, as properly performed and heard, promotes.

From the listener's point of view, Indian music offers special possibilities for which I suspect it may be hard to find parallels elsewhere. The way in which music can have 'meaning' – through reference to a rāga – brings the possibility of reaffirmation of a known structure – the 'stable element'. Of course, as in any musical language, it is to be taken for granted that the appreciative listener is enculturated – has in fact, in this case, acquired the necessary familiarity with the rāga system and with the particular rāga in question. The practice of music in India shows less interest in non-specific generalities of sound (such as timbre and dynamics), and concentrates on precision of musical structures. A tantalizing reference in one of the reference books on south Indian music states that there was once a Sanskrit manuscript in a Tanjore collection, called *Rāgacikitsā*, 'rāga therapeutics'. The work is now lost, but the title *may* suggest that it was a work using rāgas for medical therapy. It is not difficult to see how the clarity and uplifting of the mind through the experience of rāga could be turned to actual therapeutic use, given these special possibilities for a person's enhancing, purifying, or transcending the appreciation of that which is already 'in' him. Certainly there are suggestive pointers in the Indian tradition.

Notes

1.   N. Spender, 'Music Therapy', in S. Sadie (ed.), *The New Grove Dictionary of Music and Musicians* (London, 1980), vol. 12, p. 863.

2.   J. B. Katz, 'Music and Aesthetics: An Early Indian Perspective', *Early Music*, 24 (August 1996), pp. 407–20.

3.   K. H. Krishnamurthy, *A Source Book of Indian Medicine: An Anthology* (Delhi, 1991), pp. 512–14. A brief eclectic article on music therapy was included by P. Sambamoorthy in his *Dictionary of South Indian Music and Musicians*, vol. 3 (Madras, 1971), pp. 85–7; this

cited neither historical authority nor experimental success, and sought rather to establish a claim for Indian music, acknowledging that music therapy was 'largely used in the United States of America, Soviet Russia, Britain and Germany'.

4. E. te Nijenhuis, *Musicological Literature*, in J. Gonda (ed.), *History of Indian Literature*, vol. 6, fasc. 1 (Wiesbaden, 1977), and J. B. Katz, 'Indian Musicological Literature and its Context', *Puruṣārtha*, 7 (1983), pp. 57–75.

5. For a basic introduction to the history and concepts of the Indian medical systems see D. Wujastyk, 'Indian Medicine', in W. F. Bynum and R. Porter (eds), *Companion Encyclopedia of the History of Medicine* (London, 1993), vol. 1, pp. 755–77. More detailed are the pioneering study originally published in German in 1901 but available in an annotated English translation, J. Jolly, *Indian Medicine*, transl. C. G. Kashikar (Poona, 1951, repr. New Delhi, 1977), and G. Mazars, *La médecine indienne*, in the series *Que sais-je?*, no. 2962 (Paris, 1995). The development of medical theory and practice in the ancient period is described with valuable notes and references in the first two chapters of K. G. Zysk, *Asceticism and Healing in Ancient India: Medicine in the Buddhist Monastery* (New York and Oxford, 1991). A useful introduction to the classical Sanskrit texts on the classification, diagnosis and treatment of illnesses can be found in G. J. Meulenbeld's work on an important treatise concerning *nidāna* [diagnosis], *The Mādhavanidāna and its Chief Commentary, Chapters 1–10: Introduction, Translation and Notes* (Leiden, 1974). The bibliographies in these works will lead the interested reader to more specialized studies.

6. K. Zysk, 'Mantra in Āyurveda', in H. P. Alper (ed.), *Understanding Mantras* (Albany, 1989), pp. 123–43.

7. M. and J. Stutley, *A Dictionary of Hinduism: Its Mythology, Folklore and Development, 1500 BC–AD 1500* (Bombay, 1977), pp. 328–9.

8. K. Zysk, *Asceticism and Healing*, pp. 11–37, and Zysk, 'The Indian Ascetic Traditions and the Origins of Āyurvedic Medicine', *Journal of the European Āyurvedic Society*, 1 (1990), pp. 119–24.

9. The sometimes strained interplay of different concepts and traditions in Indian medicine is examined by G. J. Meulenbeld, 'The Many Faces of Āyurveda', *Journal of the European Āyurvedic Society*, 4 (1995), pp. 1–10.

10. See the edition with Sanskrit text and English translation by P. V. Sharma, *Caraka-Saṃhitā*, vol. 1 (Varanasi, 1981), p. 79, and the note (derived from the commentator Cakrapāṇidatta) in vol. 3 (Varanasi, 1985), p. 124. A more detailed note by the commentator Gaṅgādhara is available only in the Sanskrit text, *The Caraka Saṃhitā of Mahāmuni Agniveśa*, ed. N. N. Senagupta and B. C. Senagupta (with two commentaries), vol. 1, Vidya Vilas Ayurveda Series, no. 1, 2nd edn (Varanasi, 1984), p. 572.

11. Good summaries, derived from classical sources, of the essential conceptual categories of Indian medicine and therapeutics may be found in S. K. Ramachandra Rao (ed.), *Encyclopaedia of Indian*

Medicine, vol. 2: 'Basic Concepts' (Bombay, 1987); see especially the entries on 'Daiva-Vyapāśraya' (pp. 49 ff.), 'Rational Medicine' (pp. 174 ff.), and a valuable appendix which links the Āyurvedic tradition to its affiliated intellectual systems, 'Conceptual Framework of Indian Medicine' (pp. 226–36).

12. The references are collected by Jolly, *Indian Medicine*, p. 87.

13. *Carakasaṃhitā*, cikitsāsthāna 23.87; ed. P. V. Sharma, vol. 2 (Varanasi, 1983), pp. 373 ff.

14. See A. Daniélou (trans.), *The Complete Kāmasūtra* (Rochester, 1994), pp. 51 ff.

15. *Carakasaṃhitā*, Sūtrasthāna 15.7; ed. P. V. Sharma, vol. 1, p. 105.

16. K. L. Bhishagratna (ed. and trans.), *An English Translation of the Sushruta Samhita* (3 vols, Varanasi, 1963), vol. 1, p. 562.

17. On the whole subject of the origin, diffusion and widespread use of mantras see the extended essay by H. P. Alper, 'A Working Bibliography for the Study of Mantras', in Alper, *Understanding Mantras*, pp. 327–443, and the full bibliographic list that follows. Specifically on mantra and Āyurveda see pp. 391 ff. A good empirical account of the use of mantra in current practice in India is the chapter 'Tantra and Tantric Healing' in S. Kakar, *Shamans, Mystics and Doctors: A Psychological Inquiry into India and its Healing Traditions* (Delhi, 1982), pp. 151–90. On Vajrayāna survivals in Tibetan and Newar Buddhist medicine in Nepal, W. G. Stablein, 'A Medical-Cultural System Among the Tibetan and Newar Buddhists: Ceremonial Medicine', *Kailash: A Journal of Himalayan Studies*, 1.3 (Kathmandu, 1973), pp. 193–203. On Tibetan Buddhist practice, see also H. T. Clifford, *Tibetan Buddhist Medicine and Psychiatry* (Wellingborough, 1984).

18. Music is used also as a trance-inducement in the symbolic and shamanic treatments of possession in South Asia. See for example the case in Sri Lanka described by G. Obeyesekere, 'Psychocultural Exegesis of a Case of Spirit Possession in Sri Lanka', in V. Crapanzano and V. Garrison (eds), *Case Studies in Spirit Possession* (New York, 1977), pp. 235–94. A more conceptual and philosophical study of music and dance in exorcism is ch. 8, 'Music, Dance and Trance', in B. Kapferer, *A Celebration of Demons: Exorcism and the Aesthetics of Healing in Sri Lanka*, 2nd edn (Providence, RI, 1991), pp. 245–84. For a general study of psychic possession and its treatment, against the background of Indian classical ideas of divided consciousness, see R. J. Castillo, *Culture, Trance and Mental Illness* (Ann Arbor, 1993), pp. 153–372. Further Howard, Chapter 15.

19. See the description of this suite, in the more general context of Dīkṣitar's *oeuvre*, in E. te Nijenhuis and S. Gupta, *Sacred Songs of India: Dīkṣitar's Cycle of Hymns to the Goddess Kamalā*, 2 pts (Winterthur, 1987), pt 1: 'Musicological and Religious Analysis', pp. 132 ff. The transliterated text, English translation and musical notations are available in A. S. Panchapagesa Iyer, *Sri Ramajayam Navagraha Gānāmrutham* (Madras, 1995).

20.   A. K. Ramanujan (ed.), *Folktales from India: A Selection of Oral Tales from Twenty-Two Languages* (New York and London, 1994), pp. 120 ff.

21.   W. Kaufmann, *The Ragas of North India* (Bloomington, 1968), p. 12.

22.   Kaufmann, *The Ragas of North India*, p. 18. Reports of the quasi-magical influences of rāga, including physiological and therapeutic effects, were given from oral tradition by the Lucknow Muslim courtier Hakim Mohammad Karam Imam in his 1856 Treatise *Ma'dan-ul Musīqī*. See the translation of the relevant chapter by G. Vidyarthi, 'Effects of Ragas and Mannerism in Singing', *Sangeet Natak Akademi Bulletin*, 13–14 (October 1959), pp. 6–14.

23.   M. Lath, 'Ancient Indian Music and the Concept of Man', in R. Goswami (ed.), *Man and Music in India* (Shimla, 1992), p. 22.

24.   *Jaiminīya Upaniṣad Brāhmaṇa*, 1.13.7. See H. Oertel, 'The Jāiminīya or Talavakāra Upaniṣad Brāhmaṇa: Text, Translation, and Notes', *Journal of the American Oriental Society*, 16.1 (1894), pp. 79–260, at p. 93.

25.   Lath, 'Ancient Indian Music', p. 24.

26.   The sources are collected and translated (sometimes a little tendentiously) by G. U. Thite, *Music in the Vedas: Its Magico-Religious Significance* (Delhi, 1997), pp. 221–7.

27.   On the musical component of the *Nāṭyaśāstra*, see R. Widdess, *The Rāgas of Early Indian Music* (Oxford, 1995), pp. 4 ff. and 36 ff.

28.   G. K. Bhat, *Rasa Theory and Allied Problems* (Baroda, 1984), p. 4.

29.   Literature on the aesthetic theory of *rasa* is extremely voluminous. A reliable, if somewhat taxing, introduction to the subject as it arises in Sanskrit literary theory may be found in E. Gerow, *Indian Poetics*, in Gonda, *History of Indian Literature*, vol. 5, fasc. 3 (Wiesbaden, 1977), pp. 245–57. The possible intellectual precursors of the literary concept are interestingly re-examined by A. K. Warder, 'The Origins of the Technical Senses of the Word *Rasa*', *Brahmavidyā: The Adyar Library Bulletin*, 44–5 (1980–81), pp. 614–34.

30.   The discussion has been largely aimed at two questions: (1) whether in general the concept of *rasa* is at all applicable to a non-representational art form such as music; and (2) whether the perception of emotional connotation in a rāga is stable and consistent. The discussion has been not only theoretical but experimental. In the 1960s the musicologist B. C. Deva conducted tests, using behavioural and psychometric ideas as well as traditional Indian aesthetic categories; the results were re-published in his *The Music of India: A Scientific Study* (New Delhi, 1981), pp. 138–222. These in fact seem to show, perhaps unremarkably, that listeners familiar with the melodic structures within a cultural tradition are likely to respond consistently to what they hear. Specific emotional response is of course in large measure conditioned by upbringing and environment.

31.   For a good and accessible discussion leading to this point, see T. P. Ramachandran, *The Indian Philosophy of Beauty*, 2 pts (Madras, 1979–

80), pt 2, pp. 52–6 ('Is rasa one or many?'), and pp. 84–116 ('The theories of *rasa*').

32. 'The Structure of Musical Meaning: A View from Banaras', *Perspectives of New Music*, 14.2–15.1 (1976), pp. 308–334. See also D. R. Widdess, 'Sugar, Candy and Treacle: History and the Concept of Rāga in Indian Music' in M. Philipp (ed.), *Ethnomusicology and the Historical Dimension* (Ludwigsberg, 1989), pp. 71–81.

33. M. Lath, 'Creation as Transformation', *Diogenes*, 127 (1984), pp. 42–62.

34. The Sanskrit text is published with an English translation and a commentary based on old exegetical sources in *Saṅgīta-Ratnākara of Śārṅgadeva*, ed. R. K. Shringy and P. L. Sharma, vol. 1 (Delhi, 1978).

35. See P. L. Sharma, 'Mahābhūtas in Saṅgīta-Śāstra with Special Reference to Yoga and Āyurveda', in B. Bäumer (ed.), *The Āgamic Tradition and the Arts*, vol. 3 of K. Vatsyayan (ed.), *Prakṛti: The Integral Vision* (New Delhi, 1995), pp. 87–100.

36. The theory is critically examined by M. Lath, 'The Body as Instrument: A Theoretical Choice Made by Śārṅgadeva', in Bäumer, *The Āgamic Tradition*, pp. 101–13. On the Indian religious and philosophical notions of sound and its significance, see also G. L. Beck, *Sonic Theology: Hinduism and Sacred Sound* (Delhi, 1995).

37. For the link between the medical and the rhetorical uses of the Greek term, and a re-examination of Aristotle's adoption of it, see M. Nussbaum, *The Fragility of Goodness: Luck and Ethics in Greek Tragedy and Philosophy* (Cambridge, 1986), pp. 388–91.

PART II

Medieval Europe

Commentary on Part II,
with a Note on the Early Middle Ages

Peregrine Horden

I

Part I offered a *tour d'horizon* of the major traditions of learned medicine – reaching, tentatively, right across Asia. From now on, with the exception of Chapter 15, in which we revisit Asia, this collection focuses on Western Europe. So we resume the narrative begun in Chapter 2. That chapter closed with a reference to Boethius. His treatise *De Institutione Musica* (or simply *De Musica*) is the principal conduit[1] by which the ancient cosmological conception of music therapy was transmitted to medieval Europe. It gave a thorough yet accessible statement of the Pythagorean–Platonic view that individual soul (*musica humana*) could be retuned to cosmic harmony (*musica mundana*) through the intermediary of appropriate *musica intrumentalis* – music as it is nowadays conceived, vocal as well as instrumental.[2] Boethius also conveniently gathered the best anecdotes illustrating the power of *musica intrumentalis* to influence both somatic and psychic ailments. ('By means of modes, Ismenias the Theban is said to have driven away all the distresses of the Boeotians suffering the torments of sciatica', and so forth.)[3] His treatise was widely disseminated and commented upon throughout the Middle Ages and beyond. Indeed, it became an integral part of the second phase of the ideal medieval education, its study constituting the chief part of one of the 'four ways' of the *quadrivium*, which included the other mathematical disciplines of arithmetic, geometry, and astronomy.[4] *De musica* remained on some university syllabuses until the nineteenth century.[5] Knowledge of it would thus have been a prerequisite for most students of medicine at the universities (see Horden, Chapter 1; and Austern, Chapter 10).

There were, however, other intellectual currents that antiquity bequeathed to the Middle Ages, currents less favourable to the cosmological conception of music therapy. One of these can suitably be

labelled 'Aristotelian'. Aristotle, though deeply influenced by what
Plato had said about ethos, strongly doubted the audibility of the
music of the spheres. He stands at the head of that generally more
sceptical school of thought about the scope of musical healing to
which Page alludes.[6] Christianity must also, of course, be brought into
the post-antique picture. Its growth was far from being a neutral context for early medieval developments in our subject. Some theologians
held distinctive views of musical therapeutics. The Christian Church
in late antiquity and the early Middle Ages did not, some extremists
apart, find Hippocratic–Galenic medicine uncongenial.[7] But there
were certainly some Fathers who doubted the medicinal power of
music, as the Bible represented it. Considering later medieval interpretations of David's playing to Saul (on which see also Shiloah,
Chapter 3), Jones quotes the famous witch-finder's manual, the
Malleus maleficarum. Its sentiments derive ultimately from early
Christian writings such as the discussion of the uses of liturgical
singing (psalmody) by Niceta, bishop of Remesiana around AD 400.
'To absolutely all who will take it', Niceta, writes, 'the psalm offers
appropriate remedies [*apta medicamenta*]', and he expands on how
the Lord, through David, has prepared for mankind this potion with
the strength to heal wounds. He is of course using medicine as metaphor. And he has previously asserted that David subdued the evil
spirit in Saul, 'not because such was the power of his cithara, but
because a figure of the cross of Christ was mystically projected by the
wood and the stretching of the strings, so that it was the Passion itself
that was sung and that subdued the spirit of the demon'.[8]

The optimistic tradition stemming from Boethius was not, then, the
only one. And for all his prominence in medieval theorizing, what
Boethius could bequeath was no more than a background theory,
some anecdotes, and a general recommendation. We have seen in
West's chapter that, apart from the Pythagoreans, there was little in
the way of actual, systematic, music therapy in antiquity, and that,
according to at least two Roman authors, there were clear limits to its
possible effectiveness. The use of music to divert the demented
Emperor Justin II (the George III of the late sixth century) owes
nothing to the Boethian tradition, and is an isolated example in the
surviving evidence of the period. Certainly the medical writings of

Justin's time give no space to it. In the 'sub-Roman' medicine of the early Middle Ages (Byzantine and, still more, Western European), the complex disease aetiology of Galenic medicine largely disappeared. The conceptual framework that had encouraged music therapy was lost, or perhaps even dismantled.[9] Manuscripts of Boethius' treatise lay seemingly unread between his own time and the Carolingian Renaissance of the late-eighth to ninth centuries. Music might have a healing role as the vehicle for magical incantation; but that was all.

II

The early Middle Ages are thus a hiatus in the history of music therapy. Changes come with the diffusion of translations into Latin of those authors by whom the antique legacy had been developed rather than dismantled: the Arab scholars discussed by Shiloah. The flow of what is taken for superior medical wisdom is reversed. Greek learning returns to the northern Mediterranean via Spain and Italy and thence to north-western Europe and Germany. Medicine recovers its philosophical underpinning; university medical faculties burgeon; and learned therapeutics become very much in demand, therapeutics in which music therapy has once again a conceptual niche as a means of moderating the 'passions of the soul'.[10]

Those changes are, however, limited in two important respects so far as music therapy is concerned. First, as we shall see, they were slow and geographically uneven in their impact. Second, only a portion of the relevant Graeco-Arab learning became available. There were Arabic texts, discussions of 'spiritual medicine' for 'the passions of the soul', which moved beyond generalization about the usefulness of music to stipulate specific types of rhythm or melody for the inducing of particular psychological states; but, apart from one short treatise on melancholy, these were not translated because, Burnett speculates, their terminology was too difficult.[11] Nor was music therapy ever endorsed by astrology in medieval Europe as it would be in the Renaissance (see Voss, Chapter 7). European astrology is based entirely on translations from the Arabic; the Arabs brought astrology into their musicological texts but not the other way round; and the musicological texts were not the ones translated. So the sophisticated culture of music therapy which Shiloah described was only very imperfectly rendered in the new Latin scholarship.[12]

Even so, great claims have been made for the extent of musical healing in medieval Europe. In his major study discussed in Chapter 1, Kümmel deploys medieval evidence under almost every thematic heading, as if the period between the recovery of Arabic learning and the dawn of Romanticism really is all of a piece, and the Middle Ages can simply be treated as part of that larger whole.[13] In an essay of 1978, which will be cited several times in subsequent chapters, Madeleine Pelner Cosman bathes the evidence she collects from right across the later Middle Ages in a highly optimistic light: 'physicians would not perform elective surgery without the patient's prior prepa-ration by diet and music therapy ... Hospitals, clinics, and health spas sounded with rhythm and melody', and so on.[14] It is not a picture that the evidence cited is really able to sustain. A more cautious and nuanced approach seems called for. Hence the contrasting chapters by Page and Jones.

Page's world is primarily that of the thirteenth century. This was the period when Aristotle's work was recovered for the West through translation from the Arabic; and Aristotelian scepticism about the music of the spheres is taken as heralding a very subdued approach to music therapy, in which Platonist metaphysics count for little. Page's world is also very much that of Paris, and the theologians of its schools. Against a background of theological (and kindred) writings in which bold assertions of music's power are common but specific applications are few,[15] he sketches a possible music therapy which is compassionate, empirical, and unambitious, concerned with distrac-tion and comfort more than cure, and with the spirit more than the body, whether in the monastery or among lay people.

Jones's focus is later. With his chapter we move from the thirteenth to the later fifteenth century. The celebrated case of the musical treatment, for severe mental illness, of the painter Hugo van der Goes was patterned on David's playing to Saul – but only superficially so. Well before Hugo's time, biblical commentators had redefined Saul's possession by an unclean spirit in medical terms. So whereas Page writes against a background of Parisian theology, Jones's background is the larger one of university medicine, above all that of the north

Italian faculties. It is a medicine nourished by translations from the Arabic (despite the omissions mentioned above). And it issues in a substantial literature, both Latin and vernacular, which quite frequently includes music therapy in its account of the 'non-naturals'.

These contrasts of period, place, and background discipline notwithstanding, the two chapters have much in common. The subject matter of both relates closely to the monastic infirmary. Whether the infirmary stands outside thirteenth-century Canterbury or fifteenth-century Brussels, music is far from routinely welcome in it. Both authors display the connections between 'high' theory (theological and medical) and 'front-line' texts of everyday application (confessors' manuals and medical *practica*). In both sets of evidence, moreover, demonic possession is approached naturalistically: demons must use natural means to afflict mankind and can be countered only by rational medicine. Both authors are dealing with psychological ailments for which recreation and palliation are the appropriately circumscribed ambitions: if Page's is the more sceptical account, Jones could hardly be accused of overstating his case. Finally, most significantly, both authors have to depend overwhelmingly on prescriptive literature. The mad painter provides the single well-documented case history. And it is a record of failure: music brought no relief. Hugo survived, but for only a few years. The contest between Plato and Aristotle seems to have produced a clear winner.

Notes

1. Though see also Isidore, *Etymologiae*, III.17; Cassiodorus, *Institutiones*, II.5.9; Martianus Capella, *De nuptiis Philologiae et Mercurii*, bk 9, Teubner edn by A. Dick (Stuttgart, 1978), pp. 492–3.

2. The Latin text transmitted is incomplete: it breaks off in bk V out of a likely six or seven, and covers only 'instrumental music' out of the three types outlined at the start: H. Chadwick, *Boethius* (Oxford, 1981), p. 81.

3. Anicius Manlius Severinus Boethius, *The Fundamentals of Music*, trans. C. M. Bower, ed. C. V. Palisca (New Haven and London, 1989), p. 6.

4. A. White [Peden], 'Boethius in the Medieval Quadrivium', in M. Gibson (ed.), *Boethius: His Life, Thought and Influence* (Oxford, 1981), pp. 162–205. The whole volume is valuable for context and bibliography here, as is Bowers' 'Introduction' to *The Fundamentals of Music*. More recent scholarship on Boethius' medieval reception can be

sampled in F. Hentschel (ed.), *Musik – und die Geschichte der Philosophie und Naturwissenschaften im Mittelalter* (Leiden, Boston and Cologne, 1998), esp. pp. 163–83 (Bower), pp. 187–206 (M. Hochadel).

5.   J. Caldwell, 'Music in the Faculty of Arts', in J. McConica (ed.), *The Collegiate University*, The History of the University of Oxford, vol. 3 (Oxford, 1986), pp. 201–12.

6.   M. West, *Ancient Greek Music* (Oxford; 1992), pp. 249–53; Chadwick, *Boethius*, pp. 79–80.

7.   O. Temkin, *Hippocrates in a World of Pagans and Christians* (Baltimore and London, 1991); D. W. Amundsen, *Medicine, Society, and Faith in the Ancient and Medieval Worlds* (Baltimore and London, 1996).

8.   *De utilitate hymnorum*, ed. C. Turner, 'Niceta of Remesiana II', *Journal of Theological Studies*, 24 (1923), pp. 235–6, trans. adapted from J. McKinnon, *Music in Early Christian Literature* (Cambridge, 1987), pp. 135–6.

9.   F. Wallis, 'The Experience of the Book: Manuscripts, Texts, and the Role of Epistemology in Early Medieval Medicine', in D. Bates (ed.), *Knowledge and the Scholarly Medical Traditions* (Cambridge, 1995), pp. 101–26.

10. L. Conrad, M. Neve, V. Nutton, R. Porter and A. Wear, *The Western Medical Tradition 800 B.C. to A.D. 1800* (Cambridge, 1995), pp. 139–46, on the translations. N. Siraisi, *Medieval and Early Renaissance Medicine* (Chicago and London, 1990), pp. 12–16, and ch. 3, for the reception of Aristotle and the growth of medical faculties.

11. C. Burnett, '"Spiritual Medicine": Music and Healing in Islam and its Influence in Western Medicine', in P. Gouk (ed.), *Musical Healing in Cultural Contexts* (Aldershot, 2000), pp. 87–8.

12. See also L. García-Ballester, '*Artifex factivus sanitatis*: Health and Medical Care in Medieval Latin Galenism', in Bates, *Knowledge*, pp. 127–50.

13. W. F. Kümmel, *Musik und Medizin: Ihre Wechselbeziehungen in Theorie und Praxis von 800 bis 1800* (Freiburg and Munich, 1977).

14. M. P. Cosman, 'Machaut's Medical Musical World', in M. P. Cosman and B. Chandler (eds), *Machaut's World: Science and Art in the Fourteenth Century*, Annals of the New York Academy of Sciences, 314 (New York, 1978), pp. 1–36.

15. C. Page, *The Owl and the Nightingale: Musical Life and Ideas in France 1100–1300* (London, 1989), pp. 20–29, 158–60.

CHAPTER FIVE

Music and Medicine in the Thirteenth Century

Christopher Page

Around 1100 a monk of Christ Church, Canterbury, named Eadmer, wrote a biography of a great churchman who had been Archbishop of Canterbury in the tenth century and a reformer of the English church. This was St Dunstan, who died in 988. Eadmer relates that Dunstan was a gifted musician, and at one point he describes how he played his instruments for friends:[1]

> Super haec instrumentis musici generis, quorum scientia non mediocriter fultus erat, non tantum se sed et multorum animos a turbulentis mundi negotiis saepe demulcere, et in medicationem coelestis harmoniae tam per suavitatem verborum, quae modo materna modo alia lingua musicis modulis interserebat, quam et per concordem concentum quem per eos exprimebat concitare solebat.

> [In addition to these things [the arts of the scribe, sculptor and metalworker] he possessed no small skill with musical instruments, and it was his custom often to soothe himself and the spirits of many others for the troublesome occupations of the world, and to urge them towards the healing of celestial harmony as much by the sweetness of the words which, sometimes in the mother tongue, sometimes in the other, he interspersed with melodies, as by the harmonious music which he expressed with them.]

Eadmer regards the music of Dunstan as an echo of *harmonia coelestis*, perhaps the music of the spheres. Dunstan's music produces a salutary effect in his listeners, bringing them into accord with celestial harmony. Since Pythagoras, these ideas have shaped Western beliefs in music's power to soothe or even to produce what Eadmer calls a *medicatio*, a healing (see West, Chapter 2). With those beliefs in mind, I would like to introduce a second text from Canterbury. In the thirteenth century, long after the death of Eadmer, a Customary was compiled for St Augustine's Abbey, as old as Christ Church but located outside the city walls. This Customary, now in the British Library in London, contains a section on the duties of the *Infirmarius*, in charge of the monastic hospital (the reasons for presenting this text *per cola et commata* will become clear):[2]

> In infirmaria
> nullus aliquo tempore
> inconueniens fiet tumultus
> sed neque ibidem in audiencia
> manifeste alicuius instrumenti
> fiet unquam melodia
> set pro maiore necessitate
> si ad alicuius melioracionem perutile censeatur
> vt si contingat
> quod aliquis frater ita sit debilis et egrotus
> quod ad eius spiritum exhilarandum
> musici instrumenti sono
> et armonia
> quamplurimum indigeat
> poterit per infirmarium duci
> aut etiam quoquomodo in capella portari
> atque clauso hostio
> psalterium musicum coram eo absque reprehensione
> ab aliquo fratre
> seu famulo honesto et priuato
> dulciter resonari
> sed cauendum omnino est
> ne huiusmodi sonus
> siue melodia
> in aula infirmarie
> aut in cameris fratrum
> quod absit aliquo tempore audiatur

[In the infirmary, there should be no disturbing clamour at any time, but nor in that same place should there be any music of any musical instrument played openly in general hearing. But, for reasons of greater need, if it be judged very useful for improving someone's condition – as when it happens that any brother be so weak and ill that he greatly needs the sound and harmony of a musical instrument to raise his spirits – that person may be led into the chapel by the *Infirmarius*, or carried there in some manner, so that, the door being closed, a stringed instrument may be sweetly played before him by any brother, or by any reliable and discreet servant, without blame. But great care should always be taken lest music or melody of this kind be heard at any time in the hall of the infirmary or – perish the thought – in the chambers of the brothers.]

The infirmary was almost an alternative community in larger monastic houses with its own hall and chapel. This was the arrangement at St Augustine's Abbey. The infirmary hall had an aisle of nine bays, creating a few heated chambers which are presumably the ones mentioned in the passage just quoted. In order to hear the music provided for him, the ailing monk entered the chapel, east of the hall, and the music began with the door closed, *clauso hostio*.

In some ways, Eadmer's *Life* of Dunstan and the Customary of St Augustine's reflect the same monastic world. Both reveal the leisurely Latin style we expect from Benedictines. With Eadmer, this includes not only an ornate syntax but also a charged vocabulary for musical beauty (*demulcere, harmonia coelestis, suavitas, concordem concentum*, and *concitare*). In the Customary, synonymous words are placed together in ornamental pairs (*debilis et egrotus ... sono et armonia ... sonus sive melodia*), and there are some elaborate patterns of sound, carefully noted by the scribe who has marked the text into clauses and phrases for reading aloud.

The similarities between Eadmer's *Life* of Dunstan and the St Augustine's Customary make the difference which separates them more apparent. The Customary does not invoke celestial harmony, as Eadmer chooses to do, and seems to attribute no metaphysical power to music: no power of exorcism, such as David wielded over Saul (compare Jones, below), and no power of physical healing. Music may be used to lift the spirit, *ad spiritum exhilarandum*, and in that sense may produce an improvement, a *melioracio*, but only in cases of special need. In general, music is a disturbance to be banned, and the music admitted for therapeutic reasons is a substance no more mysterious than the meat that was also conceded to the monks of the infirmary.

Here is a basis for one kind of music therapy: compassionate and apparently indifferent to metaphysics. It may be no coincidence that we find the elements of such a therapy in the Customary but not in Eadmer's *Life* of Dunstan. I do not suggest that Eadmer studied Plato – or indeed that the compiler of the Customary studied Aristotle – but the difference between our two texts captures a contrast between the century of Eadmer, when the fragments of Plato known to the Latins were read with renewed interest, and the period of the Customary, when scholasticism intensified its engagement with Aristotle and entered its classic phase. The first Western European authors after the fall of Rome to venture a compassionate and empirical assessment of music's therapeutic power were not Renaissance humanists, but rather certain theologians of the thirteenth century.

Before we turn to those writers, let us pose a general question. What could thirteenth-century authors hope to accomplish in their understanding of music and medicine? If there were ways of regarding music-making as the site of a personal interaction between patients and therapist, so important in some modern therapy (see Tyler, Chapter 16) we do not know what they were. Medieval doctors had no means of recording musical sound and transporting it. If a particular piece, or a specific performance, produced a therapeutic effect, the music vanished with the malady it helped to cure; sounds could not be stored and carried to the bedside of another when needed. Nor could music be compared, for example, to an emetic herb that *usually* caused vomiting or to a soporific that *usually* induced sleep; as medieval writers often observe, the same musical sounds may induce markedly different emotions and states of mind in different persons. As we have seen, many classical sources offered generalizations about music's power to influence human health and behaviour ('the sound of trumpets excites warriors to battle'), and these were associated with some famous names including Isidore, Apuleius, Aulus Gellius, Censorinus and Plato.[3] This was an impressive thesaurus of material, but it was inert and remote from most clinical concerns. By the thirteenth century, and perhaps before, some writers had begun to record empirical observations about the curative power of music, but this was a narrow and uncertain stream of information. Around 1300, for example, the music theorist Johannes de Grocheio declares that certain kinds of songs performed by young people on feast days, especially in Normandy, have the power to quell *amor hereos*, excessive erotic desire.[4] As far as I am aware, the medical treatises which discuss *amor hereos*, the *Prose Salernitan Questions* for example, do not say this. Grocheio is giving us an enthusiast's opinion, voiced in passing (see Austern, Chapter 10).

For all of these reasons, the prescription of music for the treatment of ailments, physical or mental, was technically almost impossible, except in the most general terms. The tradition of empirical information on this subject in the Latin medical literature seems a fragile one to judge by the schoolmen whose works I have consulted; with the exception of a passing reference to al-Farabi's *De ortu scientiarum* (cited for the simple observation that music has the power to heal various maladies)[5] the theologians of the Schools give no evidence of having read anything on this topic which they think worth mentioning. So the question stands: what was there for thirteenth-century writers to accomplish in this area? My answer would be that there was much to achieve by finding a plain language for stating the essentials without consulting the dead thesaurus of references to music's curative power that had been accumulating since antiquity.

Consider William of Auvergne, Bishop of Paris. His treatise *De universo*, completed between 1231 and 1236, contains a chapter on the curative powers of music.[6] Naming Plato, but without citing any specific work by him, William summarizes what he knows of Plato's views concerning the 'soul of the universe' and the human soul. Plato ascribes a soul to the universe, says William, that is constructed according to the mathematical proportions of music. The human soul is compounded in the same way. A skilled musician can produce changes in a person's disposition because like responds to like: music has a mathematical basis and we react to it because the human soul shares the numerical motion of the soul of the universe (see West, Chapter 2).

Once William has completed this paraphrase his own judgement comes swiftly: 'Plato's position can be refuted in many ways and with many kinds of argument'. Let us follow William's track again. Like does not always respond to like; we enjoy food and drink because we are hungry and we take pleasure in warmth because we are cold. Musical consonances may have a mathematical foundation, but the pleasure we take in them does not prove the numerical constitution of the soul. Plato's position implies that we only take pleasure in things that can be numbered and measured, but this is not true; we find our ultimate joy in God, beyond all quantification. There can be no such thing as music of the spheres; sound arises from collision which sets air vibrating, and there is no such impact in the heavens.

We need not ask ourselves whether this is a well-informed critique of Plato; only a small proportion of Plato's writing was available to William, so in that sense his discussion is not well informed by the standards of a later humanist. Nor, perhaps, should a medievalist seem too triumphant about the fact that William is writing two and a half centuries before the Italian humanists admired by Claude Palisca for their sceptical view of the doctrine of celestial music.[7] More important here is the illustration which William provides of scholastic method. In comparison with Eadmer of Canterbury, with whom we began, William's Latin is a sharp instrument for uprooting flowers of poetic style like Eadmer's allusion to celestial music; his manner is forensic. William's ultimate source of inspiration is Aristotle, for in the *De caelo et mundo* (II.9) the Philosopher had already refuted the Pythagorean and Platonic belief that heavenly bodies make music as they rotate. Most important of all, William's book on the universe reveals the concern with matters of human welfare characteristic of scholasticism in its classic period. William may reject Plato's explanation of music's power to heal, but he is convinced that music has a therapeutic force. This emerges from a chapter of his book where he recognizes various forms of mental illness.[8] We speak of depression, neurosis or phobia; William refers to 'diseases of the spirit', *morbi spirituales*, including insanity [*insania*], melancholia (his word) 'and certain other mental disturbances' [*alias quasdam alienationes*]. 'Many diseases of the spirit', he writes, 'have sometimes been cured by musical sounds.' William recognizes, as we have come to do, that doctors are not always well equipped to treat mental conditions, or 'spiritual diseases', which music can touch, partly because the same musical sounds can produce such markedly different effects in people that a positive result is likely to be unrepeatable. 'Perhaps many diseases of the spirit have been cured by chance by doctors', he comments, 'the physicians knowing nothing of the sounds possessing the musical power which accomplished the cure.'

Here is an empirical and compassionate belief in music's power to alleviate various kinds of mental disturbance. Here now is another, from the *Summa de penitentia* of a Franciscan, John of Erfurt:[9]

> De citharedis et alijs qui utuntur instrumentis musicis. Nota secundum Johannem quod licite potest homo ad talibus dare et potest talia instrumenta audire vel tangere de modo ob iusticie causam faciat, scilicet ad laudem dei, ut David et Samuel qui dixit *adducite mihi psalten*, et beatus Franciscus cui dedicanti melodiam cithare angeli citharizabant. Potest etiam hec melodia audiri vel tangi causa recreacionis si debilis vel infirmus est, vel propter aliquam causam honestam vel consuetam ...

> [Concerning string players and others who play musical instruments. Note that according to Johannes a man may legitimately give alms to such persons and may hear or play such instruments in any legitimate cause, that is to say in the praise of God, as David and Samuel who said 'bring me a string player', and St Francis to whom angels played string music. One may also hear or play such music for the sake of recreation if one is weak or infirm, and for any virtuous and customary purpose ...]

This approaches the spirit of the Customary from St Augustine's; it is also close to William of Auvergne, acknowledging that music can help the weak and sick but giving no indication that any metaphysical process might be involved. And yet, this *Summa de penitentia* is unlike either the Customary prepared for St Augustine's or William of Auvergne's *De universo* written for academic theologians. It is a book for confessors dealing with lay men and women on a day-to-day basis throughout Latin Christendom. How did such books become possible, and how did the views of academics like William of Auvergne find a place in them?

Now we can untie the most important sheaf of documents produced by Rome in this period: the proceedings of the Fourth Lateran Council, convened by Pope Innocent III in 1215 'to reform the universal church, especially for liberating the Holy Land' ['*propter reformationem universalis ecclesiae ad liberatione potissimum terrae sanctae*'].[10] From the articles of the Catholic faith at the beginning, down to a ban on shoes with pointed toes in Chapter 16, the articles of this Council are a regime for a healthier Christendom. The wounds of heresy are to be cured, by painful surgery if necessary; self-interest and laxity are to be purged so that an efficient fighting force, blessed by a dutiful clergy, may recover Jerusalem. The proceedings of Fourth Lateran express the anguish of a civilization whose most holy places lay outside its own borders.

The great aims of reform and crusade required a process of inquisition throughout Christendom. These were the fears and miseries of Fourth Lateran. At least once a year, archbishops, bishops or their archdeacons were to traverse any parish defiled by a rumour of heresy and question witnesses; secular lords were required to take an oath that they had crushed any heretics within their jurisdiction (Chapter 3). For most lay persons, this process of inquisition was concentrated in the confessional. There could be neither reform nor recuperation of Jerusalem if lay men and women remained in a lax spiritual condition because bishops and their clergy were too preoccupied with other duties to preach and take confession. To remedy this, a celebrated chapter of Fourth Lateran, number 22, enjoins all Christians to be confessed at least once a year.

We do not think of confession as a medical process today, but the delegates to Fourth Lateran took a different view:[11]

> Sacerdos autem sit discretus et cautus ut, more periti medici, superinfudat vinum et oleum vulneribus sauciati, diligenter inquirens et peccatoris circumstantias et peccati, per quas prudenter intelligat quale illi consilium debeat exhibere et cujusmodi remedium adhibere, diversis experimentis utendo ad sanandum aegrotum.

> [Let the priest be discreet and cautious so that, in the manner of a skilled physician, he may pour wine and oil over the wounds of the patient, diligently inquiring into both the circumstances of the sin and of the sinner, by which means he may wisely understand what advice he should give to him and what remedy he should employ, making trial of various remedies to heal the sick man.]

At first, we might read this as a figure of speech in which priests are advised to think admiringly of physicians and to imagine themselves in a comparable role. This cannot be. Since the soul is more precious than the body, priests, who care for souls, are more important than physicians, who care for flesh. A physician from Salerno or Montpellier might be learned in his craft, but care of souls was the art of all arts: *ars artium regimen animarum*. Fourth Lateran requires every physician to advise his patient that treatment does not truly begin with a physician's work, but with a priest's:[12]

> decreto praesenti statuimus, et districte praecipimus medicis corporum, ut cum eos ad infirmos vocari contigerit, ipsos ante omnia moneant and inducant quod medicos advocent animarum ...

> [in this present decree we ordain, and firmly instruct physicians of the body that, when ˙they are summoned to the sick, they should advise and encourage their patients, before all else, to seek physicians of souls ...]

Soon after Fourth Lateran, manuals were compiled for confessors, these 'physicians of souls'. The *Summa de Penitentia* by John of Erfurt, quoted above, is one of them.

An early fourteenth-century book by an Italian Franciscan, the *Astesanus*, shows how Parisian teaching at a high academic level could flow into these books.[13] One section asks whether certain herbs and musical sounds can drive away devils, and therefore the maladies which possession can cause. The friar begins by saying that herbs and musical sounds cannot, by their own power, completely suppress a physical or spiritual trial produced by a demon – at least, not if that trial is permitted by God or by a good angel. Some herbs and melodies can mitigate the demon's effect, but they do not accomplish this by working upon the malign spirit (who, being pure spirit, has no bodily substance); they act upon the troubled individual, lifting his spirits and so giving him extra resources to combat his assailant (see also Jones, Chapter 6). A demon can cause a vexation by intensifying the prevailing humour of a person, as for example by making a melancholy person yet more melancholic; then music can produce the contrary effect, as when festive music is played to a melancholic man, somewhat mollifying the effect of the devil's attack. Given the belief in demons which animates this passage it might seem strange to refer to it as essentially rational, and yet the purpose is to deny any magical power to music and herbs. The compiler says he derived this material from a certain Richard, who proves to be Richard of Middleton.

Richard gave a lecture on this subject in Paris; we have the full text of that disquisition and the friar has followed it carefully.[14]

Within a year or so of Fourth Lateran, an Englishman from Surrey, Thomas Chobham, composed an influential manual, the *Summa confessorum*, which sheds some light on the question of musical repertory. What, for example, did the musicians who helped the patients at St Augustine's actually play? In his manual, Thomas grants that minstrels may receive absolution if 'they give comfort to others either when they are ill or when they are troubled'.[15] He also praises musicians who perform narrative songs recounting lives of saints and deeds of princes. This points us towards the Middle English romances, some of which may have had a musical dimension to their performance at some stage in their evolution, and we are perhaps to imagine the ailing brothers of St Augustine's listening to accompanied stories of Arthur, Gawayn, and many other heroes, such as Wade, who have left little trace. One thirteenth-century musician in France, Johannes de Grocheio, already mentioned, declares that narrative songs remind their listeners of the misfortunes endured by heroes such as Charlemagne, or by saints such as Stephen, so making them better able to bear their own burdens.[16] This sounds ideal material for the infirmary.

In conclusion, let us squeeze the evidence a little harder. The Customary of St Augustine's Abbey forbids any musical instruments to be played in the infirmary hall; clearly, such things had been happening. Some of the payments to minstrels which appear in monastic accounts were perhaps for services discharged in the infirmary hall or chapel. A passage in the register of Adam of Orleton, Bishop of Hereford, reveals that in 1318 the canons of Wigmore Abbey were diverted with wanton songs [*cantilenis inhonestis*] while being bled, presumably in the infirmary.[17] There seems to be no evidence that this or any other music was believed to accomplish more than to give momentary relief in cases of both bodily and mental infirmity.

Notes

1.   W. Stubbs (ed.), *Memorials of Dunstan*, Rolls Series 63 (London, 1874), p. 170.

2. MS Cotton Faustina C. xii, f. 153$^{r\text{-}v}$. The text is edited in E. M. Thompson, *Customary of the Benedictine Monasteries of St. Augustine, Canterbury, and St. Peter, Westminster*, 2 vols, Henry Bradshaw Society 23 and 28 (London, 1902 and 1904), vol. 1, pp. 329–30.

3. Isidore, *Etymologiae*, IV.13; Apuleius, *Apologia* 40–41; Aulus Gellius, *Noctes Atticae*, III.10; Censorinus, *In die natali*, 12. West, Chapter 2.

4. C. Page, 'Johannes de Grocheio on Secular Music: A Corrected Text and a New Translation', *Plainsong and Medieval Music*, 2 (1993), pp. 26–7.

5. See a section of the early fourteenth-century manual of confession, the *Summa Astensis* (Lyon edn, 1519, f. xvj$^{r\text{-}v}$), an extended paraphrase of Richard of Middleton (on whom see below), mentioning the *De ortu scientiarum* for the claim that music *valet ad curandum vel alleviandum diversas infirmitates*. On Richard of Middleton see also C. Page, *The Owl and the Nightingale: Musical Life and Ideas in France 1100–1300* (London, 1989), pp. 160–61.

6. Edition of Venice, 1591, bk I, 3.30.

7. C. Palisca, *Humanism in Italian Renaissance Musical Thought* (New Haven and London, 1985), ch. 8.

8. *De universo*, bk II, 3.20.

9. Oxford, Oriel College, MS 38, f. 102^{v}.

10. G. D. Mansi (ed.), *Sacrorum Conciliorum Nova et Amplissima Collectio* (Florence, 1759–67 and Venice, 1769–1969), vol. 22, cols 953–1086; 969.

11. Mansi, col. 969.

12. Mansi, col. 969.

13. I cite the edition of Lyon, 1519.

14. Page, *The Owl and the Nightingale*, pp. 160–61.

15. Page, *The Owl and the Nightingale*, pp. 160–61.

16. Page 'Johannes de Grocheio', pp. 22–3.

17. A. T. Bannister (ed.), *Registrum Ade de Orleton* (London, 1908), p. 102.

CHAPTER SIX

Music Therapy in the Later Middle Ages: The Case of Hugo van der Goes

Peter Murray Jones

I

This paper is an attempt to answer two questions. First, when music was used as a form of therapy in the Middle Ages, what was the rationale for its use? Second, how did the medical doctors of the period justify the use of music as a therapeutic instrument? These questions are not necessarily linked. If it could be shown that music was used therapeutically on the basis of a rationale that had nothing to do with medicine, the ideas of the medical doctors would only be of interest to students of medical history. Actually, this paper will try to show the opposite – that there is a link between the two questions, and that the rationale for the use of music as therapy did have a medical basis, and did positively influence practice.

Of course there is very little record of the practical use of music in therapy in the Middle Ages (compare Page, Chapter 5), though there is a great deal of evidence for its prescription in the writings of medical authors.[1] However, music was famously used in the case of the Flemish painter Hugo van der Goes, who suffered an episode of mental disturbance some time after 1477, while he was a *conversus*[2] brother in the house of the Red Cloister in the forest of Soignes near Brussels. His brethren, under the instructions of the prior of the time, tried to treat him with music, but apparently without much success. Gaspar Ofhuys (1456–1523), the chronicler of the community who recorded this episode more than thirty years later (*c.* 1509–13), has also left us some intriguing speculations on the nature of Hugo's illness. We can investigate the reasons why music was used in Hugo's case, as well as alternative diagnoses of the disease which accounted for his symptoms, and the lessons that Ofhuys thought could be learnt.

Later historians, unsurprisingly, have devoted much effort to unravelling the complexities of this case, coming at it from the perspectives of art history, the history of madness, and the history of medicine – but I make no excuse for returning to it once more. It is the *locus classicus* for any discussion of the practice of music therapy in the later Middle Ages.[3]

II

Ofhuys's narrative is deceptively simple:

> A few years after his profession, five or even six, it so happened that this convert brother set out for Cologne, if I remember rightly accompanied by his half brother Nicholas who had also professed here and who was a lay brother (an oblate), by brother Peter who was a canon regular at Marienthron (at that time he dwelt in the Jericho monastery in Brussels) and by others as well.
>
> As I then learned from the account of his brother Nicholas, the lay monk, on a certain evening on the way back, our brother convert Hugo incurred a strange mental disease, as a result of which he kept saying that he was a lost soul and was adjudicated eternal damnation; furthermore he was intent on injuring himself physically and committing suicide (and would have done so had he not been forcibly restrained by those who were standing by to help). As a result of this strange disease the end of that trip was overshadowed by heavy sadness.
>
> They then reached the city of Brussels in their quest for help and without delay summoned Prior Thomas[4] thither. The latter, after confirming everything with his own eyes and ears, suspected that he was vexed by the same disease by which King Saul was tormented. Thereupon, recalling how Saul had found relief when David plucked his harp, he gave permission not only that a melody be played without restraint in the presence of brother Hugo, but also that other recreative spectacles be performed; in these ways he tried to dispel the delusions. But under such treatment brother Hugo found no relief but still delirious pronounced himself the son of Perdition. Consequently in this miserable condition he entered this house.[5]

We are not told by Ofhuys how and when Hugo emerged from his illness, only that the choir brothers cared for him subsequently. Hugo had entered the Red Cloister in 1477,[6] and died in 1482, not very long after the incident Ofhuys describes. It is probable that at least one of

Hugo's paintings, the *Death of the Virgin*, now at Bruges, was painted after his recovery. It seems that he was not incapacitated by his illness from all further work.

The communal life of the Red Cloister was not receptive to music, and it is significant that Prior Thomas's attempts to treat Hugo took place before he re-entered the house. The Red Cloister [Rookloste, Roodendale, Rouge-cloitre, Rubea Vallis] belonged to the Windesheim congregation, but was originally a foundation of the Augustinian Canons Regular. The Red Cloister was one of a number of religious communities of the late fourteenth and fifteenth centuries in the Low Countries and Germany which came under the influence of the ideals of the *Devotio moderna*. The first monastery at Windesheim was founded in 1386 by six pupils of Gerard Groote (1340–1384). In 1393 the Windesheim congregation was formed by amalgamation with three other Dutch monasteries, and the constitution was con-firmed at the Council of Constance. The Red Cloister, in the forest of Soignes near Brussels, was affiliated in 1438 to a congregation which had numbered forty-five monasteries by 1430, and ninety-seven by 1500. The total number of brothers in the Red Cloister might have been twenty-five, of whom up to eight might be *conversi* at any one time.[7]

Strict enclosure was the rule for the Windesheim congregation, with a choir obligation, fast and abstinence four times a week, and the systematic practice of meditation. It is likely that the brethren were particularly sensitive to the influence of the mystic Jan van Ruysbroeck (d. 1381), who had lived at the monastery of Groenendals, very near to the Red Cloister. The focus of their devo-tions was the humanity of Christ (Thomas à Kempis was another powerful influence). Ascetic in their impulses, the brethren stressed the need for introspection and self-communing, and rejected scholas-tic learning for its own sake. Manual labour was encouraged, as was the writing and copying of books, illumination, and the production of biblical texts in the vernacular. Devotional reading of the Bible was preferred to elaborate liturgy and ornate music.

This background to Hugo's life at the Red Cloister helps to explain the tension between his contemporary fame as an artist and the ideals of the community, which may lie behind his reported obsession with divine judgement. It also shows how Prior Thomas's use of music and *spectacula recreativa* in treating Hugo could not have been predicted from religious motives alone. There is no mention of the kind of music ordered by Prior Thomas. Since instrumental music, and in particular organ music, was forbidden in the Red Cloister by the statutes of the congregation, it is not surprising that the prior prescribed music and *spectacula recreativa* before Hugo returned to his brethren in the Cloister. Once he was back it would not certainly have been appropriate to continue the music treatment, which must have been of short duration.[8]

Ofhuys tells us that he was not himself a witness to the events he describes (which probably took place in 1480–1481), but learnt the story from Hugo's brother Nicholas, and perhaps also from Prior Thomas himself or one of the other bystanders. Prior Thomas's understanding of Hugo's condition was based on what he was told by Hugo's companions about the events of the fateful return journey from Cologne, and the evidence of his own eyes and ears. Thomas arrived at a diagnosis and a course of treatment as a result of identifying Hugo's illness with that of the biblical Saul. More than thirty years later, Prior Thomas's decision and actions are narrated without comment. Ofhuys does not reflect on the accuracy of the prior's diagnosis or the likelihood that the proposed cure would succeed.

On the face of it, Prior Thomas seems to have been inspired by the story of David and Saul, and not by any medical ideas relevant to Hugo's condition. But a look at biblical exegesis of this story reveals the extent to which Saul's possession by an 'unclean spirit', as described there, had been redefined medically by the time of Prior Thomas. The most influential exegete for the fifteenth century was Nicolaus de Lyra (*c.* 1270–1349).[9] His *Postilla litteralis* on the Bible, and on I Samuel 16 where the story is told, deals with the *quaestio* 'Utrum demones virtutem melodie possint expelli a corporibus obsessis'. His *responsio* to the *quaestio* answers the question positively. Whereas the *Glossa Ordinaria*, derived from Hrabanus Maurus, saw in David's playing of the harp to Saul an allegory of the role of Christ and the church in curing sin, and in Saul's illness a humbling of the sin of pride, for Nicolaus de Lyra, by contrast, the focus is on Saul's affliction by demons, and the ways in which music, which can only operate through the senses, can somehow counteract demonic powers.

The demons are preternatural, yet they can only act in the world within the constraints of the laws of nature. Nicolaus's arguments concentrate on the natural means by which demons afflict us, and the ways that music, too, can affect the mind through the same channels. One argument suggests that demonic influence varies with the state of the moon, which in turn can influence the moist brain. Music can also work on the brain, and so can counteract demonic influence. The second of Nicolaus's arguments is that affliction by demons requires the use of human perception, and that via perception the attention of the mind can be distracted by music. What is striking about these arguments is that they concentrate on the natural effects of mental disorder, or possession by demons, and the equally natural counter-acting power of music over the human mind. The demons are preter-natural, but if they are to have any influence on humanity it must be through actions which are subject to the laws of nature.[10]

There is a parallel trend to this naturalism in the fifteenth century iconography of the story of David curing Saul. The earliest depictions of the story show Saul seated and besieged by demons. But in the mid-fifteenth century the Bible of Borso d'Este depicts Saul lying in bed. Saul is suffering from melancholy, and it is as a melancholic that he is relieved by David's music (see Figures 6.1 and 6.2).[11]

The naturalistic, or medical, interpretation of Saul's illness and cure by David is carried to its limit by Tommaso Cajetan (1469–1534). He asserted that Saul's 'unclean spirit' was not a demon, but a 'melancholy spirit' which troubled him with sensory delusions. Although sent by God, Saul's illness was natural, and hence could be treated by music, which soothed his mind, restored his tranquillity, and expanded his heart.[12] Even those committed to the existence of demons, as opposed to a 'melancholy spirit', were willing to allow music a range of natural or medical effects in Saul's case. The authors of the *Malleus maleficarum* (1486–87) were willing to allow that herbs and music can change the disposition of the body, and hence the emotions, quoting Aristotle and Boethius. But they cannot cause a man to be of such a disposition that he can be freed from molestation by the devil, even if they can alleviate the symptoms to a limited

6.1   Queen Mary Psalter, early fourteenth century. British Library Royal MS 2.B.VII, f. 51ᵛ.

6.2   Bible of Duke Borso d'Este, mid-fifteenth century. Biblioteca
Estense Universitaria, Modena, MS V.G.12, f. 119ᵛ.

extent. In Saul's case he was vexed by demons, and music alone could not have forestalled or ended that vexation:

> It must be known that it is quite true that by the playing of the harp, and the natural virtue of that harmony, the affliction of Saul was to some extent relieved, inasmuch as that music did somewhat calm his senses through hearing; through which calming he was made less prone to that vexation. But the reason why the evil spirit departed when David played the harp was because of the might of the Cross, which is clearly enough shown by the gloss [that is, the *Glossa Ordinaria*], where it says: David was learned in music, skilful in the different notes and harmonic modulations. ... David repressed the evil spirit by the harp, not because there was so much virtue in the harp, but it was made in the sign of a cross, being a cross of wood with the strings attached across. And even at that time the devils fled from this.[13]

It is only because a symbolic cross can have supernatural power that David was able to drive out the evil spirit. His power as a musician was limited to the alleviation of some of Saul's symptoms of demonic oppression.

In choosing to treat Hugo's illness as equivalent to that of the biblical Saul, Prior Thomas was not opting for a spiritual or allegorical basis for the power of music to heal. Prior Thomas is confronted in Hugh with a *mirabilem fantasialem morbum*. The symptoms ascribed to Hugo are, in the Latin of the chronicle,

> incessanter dicebat se esse dampnatum et dampnationis eterne adiudicatum, quo etiam sibi ipsi corporaliter et letaliter (nisi violenter impeditus fuisset auxilio astantium) nocere volebat.

> [he kept saying that he was judged and condemned to eternal punishment, and he also wanted to harm his own person or even commit suicide, from which he was prevented only by the help of those around him.]

Compare this to a passage from Constantinus Africanus, *De melancholia*:

> Videmus enim multos religiosos et in bone vita reverendos hanc passionem incidentes ex dei timore et future iudicii suspicione et summi boni videndi cupiditate. Quae omnia superant eorum animas. Unde nec cogitant nec investigant, nisi ut solum deum ament et timeant.[14]

[We have seen many pious people and those living a righteous life suffering from this fear of God and dread of future judgement, as well as desire to see the bliss of heaven. All these thoughts overwhelm their minds. As a result they cannot think or pursue a train of thought, only love and fear God.]

The obsession with the fear of divine judgement which seized Hugo, an oblate of the community, is just what Constantinus would have expected of a melancholic. When Ofhuys recalls the treatment ordered by Prior Thomas, he mentions *melodiam ... non modicam*, but also *alia spectacula recreativa, quibus intendebat mentales fantasias repellere*. The terms that Ofhuys uses to describe his remedies summon up not the *cythara* of David, with its symbolic cross, but the injunctions of the physicians. Avicenna's *Canon* calls for the treatment of melancholy with *cantilenis et letificantibus*, and similar phrases are used by most of the medical authorities on melancholy.[15]

III

It is not surprising that Ofhuys was able to deploy the terminology of the physicians in describing Hugo's case. Ofhuys became the infirmarer of the Red Cloister shortly after Hugo's death in 1482.[16] Knowledge of texts on practical medicine must have been expected of him. After describing Hugo's illness and Prior Thomas's attempt at therapy, Ofhuys goes on to speculate on the true nature of the illness Hugo suffered. The passage presents some puzzles, and requires careful analysis.

> Moreover, concerning the nature of the sickness of this convert different people held different opinions. Some said it was a kind of phrenitis magna. Others asserted that he was surely in the power of a demon. Some signs of either kind of misfortune were present. Nevertheless from all sources I heard that throughout the entire period of his indisposition he never wanted to injure anyone except himself. This is not heard about phrenetics or people under the power of demons; therefore I believe that God alone knew what the trouble was. Consequently we can speak about this debility of our convert painter in two ways. First we may say that it was a natural sickness and some kind of phrenitis ...
> Secondly, we can talk of this infirmity by holding that it befell him according to the most benevolent Providence of the Lord ...
> [who] not wishing him to perish, out of compassion sent him this

humiliating infirmity, by which justly he was reduced to great humility.

Ofhuys mentions in fact three candidates for the nature of Hugo's illness here. The first is *phrenitis magna*, the second the power of a demon, the third, the Providence of the Lord. Ofhuys argues that the first and second, while there are some signs in favour of each, cannot account for Hugo's unwillingness to injure others. But then, having allowed that only God can be certain of the nature of the disease, he suggests that there are two ways of looking at the episode, one in terms of a natural illness, the other as the working out of God's Providence.

One puzzle arises out of Ofhuys's mentioning the power of the demon. Is the possibility of demonic intervention ultimately ruled out by Ofhuys? Certainly the 'natural sickness' and Providence that Ofhuys talks of might seem at first glance to rule out the presence of preternatural demons. But as we have seen in discussing Nicolaus de Lyra's postills on the story of David and Saul, the activity of demons employs natural means to afflict men. Music and demonic power can both be included in a naturalistic account of possible influences on the human mind.

Ofhuys goes on to discuss the various possible causes of Hugo's sickness:

> For there are, according to the nature of this infirmity, several kinds which are engendered, sometimes by melancholy-inducing foods, sometimes by the drinking of strong wine which burns the humours and turns them into ashes by the emotions of the soul such as worry, sadness, excessive application to study or anxiety. Sometimes by the malignance of a corrupt humour which dominates in the body of a man predisposed to an infirmity of this kind.[17]

In this passage Ofhuys is quoting almost verbatim from Bartholomaeus Anglicus, *De proprietatibus rerum*, Book VII, Chapter 5, 'De amentia'. In his turn, Bartholomaeus Anglicus is paraphrasing the *Practica* of Johannes Platearius on melancholy and mania, itself based on Constantinus Africanus, *De melancholia*.[18] There is a long history behind Ofhuys's 'natural sickness'.

What is more, though Ofhuys does not say so, there is also a long tradition in such texts of calling on music as a therapy for melancholia and mania. Prior Thomas might just as easily have referred to these texts to justify his use of *melodiam ... non modicam*, as to the story of David and Saul. We shall turn to this tradition in the next section.

Although Ofhuys quoted from Bartholomaeus almost verbatim, his introduction of the diagnosis of *phrenitis magna* is puzzling. He does not draw on the chapter in Bartholomaeus on *phrenitis*, but that on *amentia*. In Bartholomaeus, as in the other medical authors, *phrenitis* is carefully distinguished from melancholia or mania (which are both included in Bartholomaeus's chapter on *amentia*). *Phrenitis* is defined by Bartholomaeus as an *apostema* in the cells of the brain, and the symptoms to which it gives rise are more violent than those of melancholy and mania. The most straightforward answer to this puzzle is that Ofhuys simply used *phrenitis* by mistake for *amentia* (or melancholia).

But there is a further complication. Ofhuys states that Hugo did not want to hurt others, only himself (*semper audivi quod nulli umquam in tota sua indispitione nocere voluit nisi semper sibi ipsi*). This is not the case with frenetics or those under the power of a demon, he averts. Which is why he leaves a final diagnosis to God alone. In fact, according to Bartholomaeus, both frenetics and melancholics wish to do harm to themselves and others. Those who suffer from *amentia* (melancholy and mania), *se et alios vulnerant*, according to Bartholomaeus. Equally frenetics *custodientem et medicantem libenter mordent et lacerant*. Hugo was apparently not dangerous to his brethren, or to others attending him. It is not clear why Ofhuys so decisively contradicts Bartholomaeus, whose text in the chapter on *amentia* he otherwise follows so closely.

It is tempting to put these confusions down to Ofhuys's sketchy understanding of his medical texts. But this does not square with the way he brings anatomy to bear in his further exploration of the lessons to be learnt from Hugo's case. Ofhuys says there are are two ways of talking about the case. First to call it a natural sickness; second to hold it to be God's Providence in reminding Hugo of the need for humility. Each has lessons for us. The lesson in humility is a straightforward one – let us do penance for our sins, and suffer earthly afflictions, rather than undergo eternal affliction after death. This is the lesson that Ofhuys tells us Hugo learnt, as on his recovery, he set about abasing himself – he took his meals with the laity rather at a table with the brethren in the refectory.[19] The other lesson is couched in medical terms, and introduces new considerations of anatomy.[20]

Ofhuys says:

> Let us assume that this infirmity resulted from a natural cause. We are taught (by this) to repress the passions of the soul, not to permit them to dominate us, otherwise we may be irreparably damaged in our natural constitution. They say that this brother, an outstanding painter, had sustained a lesion in some blood vessel in the region of the brain as a result of excessive imaginings, fantasies, and worries. For it is claimed that there is close to the brain an extremely small and tender vein which is vested with power over imagination and fantasy; therefore whenever imaginations and fantasies overabound in us this little vein is affected, but if it is affected and damaged until it ruptures, the patient falls into phrenitis or madness. Let us therefore put an end to our fantasies and imaginations, our conjectures and other vain and fruitless cogitations by which our brain is disturbed without profit, lest we fall into a danger so great and incurable. For we are human; therefore could not what happened to this convert because of fantasies and imaginings also befall us?[21]

Ofhuys does not in the end decide between the medical and Providential assumptions about the nature of Hugo's illness. However, it is clear from this passage that the medical interpretation of that illness succeeds in accounting for the effects of Hugo's worrying about his paintings, his study in a Flemish book, and wine drinking (all of which preceded his illness, according to Ofhuys).[22] The medical lesson is that we should learn never to succumb to passions of the soul, which if unchecked, will ruin our natural constitutions.

The mechanism by which that ruin is achieved is a physiological one, damage to the delicate vein in the region of the brain. I have not managed to identify the source for Ofhuys's speculations about the 'little vein' which is damaged by fantasies and imaginings. It is not to be found in Bartholomaeus Anglicus, who gives an account of the working of the inner senses, which are each localized in ventricles of the brain ; the front ventricle houses the imagination or fantasy, the second the cogitative or rational power, and the third the memory.

There is no mention of 'little veins', though Bartholomaeus recognizes the possibility of damage to the ventricles themselves.

Our best clue to Ofhuys's likely source for such a 'little vein' is to be found in the standard anatomy textbook of the later Middle Ages, the *Anatomia* of Mondino. In translation this passage on the anatomy of the skull reads:

> At the side of each *ancha*, between the aforesaid ventricles, there is a blood-red substance formed like a long worm such as an earthworm, attached by ligaments and nervules on each side: by lengthening it constricts and closes the *anchae* and the way or passage from the anterior to the middle (ventricle), and the reverse. When a man wishes to cease cogitation, and again in consideration, he raises the walls and dilates the anchae so that the spirit may pass from one ventricle to the others; it is called a worm because it resembles an earthworm in substance and form, and also in its contractive and extensive movement.[23]

It seems quite likely that what Ofhuys was remembering when he wrote the passage about the 'little vein' was not so much a *venula*, but the vermis. The blood-red appearance and function of the vermis in controlling the passage of the animal spirit between the ventricles suggest that this is what Ofhuys had in mind, rather than a vein.

After describing the vermis, Albertus Magnus in *De animalibus* goes on to point out that at the posterior end of the vermis may be found narrow extensions which are difficult to distinguish from the two veins which lie between the anterior and posterior ventricles of the brain.[24] Berengario da Carpi, in his own anatomical textbook of *c.* 1521, was later to talk of the vermis as being 'composed of veins and arteries',[25] so Ofhuys was not alone in associating veins with the vermis. Where Ofhuys does appear to be on his own is in asserting that the *venula* or vermis can be damaged physically by excessive fantasy and imaginings, for Bartholomaeus, as we have seen, refers to damage to the ventricles themselves.

I have not been able to find another author who gave the vermis such a central role in the physical effects of mental disorders. Ofhuys seems to have been pushing the medical interpretation of mental illness to a degree of materialism which even the medical doctors and the natural philosophers did not countenance.

IV

Gaspar Ofhuys showed himself to be well acquainted with the medical literature on melancholy and mania, going beyond the summary he found in the encyclopaedia of Bartholomaeus Anglicus. We do not know how he acquired this knowledge, though his role as infirmarer of the Red Cloister suggests that he had professional occasion to look out the kind of medical information that would assist him in his job. Medical texts may have been available amongst the books owned by the brethren, though we do not know what these were. But by the third quarter of the fifteenth century there was a sophisticated medical literature on which he would have been able to draw, provided he had access to books.

This literature was strongly associated with the universities of Western Europe, where the scholastic tradition of medicine proceeded by exposition and commentary of authoritative texts. These texts were often the works of classical or Arabic authors, which had first to be translated from Greek or Arabic into Latin. So it will come as no surprise that the doctrines which determine the use of music in medical therapy are actually derived from classical and Arabic sources.[26] The so-called Constantinian translations of such texts into Latin of the eleventh and twelfth centuries were studied intensively in the medical schools at the early universities. Constantinus Africanus (d. 1087) was responsible for the translation of the Arabic work on melancholy which became the starting point of the Western medical tradition on this subject. This treatise explores the nature of a particular disease, and appropriate therapies. Nevertheless, the rationale offered for those therapies can only be understood properly in the context of the systematic exposition of the nature and role of medicine which the Constantinian translations made possible.

The best starting point for understanding this context is another work translated from Arabic into Latin by Constantinus Africanus, the *Isagoge* of Johannitius.[27] This text, once Latinized, introduced the art of medicine to students in the medieval university. The *Isagoge* divides medicine into theoretical and practical parts. Theoretical medicine consists of three divisions: *res naturales* (those things which constitute the body, such as elements, humours, faculties and spirits);

res non naturales (those things which affect bodily health, such as air, food and drink, exercise); and *res contra naturam* (diseases, the causes of disease, the sequels of disease) (see also Horden, Chapter 1; and Gouk, Chapter 8). Practical medicine similarly has three parts: the proper use of the non-naturals (regimen and diet), the use of medicines, and surgery.

The use of music in medicine falls within the province of the non-naturals, which are usually listed as six. The *occasiones* of sickness and health are air, food and drink, motion and rest, sleep and waking, repletion and evacuation, and the accidents of the soul. Elsewhere in the *Isagoge* there is a slightly different list: air, exercise, baths, food and drink, sleep and waking, coitus, and accidents of the soul. Control of these factors is the most important duty of the physician. Music is a means of influencing the accidents of the soul, which have a strong impact on the health of the individual. This impact is imagined variously by different authors, but the accidents of the soul always affect the natural heat, and sometimes the *spiritus*, which animates the body. They are therefore important determinants of health. The accidents of the soul are defined in terms of emotions – anger, fear, joy, sorrow, and so on – and sometimes in terms of the workings of the imagination. It is as a result of music's capacity to stimulate or sedate these accidents of the soul that it deserves its place in the physician's armoury.[28]

A later wave of translations, notably those of hitherto unavailable texts written by the Roman author Galen, helped to foster more sophisticated theoretical discussions of the relationship of music and medicine in the fourteenth century. These new theoretical texts have a great deal to say on the use of musical knowledge in reading of the pulse,[29] and on the use of harmonic proportions in the medicinal theory of degrees;[30] they have, however, little new to offer on the role of music as it affects the accidents of the soul.[31] Yet if there are no new theoretical writings on the therapeutic use of music, there is a wealth of practical medical literature which makes use of the concept of the accidents of the soul to justify treatment of particular diseases, or to generate advice on regimen.

There are many occasions on which medical authors of practical works, whether on therapeutics or regimen, think music is of use to the physician. These include, at the opposite ends of life, pregnancy and the upbringing of infant children, and the prolongation of life in old age. Music is thought to promote digestion, bloodletting, and the medicinal uses of bathing. Music is particularly beneficial in certain illnesses, most notably fevers, lovesickness, and mental disorders: among these, melancholy and mania, frenzy, and lethargy. In times of plague music has a valuable function in boosting the spirits of individuals and communities, and hence their health.[32] These various uses of music will not all be explored here; instead I shall concentrate on the use of music as therapy for mental disorders. Whatever the illness, the rationale which lies behind the prescription of music varies little.

There is less difference between therapeutics and regimen than might at first be supposed. Whereas today we distinguish sharply between preventive medicine and therapeutics, that distinction meant far less when the role of the physician was to maintain the balance of the humours in the body or to restore it once the balance was disturbed. Frequently the means to these ends were the same. Thus the famous *Tacuinum sanitatis* by Ibn Butlan, translated into Latin in the thirteenth century, has a section on the use of music and its operation on the accidents of the soul:

> Musical instruments are aids to the maintenance of health, and to the restoration of health once lost, according to the difference in the complexions of men. For this art of music was anciently ordained to draw the mind back into healthful habits, and thus doctors are dedicated to its use to cure bodies. Therefore they employ tones for the sick mind, just as they do medicines for the sick body. And the operation of music on the mind is shown by the gait of camels, when their drivers are leading them heavy laden, and sing to comfort them ...[33]

The charming example of the camel-drivers and their songs betrays the Arabic origin of the *Tacuinum sanitatis*, but Western authors of texts on regimen show a similar attachment to music as a means of influencing the accidents of the soul for the sake of health. And they also follow the dictum that what is good for the mind is good for the body. Aldobrandino of Siena, who wrote *Le Régime du Corps* in French for Beatrix of Savoie in the mid-thirteenth century, included a chapter 'On se doit garder de corechier'. This is illustrated with a miniature of a man (perhaps David) playing a stringed instrument, and deals with the necessity of controlling the accidents of the soul for the sake of bodily health. Written in the vernacular, but building on the writings of Johannitius, Haly Abbas and Avicenna, the illustrations to Aldobrandino's text show how the writings on regimen of the Middle Ages came to identify control of the accidents of the soul with music (see Frontispiece).[34]

The most popular regimen of the Middle Ages was the *Regimen sanitatis salernitanum*, which included the verse:

> Si tibi deficiant medici, medici tibi fiant.
> Haec tria: mens hilaris, requies, moderata dieta

The standard commentary on these lines by Arnald of Villanova reinforces the message that all means to produce a mind 'laetus et gaudens', chief amongst these being music, will help man to flourish in his youth, strengthen his powers, prolong his life, sharpen his wit, and make him more skilful in all the occasions of life.[35]

Practical medical writings are framed as manuals which deal with the ailments to which the human body is subject, in order, usually, from head to toe.[36] For each ailment they list the causes, signs, prognosis and cure. More elaborate schemas were sometimes used in later writings; thus, in the fifteenth-century *Practica* of Valescus de Taranta we find diseases discussed under the headings *causa*, *signa*, *pronosticatio*, *curatio*, *dieta* and *clarificatio*. The earliest models of such texts of *Practica* are the latinized Arabic medical encyclopaedias, in particular the *Pantegni* of Haly Abbas and the *Ad Almansorem* of Rhazes.[37] The encyclopaedic authors of the Latin West, for instance Bartholomaeus Anglicus, copied the same principles of organization when they came to deal with practical medicine.

The *Practica* tradition deals with the therapeutic value of music chiefly in the sections concerning diseases of the head. The chapters where such references are to be found are those on melancholy and mania, frenzy, lethargy, and lovesickness (see Austern, Chapter 10). Because these texts are more prescriptive than descriptive in character, they do not provide much in the way of an explicit rationale for the therapeutic use of music, nor do they prescribe in any detail the kind of music that is likely to be of most value. The use of music is to distract or to soothe, in accordance with the doctrine of the accidents of the soul. The end aimed at is that of lifting the patient's spirits, inducing in him or her a moderate and tranquil cheerfulness. The means to this end are not normally specified: when they are mentioned, most frequently, *cantilenae* or instrumental music is indicated, or occasionally the patient should dance (*pulsare* or *saltare*). In cases of lethargy Valescus de Taranta recommends banging of the *timpanum* or *tuba*, in an effort to wake the patient from his or her comatose state.[38]

These illnesses are understood in terms of their humoral causes, while the authors also often seek to locate the illness within the cells of the brain which are understood to govern the mental faculties of *fantasia* or *estimativa*.[39] Under the influence of the Arabic authors, in particular Avicenna, the causes of mental disturbance are distinguished in relation to the four humours. Thus Avicenna distinguishes natural from unnatural melancholy. In natural melancholy there is simply an over-abundance of the black humour. In unnatural or secreted melancholy,

> one sort originates from the bile when burnt to ashes ... another originates from the phlegm when burnt to ashes ... another is generated from the blood when burnt to ashes ... a fourth finally comes from natural melancholy when this has become ashes.[40]

The combustion of the natural humours thus gives Avicenna the chance to distinguish four additional varieties of the illness melancholy (besides natural melancholy), each with its own causation, symptoms and cure.[41] While the authors of the *Practica* texts did not always follow Avicenna in all his elaborate distinctions, they did usually apportion different symptoms of melancholy to the combustion of the four humours, and adjust their therapeutic strategies accordingly.

There was another way of dividing up the symptoms of mental disturbance, according to their location in different areas of the brain. This approach attached the different faculties – imaginative or fantasy, cogitative or rational, and memory – to the three cells or ventricles of the brain. Damage to any of these three areas might be associated with particular symptoms: disorders of the imagination with the front cell, of understanding with the middle cell, and memory with the rear cell. The *Practica* authors undoubtedly made more use of the humoral approach to mental disorders, but they sometimes blended it with the psychological theory of localized brain disorder.[42] Gaspar Ofhuys's surprising remarks on the damage to the little vein of fantasy were probably a reference to the vermis which connects two of the ventricles, and drew their inspiration from this anatomical approach.

The most influential statement of this blend of humoral and localizable brain disorder is to be found in the *Pantegni* of Haly Abbas. In a chapter entitled 'De accidentibus animate actionis', Haly associates damage to the three cells with case histories of mental disturbance given by Galen himself.[43] The three cases are that of a patient who saw singers and musicians in his house who were not there (his *fantasia* had been damaged); another patient who threw objects through a window in his house (damaged *ratio*); and a third who forgot his own name and those of his friends (damaged *memoria*). However, Haly recognizes that changes in the humoral complexion of the patient will also give rise to mental disorders. The three examples from Galen he cites can also often be found in the *Practica* literature as examples in the chapters on frenzy, melancholy and mania, or lethargy.

Compared to the space they devote in their writings to discussion of humoral causation, faculty psychology, and the varying patterns of behaviour that the mentally ill present, music therapy occupies the doctors very little. The intervention of demons is sometimes mentioned but usually the authors follow the argument of Avicenna that it is not the business of the physician to consider demons; he must act on the humoral causes of melancholy.[44] Music gets less attention even than the demons; it is simply a tool for effecting changes in the accidents of the soul, and in the context of the practical needs of the physician this does not need further elaboration. Music distracts or soothes, and thus counteracts the effect of morbid thoughts or fantasies. The form of the music does not seem to matter much; different authors mention various instruments, song, or dance. Valescus de Taranta in his *Philonium* goes into more detail on the musical treatment of cases of melancholy and mania than most. He recommends whipping firstly, and secondly

> joy, pleasure and light-heartedness: and seek out musical instruments, and if the patient is young teach him to dance. If he does

not leap about let him hear the music. And this will help to distract him from his imaginings ...[45]

Music therefore takes its place alongside whipping, sexual intercourse, conversation, and good food and wine, as means of distracting
the patient from his imaginings. Its therapeutic use differs not at all
from its use in the context of regimen. The skill of the physician lies
in subtlety of diagnosis, not elaboration of treatment, which explains
the somewhat perfunctory references to music in the *Practica* literature. As a last resort, if the patient fails to respond to therapy
addressed to the imagination, surgery or cautery may be used on the
melancholic patient.[46]

But because music is mentioned only briefly in the context of
regimen or treatment of melancholic patients, we must not make the
mistake of underestimating the significance of its medical rationale.
As we have seen, music find its place within a complex of ideas
which derives from theorising on the accidents of the soul, as one of
the six non-naturals. In fact, music stands out as the most powerful
symbol for control of the accidents of the soul, as seen in the illustration of Aldobrandino's *Le Régime du Corps*. Gaspar Ofhuys was well
acquainted with the medical tradition which justified music's use as
therapy for melancholy and mania. Even if Prior Thomas, who
authorized the use of music to treat Hugo van der Goes, was not so
familiar with this tradition as Gaspar Ofhuys, he was inspired by the
story of David's healing of Saul, which by the fifteenth century was
itself understood in terms of the natural therapeutic effects of music.

The medical rationale for music therapy was referred to in a wide
range of therapeutic and hygienic works in the later Middle Ages.
These works were meant to be used by those with a practical interest
in healing; they were part of the reading expected of those who studied medicine at the universities, or who practised learned medicine
outside the schools. Nor was the message confined to those with a
professional interest in medicine. We find music therapy invoked in
the commentary by Arnald of Villanova to the popular poem,
Regimen sanitatis salernitatum. Music was vitally important in
restoring the mind to tranquillity, and the body to health. Although we
have so little documentary evidence for the practice of music therapy,
it comes as no surprise to find that the medical rationale for its use

played a big part in the one case we do have, that of Hugo van der Goes.[47]

Notes

1. For an entertaining conspectus of the various occasions on which music might be prescribed in the fourteenth century, see M. P. Cosman, 'Machaut's Medical Musical World', in M. P. Cosman and B. Chandler (eds), *Machaut's World: Science and Art in the Fourteenth Century*, Annals of the New York Academy of Sciences, 314 (New York, 1978), pp. 1–36.

2. *Conversus* brethren cannot leave the cloister for one year after vows; no more than eight *conversi* are allowed per house.

3. Bibliothèque Royale de Belgique, 'Originale Cenobii Rubeevallis in Zonia prope Bruxellam in Brabancia', by Gaspar Ofhuys, MS II. 48017, ff. 115ᵛ–118. See A. Wauters, *Bulletins de l'Académie Royale des Lettres et des Beaux Arts de Belgique*, 2nd series, 15 (1863), pp. 723–43; H. G. Sander, 'Beiträge zur Biographie Hugos van der Goes und zur Chronologie seiner Werke', *Repertorium für Kunstwissenschaft*, 35 (1912), pp. 519–45; J. Destrée, *Hugo van der Goes* (Brussels, Paris, 1914), pp. 215–18; W. Stechow, *Northern Renaissance Art, 1400–1600: Sources and Documents in the History of Art* (Englewood Cliffs, NJ, 1966), pp. 15–18; S. Koslow, 'The Impact of Hugo van der Goes's Mental Illness and Late-Medieval Religious Attitudes on the "Death of the Virgin"', in C. E. Rosenberg (ed.), *Healing and History: Essays for George Rosen* (Folkestone, 1979), pp. 27–50; exhibition catalogue, *Imaginair Museum Hugo van der Goes* (Ghent, 1982), doc. 43; B. Ridderbos, *De melancholie van de kunstenaar: Hugo van der Goes en de oudnederlandse schilderkunst* ('s-Gravenhage, 1991), pp. 219–21. I have examined the manuscript, and corrected the Latin text of Sander where appropriate. Translations into English are based on that in the unpublished PhD thesis (State University of Iowa, 1958) of W. A. McCloy, 'The Ofhuys Chronicle and Hugo van der Goes', pp. 16–26.

4. Thomas Vessem (Wyssem) was the fifteenth prior of the Red Cloister, elected in 1475. He died in 1485.

5. McCloy, 'Ofhuys', pp. 18–20.

6. The date of Hugo's entry to the Red Cloister has been disputed, but A. de Schryver, 'Hugo van der Goes's laatste jaren te Gent', *Gentse Bijdragen tot de Kunstgeschiedenis en Oudheidenkunde*, 16 (1955–56), pp. 193–211, shows that he rented a house in Ghent until May 1477.

7. For a brief description of Windesheim and reference to sources, see *New Catholic Encyclopedia*, s.v. 'Monastery of Windesheim'. See also *Lexikon für Theologie und Kirche*, s.v. 'Windesheim'; R. R. Post, *The Modern Devotion: Confrontation with Reformation and Humanism* (Leiden, 1968). For the Red Cloister see A. Wauters, *Histoire des environs de Bruxelles* (1851, repr. Brussels, 1969), pp. 353 ff.; *Monasticon Windeshemense*, Teil 1. Belgique, W. Kohl, E. Persoons

and A. G. Weiler (eds) (Brussels, 1976), 'Rookloster, Oudergem', pp. 108–30.

8. Sander, 'Beiträge zur Biographie Hugos van der Goes', p. 541, n. 28, referring to the Statutes of Windesheim.

9. For Nicolaus de Lyra, see F. Stegmüller, *Repertorium biblicum mediaevi*, 9 vols (Madrid, 1950–80), vol. 4, pp. 51–94; 9, pp. 310–316; E. A. Gosselin, 'A History of the Printed Editions of Nicolaus de Lyra', *Traditio*, 26 (1970), pp. 399–426. I have used *Biblia latina cum postillis Nicholai de Lira* (Venice 1495), vol. 2, f. 296ᵛ. W. F. Kümmel, 'Melancholie und die Macht der Musik: Die Krankheit König Sauls in der historischen Diskussion', *Medizinhistorisches Journal*, 4 (1969), pp. 189–209, first drew attention to the importance of these postills for interpretation of the story of David and Saul.

10. Contemporary demonologists held that demons not only exist in nature (and are hence not supernatural beings), but act according to its laws: S. Clark, *Thinking with Demons: The Idea of Witchcraft in Early Modern Europe* (Oxford, 1997), pp. 151–6.

11. Kümmel, 'Melancholie', pp. 195–6. L. Réau, *Iconographie de l'art chrétien* (Paris, 1955–59), vol. 2, pp. 263–4; Bible of Borso d'Este, vol. 1, f. 119ᵛ, facsimile, ed. G. Treccani degli Alfieri (Bergamo, 1961).

12. T. Cajetan, *In omnis authenticos veteris testamenti historiales libros commentarii* (Paris, 1546), ff. 125–6. Later still, the story of David playing to Saul was interpreted in terms of the operation of music on a subtle *spiritus* which in turn affected the humours: M. Mersenne, *Quaestiones celeberrima* (Paris, 1623), p. 1708, as cited by J. Haar, '*Musica mundana*: variations on a Pythagorean theme' (PhD thesis, Harvard, 1960), pp. 501–2.

13. J. Sprenger and H. Institoris, *Malleus maleficarum*, trans. M. Summers (London, 1948), p. 41.

14. K. Garbers (ed.), *Ishaq ibn Imran Maqala fi l-malihuliya (Abhandlung über die Melancholie) und Constantini 'Libri duo de melancholia'* (Hamburg, 1977), p. 103. The Arabic author's work was in turn based on Rufus of Ephesus, *On Melancholy*, c. 100 AD, now lost. See R. Klibansky, E. Panofsky and F. Saxl, *Saturn and Melancholy* (London, 1964), pp. 82–6.

15. Avicenna, *Canon*, 3. i. 4. 21 (Venice, 1507), f. 190ʳ.

16. See Sander, 'Beiträge zur Biographie Hugos van der Goes', p. 545, n. 83.

17. McCloy, 'Ofhuys', pp. 21–2.

18. Bartholomaeus Anglicus, *De proprietatibus rerum* (Strasburg, 1505), gathering i, 1ᵛ; J. Platearius, *Practica* (Lyon, 1525), ff. 207ᵛ–208; *On the Properties of Things: John Trevisa's Translation of Bartholomaeus Anglicus De Proprietatibus Rerum*, ed. M. Andrew (Oxford, 1975), vol. 1, bk 7, pp. 349–50. Constantinus Africanus, *De melancholia*, ed. Garbers. McCloy, 'Ofhuys', was the first to note the dependence of Ofhuys on Bartholomaeus Anglicus.

19. Ofhuys may well have remembered that Saul was a figure representing spiritual pride, humbled by God. See P. B. R. Doob, *Nebuchadnezzar's Children: Conventions of Madness in Middle English Literature* (New Haven, 1974). The emphasis that he put on the humility which marked Hugo's recovery certainly points that way. The great painter was taught the value of humbling himself before his brethren. Some modern commentators on Ofhuys' chronicle have identified more than a touch of *Schadenfreude* in Ofhuys' description of the lesson Hugo was taught.

20. In drawing lessons from his story Ofhuys is following the model both of the *consilium* (which is a letter of advice from a physician to another doctor in the case of a particular patient) and the *exemplum* (a brief narrative used to illustrate a sermon), for in both genres the recital of the story is followed by the drawing of its lesson. See J. Agrimi and C. Crisciani, *Les 'Consilia' médicaux* (Turnhout, 1994); C. Bremond, J. Le Goff and J.-C. Schmitt, *L'Exemplum* (Turnhout, 1982), nos 69 and 40 of *Typologie des Sources du Moyen Age Occidental*.

21. McCloy, 'Ofhuys', pp. 24–5.

22. McCloy, 'Ofhuys', p. 22.

23. Translation from E. Clarke and C. D. O'Malley, *The Human Brain and Spinal Cord* (Berkeley, 1968), p. 24. A well-known thirteenth-century description of the vermis was that given by Albertus Magnus in his *De animalibus*, XII.2.4, in turn based on Avicenna, *Canon*, 3.i.1.2, (Venice, 1507; facs. 1964), ff. 165[vb]–166[ra]; N. H. Steneck, 'Albert the Great on the Classification and Localization of the Internal Senses', *Isis*, 65 (1974), pp. 193–211 (the 'vermis' passage is translated on pp. 207–8). See also Costa Ben Luca, *De differentia animae et spiritus*, ed. K. S. Barach, *Bibliotheca philosophorum mediae aetatis*, 2 (Innsbruck, 1878), pp. 124–5.

24. 'Vermiculus autem posterior minor est anteriore: et additamenta ista vermicularia quasi duabus venis sunt similia: et ideo a quibusdam due vene vocantur.' Albertus Magnus, *De animalibus*, XII.2.4, ed. H. Stadler, in *Beiträge zur Geschichte der Philosophie des Mittelalters*, 15 (Munich, 1916), p. 850.

25. J. Berengario da Carpi, *A Short Introduction to Anatomy*, trans. L. R. Lind (Chicago, 1959), p. 12

26. C. Burnett, 'European Knowledge of Arabic Texts Referring to Music: Some New Materials', *Early Music History*, 12 (1993), pp. 1–17, and esp. the sources listed there in n. 1; Burnett, '"Spiritual Medicine": Music and Healing in Islam and its Influence in Western Medicine', in P. Gouk (ed.), *Musical Healing in Cultural Contexts* (Aldershot, 2000), pp. 85–91; and Shiloah, Chapter 3.

27. This work is an abbreviated version of the 'Questions on medicine' by Hunain ibn Ishaq, a prolific translator from Greek into Arabic of the ninth century. 'Johannicius, Isagoge ad Techne Galieni', ed. G. Maurach, *Sudhoffs Archiv*, 62 (1978), pp. 148–74.

28. For a useful introduction to the 'hygienic' implications of the doctrine of accidents of the soul, see G. Olson, *Literature as Recreation in the Later Middle Ages* (Ithaca, 1982), ch. 2.

29. N. Siraisi, 'The Music of Pulse in the Writings of Italian Academic Physicians (Fourteenth and Fifteenth Centuries)', *Speculum*, 50 (1975), pp. 689–710; L. Holford-Strevens, 'The Harmonious Pulse', *Classical Quarterly*, 43 (1993), pp. 475–9.

30. *Aphorismi de gradibus*, ed. M. R. McVaugh, *Arnaldi de Villanova Opera Medica Omnia*, 15 (Barcelona, 1975).

31. This may have been in part because the advanced discussions of Arab authors on the relationship between particular modes and emotional states were never translated into Latin. For instance a crucial section on 'spiritual medicine' in the influential work known as the *Secretum secretorum* was for some reason untranslated in both Latin versions. See Burnett, '"Spiritual Medicine"'. English translation of the Arabic by A. S. Fulton in *Opera hactenus inedita Rogeri Baconi*, ed. R. Steele, vol. 5 (Oxford, 1920), pp. 217–18.

32. Uses of music for various conditions of life and diseases are surveyed exhaustively by W. F. Kümmel, *Musik und Medizin: Ihre Wechsel-beziehungen in Theorie und Praxis von 800 bis 1800* (Freiburg and Munich, 1977), though compare Horden, Chapter 1. See also Cosman, 'Machaut'. On plague, see Olson, *Literature*, esp. ch. 5, 'From Plague to Pleasure'. He cites several examples of music's being prescribed in plague tracts to counteract gloomy thoughts.

33. Ibn Butlan, *Tacuini Sanitatis Elluchasem Elimithar* (Strasburg, 1531), p. 28: 'Musicae instrumenta sunt iuvativa ad conservandam sanitatem, et restituendam amissam, iuxta diversitates complexionum hominum. Nam et antiquitus ordinata erat haec ars, ad retrahendum animos ad salutiferos mores et deinde medici exercitati vel sciscitati sunt ad curandum per ea corpora aegra. Et operatio musicae ad animos est manifesta in incessu camelorum, quando confortantur ex hoc ...'. See also *Le Taqwim al-Sihha (Tacuini Sanitatis) d'Ibn Butlan: un traité médical du XIe siècle*, ed. H. Elkhadem (Louvain, 1990), pp. 269–70.

34. *Le Régime du Corps de Maitre Aldebrandin de Sienne*, ed. L. Landouzy, R. Pépin (Paris, 1911), pp. 31–2. P. Jones, 'Il regime del corpo: medicina e francesismi', *Kos*, 2 (1985), pp. 42–51.

35. Arnaldus de Villanova, *Regimen salernitanum*, in *Opera omnia* (Basel, 1585), col. 1875.

36. The medieval *Practica* is discussed by J. Agrimi and C. Crisciani, *Edocere medicos: medicina scolastica nei secoli XIII–XV* (Naples, 1988), ch. 6, and by A. Wear, 'Explorations in Renaissance Writings on the Practice of Medicine', in A. Wear, R. K. French and M. Lonie (eds), *The Medical Renaissance of the Sixteenth Century* (Cambridge, 1985), pp. 118–45.

37. Many *Practica* texts are in effect, if not in title, commentaries on the ninth book of the *Ad Almansorem* of Rhazes.

38. Valescus de Taranta, *Philonium* (Lyon, 1535), cap. 15, 'de litargia' (f. 31ʳ).

39. W. Sudhoff, 'Die Lehre von der Hirnventrikeln in textlicher und graphischer Tradition des Altertums und Mittelalters', *Archiv für Geschichte der Medizin*, 7 (1913), pp. 149–205.

40. Avicenna, *Canon*, I.i.4.1 (Venice 1507), ff. 5^v–6^r, quoted by Klibansky et al., *Saturn*, p. 88.

41. Note that the symptoms of melancholy caused by combustion of the sanguine humour include delight in instrumental music (Arnaldus de Villanova, *Breviarium*, cap. 18, 'De mania et melancholia', *Opera omnia* (Basel, 1585), col. 1093); A. Guainerius, *Practica* (Venice, 1508), tr. 15, cap. 3, f. 22^v.

42. Klibansky et al., *Saturn*, pp. 90–93. Y. V. O'Neill, 'Meningeal Localization: A New Key to Some Medical Texts, Diagrams, and Practice of the Middle Ages', *Mediaevistik*, 6 (1993), pp. 211–36, is a valuable guide to this tradition.

43. Haly Abbas, *Pantegni*, Theorica, 6.11.

44. As in Valescus de Taranta, *Philonium* (Lyon, 1525), cap. 13, f. 26^r, following Avicenna, *Canon*, 3.i.4.19 (Venice, 1507), f. 188^v.

45. Rhazes, *Ad Almansorem*, bk 9, cap. 13, recommends 'cantilenas', and is followed by many authors. Valescus de Taranta, *Philonium* (Lyon, 1535), cap. 13, f. 27^r: 'gaudium letitia et iocunditas: et querantur instrumenta musicalia et si est iuvenis addiscat pulsare: si non saltem illa audiat. Et hoc fit ut distrahantur ab imaginatione sua …'. This course of treatment is not however recommended for 'sanguine' melancholy (see n. 41 above), which on the principle of allopathy requires by contrast soberness and quiet.

46. Platearius, *Practica* (Lyon, 1525), f. 208^v; A. Guainerius, *Practica* (Venice, 1508), tr. 15, cap. 8, ff. 58^v–59.

47. I would like to thank Iain Fenlon and Charles Burnett for assistance with this article, also those attending the Fondazione Levi seminar on 'Miti musicali nel Medioevo e nel Rinascimento' in October 1995, and the medieval seminar of the Wellcome Unit for the History of Medicine, University of Cambridge, in 1996, who commented on earlier versions. All faults are, of course, my own.

PART III

Renaissance and Early Modern Europe

Commentary on Part III,
with a Note on Paracelsus

Peregrine Horden

I

The creative revival of interest in classical antiquity that we – like those who brought it about – call a Renaissance or rebirth was a movement that came at differing times and in differing forms in the visual arts, in letters, in philosophy, in music, and in medicine.[1] But so far as the history of music as therapy is concerned, one development was crucial. This development is what gives the subject its Renaissance, a period that differs from the preceding Middle Ages (which are, of course, 'middle' only because Renaissance scholars saw them as an intermediate embarrassment between antiquity and its rebirth). It distinguishes the fifteenth, sixteenth, and early seventeenth centuries[2] as an era when musical therapeutics attained a philosophical centrality, a cultural resonance, among educated Europeans greater than it has enjoyed at any time before or since – and greater than it seems likely to enjoy in the future, at least until the 'New Age' truly dawns.

The development in question was the re-establishment in European thought of an integrated vision of music which embraced both ethos and cosmos. Music could have salutary effects on human beings because of its astrological significance as a mirror of the universe's 'deep structure'. Two currents within theorizing about music, the 'ethical' and the 'astrological', had come together in the Pythagorean–Platonic tradition in antiquity but had never been fully integrated (see West, Chapter 2). Correspondences between planets, signs of the zodiac, musical tones, elements, and bodily humours had then been systematically elaborated by Muslim scholars (see Shiloah, Chapter 3). But this integration could not influence European thought because the most pertinent texts had not been translated into Latin (see Commentary on Part II). If Plato is the key figure for us in antiquity, then Aristotle, with his scepticism about the music of the spheres, sup-

plants him in the Middle Ages (see Page, Chapter 5). Music is therapeutic in that period because of its power to moderate the 'accidents
of the soul', not (or not usually) because it replicates the harmony of
the cosmos within the human frame (Jones). Thus the Commentary on
Part II could close, without being unduly schematic, by asserting the
triumph of Aristotle. The Renaissance in music therapy is the rebirth
of Platonism in the mid-fifteenth century and its absorption into the
larger framework of natural magic. This is not the magic of the village
enchanter whose incantations have been relegated to the margins of
our topic (see Horden, Chapter 1; and West, Chapter 2). It is a magic
that is fundamental to a thoroughly articulated and, given its premises,
highly rational world-view, which is better called 'occult philosophy'.[3]

The sources of that philosophy are various, but they certainly
include Arabic texts (eventually accessible to interested Christian
scholars in a Spain reconquered from Islam), as well the Jewish
numerological mysticism of the Kabbalah. There are several early
figures whose writings exemplify the Platonist revival.[4] Yet by far the
most influential of them was the physician–philosopher–musician
Marsilio Ficino (1433–99). This part of the collection therefore begins
with him (Voss, Chapter 7). The inspired songs of the 'second
Orpheus' were intended, 'through fitting [musical] tones to the stars',
to 'banish vexations of both soul and body', not just to provide diver-
sion in discomfort. Ficino looked to newly-recovered texts from both
classical and late antiquity for a therapy that was far more ambitious
in conception than anything detectable in medieval evidence. His
work provided the starting point for many subsequent discussions –
not, Gouk argues, particularly among theorists of music and medicine
(as we might now style them) so much as in the writings of 'occult
philosophers'. Physicians and musicologists reproduce ancient
commonplaces, biblical and Pythagorean, about the power of music.
(See, for instance, the *Istitutione harmoniche* [1558], bk 1, ch. 2, of
Gioseffo Zarlino [1517–90], so often taken as the paradigmatic text of
early modern music therapy.)[5] Under this heading, nothing substan-
tially new is added. The occult philosophers, by contrast, innovate by
the subtlety and thoroughness with which they reinvent Pythagorean
cosmology. And they are important not just in their own right but also

for their profound yet equivocal connections with what can still (controversially) be called the Scientific Revolution, as well as with the religious reformations of the early modern period, both Catholic and Protestant.[6]

Superimposed on the conception of music as regulator of the 'non-naturals' (a conception with a more or less continuous life from antiquity to the start of the nineteenth century: see Chapter 1) Ficino's astrological model, once publicized, proved comparably durable, lasting to the close of the eighteenth century, when explanations of musical healing were couched in mechanical or neurological terms that Ficino would not have recognized. Gouk's chapter guides us through all this, and then settles on the figure of Robert Burton (perhaps inspired by Ficino above all), thus for the first time in the collection bringing into play a major work written in English. As in antiquity so in the period of its rebirth, music therapy is apparently of far more widespread interest among philosophers than among physicians. Voss can cite one example of an apparently successful Ficinian cure. But, on the whole, early modern university-educated doctors were no more prone to 'dispense' music than were their medieval predecessors – or rather, they have covered their traces if they did, because neither Gouk nor Austern has a collection of case histories of music therapy at her disposal. A handful of anecdotes apart, music therapy flourishes most obviously – and perhaps to an unprecedented degree – in the realm of 'high culture'.

Voss and Gouk reveal its ambient philosophy. In the chapter that follows them, Heather's task is to show how deeply French literature of the period is imbued with the theme of cosmological music. There is much that could be said about such figures as Molière.[7] Heather's focus is earlier, however. Du Bartas is seemingly a minor author in that his name is now familiar principally to specialists. Yet he was (in Heather's words) 'the most popular non-theological writer of Renaissance Europe', and his *Semaines* were translated into all the main European languages as well as into Latin, the lingua franca of the educated. There could be no better testimony to the diffusion of Renaissance Platonism and to its attractiveness in a world riven by religious hostilities. Here again, the protagonist is a second Orpheus (and David, and Adam). By means of his verses the poet reharmonizes creation, curing not just individual human beings but, indeed, the cosmos as a whole – the divinity.

It would be a great mistake to dismiss such refractions of our theme as marginal to the history of therapy. First, they are not mere metaphor:[8]

> Historians ... who depict a sixteenth- and seventeenth-century 'trivialization' of ideas of cosmic harmony into fiction or 'decorative metaphor and mere turns of wit' do not fully appreciate the staying power of this discourse. Their histories cannot account for the dispersion of the general idea of cosmic harmony across the conceptual and practical landscape ... of magic and astrology, courtly ritual and pageantry, and writings by [diverse] authors ... Faced with such persistence and pervasiveness, we should heed Haar's admonition 'to be cautious about labelling as metaphor only what was for so long believed in so earnestly'.

Secondly, cultural representations, whether in didactic verse or some other medium, should not be seen as separable from the history of what they represent. Image can encourage and mould practice; the contemplation of an image of healing can itself be therapeutic.

Those are crude formulations. But they are given full and subtle exemplification in Austern's chapter. Her subject is a cluster of pathologies associated with erotic longing: pathologies for which modern erotomania (scourge of film stars and celebrities) is only an approximation. Lovesickness has been mentioned in passing in several previous chapters (see West, Chapter 2; Page, Chapter 5; Jones, Chapter 6; and Gouk, Chapter 8). Its treatment by music had been recommended occasionally in the learned medical tradition since the time of Rufus of Ephesus (Chapter 2). But nothing has prepared us for the Renaissance estimation of love as both the *vinculum mundi* (that holds the universe together) and as its potential undoing. Nor could we have anticipated the range of evidence that Austern is able to present. It runs from emblem books (those most widely read of Renaissance publications),[9] to paintings, instrument decorations, music books, and more. And all of them variously condense and reinforce the medical–philosophical message of music as doubly remedial for unsatisfied love: a means of seduction on one hand; on the other, a distraction when seduction fails (or, alternatively, a way of sublimating profane into sacred love).

II

The cosmology against which all this needs to be projected did not supply the only way in which musical therapeutics could be conceptualized during the sixteenth and seventeenth centuries. That is, the Platonic model did not entirely achieve 'market dominance'. A different, though not unrelated, kind of musical healing, which emerges clearly for the first time in the sixteenth century, is the subject of Part IV. A rather more eccentric instance comes from the writings of the man whose medicine offered, for a long time, the only potent alternative to the Galenic humoralism upon which Renaissance Platonists predicated their understanding of *musica humana*. That man is Paracelsus.[10]

Theophrastus Philippus Aureolus Bombastus von Hohenheim (1493–1541) adopted the name Paracelsus, not (as is sometimes thought) in qualified homage to the first-century Roman medical authority Celsus, but as a Latinization of his 'surname', Hohenheim. Little known in his own lifetime, Paracelsus' writings were widely diffused across Europe in numerous editions from around 1560 onwards. For the four humours of Hippocratic–Galenic tradition, Paracelsian medicine substituted salt, sulphur and mercury as the primary substances. To the humoral imbalance as the systemic cause of disease, it preferred a quasi-ontological conception in which each disease was a distinct entity with a specific cause external to the patient. Against the allopathic medicine of the Galenists (countering humoral excess or deficiency with its opposite) it substituted a type of homoeopathy derived from the similarity of medicament and disease.

Admittedly, Paracelsus' belief in the detailed correspondence between body and cosmos (microcosm and macrocosm) and the role of spiritual essences in his physiology place him in broadly the same company as the occult philosophers; and his acceptance that beliefs were potentially pathogenic can be reconciled with the medieval conception of the accidents of the soul.[11] None the less, there is little in the fundamentals of his thinking that should obviously have predis-

posed him to find curative virtue in music. His religious radicalism
made him generally hostile to liturgy and ritual incantation.[12] His contempt for ancient wisdom, together with the alchemical basis of his
therapeutics, seem to leave no opportunities for soothing sound.[13]

It is the more surprising, then, to find in Paracelsus' early treatise,
De religione perpetua [*On the perennial religion*], the contention –
rare or even perhaps unique in his massive literary output – that
'music is a cure for those troubled by melancholy and morbid imagination [*Fantasey*],' and that 'on the same account music drives away
the spirits used by witches, by malefactors, and in sorcery'.[14] The context is a discussion of the benefits that accrue to a doctor armed with
the 'religion of medicine', a doctor of upright character and genuine
spirituality. Such a doctor will appreciate that a beneficent God has
provided – and provided locally – all the appropriate remedies for
local ills. Paracelsus' 'doctrine of signatures', according to which the
remedy resembles the ailment, is intelligible by the light of nature; it
requires no university learning. And just as in a garden there grow the
plants that the physician needs, so there are kinds of music that will be
efficacious against particular forms of insanity: listening to music
resembles lunacy in that both involve the mind.

This is a music therapy which of course has some affinities with
those of medieval Aristotelians and Renaissance Platonists, despite
their general refusal to countenance the possibility that music could
directly affect demons. Moreover, as later generations of Paracelsians
syncretized their master's medicine with the Galenic mainstream, so
the affinities would be magnified. Yet at this early stage, in the master's own hands, it was, and remains, uncomfortably distinct.

Notes

1.   For music see, for example, L. L. Perkins, *Music in the Age of the
      Renaissance* (New York and London, 1999). For philosophy, B. P.
      Copenhaver and C. B. Schmitt, *Renaissance Philosophy* (Oxford,
      1992); further, C. B. Schmitt, Q. Skinner and J. Kraye (eds), *The
      Cambridge History of Renaissance Philosophy* (Cambridge, 1988).
      Medicine: N. Siraisi, *Avicenna in Renaissance Italy* (Princeton, NJ,
      1987); A. Wear, R. K. French and I. M. Lonie (eds), *The Medical
      Renaissance of the Sixteenth Century* (Cambridge, 1985).

2.   For present purposes, it is not important to distinguish the Renaissance
      from a supposedly succeeding Baroque age.

3.   As by Agrippa, cited by Gouk. For context see G. Tomlinson, *Music in Renaissance Magic: Toward a Historiography of Others* (Chicago and London, 1993), ch. 3, with the review essay by P. Gouk, *Early Music History*, 13 (1994), pp. 291–306. Also P. G. Maxwell-Stuart (ed. and trans.), *The Occult in Early Modern Europe: A Documentary History* (Houndmills, London and New York, 1999); B. Vickers (ed.), *Occult and Scientific Mentalities in the Renaissance* (Cambridge, 1984).

4.   Tomlinson, *Music in Renaissance Magic*, pp. 77 ff.

5.   Trans. in O. Strunk (ed.), revised L. Treitler, *Source Readings in Music History* (New York and London, 1998), and discussed briefly by P. Gouk, 'Sister Disciplines? *Music and Medicine* in Historical Perspective', in Gouk (ed.), *Musical Healing in Cultural Contexts* (Aldershot, 2000), pp. 190–91. For a medical parallel, Epifanio Ferdinando, *Centum historiae seu observationes et casus medici* (Venice, 1621), pp. 266–8, 321. Peter Lauremberg, *Laurus Delphica seu consilium quo describitur methodus perfacilis ad medicinam* (Leiden, 1621), p. 31, supports his plea for musical knowledge in a physician with reminiscences of auto-therapy in his youth.

6.   C. Webster, *From Paracelsus to Newton: Magic and the Making of Modern Science* (Cambridge, 1982); Vickers, *Occult and Scientific Mentalities*; D. C. Lindberg and R. S. Westman (eds), *Reappraisals of the Scientific Revolution* (Cambridge, 1990).

7.   E. Forman, 'Music has Charms ... Music and Healing in Seventeenth-Century France', *Seventeenth-Century French Studies*, 6 (1984), pp. 81–91. For context, L. Brockliss and C. Jones, *The Medical World of Early Modern France* (Oxford, 1997), for example p. 462.

8.   Tomlinson, *Music in Renaissance Magic*, p. 98, citing J. Haar, '*Musica mundana*: Variations on a Pythagorean Theme' (PhD thesis, Harvard, 1960), p. 444.

9.   M. Bath, *Speaking Pictures: English Emblem Books and Renaissance Culture* (London, 1994).

10. H. R. Trevor-Roper, 'The Paracelsian Movement', in his *Renaissance Essays* (London, 1985), pp. 149–99; O. P. Grell (ed.), *Paracelsus: The Man and His Reputation, His Ideas and Their Transformation* (Leiden, 1998).

11. H. Schott, '"Invisible Diseases" – Imagination and Magnetism: Paracelsus and the Consequences', in Grell, *Paracelsus*, pp. 315–16.

12. C. Webster, 'Paracelsus Confronts the Saints: Miracles, Healing and the Secularization of Magic', *Social History of Medicine*, 8 (1995), pp. 403–21.

13. Contrast A. Hayum, *The Isenheim Altarpiece* (Princeton, NJ, 1989), p. 46, who takes Paracelsus, uncontroversially, as a music therapist.

14. Leiden University, Codex Vossianus Chymicus 25, ff. 511–12a, ed. K. Sudhoff, *Versuch einer Kritik der Echtheit der Paracelsischen Schriften*, pt 2.1 (Berlin, 1898), no. 89, p. 419, trans. Charles Webster (personal communication).

CHAPTER SEVEN

Marsilio Ficino, the Second Orpheus

Angela Voss

Through his revival of Platonic thought, the Florentine philosopher Marsilio Ficino (1433–99) stands at the forefront of the great spiritual and cultural rebirth we call the Renaissance. Priest, theologian, astrologer, physician, musician and magician, his life was dedicated to the reconciliation of faith and reason in the quest for self-knowledge, and knowledge of God. On an intellectual level he sought to unite Platonism and Christianity, and on a practical level his holistic approach to healing revealed a new way of understanding and participating in the world: what he was to call natural magic. Ficino's practice of magic was firmly based on his reading of Hermetic, neo-Platonic and Arabic texts combined with his medical, astrological and musical skills. It was directed towards bringing the human soul – understood as the intermediary between mind and body – into harmony with the soul of the world, the mediator of heaven and earth. Ficino understood that the most powerful means of restoring such unity was through the careful preparation and performance of music. In short, music therapy.

In this paper, following a Platonic progression from speculative principles to practical demonstration, I shall explore Ficino's understanding of the power of music in relation to his concept of natural magic. In addition to his writing on the subject, we have plenty of evidence that Ficino's own inspired performance led those who heard him play to regard him as Orpheus reborn. Most importantly, his friend the poet Poliziano associated his music-making with the resurgence of Platonic philosophy:

> his lyre ... far more successful than the lyre of Thracian Orpheus, has brought back from the underworld what is, if I am not mistaken, the true Eurydice, that is Platonic wisdom with its all-embracing scope and understanding [*amplissimi iudici*].[1]

And Lorenzo de' Medici, on hearing the sound of Ficino's lyre in the countryside, wrote in his poem 'Altercazione':

> ... una nuova voce a se gli trasse
> da più harmonia legati e presi,
> *Pensai che Orfeo al mondo ritornasse.*
> [...I thought that Orpheus had returned to the world.][2]

It would seem that Ficino was destined for a vocation as spiritual healer from an early age. He himself tells us that when still a boy, Cosimo de' Medici had selected him to run his projected Platonic Academy. By his own account, Cosimo said to Marsilio's father, who was a physician, 'You, Ficino, have been sent to us to heal bodies, but your Marsilio here has been sent down from heaven to heal souls.'[3] In 1462 Cosimo de' Medici founded the Platonic Academy in the hills at Careggi and invited Ficino to install himself there and begin the task of translating and commenting on the entire works of Plato, along with the newly discovered *Corpus Hermeticum* attributed to the mythical Hermes Trismegistus, an ancient magus whose spiritual revelation was understood to prefigure the religious philosophy of Plato and ultimately to have been fulfilled in the mysteries of Christ.

However, even before he embarked on the Hermetic texts, Ficino had discovered Orpheus, and having translated his Hymns into Latin, was already describing their mysterious power. In September 1462, Ficino wrote a letter to Cosimo, having just received news of his patronage.[4] Here we find the first indication of Ficino's easy appreciation of the significance of coincidental events in his everyday life. In the letter he says that a few days previously he had been singing a 'hymn of the divine Orpheus' to the Cosmos (*Cosmus* being the Latin for 'Cosimo'), and he gives us the text of the hymn which he had translated from Greek, the last line of which runs: 'Listen to our prayers, Cosmos, and grant a peaceful life to a virtuous young man'. Soon after performing this 'Orphic rite', letters were brought to him with news of Cosimo's patronage and of his bestowal of the villa at Careggi. Ficino had no doubt that through a 'certain heavenly inspiration [*celestis quodam afflatus instinctu*]' Cosimo was granting his wish at the same time as Orpheus himself was speaking to him through the hymn. The important point to realize here is that it was not Ficino's conscious intention to ask Cosimo directly for patronage or otherwise to manipulate him through a purposive magical rite; it happened, he believed, through the sympathetic action of the heavenly inspiration, a completion or fulfilment of an event in accordance with the co-ordinating motion of higher will, beyond the cause-and-effect assumptions of logical reasoning. Ficino's interpretation of the meaningfulness of such moments, and his ability to 'set up' carefully the conditions in which such connections might spontaneously arise, was to form the basis of his natural magic.

Further, in Ficino's general preface to his Commentaries on Plato, we find the suggestion that true self-knowledge can be gained through an understanding and practice of an astrology which is far from the deterministic science of classical tradition. Ficino sees Philosophy, the daughter of Minerva, extending encouragement to Lorenzo de Medici, the dedicatee, to enter the Platonic Academy. This invitation to join the elite at Careggi, where the gods themselves were said to inspire and instruct, can be seen as a universal and timeless exhortation to mankind to embark on the journey towards wisdom: Mercury declaims at the entrance, Apollo sings in the garden, Jupiter pronounces Justice, and, most importantly, in Ficino's words, 'within the innermost sanctuary, philosophers will come to know their Saturn *contemplating the secrets of the heavens'*.[5] The position of Saturn in Ficino's own natal horoscope was a dominant one, and his lifelong attempt to come to terms with this 'seal of melancholy'[6] resulted in a highly original reformulation and transformation of Saturn's traditionally malefic qualities into positive attributes of philosophical contemplation and spiritual purification.

Ficino lived and breathed astrology as a symbolic language – a language which could reveal the inner workings of divinity. 'As above, so below' – in the neo-Platonic and Hermetic vision of the cosmos the heavenly bodies are gods, their movements indicating the will of the supreme One, their souls participating in the vast web of animated being which reaches down to matter. Thus in the human soul, as microcosm, their energies can be understood, tempered and directed towards a harmonious interplay – and what better medium to aid this process than music, for the Platonists understood audible sound to be an echo of the perfect concord in the heavens. In imitating the music of the spheres it may arouse the soul out of its forgetful earthly slumber, to a memory of its former, pristine condition.

The source for this idea is found in Plato's *Timaeus*, where we find the contemplation of the visible heavens and the hearing of music as essential aids to self-understanding:

> the cause and purpose of god's invention and gift to us of sight was that we should see the revolutions of intelligence in the heavens and use their untroubled course to guide the troubled revolutions in our own understanding, which are akin to them, and so, by learning what they are and how to calculate them accurately according to their nature, correct the disorder of our own revolutions by the standard of the invariability of those of god. The same applies again to sound and hearing, which were given by the gods for the same end and purpose ... all audible musical sound is given us for the sake of harmony, which has motions akin to the orbits in our soul, and which, as anyone who makes intelligent use of the arts knows, is not to be used ... to give irrational pleasure, but as a heaven-sent ally in reducing to order and harmony any disharmony in the revolutions within us.[7]

It is also in this text that we find a creation myth which demonstrates the musical principle of proportionality underlying the whole cosmos, for the Demiurge divides the mixture of Cosmic Mind and Matter into the ratios of 2:1, 3:2 and 4:3. These produce the perfect intervals of the octave, fourth and fifth, which were understood to represent in sound the very structure and fabric of creation. In the Intelligible realm, these sounds ring pure and clear; in the sublunar world, they become necessarily more compound and differentiated, and are easily muddled and sullied by the human soul afflicted by diverse material influences.

It was chiefly in the works of the neo-Platonic Plotinus (third century AD) that Ficino found a philosophical basis for the efficacy of his magical practice. For Plotinus, the cosmos is ensouled. It is the soul of the world, the *anima mundi*, which connects the pure Ideas of the Divine Mind with the middling realm of the stars and planets and the earthly realms of matter. It is the soul which converts the Ideas into the instrumental causes which move the sublunary world, sowing in each living being a seed of divinity, which Plotinus was to call the seminal reason. The spiritual energy moving between Mind, Soul and Nature forms what Ficino calls a *circuitus spiritualis*, a 'divine influence emanating from God, penetrating the heavens, descending through the elements, and coming to an end in matter'.[8] We can know, says Ficino, of the interpenetration of the World Soul through its effects in the spiritual circuit – particularly via man's own *spiritus*, the airy body which joins soul to the material body. For Ficino, astrology as a symbolic system became a means of working with and on these effects as they manifested as planetary energies in the psyche of human beings.

The whole process of sympathetic magic is made possible by the mediating function of the World Soul. In this system of cosmic sympathy, all emanating from the One in a complex web to the furthest reaches of matter, like resonating with like, all elements connected through their inner kernels of divinity implanted by the Soul, Plotinus sets a precedent for a 'magical' experience as a non-quantifiable moment of meaningful connection between the participator and his chosen set of cosmic 'mirroring' devices, whether they be observed as stars, birds or entrails, or actively created in the forms of prayers, invocations, remedies or bodily movements. Magical operations work, he says, 'by sympathy and by the fact that there is a natural concord of things that are alike and opposition of things that are different, and by the rich variety of the many powers which go to make up the life of the one living creature'.[9]

He goes on to emphasize how incantations, together with the attitude and intent of the participator, exert a wholly natural (that is involuntary) power over the 'irrational' portion of the soul, which needs to be shaken up and out into a more ordered state. These natural powers, such as may be drawn down from the stars, do not have autonomous wills, and so may not be directly petitioned, but operate within the overall ebb and flow of the cosmos. Plotinus suggests that it is the role of the doctor or magic-healer to enter into this play of natural forces and 'by [their] arts one thing is compelled to give something of its power to another ...'.[10] So the drawing-down of the Soul's qualities is dependent on an affinity between the operator and the natural forces of cosmic interplay, the careful alignment of particular quality and specific time, the right moment when like is drawn to like by virtue of natural coincidence or human preparation and intervention.

In Ficinian magic, the concrete level (accessible to sense) of instrumental and vocal music [*musica instrumentalis*], whether literally in the form of musical performances, or when manifest as works of art, herbal remedies, talismans or even specific friendships, becomes a necessary vehicle for clarifying and harmonising the soul [*musica humana*] and leading it to participation in the great cosmic dance – 'Fitting One's Life to the Heavens' [*De vita coelitus comparanda*] as Ficino called the third part of his treatise on natural magic, the *Book of Life*. Following Plotinus, he stresses that the kind of magic he advocates is of a different order from the profanity of love philtres or demonology, calling it 'natural magic, which, by natural things, seeks to obtain the benefits of the heavens for the prosperous health of our bodies'.[11] If one has inner eyes to see them, the 'natural things' of the changeable world perceived by the senses are signs, or 'divine lures' which provide an unending reminder of enduring reality. In this sense, the act of living itself can be seen as a magical rite – if one seizes its gifts via the immediacy of intuitive apprehension and the transforming power of the imagination.

It is in this context that we can begin to realize the significance of Ficino's Orphic singing, for instrumental and vocal music, the earthly counterpart to the pure music of the Cosmic Mind, can be used to effect harmony of the soul via the *spiritus*, through the close imitation of the *musica mundana*, the harmony of the spheres.

There are, too, the implications of the kind of 'seeing' (in the intuitive 'grasping of the moment' sense) which we glimpsed in Ficino's letter to Cosimo, for only by making a turnaround from linear, cause-and-effect thought to an awareness of participation on some deeper level can one experience such coincidences, and such a mode of perception lies at the heart of 'magical' operations. Indeed it is prerequisite for spiritual transformation in the Plotinian sense. Plotinus exhorts man to 'shut your eyes and change to and wake another way of seeing, *which everyone has but few use*'.[12] For Plotinus, this could be cultivated through prayer, a 'tension of the soul', an act of reconnection in the true sense of *religio*. If our deepest desires – and there must be a personal desire on the part of the individual to effect a change – are to resonate with the harmonious play of forces in the cosmos, the very act of discerning, conscious connection will open the channel for

their flowing in, beautifully expressed by Ficino in his Commentary
on Plotinus:

> Our spiritus is in conformity with the rays of the heavenly
> spiritus, which penetrates everything either secretly or obviously.
> It shows a far greater kinship when we have a strong desire for
> that life and are seeking a benefit that is consistent with it, and
> thus transfer our own spiritus into its rays by means of love,
> particularly if we make use of song and light and the perfume
> appropriate to the deity like the hymns that Orpheus consecrated
> to the cosmic deities.[13]

Such a ritual facilitates mixing and fusion of *spiritus* through the
subjective transformation of the worshipper's imagination with the
powerful aid of invocations. This altered condition of awareness
involves the suspension of logical thought processes, and can be
brought about through the practice of specific rites. The importance of
such a 'ritual attitude' is addressed by Iamblichus, another of Ficino's
neo-Platonic authorities, in his treatise on theurgy, the hieratic art of
the Egyptian priests:

> a conception of the mind does not conjoin theurgists with the
> Gods; since, if this were the case, what would hinder those who
> philosophise *theoretically*, from having a theurgic union with the
> gods? In reality, this is not the case. For the perfect efficacy of
> ineffable works, which are divinely performed in a way
> surpassing all intelligence, and the *power of inexplicable
> symbols*, which are known only to the Gods, impart theurgic
> union.[14] [my italics]

Gemisthos Pletho, the Byzantine Platonist who brought to
fifteenth-century Florence an elaborate system of ritual hymn-singing
which may well have influenced Ficino, saw the process as one of
self-purification; of 'moulding and stamping our own imagination'
and making it 'tractable and obedient to that which is divine in us'.[15]
Since, in the elaborate system of correspondences between levels of
creation the human heart came to be regarded as the physiological seat
of divine energy in the body, as the sun in the visible universe, the
alignment required would necessarily involve a mode of understanding which incorporated the non-rational quickenings of heartfelt
desire, far beyond the intellectual energizing of the mind.

For Ficino, Plato's own use of language itself could rhetorically captivate and seduce the mind away from rational concerns, and such a way of using words to express the ultimately inexpressible parallels the task of the practical musician, who, if he wishes to truly move both himself and the listener into alignment with cosmic harmony, must convey through his audible performance a sense of another order of music which can only be heard with 'the ears of the mind'. We are back to Orpheus, for such, by all accounts, was *his* ability, and such was the aim of the ritual of Ficino's Orphic singing.

So, what was the nature of Ficino's astrological music therapy? What sort of music did he actually perform? He clearly considered that his vocation as a healer involved curing both physical and psychological disorders, and that music was a powerful agent for such work. Indeed, in harmonizing the mind, the regulation of the body will follow: 'sound and song easily arouse the fantasy, affect the heart and reach the inmost recesses of the mind; they still, and also set in motion, the humours and the limbs of the body ... Nearly all living beings are made captive by harmony' he asserts in a letter to Antonio Canigiani, and on a personal note, adds 'For myself ... I often resort to the solemn sound of the lyre and to singing, to avoid other sensual pleasures entirely. I do it also to banish vexations of both soul and body, and to raise the mind to the highest considerations and to God as much as I may.'[16]

It is evident that Ficino's music-making was not just for his own delectation, for the therapeutic effects that he and his friends experienced through hearing his 'orphic lyre' are constantly mentioned in his correspondence. Taking his leave as he concludes a letter to his friend Sebastiano Foresi he adds 'we play the lyre precisely to avoid becoming unstrung ... may the well-tempered lyre always be our salvation when we apply ourselves to it rightly'.[17] And at another time: 'after I wrote Farewell to you, I got up and hurriedly picked up my lyre. I began a long song from the Orphic liturgy. You also, when you have read this 'farewell' again, if you are wise, will get up without delay, and pick up your lyre willingly, the sweet solace for labour.'[18] To his intimate 'Platonic friend' Giovanni Cavalcanti, who accused him of complaining too much about the trials of his Saturnian temperament, he wrote: 'You command me, my Giovanni, to sing a hymn of recantation to Saturn, about whom I have recently complained a great deal. I accuse a certain melancholy disposition, a thing which seems to be very bitter unless, having been softened, it may in a measure be made sweet for us by frequent use of the lyre.'[19] We have at least one example of a successful treatment; to Francesco Musano Ficino writes: 'As soon as you were cured of your wrongly diagnosed tertian fever by our medicines, both you and Giovanni Aurelio paid your respects to our Academy, as if it were your own doctor. You then asked for and heard the sound of the lyre and the singing of hymns.'[20]

In a rare eye-witness account, one admirer, Bishop Campano, enthuses about Ficino's performance: ' ... then his eyes burn, then he leaps to his feet, and he discovers music which he never learnt by rote'.[21]

Like that of the lover, Ficino's song causes a sympathetic reaction in his audience. But what is this frenzied inspiration which enables him to improvise with such skill and achieve such an effect? It is the Platonic *furor divinus* of the poet, the state of spiritual possession which is a prerequisite for the communication of divine truth, the experience of the flooding of the soul in the act of reconnection with its source. Plato tells us that there are four types of *furor*: that of the poet, the priest, the prophet and the lover, for all of these, when in an enraptured state, have a direct visionary or intuitive channel to the Intelligible realm.[22] The creation of the 'inspired madman' as Plato calls him in the *Phaedrus*, utterly eclipses the efforts of those who think that technique alone will make them good artists, and this inspiration, springing from the Muses, will communicate itself from poet to performer to audience like the force of a magnet. So highly does Ficino regard the frenzy of the musician, that he goes even further than Plato in his view that 'any madness, whether the prophetic, hieratic or amatory, justly seems to be released as poetic madness when it proceeds to songs and poems'.[23] In other words, musical frenzy is the outward vocal expression of the other three, and elevates the stature of the musician to that of divine messenger.

The figure of Orpheus takes on further significance when we read that Ficino believed him to have been seized by all four madnesses: as a priest and prophet through his Hymns and authority as an ancient theologian, as a lover through his passion for Eurydice which led him to the underworld, and as a musician through the inspiration of his lyre-playing. In all these guises it is the power of love which Orpheus brings into the world, and neo-Platonic magic can only be effective by virtue of the all-pervading force of love's harmonious co-ordination of events within the cosmic hierarchies. Just as earthly music-making can lead one to an awareness of the harmony of the spheres, so the earthly Venus can lead to her heavenly counterpart. Ficino was in fact first to coin the term 'Platonic love', meaning the love of two persons which derives from the love of each individual for God.

What were these 'songs to the Orphic lyre', the singing of which Ficino considered to be one of the liberal arts rescued from near-extinction by his circle of Florentine *illuminati?* What texts did Ficino use, and what was the power contained in them? Ficino's precocious disciple Pico della Mirandola tells us that 'Nothing is more effective in natural magic than the hymns of Orpheus, if the correct music, intent of the soul and other circumstances known to the wise were to be applied.'[24] Pico's thirty-one 'Orphic conclusions' tell us much about the rarefied mysticism surrounding the use of the Orphic Hymns in the Platonic Academy, and one in particular points us towards their function as keys for unlocking the doors of supra-rational insight: 'Whoever denies that it is possible to understand, intellectually and perfectly, sensible properties by the way of secret or occult analogy, will not understand the essence of the Orphic Hymns.'[25] In other words, the hymns became the very means by which sense perception could be transmuted into the lucid insights of the Intelligible realm, but only for those who could grasp the function of analogy and symbol.

The texts of the Orphic Hymns, mainly consisting of epithets to various gods, were discovered in Constantinople in 1423, and were evidently used for ritual purposes as they included instructions for burning specific fumigations. Although they probably originated in the early centuries AD, for the fifteenth century humanists they stemmed from the pen of Orpheus himself, who was revered as both a legendary musician and singer and as a *priscus theologus* – the foun-der of a mystery religion from whose disciples Pythagoras himself was believed to have learned his theory of musical proportion. The early neo-Platonists testified to Orpheus' role as a representative of

that perennial wisdom known as the Ancient Theology, and he was
even regarded as a precursor of Christianity by St Augustine. Thus as
a primary source of esoteric Greek religion, his importance as a spiritual authority for the Renaissance Christian Platonists was profound.
For Ficino the musician, Orpheus' stature as founder of the 'mysteries' meant that the hymns could be appropriate vehicles for his
therapy of soul-purification; indeed in performing them in the context
of his ritual of natural magic, Ficino would consciously have been
drawing on a venerable tradition of occult knowledge. He translated
them into Latin very early in his career, and his biographer Corsi tells
us: 'it is said that he sang them to the lyre in the ancient style with
remarkable sweetness'.[26]

It is in 'Fitting One's Life to the Heavens' that we find Ficino
immersed in the intoxicating realm of natural magic where talismans,
herbs, plants, animals, colours, unguents and fragrances all play their
part in the 'tempering' of the human psyche – and music above all.
Ficino's approach is holistic and eminently practical: 'the intention of
the imagination', he asserts, 'does not have its power so much in
fashioning images or medicines as it does in applying and swallowing
them'[27] – in other words, it is the individual's attitude towards his
remedy wherein the power lies, not in any independent constitution of
the substance. When Ficino sings to the planetary gods, it is through
his own personal and subjective relationship with the divine realm,
together with his unremitting faith in its power, that the listener is
moved; as he wrote to Lorenzo Lippi: 'the speaker who is most deeply
moved himself will move others most deeply, whereas the man who
sings one tune and plucks another from his lyre totally offends the
ear'.[28] And he elaborates in his Commentary on the *Timaeus*:
'Musical sound, more than anything else perceived by the senses,
conveys, as if animated, the emotions and thoughts of the singer's or
player's soul to the listener's souls: thus it pre-eminently corresponds
with the soul ...'.[29]

Chapter 21 of 'Fitting One's Life to the Heavens' is devoted to 'the
power of words and songs in obtaining heavenly gifts'. It is here that
Ficino gives us his rules for composing, or improvising, astrological
music. He begins by stressing the power that words hold in themselves when they are used in conjunction with images, and then

explains how musical harmony is drawn from higher to lower things in the cosmic hierarchy through seven steps which correspond to the seven planets; these range from stones and metals, which correspond to the moon, to the 'secret and simple intelligences' of Saturn's realm. Words, songs and sounds, dedicated to Apollo or the sun, hold, most powerfully, the middle place. In this way the divine harmony is reflected and refracted, moving throughout creation in the vast web of cosmic sympathy described by Plotinus.

Via this system of correspondences, natural substances are impregnated with the *divinus influxus* from a particular planet, for, through their seminal reasons discriminatingly implanted by the World Soul, all levels of creation partake of the divine, and effective remedies can then be made from these substances using the arts of both medicine and astrology. Similarly, music can be given a 'heavenly strength' by taking into account what Ficino calls the 'pattern' or 'model' [*norma*] of the stars – choosing the tones which correspond to this pattern, then composing them into an order and harmony in a way which reflects in musical sound the arrangement of the heavens. How much closer could one get to an imitation of the music of the spheres? Concerning the choice of remedy, music or time to suit the individual, attention must be paid to the particular energies to which he is susceptible – that is, to his dominant planets at birth whose qualities the soul indelibly imprints on his *spiritus*, the medium through which musical sound can reach 'the inmost recesses of the mind'.

In practical terms, Ficino suggests that it is an extremely difficult task to decide which tones agree with which stars and aspects, but that we can come to find out partly through our diligence, and partly through a *divina sorte* or divine fortune. This immediate intuition of the 'transpersonal' imperative of the moment – which perhaps could be described as the flowing of grace – gives rise to the exactly appropriate action, a perfect alignment which spontaneously occurs after perseverance and discipline. Its intensified manifestation results in the condition of frenzy [*furor*], when the soul is so aligned with the power of God that it becomes insensible to its embodied condition.

Ficino goes on to give three rules for 'fitting tones to the stars', which are intriguing from both a musical and astrological point of view. But first he warns us that we must not think he is idolatrously adoring the stars, but rather 'imitating them and thereby trying to capture [*captandis*] them by imitation'.[30] Following Plotinus, he stresses that the stars do not give their gifts through their own willed choice, but through the natural influx [*influxus naturalis*] of their emanations. Here are his instructions:

> The first [rule] is, to inquire diligently what powers in itself or what effects from itself a given star, constellation, or aspect has – what do they remove, what do they bring? – and to insert these meanings into the meaning of our words, so as to detest what they remove and to approve what they bring. The second rule is to take note of what special star rules what place or person and then to observe what sorts of tones and songs these regions and persons generally use, so that you may supply similar ones, together with the meanings I have just mentioned, to the words which you are trying to expose to the same stars. Thirdly, observe the daily positions and aspects of the stars and discover to what principal speeches, songs, motions, dances, moral behaviour, and actions most people are usually incited by these, so that you may imitate such things as far as possible in your song, which aims to please the particular part of heaven that resembles them and to catch an influence that resembles them.[31]

The power of such appropriate fitting of words to music to planetary positions and qualities is such that the spirit of the performer will be opened to the *influxus celestis* which will then open itself to him, and the music spirit will have access to his spirit, and so to the spirits of his listeners. Ficino then tells us what sort of music is suitable for each planet; stressing that all music comes from Apollo or the sun, and that Jupiter is only musical when it is in harmony with him. Venus and Mercury also carry music when they are close to the sun. We learn that Saturn, Mars and the moon have voices, or sounds [*voces*] but no song [*cantus*] – Saturn's sounds are slow, deep, harsh and plaintive; Mars' sounds are quick, sharp, fierce and menacing; the sounds of the moon are 'in between'. As for the music of the other planets, Jupiter has harmonies which are deep and intense, 'sweet and joyful in their constancy', Venus' songs are 'voluptuous with wantonness and softness'. Apollo's music is characterized by grace, reverence and simplicity, and Mercury's by vigour and gaiety. By choosing to invoke a particular god with suitable music at 'the right astrological hour', Ficino says, you will naturally attract their gifts, for the appropriate planetary music spirit will vibrate in sympathy. Ficino says that if we practice this frequently, our spirit will become more naturally Jovial, Mercurial or Venusian at the same time as strengthening its solar properties, and it will carry these benefits to the soul and body. 'Remember', he says, 'that a prayer [*oratio*], when it has been suitably and seasonably composed and is full of emotion and forceful, has a power similar to a song.'[32]

Just as we expose our body to the beneficial rays of the sun, Ficino says, we can, through this process of natural magic, expose our spirit to the 'hidden' powers of the other planets. Because the cosmic spirit conveys their properties to our soul, the seat of our imagination, reason and mind, they will effect each of these faculties; *by the quality and movement of the spirit, or through our own choice, or both*. In acknowledging the responsibility of the individual to effect or enhance his own healing process through both the positive direction of thought and the freeing of his imagination, Ficino's therapy describes a potent confluence of subjective and objective experience. When he tells us that Mars and the sun will affect our imaginative processes, Jupiter our reason, and Saturn our contemplative mind, Ficino is expressing through the symbolic language of astrology an insight into archetypal principles as they manifest in the human soul. He is suggesting that changes can be facilitated when both performer and listener (or we might say therapist and client) meet in this middle ground of psychic imagery – only here can access to higher realms be mediated, and only here can true spiritual healing be generated.

The instructions in the *Liber de vita* are somewhat vague on the exact techniques for imitating positions and aspects of planets in words and music. However, in 'The Principles of Music', a letter Ficino wrote to Domenico Benivieni, he goes a stage further in uniting astrological aspects with audible musical intervals. In this sole excursion into music theory Ficino tells us, on the authority of Hermes Trismegistus, that God gave us both 'true music', that is harmony of mind, and its reflection or echo, that is, audible music, 'so that through the former we may continually imitate God Himself in our reflections and dispositions and through the latter we may regularly honour the name of God in hymns and sounds'.[33] He goes on to describe the nature of musical consonances. Ficino may have been influenced here by his contemporary Ramos de Pareja, a music theorist working in Bologna, who two years before wrote a treatise on practical music which discarded the 'ill-fitting' Pythagorean ratios for thirds in favour of consonant ones. Ramos in fact went further than any previous theorist in specifying the kind of practical music which might correspond to the planets, aligning Muses, planets, musical pitches and the emotional effects of the various modes according to traditional ancient Greek theory.[34] He was attempting to connect the music of the spheres with auditory experience in a theoretical model; Ficino was concerned with the transformative effects experienced by in the psyche of the individual.

In his letter Ficino talks of the 'gentle harmony of the third', recalling Cupid and Adonis, and of the perfect triad reminding us of the three Graces, whose unity was a crucial philosophical tenet in the neo-Platonic ascent to the One. In vivid and imaginative language, he describes the qualities of the discords and concords in a musical scale, whose culmination in the perfection of the octave he sees as a reflection of the Hermetic procession of the soul: the still state, the fall, the arising and the return, or the neo-Platonic emanation, conversion and return. In the 'general causes of harmony' Ficino gives a technical description of how different intervals can be produced and recognized by tensioning string-lengths against each other, and in the 'physical causes of harmony' he considers how the varying degrees of earth, air, fire and water which constitute hearing correspond to the ratios of the consonances. Of particular interest are the 'astronomical causes of harmony'. Evidently influenced by Book 3 of Ptolemy's *Harmonics*, Ficino compares the qualities of the astrological aspects with musical intervals:

> If you begin from the head of the twelve celestial signs and progress in sequence, you will find that the second sign falls away from the first in some way, and just as in a musical scale we perceive the second note as dissonant with the first, so here the second sign is in some way dissonant from the first: but then the third sign, as if a model for the third note, looks on the first sign with that friendly aspect which the astronomers call a sextile; the fourth sign, although dissonant, nevertheless is as [the astronomers] say, a middling dissonance which is in the view of musicians the nature of the fourth …[35]

He continues in similar fashion through to the twelfth sign. Is this what Ficino had in mind when he instructs us to find tones which correspond to the pattern of the heavens in the *Liber de vita*? Ptolemy quite clearly states that our souls' movements correspond to the movements of musical intervals within a melody, and that they can be thus moulded by the specific idiosyncrasies of its intervallic steps. However Ptolemy compares the opposition aspect to an octave, whereas for Ficino the dissonance of the seventh most clearly corresponded to the experienced tension of the opposition in practice, for the intervallic resolution of the seventh into the perfection of the octave musically embodies psychological and metaphysical potential: firstly for the resolution of the tension of opposites within the individual, and secondly for the resolution, within the Platonic hierarchy, of the dissonance and tension of earthly existence into the harmony of the divine realm through the transcendence of death, as symbolized by the eighth sign of Scorpio.

We can only speculate about how Ficino incorporated this theory into his Orphic singing since none of his music survives. We know there was a strong indigenous tradition of *improvvisatori* – self-accompanied singers who would declaim poetry to the lute or *lira da braccio*, and the *lira* is possibly the instrument Ficino called his 'orphic lyre'. To judge from the quantity of pictorial evidence, the *lira* was certainly associated with Orpheus, and we know that the singer Baccio Ugolino played it in the performance of Poliziano's musical drama *Orfeo* in Mantua in 1471. But it is also possible that Ficino played a harp, suggested by the bust by Ferrucci in Santa Maria del Fiore, Florence, where Ficino is portrayed holding a volume of Plato in the position of such an instrument; or even a lute, for we find several references to a plectrum in his letters. Whatever his instrument, it would have been able to reproduce the perfect intonation of the Pythagorean scale, and would also have been rich in symbolic association – in particular the lyres of Apollo and Orpheus, whose instruments were seen to mirror the cosmos in the four-fold and seven-fold arrangement of their strings.[36] I think we can safely assume that Ficino's music was self-accompanied monodic semi-improvisation, set to either Orphic hymns or self-composed astrological or mythological texts.

I shall end this paper with two examples of Ficinian magic in practice. Firstly, a letter which Ficino wrote to Giovanni Cavalcanti.[37] Here the doctor of souls is found in playful mode – he wants his friend to visit him at Careggi, and says that he often, while walking at sunrise through the woods, prayed to Apollo with his lyre, for as Orpheus moved oaks and stones with his playing, so he, Ficino, should be able to move the wooden and stony Giovanni to Careggi. But Apollo replies that his prayers will not work, for Giovanni is not made of stone and wood but of iron. He says Ficino had better use the magical art of Zoroaster to transform the stone of the hills into a magnet, and draw his friend there by attraction. So, says Ficino, that is what he is doing, but it seems to be in vain. It would be so much better and easier than trying to change stones by this work if Giovanni would just change his mind and decide to visit – for as long as he wants to remain iron-like, Ficino's musical and magical efforts are to no avail.

On receiving that letter, how could his friend not change his mind and visit! The letter itself achieves the magical effect, which was initiated in the ritual singing, we may imagine, of an Orphic hymn to Apollo at dawn. Natural magic does not require entreaties and effort to achieve its transformations. All it takes, implies Ficino, is a subtle appreciation of the coincidence of outer and inner circumstance and willingness to enter into the meaningful play of everyday life as poetry, metaphor, imaginative gesture. As Plotinus observed, 'all things are filled full of signs, and it is a wise man who can learn about one thing from another'.[38]

On a more elevated note, the letter that Ficino wrote to the young Lorenzo de Pierfrancesco de' Medici to accompany, it has been suggested, the gift of Botticelli's painting *Primavera*. Here we find Ficino the humanistic astrologer at his most eloquent, as he encourages the young man to embark on the road to self-knowledge:

> ... approach the task with good hope, free-born Lorenzo; far greater than the heavens is he who made you; and you yourself will be greater than the heavens as soon as you resolve upon the task. For these celestial bodies are not to be sought by us outside in some other place; for the heavens in their entirety are within us, in whom the light of life and the origin of heaven dwell.[39]

He urges Lorenzo to achieve inner equilibrium by concentrating on the fluctuations of the moon as it manifests in the continuous movements of mind and body – 'let this Moon within you continually turn towards the Sun, that is God himself', he says, and encompass the virtues of all the other planets, for unless we achieve self-possession, we can possess nothing on earth: 'Men can be taken by no other bait whatsoever than their own nature.' Finally, he instructs him to fully embrace Venus, in her higher manifestation of human nature at its most dignified, through her earthly counterpart in his new state of wedlock. He ends the letter:

> if by this reasoning you prudently temper within yourself the heavenly signs and the heavenly gifts, you will flee far from all the menaces of the fates and without doubt will live a blessed life under divine auspices.

If indeed this 'tempering of heavenly signs and gifts' is what Ficino set out to achieve in his 'singing of songs to the Orphic lyre', the spirit of Orpheus could hardly have received a more noble embodiment and expression.

Notes

1. A. Poliziano, *Opere* (Basle, 1553), p. 310.
2. Lorenzo de' Medici, *L'Altercazione*, in *Opere*, ed. A. Simioni (Bari 1914), vol. 2, p. 41.
3. M. Ficino, *Opera omnia* (Basle, 1576), vol. 2, pp. 1537–8.
4. P. O. Kristeller (ed.), *Supplementum Ficinianum* (Florence 1937), vol. 2, pp. 87–8.
5. Ficino, *Opera*, vol. 2, p. 1129.
6. See *The Letters of Marsilio Ficino*, ed. Members of the School of Economic Science, 5 vols (London, 1975–94), vol. 2, pp. 33–4.
7. Plato, *Timaeus*, 47 c–d (compare West, Chapter 2).
8. Ficino, *Opera*, vol. 1, p. 234.
9. Plotinus, *Ennead* IV.4.40, ed. A. H. Armstrong, 7 vols (Cambridge and London, 1966–88), vol. 4, p. 261.
10. Plotinus, IV.4.42, p. 267.
11. Ficino, 'Apology', in *Three Books on Life*, ed. C. Kaske and J. Clark (Binghamton, NY, 1989), p. 397.
12. Plotinus, I.6.8, vol. 1, p. 259.
13. Ficino, *Opera*, vol. 2, p. 1747.

14. Iamblichus, *De mysteriis*, II.11, ed. S. Ronan (Tunbridge Wells, 1989), p. 62.

15. Quoted in D. P. Walker, *Spiritual and Demonic Magic from Ficino to Campanella* (London, 1958), p. 61.

16. Ficino, *Letters*, vol. 1, pp. 141–4.

17. Ficino, *Letters*, vol. 4, pp. 16–17.

18. Ficino, *Opera*, vol. 1, pp. 823–4.

19. Ficino, *Letters*, vol. 2, p. 33.

20. Ficino, *Opera*, vol. 1, p. 609.

21. Quoted in A. della Torre, *Storia dell'Accademia Platonica di Firenze* (Florence, 1902), p. 791.

22. Plato, *Phaedrus*, 244a–245c.

23. Ficino, *Commentarium in Platonis Phaedrum*, IV.3, in M. Allen (ed.), *Marsilio Ficino and the Phaedran Charioteer* (California, 1981), p. 84.

24. G. Pico della Mirandola, *Conclusiones* XXXI, no. 2, in *Omnia quae extant opera* (Venice 1557), p. 159.

25. Pico della Mirandola, *Conclusiones* XXXI, no. 7, p. 159.

26. G. Corsi, 'The Life of Marsilio Ficino', in Ficino, *Letters*, vol. 3, p. 138.

27. Ficino, *Three Books on Life*, III.20, p. 353.

28. Ficino, *Letters*, vol. 1, pp. 162–4.

29. Ficino, *Opera*, vol. 1, p. 1417.

30. Ficino, *Three Books on Life,* III.21, p. 357.

31. Ficino, *Three Books on Life,* III.21, pp. 357–8.

32. Ficino, *Three Books on Life,* III.21, pp. 362–3.

33. Ficino, *De rationibus musicae*, in Kristeller, *Supplementum Ficinianum*, vol. 1, pp. 51–5.

34. See Ramos de Pareja, *Practica Musica*, ed. J. Wolf, *Publikationen der internationalen Musikgesellschaft* 2 (Leipzig, 1901).

35. Ficino, *De rationibus musicae*, p. 54. See also Ptolemy, *Harmonics*, trans. A. Barker in *Greek Musical Writings*, vol. 2 (Cambridge, 1989), pp. 275–391.

36. See Ficino, *Commentarium in Platonis Philebum*, ed. M. Allen, *The Philebus Commentary* (California, 1975), p. 266; M. L. West, *The Orphic Poems* (Oxford, 1983), p. 29.

37. Ficino, *Opera*, vol. 1, p. 844.

38. Plotinus, II.3.7, vol. 2, p. 69.

39. Ficino, *Letters,* vol. 4, pp. 61–3.

CHAPTER EIGHT

Music, Melancholy, and Medical Spirits in Early Modern Thought

Penelope Gouk

I

Early modern medical practitioners and the educated lay public had very clear ideas about how music could cure sickness, what diseases it was associated with, and why it could heal or harm people.[1] In the literature of the period, music's relationship to medicine is typically manifested in two distinct, but ultimately connected, ways. First, the activity of listening to or performing music may be conceived of as a remedy for particular diseases, as a general aid to convalescence, or conversely as a cause of sickness. With few exceptions the diseases involved were those associated with the passions of the mind. In the sixteenth and seventeenth centuries such ailments were most often addressed in terms of melancholy, but during the eighteenth century emphasis shifted to the nerves and their associated problems.

The second important role that music plays in medical thought of the period is as a model for occult (that is, hidden) phenomena, above all as a means of understanding the relationship between body, mind and soul (the meaning of occult will be taken up shortly). This link was normally conceptualized either in terms of the action of 'spirits', or else in terms of an analogy with musical strings and their vibration (see also West, Chapter 2; and Voss, Chapter 7). In fact both models could be invoked at the same time to account for particular phenomena.[2]

In the sixteenth and early seventeenth centuries these occult relationships were most often talked about in terms of 'sympathy', and framed within the context of natural magic.[3] By the eighteenth century, however, natural magic was no longer fashionable among the academic medical elite, whose preferred discourse was drawn from the fields of mechanics, hydraulics and chemistry which were at the heart of the new experimental philosophy taught at Leiden and Edinburgh.[4] Despite apparent changes in terminology, however, there appears a remarkable continuity in ideas over the period. This should not be surprising, for although the *Principia* is seen as marking a decisive turning-point in natural philosophy, there were features of the Newtonian synthesis which had much in common with the natural magic tradition that had reached its zenith in the early seventeenth century.[5]

II

A central figure in the development of musico-magical doctrine was Marsilio Ficino, whom Angela Voss discussed in the previous chapter.[6] Ficino's learned editions of Hermes Trismegistus and Plato (including later neo-Platonic texts), and especially his own *De triplici vita* or *Three Books on Life* (1489), provided the philosophical underpinnings for most sixteenth- and seventeenth-century texts on magic. The *De vita* also proved to be the starting point for all later discussions of melancholy, including its intimate relationship with both philosophy and music. This work was intended as a self-help manual for scholars: the first book dealt with preserving their health, the second with prolonging their life, and the third with astral influences on them. It was here that Ficino proffered an essentially new explanation for the affective powers of music which not only took into account the similarity between air moved by music and the motion of the human spirit, but also linked these to the *spiritus mundi* which served as a channel of influence between the heavenly bodies and the sublunar world.[7]

Although most sixteenth-century music theorists as well as medical theorists appear to have ignored Ficino, his music–spirit theory was widely disseminated via such popular works as Gregor Reisch's *Margarita philosophica* (1503) and Heinrich Cornelius Agrippa's *De occulta philosophia* (1510, enlarged edition 1533), which also proved an important source for astrological medicine and the psychology of temperaments. Seventeenth-century works which explicitly took up the music–spirit theory include Robert Burton's *Anatomy of*

Melancholy (1620) and Athanasius Kircher's *Musurgia universalis* (1650).

The most striking visual representations of Ficino's essentially neo-Platonic theory, however, are found in Robert Fludd's monumental *Utriusque cosmi ... historia*, or *History of the Macrocosm and Micro-cosm* (Oppenheim, 1619).[8] The two engravings depicted here (Figures 8.1 and 8.2) represent the relationships between God and His creation (the macrocosm), and also between the soul and the body (the microcosm) in explicitly musical terms. The first image represents the harmonic structure of the universe (*musica mundana*) by the musical scale on a monochord. The scale of levels of existence descends from the immaterial realm of God, via the empyrean realm of angels and the ethereal realm of the stars and planets, to the Earth. In the second image, of man the microcosm, the musical string not only represents the *spiritus mundi* or world soul, but also corresponds to the medical spirits that link the soul to the body and which act as the principal vehicle for the imagination. Invisible, corporeal, and also extremely active, *spiritus* can intermingle with earthly matter and bring about changes in its form (for example in alchemical processes, generation and growth). At the same time, as Burton explains in his *Anatomy*,

> Spirit is a most subtle vapour, which is expressed from the blood, and the instrument of the soul, to perform all his actions; a common tie or medium between the body and the soul, as some will have it; or as Paracelsus, a fourth soul of itself.[9]

Sympathy – that is, the interaction and affinity of different parts of the cosmos – is maintained by *tonos*, or tension, a dynamic property of the *spiritus*. This was an originally Stoic concept that was taken up by the neo-Platonists, notably in Plotinus's *Enneads* edited by Ficino in 1492. Thus, for example, the invisible power of music to affect the passions and the soul can be explained in terms of universal sympathy. The metaphor most commonly invoked to explain such action at a distance was sympathetic resonance between two stringed instruments. While the ancients employed the lyre for this analogy, early modern authors tended to use the lute because it was one of the most popular amateur instruments of the sixteenth and early seventeenth centuries.[10]

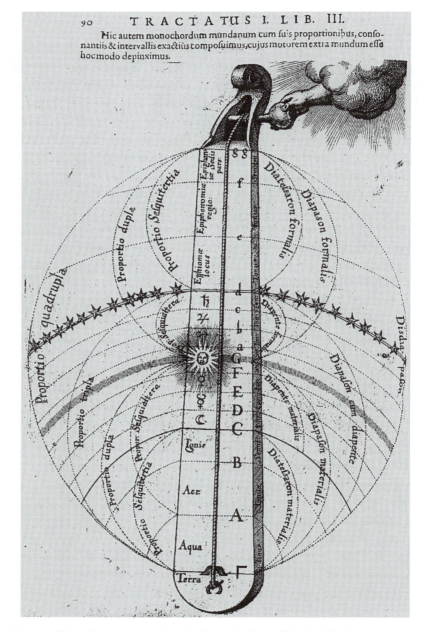

8.1 The divine monochord, from Robert Fludd, *Utriusque cosmi historia*, vol. 1 (1617), p. 90.

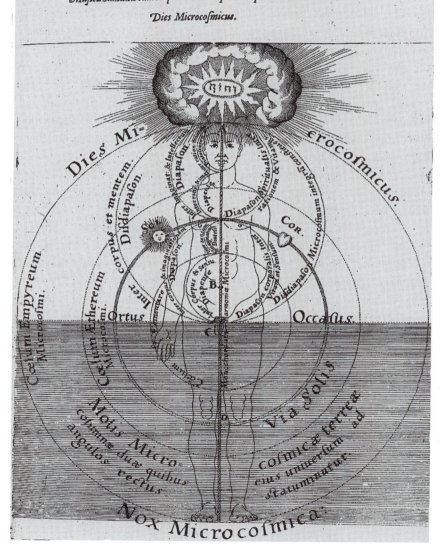

8.2 Man the microcosm, from Robert Fludd, *Utriusque cosmi historia*, vol. 2 (1619), p. 275.

As we shall see, this concept of musical harmony linking body and soul, God and His creation, was still being used during the eighteenth century, and Ficino's own writings also continued to exercise a lasting, if not always explicitly recognized, influence on the subject. Thus, for example, we find that the mechanisms invoked in Richard Browne's *Medicina Musica: or a Mechanical Essay on the Effects of Singing, Music, and Dancing* (London, 1729) to explain music's therapeutic effects are remarkably similar to those used by Ficino in the *De vita*. Browne explains how singing communicates pleasure to the soul by means of the vibration of the nerves and their action on the animal spirits. Although making no direct reference either to Ficino or his astrological theories, Browne nevertheless conceived of the mind–body relationship in a broadly similar way, and also placed a similarly high value on the benefits of music to health.

Given that music and medicine are supposed to have such a long-standing and natural affinity with each other – an intimate connection that is always traced back to Apollo – it is surprising to find that Browne's essay is actually the first English book to be wholly devoted to this subject. The second was Richard Brocklesby's *Reflections on Ancient and Modern Musick, with the Application to the Cure of Diseases* (London, 1749). In this work Brocklesby explicitly cites Ficino (his *Commentary on Plato*) to support a discussion of mental disorders and how music composes the motion of both the animal spirits and the mind.[11] At the same time, however, Brocklesby also refers to more recent literature, most notably two articles in the *Histoire de l'Académie Royale des Sciences* (1707 and 1708).[12] These had recently been cited in the *Gentleman's Magazine* (1743) in an influential article on the tarantula, and the same stories were repeated into the nineteenth century.[13]

A similar approach to music and its effects is found in French medical literature over the same period. Thus, for example, although there are numerous references to classical anecdotes of music's healing powers in sixteenth- and seventeenth-century texts, it appears that the Montpellier physician Louis Roger's *Tentamen de vi soni et musices in corpus humanum* (1748) represents 'the first clear support for music therapy in the French medical profession', at least in the early modern period.[14] Before the eighteenth century few French physicians actually seem to have treated music in any depth in their medical writings. Indeed, as other contributors to this volume have observed (compare Page and Jones), this absence seems to have been a general characteristic of Western medical literature since Galen.

Yet while early modern medical textbooks have little to say about the subject, music's healing powers – and indeed its properties more generally – were increasingly being explored by composers and poets who sought to arouse particular emotional responses in their audiences, often with a view to recreating or at least imitating the miraculous effects described in ancient Greek mythology. In fact it was chiefly through the medium of courtly entertainments (especially masques, ballets, and eventually opera) that Ficino's neo-Platonic and magical doctrine became so fashionable in the late sixteenth and early seventeenth centuries. The dominant theme of these elaborately choreographed entertainments was harmony and the taming of the beasts of the passions, expressed chiefly through the medium of musical sound.[15] The harmonic language and musical conventions that were being developed by seventeenth-century composers to express the whole gamut of human passions eventually became so sophisticated that by the mid-eighteenth century theorists were able to offer far more detailed explanations for music's effects than had hitherto been possible.[16]

III

Robert Burton's *Anatomy of Melancholy* (first published in 1621, and appearing in numerous editions thereafter) was the first major work in English to treat diseases of the mind, and as we have already suggested it is these which have most connection with music. The *Anatomy* not only summarized all earlier writing on melancholy but also became an essential reference work on the subject for later authors (see Austern, Chapter 10).[17]

According to Burton, most authorities defined disease in negative terms, as 'an affection of the body contrary to nature', 'a hindrance, or alteration of any action of the body', or else as an imbalance between the body and the soul. While Burton was writing from the perspective of an ordained minister who also had an Oxford degree in divinity, most early modern medical practitioners and their clients would have agreed with his claim that the origins of disease and death could ultimately to be traced to man's fall from grace in the garden of Eden. Even the most progressive medical writers believed that new forms of plague and other virulent diseases recently visited on European society were divine retribution for sin. Yet while God could bring about such ailments directly through supernatural means, the usual assumption was that He worked through secondary causes, so that medical intervention remained a viable response to disease, alongside prayer and other religious rituals. These natural causes ranged from the influence of the stars and the elements to the actions of animals and other men. Significantly, such causes also included those instigated by the devil, whose actions were thought to be constrained by nature just like those of man and all God's creatures.

The cures of disease, just like their causes, might be similarly classified. Writing some three decades after Burton, the Jesuit polymath Kircher identified three categories of cure which follow a similar form of reasoning: one kind relies on God-given miracles, a second involves illicit pacts with the devil, while the third type is brought about by purely natural means (see also Jones). Kircher was concerned to show that most strange diseases and amazing cures are neither a result of supernatural intervention, nor of demonic action. Instead he emphasized that there are many prodigious powers in the natural realm which can bring about equally amazing effects. This view seems little different from that expressed a century later in Richard Mead's *Medica sacra* (1749), which argued that the physician held a priestly role because his ability to cure was divinely given, but worked through natural causes. Indeed, although God retained the power to cause or cure diseases by miraculous means, most illnesses, including those in the Bible, were natural afflictions.[18]

Noting that Galen and others had 'methodically and elaborately written' about all manner of diseases, Burton simply divided them into those of the body and mind, and classified these mental diseases according to which part of the head and brain they affect. Headaches, for example, are diseases of the *pia mater* and *pia dura* (the hard protective shell around the brain), falling sickness (epilepsy) is a disease of the ventricles, stupor and tremor are diseases of the nerves, while

those arising in the substance of the brain come under the broad
heading of 'folly', which can be further divided into frenzy, madness
and melancholy. Burton notes that although some authors confound
these three types, he follows those who distinguish them according to
their different symptoms.

Burton says little about madness as such, which he defines as 'a
vehement dotage, or raving without a fever, far more violent than
melancholy, full of anger and clamour, horrible looks, actions, gestures ...' By contrast, frenzy or *phrenitis* is a disease 'which hath an
acute fever annexed, or else an inflammation of the brain'. It is this
fever which allows the physician to distinguish frenzy from either
madness or melancholy. Many types of frenzy appear to be self-
induced, and Burton notes that in some cultures they are considered
favourably. Ecstasy, for example, is the state 'in which the Indian
priests deliver their oracles, and the witches in Lapland ... answer all
questions in an ecstasy you will ask'. The other species of frenzy
identified by Burton are 'enthusiasms, revelations, and visions ...
obsession or possession of devils, sibylline prophets, and poetical
furies'.

Two types of frenzy which Burton mentions as being especially
affected by music are tarantism, to which later chapters return, and the
phenomenon known as *chorus Sancti Viti*. He notes that Paracelsus
called St Vitus's dance the 'lascivious dance' because 'they that are
taken from it can do nothing but dance till they be dead or cured'. One
of the most important symptoms of both these diseases is frenetic
dancing, often for days at a time, by the afflicted. In each case music's
role is highly ambiguous, since it clearly acts as a stimulus to further
dancing even while being identified as a remedy in itself. St Vitus's
dance was apparently common in medieval Germany but seems to
have mostly died out later. By contrast, although tarantism was similarly identified in the Middle Ages, it continued, as we shall see, to be
the object of medical and anthropological interest into the twentieth
century.[19]

Significantly, Burton does not explicitly refer to the Platonic concept of divine madness or frenzy which was a stock feature of courtly
masques at the time he wrote his *Anatomy*.[20] One of the most influential sources for Thomas Campion's treatment of this theme in *The*

Lord's Masque (1613), for example, was the French philosopher Pontus de Tyard's *Dialogue de la fureur poetique* (1552).[21] This work, which was ultimately derived from Ficino, describes the fourfold ascent to the divine via poetic frenzy, spiritual revelation, prophetic madness or enthusiasm, and rapture. Renaissance poets and musicians used this tradition not only as a source of subject matter, but also as a source of legitimation for their own artistic creativity. Beyond the confines of the courtly circles where such practitioners exercised their skills, however, the powers of music were by no means universally applauded, and were often seen as dangerous.

The problem with this concept of divine creative madness (which became popular again in the Romantic period: see Kramer, Chapter 14) was the difficulty of distinguishing it from madness brought about by natural causes, and also its association with demonic possession. How far demons could affect people's behaviour, and whether their operations should be considered natural or not, was a highly contentious issue in this period. While poets and musicians might want to identify their own frenzy as divine, moralists and theologians were more concerned with the disruptive effects and potentially evil sources of such behaviour. Given this context, it is perhaps not surprising that Burton himself is rather circumspect about diseases brought about by demonic possession.

Burton is of course most interested in melancholic diseases, which particularly affect the imagination and reason.[22] He identifies melancholy as being of two kinds. The first of these is 'transitory melancholy', a temporary disposition which affects everyone from time to time as part of their everyday complexion. However, he is concerned chiefly with the second kind of melancholy, which is a chronic and continuing condition, a 'settled humour' that is a fixed habit. Implicitly following Ficino, he observes that scholars are particularly prone to melancholy, because their sedentary and isolated habits lend themselves to this imbalance, but its effects are far more widespread throughout society. Despite a bewildering variety of forms, all melancholic diseases can ultimately be attributed to an excess of black bile or melancholy humour which can wreak dramatic effects on people's behaviour. Among its most characteristic symptoms are unnatural silence, anguish of the mind, vivid dreams, and fear and sadness without any discernible cause.

Remarkably similar sentiments are still to be found in eighteenth-century medical writings. Thus, for example, in his popular *Domestic Medicine* the Edinburgh physician William Buchan notes that 'delerium, melancholy, and even madness, are often the effect of close application to study' and suggests that 'music has a very happy effect in relieving the mind when fatigued with study'.[23] Even as late as 1792 the cleric and physician William Pargeter considered that physicians need to distinguish between sanguine and melancholic temperaments when managing the insane, and listed music among the external remedies for the treatment of madness.[24]

Although it obviously has a direct relationship to melancholy, music has a surprisingly small part to play in the *Anatomy*'s overall structure. A short chapter entitled 'Music a remedy' appears in the section on cures relating to the sixth category of non-naturals, namely the passions of the mind (see also Horden, Chapter 1; and Jones, Chapter 6).[25] The two most important sources for Burton's treatment of this subject were the Cambridge physician and cleric Timothy Bright's *Treatise on Melancholy* (London, 1586) and the Jesuit Thomas Wright's *The Passions of the Minde* (enlarged edition, London, 1604).[26] Yet while Burton surveys the literature celebrating the power of music, it is clear that he is not at all interested in the details of how real music might actually be applied therapeutically in a given context.

As we have already suggested, this kind of superficial treatment of music's powers is absolutely typical of most sixteenth- and seventeenth-century sources on the subject. It is not surprising, therefore, that later authors often drew on the unusually extensive discussion of music's therapeutic powers found in Kircher's *Musurgia*.[27] The key topics identified in the second part of Book 9 (entitled 'De magia musurgo-iatrica') include David's cure of Saul's melancholy, the cure of a Danish king's madness, tarantism, how music helps prophecy and divination, the great effect music can have on excited bodies, and whether musical motion can increase the curative powers of plants and animals. Kircher situated all these phenomena within the explanatory framework of natural magic. Although eighteenth-century authors appear not to have accepted this conceptual framework, they essentially address the same musically-related topics identified by Burton and Kircher.

IV

Early modern understandings of disease and health evidently went far beyond the boundaries of professional medical discourse, if by this we simply mean the writings of qualified lay physicians. In the turbulent climate of Reformation and Counter-Reformation struggle, the proper relationship between the cure of bodies and the cure of souls was an especially vexed issue. Where was the rational, immaterial and immortal soul insisted on by Christian theology located in the human body, and how were body and soul connected? If God is to be reached primarily through the Word, what role should music play in the relationship between man and his creator?

Not surprisingly, a number of the authors who addressed the medical implications of such questions were themselves men of the church (Ficino himself, for example, had become a priest at the age of forty). Thus although neither Burton nor Kircher practised medicine for a living, their university training prior to ordination qualified them to write learnedly about medically-related subjects. Generally speaking, the term 'medicine' was normally used to denote the empirical treatment of disease through the application of surgical or medicinal therapies.[28] To practice medicine it was not necessary to have either a specialist training or a licence, and could be practised by anyone either on themselves or on other people with their permission. There was no need to understand why particular treatments worked, but the goal was to produce desirable effects. However, a very different approach to healing was signified by the term 'physic', and it is within this academic domain that most attempts to provide systematic explanations for music's effects are to be found.[29]

In the early modern period, 'physic' was defined as primarily as 'natural philosophy', and only secondarily as 'the Art of curing by Medicines'.[30] Like other kinds of university qualification, the medical degree automatically conferred scientific, or rather philosophical, status on the recipient's learning.[31] To gain this qualification it was necessary to have studied natural philosophy. This study of nature was conducted chiefly through the medium of texts, and was overwhelmingly theoretical in orientation. Medical degrees were normally only awarded to candidates who displayed a thorough knowledge of the philosophical writings of Galen.[32] While it is clear that the Galenism of eighteenth-century physicians was in some respects very different from sixteenth-century understandings of Galenism, this systematic body of doctrine provided the dominant conceptual framework for university medical education throughout this period.

Within this Galenic framework the preservation of health and the understanding of its principles was regarded as more important than the actual cure of disease. Illness was the result of a disturbance in the natural balance of the bodily humours, fluids which provided the main explanation for physiological and psychological change.[33] The four humours – blood, phlegm, choler or yellow bile, and melancholy or black bile – were thought to be made up of and affected by the four elements (earth, air, fire and water) and the four qualities (hot, cold, wet and dry). Most emphasis was placed on 'dietetic' medicine, which focused on the particular temperament and complexion of the individual. Each person had an innate complexion, but this varied according to both internal and external circumstances. The physician needed his training in natural philosophy in order to assess how someone's temperament should be balanced in relation to their changing environment, and to advise on a proper daily regimen.

Such a regimen would be framed in relation to the concept of the six Galenic non-naturals, the regulation of which determined whether one would be healthy or ill. Within this overall framework the act of making music (especially singing) could simply be regarded as a form of exercise which stimulates the pulse and thereby rebalances the humours.[34] At the same time musical rhythm was recognized as a useful diagnostic tool for the physician in his reading of the pulse.[35] Listening to music might also be considered beneficial, serving as an aid to digestion, to women in labour, or relaxation before sleep. Above all, however, music was recognized as having a particular affinity with the passions of the mind. These were thought to lie midway between the reason and the sense, and were responsible for bringing about alterations in the body's humours.

V

We can now focus in more detail on the various mechanisms that were invoked to explain melancholy and nervous diseases. At bottom, the fundamental cause of melancholy was due to an excess of black bile interfering with the proper flow of the bodily fluids and spirits. It could be brought on by a range of organic and non-organic factors, such as too much study, the wrong kinds of foods, and strong passions. It is helpful to follow Burton's 'brief digression of the anatomy of the body and faculties of the soul' as a means of sketching out how such physiological mechanisms were generally thought to work by the early seventeenth century.

The four humours were traditionally associated with specific parts of the body and particular kinds of spirit, to which were attributed different bodily functions. The body itself was divided into three parts, based on the principal cavities of head, thorax, and abdomen or lower belly. Each had a primary life function and dominant organ, exerting its effects through vessels containing a particular fluid or spirit. The natural functions of the belly were nutrition, excretion, and procreation, and the veins its principal vessels. Waste drawn off from the venous system included urine extracted by the kidneys, yellow bile extracted by the gall bladder, and black bile or melancholy by the spleen. At the centre of the body, the thorax served the vital functions of maintaining and distributing life through the body. Its principal organ was the heart, which Burton describes as 'the seat and fountain of life, of heat, of spirits, of pulse and respiration ... the seat and organ of all passions and affections'. Heat was carried by the vital spirits created in the hot left ventricle out of blood and air, and these were distributed through the arteries which maintained inherent natural heat. Even after Harvey's discovery of pulmonary circulation the arterial system was thought to be completely separate from the venous system.[36]

Lastly, the head contained the brain, which Galen maintained was the seat of intelligence, motion and sensation. The arteries brought the vital spirits to the base of the brain, and these were converted into extremely rare animal spirits that were the instrument through which the brain received external sense impressions, and by which it initiated muscular motion. These spirits were stored in the ventricles and from thence entered the nerves, which acted as conduits for their operation throughout the body. The front ventricles were often thought of as the seat of common sense; the imagination and reason were located somewhere the middle of the brain; while the third ventricle contained memory.[37]

At this point this purely medical description begins to encroach on the domains of theology. For as Burton and his contemporaries were well aware, although it might be agreed that the animal spirits performed sensation and motor functions, there was a danger these might be seen as removing the need for a rational soul altogether. Burton himself simply observes that the actions of the soul are normally divided into three kinds: vegetal, sensitive and rational. The sensible soul is an apprehending power divided into the five outward and three inward senses, and a moving power divided into locomotion and appetites. These appetites are also divided into vegetal, sensitive and rational. The rational or voluntary appetite is meant to curb the other appetites, but for the most part is captivated and overruled by them, 'and men are led like beasts by sense, giving rein to their concupiscence and several lusts'.

In his account of the passions Burton relies heavily on Wright's *Passions of the Mind*, which includes an extensive discussion of music's effects on the passions.[38] Following Aristotle, Wright classified the passions as either pleasurable (concupiscible) or painful (irascible). Pleasurable passions occur when the sensitive faculty signifies to the soul that the appetite should be followed. Animal spirits accordingly flock from the brain, the seat of the sensitive soul, via certain 'secret channels' (that is, the nerves) to the heart, the seat of the passions, which thereby become dilated. Conversely, a painful appetite leads to the contracting of the heart and the gathering of melancholy blood around it, leading to an imbalance of the humours and mental disquiet. There was strong disagreement, however, about the ultimate causes of such changes. As Burton observes,

> Scaliger, *exercit 302*, give a reason of these effects, 'because the spirits about the heart take in that trembling and dancing air into the body, are moved together, and stirred up with it', or else the mind, as some suppose, harmonically composed, is roused up at

the tunes of music. And 'tis not only men that are so affected, but almost all other creatures.[39]

Here in outline are the mechanics of hearing and response to musical stimuli as they were broadly understood in the early seventeenth century. The most striking thing about this conceptualization is that although later authors begin to focus in more detail on the functions of different bodily parts (for example Thomas Willis's neurophysiology of the brain), they nevertheless continued to accept this broad outline as the starting-point for discussion.

The way that earlier humoral theories could simply be translated into the language of experimental philosophy and mechanics can be exemplified in the work of the Scottish medical practitioner George Cheyne (1671–1743).[40] From the outset of his career, Cheyne (who was an Episcopalian) concerned himself with the religious and moral implications of medical thought. His *Philosophical Principles of Natural Religion* (London, 1705), for example, used Newtonian mechanics as a means of proving the existence of a deity, much as Richard Bentley and other Boyle lecturers were also doing around this time.[41] In 1706, however, Cheyne experienced a conversion to mysticism that came to have a profound impact on his medical theories, which became increasingly vitalist. As Guerrini has noted, analogy now became for Cheyne the unifying principle between God and nature, a 'Simple, yet Beautiful *Harmony*, running through all Works of Nature in an uninterrupted chain of Causes and Effects'.[42] It is not altogether surprising to find that Ficino's *spiritus*, in the guise of Newton's aether theory, now also came to play an important explanatory role in his work.[43]

In his *Essay on Health and Long Life* (London, 1724), Cheyne was concerned to show the direct and causal connection between immorality and ill health. Here the six Galenic non-naturals, are equated with the seven deadly sins, so that the prevalence of nervous diseases (in his own practice at Bath, for example) is taken as evidence of overexcited passions. And while diseases brought on by the passions may be cured by medicine, Cheyne claims that the preventing or calming the passions themselves – which is the secret of long life – 'is the business, not of Physick, but of Virtue and Religion'.[44]

It is notable that unlike Brocklesby, for example, Cheyne does not mention music as either a remedy or a cause of particular diseases in his discussion of the passions. It is, however, invoked as a means of conceptualizing the harmony between soul and body. First, Cheyne claims that the soul resides in the brain, 'where all the Nervous fibres terminate inwardly, like a *Musician* by a well-tuned *Instrument*'. On the basis of this analogy it can be said that if the organ of the human body is in tune, its 'music' will be distinct and harmonious, but if it is spoiled or 'broken', it will not yield 'true Harmony'. Cheyne continues the analogy by suggesting that men who have 'springy, lively and elastic fibres' for nerves have the quickest sensations, and 'generally excel in the faculty of imagination'. They are also, however, most susceptible to nervous diseases. By contrast, idiots, peasants and mechanics have rigid and unyielding fibres, which means that they have fewer passions and are therefore more healthy.

Cheyne developed this musical model further in his *English Malady: Or a Treatise of Nervous Diseases* (London, 1733). Here he considers that that elasticity of the nervous fibres might be due to an extremely fine and active spirit which

> may make the cement between the human Soul and Body, and may be the Instrument or *Medium* of all its Actions and Functions, where material Organs are not manifest: And may possibly be the cause of the other Secret and Inscrutable Mysteries of nature, and the same (for ought I know) with Sir Isaac Newton's infinitely fine and elastic fluid or Spirit. ... To conclude this dark subject of animal Spirits if they must be Suppos'd, we may affirm they cannot be of the Nature of any Fluid we have notion of.[45]

Few of Cheyne's medical contemporaries may have shared his beliefs that nature was the sensorium of God, that gravity and God's love were aspects of the same universal principle, or that body and spirit were part of a continuum and capable of changing into each other. Yet they implicitly endorsed his musical model of nervous action, and continued to wonder about the manner in which the mind and body interact.

For as Charles Nicholas Jenty explains in his *Course of Anatomical and Physiological Lectures* (1757), there was general consensus that the nerves 'are the principal instruments of our sensations and motion', although authors were divided on the means by which this influence was communicated. Some claimed that nerves were like solid strings (a view Jenty himself rejected), while others conceived of them as pipes through which an extremely fine liquor flowed, a medium which served as the 'principle instrument which the mind makes use of to influence the actions of the body'.[46] In short, both camps relied on their understanding of the way musical instruments worked for their grasp of the inner workings of the body, just as Ficino had done nearly 300 years previously. The chief difference was that in the interim natural philosophers had succeeded in translating the vibration of musical strings and the dynamics of wave motion into abstract mathematical relationships. It was their appeal to the higher laws of physics which mostly distinguished eighteenth-century explanations of melancholy from earlier qualitative accounts. Otherwise, not much seems to have changed between the late fifteenth century and the middle of the eighteenth century in terms of the kind of diseases music was associated with and its effects on the spirits. Thus we find, for example, that Brocklesby emphasizes the particular value of music in countering lovesickness and religious melancholy, and even discusses the retardation of old age through music in a way that Ficino himself would have greatly appreciated.[47]

Notes

1. W. F. Kümmel, *Musik und Medizin: Ihre Wechselbeziehungen in Theorie und Praxis von 800 bis 1800* (Freiburg and Munich, 1977). See also A. Carapetyan, 'Music and Medicine in the Renaissance and in the Seventeenth and Eighteenth Centuries', in D. M. Schullian and M. Schoen (eds), *Music and Medicine* (New York, 1948), pp. 117–57.

2. J. C. Kassler, 'Music as a Model in Early Science', *History of Science* 20 (1982), pp. 103–39; Kassler, 'Man – A Musical Instrument: Models of the Brain and Mental Functioning before the Computer', *History of Science*, 22 (1984), pp. 59–92; Kassler, *Inner Music: Hobbes, Hooke and North on Internal Character* (London, 1995).

3. Natural magic was the ability to bring about amazing effects by occult but natural means (see Voss, Chapter 7). For an explanation of the term 'occult', which was used to describe phenomena that were not directly amenable to the senses (such as magnetism, gravity and musical resonance), see K. Hutchison, 'What happened to Occult Qualities in the Renaissance?', *Isis*, 73 (1982), pp. 233–53. For natural magic more generally, see J. Henry, 'Magic and Science in the Sixteenth and

Seventeenth Centuries', in R. C. Olby, G. N. Cantor, J. R. R. Christie and M. J. S. Hodge (eds), *A Companion to the History of Modern Science* (London and New York, 1990), pp. 583–96; and B. Copenhaver, 'Natural Magic, Hermetism, and Occultism', in D. C. Lindberg and R. S. Westman (eds), *Reappraisals of the Scientific Revolution* (Cambridge, 1990), pp. 261–301. See also notes 5 and 6 below.

4. A. Cunningham, 'Medicine to Calm the Mind: Boerhaave's Medical System, and Why it was Adopted in Edinburgh', in A. Cunningham and R. French (eds), *The Medical Enlightenment of the Eighteenth Century*, (Cambridge, 1990), pp. 40–66; A. Guerrini, 'Newtonianism, Medicine and Religion', in O. P. Grell and A. Cunningham (eds), *Religio Medici: Medicine and Religion in Seventeenth-Century England* (Aldershot, 1996), pp. 293–312.

5. P. M. Gouk, 'Natural Philosophy and Natural Magic', in E. Fuciková (ed.), *Rudolf II and Prague: The Court and the City* (London, 1997), pp. 231–8. On Newton's appropriation of the occult tradition, see Gouk, *Music, Science and Natural Magic in Seventeenth Century England* (New Haven and London, 1999), esp. pp. 224–57. See also J. Henry, 'Occult Qualities in the Experimental Philosophy: Active Principles in Pre-Newtonian Matter Theory', *History of Science*, 24 (1986), pp. 335–81, and S. Schaffer, 'Godly Men and Mechanical Philosophers', *Science in Context*, 1 (1987), pp. 55–85.

6. On Ficino's theory of magic, see also D. P. Walker, *Spiritual and Demonic Magic from Ficino to Campanella* (London, 1958), esp. pp. 36–44, 75–84; F. Yates, *Giordano Bruno and the Hermetic Tradition* (London, 1964, repr. 1982), pp. 20–83; B. Copenhaver, 'Astrology and Magic', in C. B. Schmitt, Q. Skinner and J. Kraye (eds), *The Cambridge History of Renaissance Philosophy* (Cambridge, 1988), pp. 264–300, esp. pp. 274–85.

7. Walker, *Spiritual and Demonic Magic*, pp. 1–24; see also D. P. Walker, 'Medical Spirits in Philosophy and Theology from Ficino to Newton', in *Arts du spectacle et histoire des ideés* (Tours, 1984), pp. 287–300, reprinted in Walker, *Music, Spirit and Language in the Renaissance*, ed. P. M. Gouk (London, 1985).

8. P. Ammann, 'The Music Theory and Philosophy of Robert Fludd', *Journal of the Warburg and Courtauld Institutes*, 30 (1967), pp. 198–227; J. Godwin, *Robert Fludd: Hermetic Philosopher and Surveyor of Two Worlds* (London, 1979); W. H. Huffman, *Robert Fludd and the End of the Renaissance* (London, 1988). See also Gouk, *Music, Science and Natural Magic*, pp. 95–101, 146–7.

9. R. Burton, *Anatomy of Melancholy* (London, 1621), pt 1, mem. 2, subs. 2.

10. For example, in Century 2, experiment 225, of the *Sylva Sylvarum* (London, 1627), Francis Bacon describes the 'common observation' that

  if a *Lute*, or *Viall*, bee layed upon the back with a small Straw upon one of the *Strings*; and another *Lute* or *Viall*

bee laid by it; And in the other *Lute* or *Viall*, the *Unison* to
that *String* bee strucken; it will make the *String* move.

See also P. M. Gouk, 'Music in Francis Bacon's Natural Philosophy',
in M. Fattori (ed.), *Francis Bacon: terminologia e fortuna nel XVII
secolo* (Rome, 1985), pp. 139–54, and Gouk, *Music, Science and
Natural Magic*, pp. 120, 169–70.

11.   Brocklesby, *Reflections*, p. 26.

12.   Brocklesby, *Reflections*, pp. 50, 61. See *Histoire de l'Académie des
Sciences* (Paris 1707), pp. 7–8; (1708), p. 27.

13.   'Surprising Instances of the Effects of Musick in Acute Fevers, and for
the Cure of the Bite of the Tarantula', in *The Gentleman's Magazine*,
13 (1743), pp. 422–4. The same material appears in a satirical account
of a German doctor's claim to heal all disease by music in *The
Gentleman's Magazine* for November 1807, pp. 1005–8.

14.   E. Forman, 'Musick has charms ... Music and Healing in Seventeenth-
Century France', *Seventeenth-Century French Studies*, 6 (1984), pp.
81–91; Carapetyan, 'Music and Medicine in the Renaissance', pp. 146–
50.

15.   F. A. Yates, *The French Academies of the Sixteenth Century* (London,
1947); R. M. Isherwood, *Music in the Service of the King: France in
the Seventeenth Century* (Ithaca and London, 1973), pp. 1–38, 67–113;
S. Orgel, *The Jonsonian Masque* (Cambridge, MA, 1967).

16.   Most of the secondary literature addresses French thought on the
doctrine of the affections since Marin Mersenne; see, for example, the
articles in G. Cowart (ed.), *French Musical Thought, 1660–1800* (Ann
Arbor and London, 1989), and T. Christensen, *Rameau and Musical
Thought in the Enlightenment* (Cambridge, 1993), pp. 236–41.

17.   See R. Hunter and I. MacAlpine (eds), *Three Hundred Years of
Psychiatry* (London, 1963). On Burton's broader religious aims in
publishing this work, see M. Heyd, 'Robert Burton's Sources on
Enthusiasm and Melancholy: From a Medical Tradition to Religious
Controversy', *History of European Ideas*, 5 (1984), pp. 17–44.

18.   Richard Mead, *Medica sacra*, trans. in *The Medical Works of Richard
Mead, M.D.* (London, 1762); Guerrini, 'Newtonianism, Medicine and
Religion', p. 307. See also C. Webster, 'Paracelsus Confronts the
Saints: Miracles, Healing and the Secularization of Magic', *Social
History of Medicine*, 8 (1995), pp. 403–21.

19.   See Lüdtke, Chapter 13.

20.   J. P. Cutts, 'Jacobean Masque and Stage Music', *Music and Letters*, 35
(1954), pp. 185–200; A. J. Sabol (ed.), *A Score for the Lords' Masque
by Thomas Campion* (Hanover, NH, 1993).

21.   P. de Tyard, *Solitaire premier, ou, Prose des muses & de la fureur
Poetique* (Lyons, 1552), expounds a theory of poetic inspiration;
Solitaire second, ou discours de la musique (Lyons, 1552) is on the
effects of music; while his *Discours philosophiques* (Paris, 1587)
collected these and related dialogues. Yates, *French Academies*, pp.
77–94; Walker, *Spiritual and Demonic Magic*, pp. 119–22.

22. L. Babb, *The Elizabethan Malady. A Study of Melancholia in English Literature 1580–1642* (East Lansing, 1951); F. D Hoeniger, 'Musical Cures of Melancholy and Mania in Shakespeare', in J. C. Gray (ed.), *Mirror up to Shakespeare* (Toronto, 1984), pp. 55–67.

23. W. Buchan, *Domestic Medicine; or a Treatise on the Prevention and Cure of Diseases by Regimen and Simple Medicines* (2nd edn, Edinburgh, 1772), pp. 70, 73.

24. W. Pargeter, *Observations on Maniacal Disorders* (Reading, 1792), pp. 104–8.

25. Burton, *Anatomy of Melancholy*, pt 2, sec. 2, mem. 6, subs. 3, 'Music a remedy'.

26. P. M. Gouk, 'Some English Theories of Hearing in the Seventeenth Century: Before and After Descartes', in C. S. F. Burnett, M. Fend and P. M. Gouk (eds), *The Second Sense: Studies in Hearing and Musical Judgement from Antiquity to the Seventeenth Century* (London, 1991), pp. 95–113; K. S. Park, 'The Organic Soul', in Schmitt et al., *History of Renaissance Philosophy*, pp. 464–84.

27. J. Godwin, *Athanasius Kircher: A Renaissance Man and the Quest for Lost Knowledge* (London, 1979); P. Findlen, *Possessing Nature: Museums, Collecting, and Scientific Culture in Early Modern Italy* (Berkeley, Los Angeles and London, 1994), pp. 334–45; Gouk, *Music, Science and Natural Magic*, pp. 101–9.

28. Derived from the Latin term *medico* [I drug]. See H. Cook, 'The New Philosophy and Medicine', in Lindberg and Westman, *Reappraisals of the Scientific Revolution*, pp. 397–436 at 398–9.

29. Derived from the Greek noun *phusis* meaning 'nature'; see Cook, 'The New Philosophy', pp. 398–9.

30. E. Phillips, *The New World of English Words, or a General Dictionary* (London, 1598), sig. Hh^v.

31. In this period the term 'science' [*scientia*] was normally used to refer to a body of learning about a specific subject acquired by study that was normally written down. Philosophy overlapped with science, but was distinct from and also superior to it because it involved the study of wisdom and a knowledge of causes. For further discussion, see Gouk, *Music, Science and Natural Magic*, pp. 7–11, 67–72.

32. V. Nutton, 'Greek Science in the Sixteenth-Century Renaissance', in J. V. Field and F. A. L. James (eds), *Renaissance and Reformation: Humanists, Scholars, Craftsmen and Natural Philosophers in Early Modern Europe* (Cambridge, 1993), pp. 15–28; P. Jones, 'Reading Medicine in Tudor Cambridge', in V. Nutton and R. Porter (eds), *The History of Medical Education in Britain* (Amsterdam, 1995), pp. 153–83; C. Lawrence, 'Ornate Physicians and Learned Artisans', in W. F. Bynum and R. Porter (eds), *William Hunter and the Eighteenth Century Medical World* (Cambridge, 1985), pp. 153–76.

33. V. Nutton, 'Humoralism', in W. F. Bynum and R. Porter (eds), *Companion Encyclopedia of the History of Medicine* (London and New York, 1993), vol. 1, pp. 281–91.

34. G. L. Finney, 'Medical Theories of Vocal Exercises and Health', *Bulletin of the History of Medicine*, 40 (1966), pp. 395–406; Finney, 'Vocal Exercise in the Sixteenth Century', *Bulletin of the History of Medicine*, 42 (1968), pp. 422–49.

35. N. Siraisi, 'The Music of the Pulse in the Writings of Italian Academic Physicians (Fourteenth and Fifteenth Centuries)', *Speculum*, 50 (1975), pp. 689–710.

36. For details see R. G. Frank, *Harvey and the Oxford Physiologists: Scientific Ideas and Social Interaction* (Berkeley, Los Angeles and London, 1980), pp. 1–20.

37. K. Park, 'The Organic Soul'; see also E. Clarke and K. Dewhurst, *An Illustrated History of Brain Function* (Oxford, 1972).

38. T. Wright, *The Passions of the Mind* (2nd edn, n.p., 1604), esp. pp. 159–72, 300–308; see Gouk, 'English Theories of Hearing', pp. 97–8, 101–3.

39. Burton, *Anatomy*, pt 2, sect. 2, mem. 6, subs. 3. See Gouk, 'English Theories of Hearing', pp. 100–103.

40. A. Guerrini, 'Isaac Newton, George Cheyne and the *Principia Medicinae*', in R. French and A. Wear (eds), *The Medical Revolution of the Seventeenth Century* (Cambridge, 1989), pp. 222–45; G. Cheyne, *The English Malady*, ed. R. Porter (London, 1991), 'Introduction'.

41. Robert Boyle endowed a series of sermons to provide proof of Christianity against atheists and infidels; they commenced after his death in 1691. See M. C. Jacob, *The Newtonians and the English Revolution* (Ithaca, 1976).

42. G. Cheyne, *The Philosophical Principles of Religion, Natural and Revealed* (London, 1715), p. 42; quoted in Guerrini, 'Newtonianism', p. 302.

43. The 'General Scholium' of the second edition of Newton's *Principia* (London, 1713) refers to 'a certain most subtle spirit' as a possible explanation for gravity, a fluid which is tentatively identified with the animal spirits or nervous fluid. Drawing on alchemical sources that assume the existence of *spiritus*, Newton had already discussed the possibility of a universal aether in his 'Hypothesis explaining the properties of light' which he sent to the Royal Society in 1675. See J. Henry, 'Newton, Matter and Magic', in J. Fauvel, R. Flood, M. Shortland and R. Wilson (eds), *Let Newton Be! A New Perspective on his Life and Works* (Oxford, 1988), pp. 127–45.

44. Cheyne, *Essay*, p. 171.

45. Cheyne, *English Malady*, pp. 88–9.

46. C. N. Jenty, *A Course of Anatomical and Physiological Lectures on the Human Structure and Animal Oeconomy*, 3 vols (London, 1757), vol. 2, pp. 501–3.

47. Brockelsby, *Reflections*, p. 69. For lovesickness, see Austern, Chapter 10.

CHAPTER NINE

Curing Man and the Cosmos: The Power of Music in French Renaissance Poetry

Noel Heather

I

Guillaume Du Bartas (1544–90), a Gascon minor nobleman, was possibly the most popular non-theological writer of Renaissance Europe, and even attracted a following in the American colonies of the seventeenth century.[1] The power of music and poetry were central to his concerns, and he must have had considerable influence as a common source of ideas in these areas during the later Renaissance. His main works were the two *Semaines*, the first of which was published in 1578, and the second in sections from 1584–1603. At least nine attempts were made to translate all or parts of his work into English (Sidney's was one of them), and versions appeared in all the main European languages, as well as in Latin.[2] During the thirty-five years following the publication of the *Premiere Semaine* in 1578, about two hundred editions of the whole or parts of Du Bartas's writings appeared. Interest in his work lapsed for many years, but there is currently a considerable revival in the level of critical study of his verse in the francophone world – a fact which can be confirmed by a glance through recent numbers of, for example, the *Bulletin d'Humanisme et Renaissance* and the *Nouvelle Revue du XVIe Siècle*.

Du Bartas owed his wide popularity in the Renaissance largely to the way the two *Semaines* develop ancient and medieval traditions within the framework of current religious and philosophical beliefs and contemporary poetic theory. An important aspect of Du Bartas's appeal was that his work lies within the broad strand of a particular type of verse popular at the time: scientific and philosophical poetry in which observations on the history and qualities of mankind and the natural world are imbued with the insights of the artistic visionary.[3]

II

Du Bartas's poetic vision reflects an image of a world under threat from changing cosmological models as well as from religious and political strife. The *Semaines* are literary commentaries on the week of creation and early biblical history written by a surprisingly unsectarian Huguenot during the religious wars which occurred spasmodically in France from the 1560s to the 1590s. Amidst a culture under threat in various ways and from a variety of sources, Platonism and its promise of another harmonious world must have seemed an attractive proposition. Furthermore, the Platonic discourse offered ways of 'holding together' the visible *mundus* – there was a tendency to fear that chaos might return – by a number of means, one of which was music. Order could be imposed by means of contiguity (the connections of the chain of being), by correspondences (the reflecting planes pointing upward to God), and by *concordia discors*.[4] To this day this train of thought is reflected in the christening of a child which recalls that the family, church and state are all corresponding planes which – among other features – have primates which direct the contemplative mind up to the Deity, the universal primate. The family could also be seen as a convenient expression of *concordia discors*: it exemplified a 'balance of contraries' in the father–mother, parents–children distinctions. In addition a main thrust of *concordia discors* is towards seeing the world in terms of the harmony of music (most strongly associated with the music of the spheres) which was used by God in His work of creation:

> Le discordant accord, la sacree harmonie,
> Et la nombreuse loy, qui tenait compagnie
> A Dieu, lors qu'il voulut donner, ingenieux,
> A la terre repos, et des ailes aux cieux.   (*Les Colomnes* 687–90)[5]

> Th'Accord of Discords: sacred *Harmonie*,
> And numbrie Law, which did accompanie
> Th'Almighty-most, when first his Ordinance
> Appointed Earth to Rest, and Heav'n to Daunce.
>   (*The Columnes* 707–10)

The ultimate means of re-establishing the threatened *mundus* was to recreate the harmony between higher and lower which was lost through the Fall. This was a kind of curing of the cosmos which could be accomplished thanks to the poet and his equivalent of the Orphic – or the Davidic – lyre. The latter, in tune with the harmonies of the sky, might allow the lower to re-establish balance, as well as calm the human soul (compare Voss, Chapter 7; and Gouk, Chapter 8).

In Christian Platonism one strand of belief in the power of music to heal can be traced to an interpretation of a verse from the Apocrypha popular in the medieval and Renaissance eras. According to Wisdom 11.21, creation was accomplished by 'number, waight [*sic*], and measure' (*DW* I, I.314; 'poids, nombre et mesure', *PS*, II.298). This verse was taken to fit neatly with the belief that the Creator made use of arithmetic, geometry and music in the course of his work.[6] With regard to poetic creation, Wisdom 11.21 was interpreted in two ways. In a broad sense the verse was linked to the general notion of poetic harmony. Thus, in a poem dedicated to his muse Urania (who will later also inspire Milton), Du Bartas refers to 'L'armonie qui naist du ton, nombre et mesure, / Dont les vers on compose' ['*Tunes, Notes, and Numbers*, whence we doo transferre / Th'harmonious power that makes our *verse* so pleasing'] (*L'Uranie* 85–6 [153–4]). Marvell evokes the same associations in his prefatory poem to *Paradise Lost*: 'Thy verse created like thy theme sublime, / In number, weight and mesure, needs not rhyme.' And in Book III of *Paradise Lost* Milton has the same tradition in mind when he refers to the process of poetic creation: 'Then feed on thoughts that voluntary move / Harmonious numbers' (37–8).

The concepts of 'number, weight and measure' could also, according to a second tradition, be related to the processes of creation – both divine and poetic – in more precise ways. Thus Wisdom 11.21 was interpreted by reference to the idea of poetic creation by number, measure or geometrical structure, and music. In this context music was understood in a mathematical sense, a viewpoint popularly traced back to the traditional belief that Pythagoras discovered the nature of musical harmonies through listening to the blows made by a black-smith's hammer (see also West, Chapter 2). The numerical ratios at the basis of music were usually conceived in terms of the so-called *lambda formula* (the first three numbers with their squares and cubes):[7]

Derived from the *Timaeus* and Judaeo-Christian traditions, the
lambda formula was used to link musical tones with numerically-
defined measurements in space. (The ratio 1:2 provides the octave,
2:3 the musical fifth, and so on.) For the contemplative mind such a
formula provided one way of representing *musica mundana* – ultimately the divine music which maintains the harmony of nature. This
is suggested in Figure 9.1 by the numbers 1–28 (the One of the
Divinity is added) included along the length of the chain of being
detailed by Nicolas Lefèvre de la Boderie in 1578. This diagram was
published in the introduction to a translation (by the author's brother)
of Giorgi's *De Harmonia Mundi* – one of the great Renaissance
expressions of ideas surrounding musical harmony. The brother, Guy
Lefèvre de la Boderie (1541–98), was, next to Du Bartas, the most
prolific scientific poet of late sixteenth-century France. His main
works (both of which are divided numerically into *Cercles*) are the
Encyclie des secrets de l'éternité (1571) and *La Galliade, ou de la
revolution des arts et sciences* (1578). These works provide encyclopaedic coverage of nature, man and the arts, and explore even further
into areas of esoteric interest than do the *Semaines*. Central to the perspectives of both Du Bartas and Guy Lefèvre is belief in the almost
magical effect both music and verse can have in restoring harmony to
humankind.

The power of music and poetry were closely linked through the
figure of the mythic bard, especially that of Orpheus (see West,
Chapter 2; and Voss, Chapter 7). Under inspiration analogous to that
enjoyed by Orpheus, Du Bartas's poetic persona both acts as mediator
with the divine, and exercises a harmonizing and civilizing effect on
his hearers. This was of course a popular view of the time; Peletier du
Mans, a prominent theorist, writes (after Horace) in his *Art poëtique*
(Lyon, 1555):

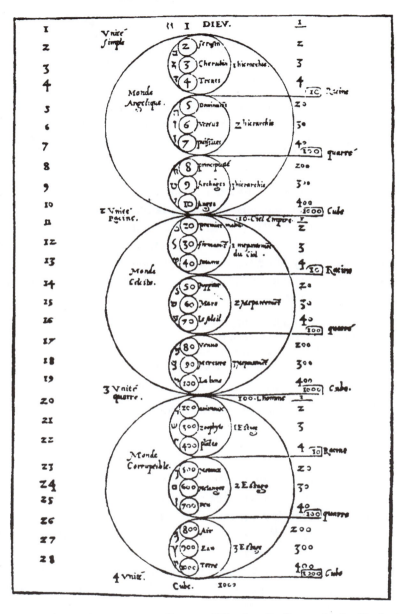

9.1 The universe according to Nicolas Lefèvre de la Boderie, from the opening to 'Introduction sur l'harmonie du monde', in Guy Lefèvre de la Boderie (trans.), *L'harmonie du monde* (Paris, 1578).

La Poésie a congrégé les hommes, qui étaient sauvages, brutaux
et épaves: et d'une horreur de vie, les a retirés à la civilité, police
et société ... par le son de leurs Lyre, ils [Amphion and Orpheus]
tiraient les Arbres et les Pierres après eux. La Poésie a été cause
des édifications des Villes ... (pp. 67–8)

[Poetry introduced to the communal state men who were wild,
brutish and depraved, bringing civilisation and government ...
through the music of the lyre Amphion and Orpheus drew trees
and rocks after them. Poetry was the moving force in the
founding of city settlements ...]

Orpheus was the principal figure associated with these powers, and he
was particularly renowned as 'celui dont la lyre / Oreilloit (comme on
dit) les rocs et les forets' ['Whereof the first Charm'd stockes and
stones (they say)'] (*L'Uranie* 145–6 [214]). Orpheus' authority over
nature is echoed by Du Bartas in a story about Jubal Cain who, as a
Judaeo-Christian version of the mythic bard, invents the lyre on the
model of the turtle shell:

> un Luth harmonieux,
> Qui meine au bal les monts, retrograde les cieux,
> Oreille les forests, les Lyons dessauvage,
> Impose aux vents silence, et sereine l'orage.
>
> (*Les Artifices* 503–6)
>
>   the melodious Lute
> That makes woods harken, and the winds be mute;
> The hils to daunce, the heav'ns to retro-grade,
> Lyons be tame, and tempests quickly vade.
>
> (*The Handy-Crafts* 545–8)

Here the music and poetry associated with the lyre is portrayed as
having a profound influence over many aspects of nature. The reference to power over one aspect of nature – 'sereine l'orage' (506)
['tempests quickly vade', 548] – recalls the ability of Christ to calm
the storm (Matthew 14.24–33).

Du Bartas places his poetic persona in the traditions associated with
the mythic figures of Orpheus, Arion and Amphion. However, when
he charts a course through pagan beliefs he usually attempts to follow
a Judaeo-Christian route, and this case is no exception. The poet links
his name most overtly with David, the biblical character most prominently likened to Orpheus. David was, of course, celebrated not just

for writing the Psalms, but also for his ability to calm Saul through his music (see Shiloah, Chapter 3; and Jones, Chapter 6). Lefèvre de la Boderie draws out a variety of points of comparison between the Psalmist and Orpheus:

> David conduit aus mons les troupeaus de sa Lyre,
> Et de sa Lyre Orfée à soy les bestes tire ...
>
> Il [Orpheus] sceut si bien de Dieu les ouvrages priser,
> Et Nature sonder en toute chose infuse,
> Que plus grand que Nature on feint l'art de sa Muse ...
>
> Et que dirai-je plus? David chante en esprit
> Le beau Chant nuptial de l'Eglise et de Christ,
> Et Orfée a conjoint par sa Muse discréte
> La Nature avec Dieu d'alliance secréte.
>
> (*Anagrammatismes* 195–6)

[By the aid of the lyre David leads flocks to the mountains and Orpheus draws beasts after him ...
So well does Orpheus appreciate the works of the Creator and plumb the depths of Nature that the art of his muse is imagined as greater than Nature herself ...

And what more shall I tell? In the Spirit David sings the beautiful marriage song of Christ and the Church,
And Orpheus by his discreet muse joins in secret alliance Nature and God.]

Like Du Bartas, Lefèvre perceives the power of Orpheus over nature to be great indeed – 'plus grand que Nature on feint l'art de sa Muse' [the art of his muse is imagined as greater than Nature herself]. Du Bartas follows Lefèvre in likening David to Orpheus in *Les Trophees*. He addresses the infant David in terms which clearly evoke a comparison with the mythic bard:

> Voy s'entre-coudoyer à l'entour de ton bers
> Les bois, mais oreillez: les mers, mais non vagueuses:
> Les Tigres, mais privez: les roches, mais dançeuses.
> Voy comme tout le Ciel ravy d'un si doux ton,
> Quitte, pour escouter ton bal et ta chanson. (823–7)
>
> About thy Cradle here are thronging (round)
> Woods, but with ears: floods, but their furie stopping:
> Tigres [*sic*], but tame: Mountaines, but alwayes hopping:

> See how the Heav'ns, rapt with so sweet a tongue,
> To list to thine, leave their owne Dance and Song.
>
> (*The Tropheis* [*sic*] 960–64)

Here David's mystic power stretches over land, sea, the animal kingdom and even the domain of the spheres. Du Bartas was strongly attracted, as we have seen, by the idea that power of this kind could be associated with the abilities enjoyed by the vatic poet. There are some suggestions that Du Bartas's confidence that his poetic talents could be seen in these terms increased following the remarkable success of the *Premiere Semaine* on its publication in 1578. In the following year, when he republished *L'Uranie* – his *art poétique* – Du Bartas included additional lines which compare his powers with those of David, son of Jesse: in both the 1579 and 1585 editions Urania tells the poet,

> Pren-moi donques pour guide, eleve au ciel ton aile!
> Salluste, chante-moy du Tout-puissant l'honneur,
> Et remontant le lut du Jesséan soneur,
> Courageus, brosse apres la corone eternele!   (65–8)

> Then, take me (BARTAS) to conduct thy Pen,
> Soare-up to Heav'n; Sing-me th'Almighties [*sic*] praise;
> And tuning now the Jessean Harpe againe,
> Gaine thee the *Garland* of eternall *Bayes*.   (65–8)

So the power and dignity of his divine poetic song is like that of the 'lut du Jesséan soneur' ['Jessean Harpe'].

The poet's association with David strengthens his claim to be able to restore a special kind of harmony. He tells David, as we have seen, that 'the Heav'ns, rapt with so sweet a tongue, / To list to thine, leave their owne Dance and Song' (*The Tropheis* 963–4). In a similar vein Du Bartas portrays his own Orphic poetic song as a force re-connecting mankind with the harmony of the superlunary realm. This poetic linking with the perfection of the sky suggests for the divine poet a re-establishment of the bond between earth and heaven which was lost though the Fall. In *Les Furies* the reader is informed that the sympathies which (according to contemporary lore) bind together parts of postlapsarian creation, are only

> une trace, un umbrage
> De l'amour qui regnoit durant le premier age:

Où *les Muses d'icy* d'un son harmonieux,
Divines, sous-chantoient avec celles des cieux.

(41–4, my italics)

a spark or shadow of that Love
Which at the first every thing did move,
When as th'Earthes *Muses* with harmonious sound
To Heavens sweet *Musike* humblie did resound.

(*The Furies* 61–4)

The suggestion is that the poet can re-create these former conditions and reinstate cosmic harmonies: he can parallel the activities and the effects of the erstwhile 'Muses d'icy' ['Earthes *Muses*'] through his *divine* poetic song. His muse, by harmonizing with the music of the spheres, will rejoin earth and heaven. This idea is given greater emphasis after the success of the *Premiere Semaine* (1578) which, as we have seen, appears to have encouraged Du Bartas's view of himself as a divine poet. In the post-1578 versions of *L'Uranie* he adds lines which underscore the harmony brought about by his verse – presented in strongly musical terms – with both the celestial and divine regions; in the 1579 and 1585 editions his muse is described as follows:

Sa face est angelique, angelique son geste;
Son discours tout divin, et tout parfait son cors;
Et sa bouche à neuf vois imite en ses accors
Le son harmonieus de la dance celeste. (33–6)

Angelicall her gesture and her gate;
Devinely-sweet her speech and countenance,
Her *Nine*-fold Voice did choicely imitate
Th'*Harmonious* Musike of *Heavens* nimble Dance. (33–6)

Du Bartas's muse, then, is closely linked to the harmony of the visible heavens – including that expressed in the music and dance of the spheres. Urania also attracts the epithets 'angelique', 'divin' and 'parfait', reflecting qualities which connect the harmony of the superlunary region with that of the invisible, heavenly realm.

Further associations accrue to Du Bartas's poetic song through another area which 'stands between' two worlds: Eden. In the Garden, as in the sky, are found many expressions of harmony. For example, the music of birds harmonizes with angelic song, and is likened to the music of the Orphic poets; the birds of Eden,

> marians leurs tons aux doux accents des Anges,
> Chantoient et l'heur d'Adam et de Dieu les louanges.
> Car pour lors les Corbeaux, Oriots, et Hiboux
> Avoient des Rossignols le chant doctement doux,
> Et les doux Rossignols avoient la voix divine
> D'Orphee, d'Amphion, d'Arion, et de Line.   (*Eden* 85–90)

> marrying their sweet tunes to th'Angels layes
> Sung *Adams* blisse, and their great makers praise.
> For then the Crowes, night-ravens, and howlets noise
> Was like the Nightingales sweet-tuned voice;
> And Nightingales sung like divine *Arion*,
> Like Thracian Orpheus, Linus and Amphion.   (*Eden* 115–20)

Here readers may again recall the poet's work as they contemplate the song of 'les doux Rossignols' ['the Nightingales sweet-tuned voice'], which in the prelapsarian state enjoyed the higher level, harmonizing powers possessed by the 'voix divine / D'Orphee' [Orpheus' divine song]. Seeking echoes to highlight the power of his own poetic song to re-establish harmony, Du Bartas uses a description of nightingales in *PS* V to convey an elaborate and witty image of the poet who sings the 'song of creation'.[8]

The poet is further associated with the harmony of Eden through a parallel between his song and one of the activities of Adam. The poet can tame the animals by the power of his verse as Adam did in Eden by naming them. In *PS* VI Du Bartas alludes to his status and that of Adam in his request for divine aid in calming the animals he sees in his poetic vision:

> O Pere tout-puissant, sois guide de leur guide:
> Verse le miel plus doux de l'humeur Castalide:
> Sur ma langue indiserte, et par mes chants veincueurs
> Des tigres furieux aprivoise les coeurs,
> Dompte les fiers lions: fay, qu'acoisant sa rage,
> Tout genre d'animaux me viene faire hommage.   (17–22)

> Almightie [*sic*], Father, guide their Guide along
> And poure upon my faint un-fluent tongue
> The sweetest hunnie of th'*Hyantian* Fount,
> Which freshly purleth from the Muses Mount.
> With the sweet charme of my Victorious Verse,
> Tame furious Lyons, Bears, and Tigers fierce,
> Make all the wilde Beasts, laying furie by,
> To come with Homage to my Harmonie.   (*Sixth Day* 17–24)

These lines playfully develop popular beliefs of the time surrounding Adam's naming of the beasts in the Garden. Later in the same 'Jour' these ideas are evoked more explicitly when the poet says of Adam's power:

> Il vivoit Roy d'Eden ...
>
> Les plus fiers animaux volontiers fleschissoyent
> Leur col dessous son joug, et prompts obeissoyent
> A sa voix ...   (185, 187–9)
>
> He lived King of *Eden* ...
>
> The fiercest Beasts, would at his word, or beck,
> Bow to his yoake their self-obedient neck ...   (199, 201–2)

Both in this description of Adam's abilities, as at the beginning of *PS* VI in the account of the poet's harmonizing force, dominance over the animals is associated with poetic song. The poet wishes to tame wild beasts by his 'chants veincueurs' (19) ['Victorious Verse', 21], paralleling the way Adam's voice elicits obedience ('obeissoyent / A sa voix' (188–9) ['at his word, or beck, / Bow to his yoake', 201–2]. Similarly, the poet claims sway over another aspect of nature when, in recommending people to take note of the moral exempla he represents in his portrayal of the sea, he declares: 'Visitez ceste mer, *par mes chants acoisee* ...' ['Looke on these Seas *my Songs have calmed* thus'] (*PS*, V.303; *DW* I, V.317, my italics). This reference to the power exercised by the poet over the waves recalls the biblical account of Christ's ability to calm the storm which we noted earlier. The same biblical episode is also echoed earlier in *PS* V when the poet addresses the Creator about his command over the sea: 'Et toy, Pere eternel, qui *d'un mot seulement / Acoises la fureur* de l'ondeux element' ['And thou eternall Father *at whose winke / The wrathfull* Oceans swelling *pride doth sinke*'] (13–14 in both, my italics).

III

We saw in passing how the Renaissance fascination for David had a special focus on one of his abilities: his skill in calming Saul with the lyre. The possession of this power helped to confer on David a status similar to that of Orpheus, the great tamer of nature in classical myth.

The similarities between the two figures could be understood at more than one level. At a surface level references to the comparable powers of David and Orpheus provide support for syncretistic beliefs which combine biblical and classical ideas in a general way. At a deeper level the David–Orpheus parallel contributes to a set of beliefs which justify the existence of *musica mundana* and *musica humana*. Reflections of this system of ideas are found in Du Bartas's conception of the power of his poetic song.

Following a well-trodden route in Renaissance discussions of musical effects, Du Bartas explains the influence of David's music on Saul in terms of the neo-Platonic notions of his day. Like the harmonies of *musica mundana*, those of *musica humana* could be defined in numerical terms. So the harmony of the human soul could be explained by reference to musical harmonies expressed numerically. Du Bartas alludes to this idea in *Les Artifices* when, in a passage deeply imbued with Christian Platonism, he describes how the 'nombreux esprit' ['numb'ry soule'] of Jubal Cain resonates to musical harmonies recalled from before birth:

> L'imparfaite harmonie
> Des marteaux inegaux, qu'un bras divers manie,
> Esveille les accords, que son [Jubal Cain's] nombreux esprit
> Des Anges bien-heureux avant que naistre apprit.
>
> (489–92)

> th'un-ful harmonie
> Of un-even hammers beating diverslie,
> Wakens the tunes that his sweet numb'ry soule
> Yer birth (some thinke) learnd of the warbling *Pole*.
> ['of the blissful angels' in the original]
>
> (*The Handy-Crafts* 529–32)

Here Du Bartas transposes to the life of Jubal Cain the traditional story of how, as we have seen, Pythagoras was said to have discovered the nature of musical harmonies through listening to hammer blows. He also draws in a Christianized version of a Platonic notion to claim that Jubal Cain had learned harmonies from the angels in a pre-existent state. Central to all this is the concept of the numerically-based musical harmony of the soul.

The system formed by these Pythagoro–Platonic ideas could easily assimilate the concept of the harmony of poetic song. This was possible because of the association of verse with music in general, as well as with 'number, weight and measure'. When David sang to his lyre, his music brought back into harmony the *musica humana* of Saul's soul which could be expressed in numerical terms:[9]

> Ainsi au ton devot de l'airain doux-tremblant,
> Le Prophete sacré l'ame a son ame emblant,
> Peu à peu se decrasse et dans sa fantaisie
> Profondement empreint le seau de Prophetie.
> Si nostre esprit est nombre (ainsi qu'on a chanté)
> Il doit estre souvent du nombre alimenté,
> Ou s'il est fait par nombre (et de vray je l'estime)
> Il le faut r'amener par une douce rime
> A quelque bon accord, tout ainsi que la voix
> Qui chantant un trio s'esgare quelque fois,
> Est ramenée au son par la voix mesurée.
> Qui coule selon l'art d'une bouche asseurée.
>
> (*Les Trophees* 393–404)

> So, at the sound of the sweet-warbling brasse,
> The Prophet rapting his soule's soule a space,
> Refines him selfe, and in his fantasie
> Graves deepe the seale of sacred Prophesie.
> For, if our Soule bee Number (some so thought)
> It must with Number be refreshed oft;
> Or, made by Number (so I yeeld to sing)
> We must the same with some sweet Numbers bring
> To some good Tune: even as a voyce (sometime)
> That in its Part sings out of tune and time,
> Is by another voice (whose measur'd straine
> Custome and Arte confirmes) brought in againe.
>
> (*The Tropheis* 429–40)[10]

Once again, in these lines Du Bartas seems to give strong credence to quite advanced numerological and musicological beliefs ('Si nostre esprit est nombre ... / ... doit estre souvent du nombre alimenté, / ... est fait par nombre', 397–9 ['if our Soule bee Number ... / ... must with Number be refreshed oft; ... [is] made by Number', 413–15]). In addition, the first four lines of this section evoke mystic, neo-Platonic suggestions which emphasize the remarkable impact of the numerically-based influence of music: the effect of David's prophetic inspiration with musical support is likened to the impact of a seal on matter. Similar allusions are present in *L'Uranie*, where Du Bartas

compares the effect on the reader of the number, weight and measure
of poetic song to the impact of a seal on wax:

> Les tons, nombres et tans, dont se fait l'harmonie,
> Qui fait le vers si beau, ont sur nous tel pouvoir,
> Que les plus durs Catons ils peuvent emouvoir,
> Agitant nos espris d'une douce manie.
>   Ainsi que le cachet dedans la cire forme
> Presque un autre cachet, le poete sçavant
> Va si bien dans nos coeurs ses passions gravant,
> Que presque l'auditeur en l'autheur se transforme.
>
> (85–8 [1574], 89–92 [1585])

> *Tunes, Notes, and Numbers*, whence we doo transferre
> Th'harmonious power that makes our *verse* so pleasing,
> The sternest *Catoes* are of force to stirre,
> Mans noblest spirits with *gentle Furie* seazing.
> And, as a Seale printeth in waxe (almost)
> Another Seale: A learned *Poet* graveth
> So deepe his passions in his Readers Ghost;
> That oft the Reader, th'Authors forme receiveth.   (153–60)

This great power of music which could move even the stern Cato was
also exemplified elsewhere in the ancient world. The effect of David's
lyre on Saul is echoed in the popular story of the power of Timotheus'
music over the moods of Alexander the Great:

> ... ainsi ton Timothee,
> O fameux Pellean, tient de ton couer le frein,
> Arme quand il luy plaist et desarme ta main ...
>
> (*Les Trophees* 384–6)

> Princely *Pellean*,
> Holding thy hart's raines in his Tune-full hand,
> Thy *Timothie* with his Melodious skill
> Armes and dis-armes thy Worlds-dread arme (at will) ...
>
> (*The Tropheis* 419–22)

The secret of music's power, Du Bartas reminds the reader, arises
from the fact that it is numerically based; it is at this level that *musica
mundana* and *musica humana* find their deepest correspondence. This
principle is illustrated by correspondences between major tetrads of
the macrocosm and microcosm (the elements, humours, seasons and
the four divisions of part singing):

Or tous ces contr'accents enchanteusement dous
Plus clairs que dans le ciel s'entendent parmy nous.
La plus pesante humeur, l'hyver, la terre basse,
Vont tenant la partie et plus lente, et plus casse.

(Les Colomnes 709–12)

But, brimmer farre then in the Heav'ns, here
All these sweet-charming Counter-Tunes we heare:
For Melancholie, Winter, Earth below
Beare aye the *Base*; deepe, hollow, sad, and slow:

(The Columnes 731–4)

These lines, which reach a climax in an account of the analogies between choler, summer, fire and soprano, lead into a passage which highlights the effect of *musica instrumentalis* on mankind. The correspondences between the four categories described explain why

les plus rebelles choses
Se laissent veincre au chant, comme tenant encloses
Les semences du nombre; et, foibles, ne vivant
Qu'en vertu de l'Esprit qui va les cieux mouvant.

(Les Colomnes 719–22)

stubborn'st things
Are stoopt by *Musike*; as reteyning springs
Of Nombre in them: and, they feebly live
But by that Spirit which the Heav'ns dance doth drive.

(The Columnes 741–4)

IV

Supported by the status and power of a numerical basis, singing can conquer 'les plus rebelles choses' ['the stubborn'st things'] of the natural and human worlds. There is then one more step which can be taken – into the divine realm. This is perhaps surprising to modern conceptions of Renaissance – especially reformed – religious beliefs as an outworking of conservative systematic theology (compare, for example, Calvin's rejection of judicial astrology). In this area the systemic ideas of Renaissance Platonism were sometimes well mixed into more orthodox Christian beliefs: the musical theories which explained how David brought calm to Saul could be used to suggest that music can play a role in divine propitiation.

Du Bartas repeats the notion current at least among the Huguenots that hymn singing can calm the Almighty himself; music must be very powerful:

> Veu que quand l'Eternel en sa fureur plus grande
> Fume, tonne, treluit : que tous ses nerfs il bande …
>
> L'accord melodieux, qu'un coeur devot souspire,
> Destrempe ses tendons, fait rendormir son ire,
> Et Clemence aux-doux-yeux emble d'entre ses mains
> Le supplice ensouffré des rebelles humains.
>   (*Les Colomnes* 739–40, 743–6)
>
> Sith, when the Lord (most moved) threatneth most,
> With wrathfull tempest arming all his Hoast …
>
> Th'harmonious sighes of his hart-turning Sheepe
> Supple his sinnewes, lull his wrath a-sleepe;
> While milde-ey'd Mercy stealeth from his hand
> The sulphry Plagues prepar'd for sinfull Man?
>   (*Les Columnes* 765–6, 769–72)

So even God himself could be deeply affected by the 'accord melodieux' [melodious harmony] of music – and in a quasi-physical (or metaphysical) way. Underlying this suggestion are echoes of the belief that ultimately, like the human soul, the divine soul (which has affinities here with the Platonic *World Soul*) can be described in numerically-based musical terms. If, as we have seen, the human soul 'bee Number', it must 'with Number be refreshed oft'; or, if it is 'made by Number', then 'We must the same with some sweet Numbers bring / To some good Tune'. The calming, harmonizing of the divinity can be understood to operate in a similar manner.

Against the background of the Renaissance beliefs we have considered, it is understandable how so much power was ascribed to music in a clinical setting. Biblical and classical stories provided cogent examples. Influential philosophico-theological ideas afforded persuasive arguments for believing in the healing power of music. After all, what was a kind of cosmic madness – a loss of harmony and calm – following the Fall could potentially be alleviated by the music of Orpheus–David as well as by latter-day poetic song. And this musical power could reach even to God himself.

Sweet *Musike*, makes the sternest men-at-Armes,
Let-fall at once their anger and their Armes:
It cheeres sad soules, and charmes the frantike fits
Of Lunatikes that are bereft their wits:
It kills the flame, and curbes the fond desire
Of him that burnes in Beauties blazing Fire
(Whose soule seduced by erring eyes,
Doth some proud Dame devoutly Idolize):
It cureth Serpents bane-full bit, whose anguish
In deadly torment makes men madly languish: ...

O, what is it that *Musike* cannot doo;
Sith th'all-inspiring Spirit it conquers too ...

(*The Columnes* 745–54, 759–60)

Notes

1. See, for example, the poem by the New England author Anne
    Bradstreet (perhaps his most fervent admirer): 'In Honour of Du
    Bartas, 1641', in *The Works of A. Bradstreet* (Cambridge, MA, 1967),
    pp. 192–4.

2. All quotations from the two *Semaines* are drawn from the most recent
    critical edition by Y. Bellenger et al., 5 vols (Paris, 1981, 1991–92,
    1994). The seven parts of the *Premiere* [*sic*] *Semaine* (hereafter *PS*) are
    cited by part and line number. References following quotations in
    English are to the translation of Du Bartas's works by Joshua
    Sylvester, *The Divine Weeks and Works*, ed. S. Snyder, 2 vols (Oxford,
    1979). Sylvester's version of the first of the two *Divine Weekes*
    (hereafter *DW* I) is cited by part and line.
        Du Bartas also published *La Muse chrestiene* (1574), a collection of
    minor works – *La Judit*, *Le Triomphe de la Foi*, and *L'Uranie* – which
    fulfils the role of an *ars poetica*. Quotations from Sylvester's
    translation of *L'Uranie* are from *Urania, or the Heavenly Muse*
    (London, 1800).
        Du Bartas's initial fame and subsequent fluctuating fortunes are
    ably summed up by Wordsworth: 'who is there that now reads the
    "Creation" of Dubartas? Yet all Europe once resounded with his praise;
    he was caressed by kings; and, when his Poem was translated into our
    language, the Faery Queen faded before it.' *Selected Prose* (Harmonds-
    worth, 1988), p. 393. Goethe was another admirer of Du Bartas who
    expressed surprise at the fall in his reputation: see Goethe's note
    translated into French by Sainte-Beuve: *Tableau de la poésie française
    au XVIe siècle* (Paris, 1876), vol. 2, pp. 209–10.

3. See in particular *Renaissance Studies*, 5.3 (1991), ed. L. Panizza,
    devoted to scientific and philosophical poetry; also A.-M. Schmidt, *La
    Poésie scientifique en France au seizième siècle* (Paris, 1938). For a
    selection of the poems, see D. B. Wilson, *French Renaissance
    Scientific Poetry* (London, 1974).

4.   For a good modern discussion of the importance of correspondences and related ideas in the Renaissance, see M. Foucault, *The Order of Things: an Archaeology of the Human Sciences* (London, 1991), esp. chs 2 and 3.

5.   The *Seconde Semaine* is cited, from both the original and the Sylvester translation, by name of the constituent part and line.

6.   See Giorgi, *De Harmonia Mundi* (Venice, 1525), f. 95[v]. An alternative, though apparently less popular view, interpreted 'weight' as evoking the *gravitas* rather than the musicality of the creative process.

7.   An amusing parody of the formula is included in Rabelais's *Fifth Book*. This work contains a satire on the quest for the Holy Grail in which, following Rabelais's *bon viveur* theme, the protagonists' object of desire is the 'divine bottle'. When they reach the Temple of the Bottle they find the steps leading down into the building are laid out in a numerologically significant manner. The 'tetradic steps' are arranged according to the *lambda formula*. A more conventional account of that formula and its relation to *musica mundana* is found in the work of Pontus de Tyard, the Pléiade poets' principal theorist on scientific matters; esp. *Solitaire second ou prose de la musique* (Lyon, 1555), pp. 142–3.

8.   See ch. 5 of my *Du Bartas, French Huguenot Poet, and his Humorous Ambivalence* (Lewiston and Lampeter, 1998).

9.   The same ideas linking poetry, music, number and harmony also underlie lines in Saint-Marthe's 'Chant premier de la providence de Dieu' (*Les Premieres oeuvres*, Paris, 1569), in which he declares a wish to 'chanter sus ma lyre / ... et . . . / Luy [à l'Eternel] dedier les nombres de ma voix' ['sing to my lyre / ... and ... / dedicate to the Eternal the numbers of my voice'] (f. 56[v]).

10.   Besides seeing this curative power in terms of the effect of the musical aspects of poetry, Du Bartas also suggests that David's words may perhaps also have brought relief to Saul's troubled mind (*Les Trophees* 405–8; *The Tropheis* 441–4).

CHAPTER TEN

Musical Treatments for Lovesickness: The Early Modern Heritage

Linda Phyllis Austern

I

Even after centuries, Philip Ayres's emblematic image *Amans quod suspicatur, vigilans somniat* of 1683 (Figure 10.1) retains its power to disturb. The shadowy figure of a man, eyes still sealed in sleep, reaches for the luminous body of a woman standing in naked perfection beside him. Twisted bedclothes reveal his restless agitation. Erotic energy animates her mobile limbs as she hovers over him with parted legs and coyly outstretched arms. Light and shadow caress her voluptuous form to emphasize its most sexual parts, rendering her an object of desire to the heterosexual male viewer as well as to the dreamer. Yet in spite of her proximity and unsettled pose, she eludes his grasp. The accompanying epigram explains in four European languages that she is but a ghostly figure, haunting his memory and his every thought. Its graphic verbal imagery raises further spectres of the dark, uncontrollable aspects of love, which lead to obsession, madness and death. His life hovers impossibly between sleep and wakefulness, his capacity to distinguish between internal and external cognitive signals destroyed. Here is erotic longing at its most extreme, transformed into a serious illness that threatens mind and body.

Surrounding the woman's glowing form are objects that would have suggested well-known and long-accepted remedies for the lover's desperate condition to the original viewers. The globe beside his bed evokes the vigorous distractions of travel. Toilet vessels bring to mind the importance of balanced care of the body. More significantly, just beyond the remembered form of the beloved and mirroring her curvaceous shape, rests a violin with its bow and an open music-book. The instrument's neck and the bow's frog point toward the

Emblemi d'Amore.

Emblemata Amatoria.
EMB. 20.

Amans quod suspicatur,
vigilans somniat.

Te loquor absentem, te vox mea nominat unâ,
Te sine nulla venit nox mihi, nulla dies,
Quid Ante meos oculos præsto est tua semper Imago,
Et videor vultus mente videre tuos.
Io.) Ad qui amant, ipsi sibi somnia fingunt.

Ever present.

Her name is at my tongue, when ere I speak,
Her shape's before my Eyes wher ere I stir
Both day, and night, as if her ghost did walk,
And not the mee, but I had murdred her.

Vani e dolci sogni.

Forma l'amante ne la mente vaga
Gran sogni, e crede al suo desir fèn folle,
Illa nel mar caccia, e caçe in aria citale.
Di men sogne l'amante anchi s'apaga.

Heureux en Songe.

Malgré les cruautez d'une injusta Maitresse,
d'Vn Songe officieux, voulage un pauvor Amant,
Il porte entre ses bras, son aimable tygresse,
Mais le facheux reveils, en tire un instant.

Emblemes d'Amour.

10.1 Philip Ayres, *Emblemata amatoria* (London, 1683), sigs. E3ᵛ–E4.

unquiet lover, where he might reach them easily to banish care and restore inner harmony. This tiny tableau was published in the twilight years of ancient understanding of the powers of music and the self-regulation of psycho-physical health. It represents an almost perfect encodement of complementary attitudes toward the powers of music over lovesickness. Typically, we see the suggestion of music among other recognizable therapies for private use at the sufferer's discretion. We also see, through publication of this emblem in a book clearly meant for multinational circulation among learned readers of Latin and less erudite vernaculars, the commodification of an ancient form of self-care for an almost universal disorder. Such evidence reminds modern historians that the use of musical therapy for lovesickness had become a verbal and visual cliché by the early modern era, ultimately founded on the venerable philosophical relationship between literal and metaphorical notions of harmony. However, virtually no medical records, prescriptions, or other recommendations survive to indicate what sort of sound or musical repertory may have actually been used by whom to quell the dark flames of all-consuming love. Images like Ayres's, however, combine with medical manuals and certain music-books and instruments to suggest a flourishing practical tradition built on ancient theory, so well understood and highly individualized that it required no additional description.

II

By the time Ayres compiled his collection of emblems, European sufferers, healers, and other thinkers had had centuries' worth of access to a bewildering variety of intellectual and cultural assumptions about love and its role in human wholeness. The ancient Greek, Roman, Jewish, early Christian, and medieval Arabic writers to whom sixteenth- and seventeenth-century European intellectuals most often turned for information had left copious and occasionally contradictory advice. For an early modern investigator, love thus proved anything but simple. It belonged to the realm of metaphysics, but produced clinically measurable effects. It fell into the contrasting domains of the sacred and the secular by virtue of popular and learned traditions.

Scholars and healers could synthesize all of this information in an infinite number of ways.

Love affected not only human beings, but every aspect of a cosmos that pulsed with hidden energies. Because of its universal nature, its uncontrollable power, and its central positions in philosophy and theology, in science and in medicine, Western love had traditionally had aspects bright and dark. It was continually likened to fire, to poison, to agents that pierce, sting, burn, prick or discharge venom. The flames of love blazed like those of war or inner contemplation, a combustible enigma ever shifting between death and renewal.[1]

For over two thousand years, love's processes had been analysed principally in terms of the subtle mechanical interplay between the almost irreconcilable elements of mind and body. Medieval and early modern thinkers had first and foremost inherited ancient Greek notions that Eros was a disordered force of nature, particularly dangerous because of the sweet deceptions promised by desire and gratification. Love knew no reason. Any excess of passion, midway between the exterior life of the body and interior life of the mind, threatened to grow into insanity and loss of control. Love was the most dangerous of these. It was a particularly destructive agent that acted on the soul, threatening to weaken its tenuous control over the body that was its base opposite, admitting disease, madness, violence, bestiality, and servility. As codified most influentially by Plato and by Aristotle, the complexities of Greek love shifted between sexual idealism and sexual pessimism, bespeaking divine inspiration and bodily demand. These two axes have served as the base of the grid on which Western attitudes toward love have been laid out for two and a half millennia, through the most un-Hellenic Christian asceticism and Victorian sentimentality all the way to postmodern cynicism in an age of AIDS.[2]

Early Christian thought instituted new forms of antagonism between body and soul in matters of love, and additionally introduced the notion of *agape* to the utterly incommensurate *eros* of antiquity. To an ascetic culture that held mind over matter, love metamorphosed into an extension of human spirituality and psychic wilfulness. It thus came closer to theology than to social or biological science. After Aristotle and his adherents had removed the erotic apparatus from the exclusive dominion of the psyche, the Christian West came to regard the body as the highly flawed instrument of a soul that constantly risked carrying it beyond its basic needs and capacities. The passions and imagination, imperfect intermediaries between bodily sensation and inner knowledge, led people even further astray in matters of desire. Eroticism finally became an aspect of inner life, potentially governable by the will. True love transcended both perception and cognition to seek solace in the God who could not be reached by living flesh. Augustinian doctrine in particular linked the great complexities of love to the spiritual confusion of a fallen creature who could occasionally and tragically glimpse what he had lost.[3]

III

Since love itself was so powerful, so universal, yet so closely allied even in its normal progress to pathological conditions, it is hardly surprising that erotic disorders were among the most frequently discussed in Western medical and spiritual writings before 1700. The magnetic force that moved the very cosmos and drew the soul toward God was most often considered a compelling, violent disability that completely commanded the sufferer's mind and body beyond the point of health or rationality even at its most banal. So central has this idea been to Western thought that it still survives in modern clinical and psychological literature.[4] In earlier eras, love was often personified as the most ancient and powerful of the pagan gods and was accounted 'the cause of all good'[5] and 'the bond of all perfections'.[6] But yet

> the diverse and violent perturbations which affect the mind of a Passionate Lover, [were] the causes of greater mischiefs, then any other passion of the mind whatsoever.[7]

The sickness arising from unrequited love was terrible indeed, slowly consuming the entire somatic system and the very soul. It was an invasive illness that could lead to self-destruction, madness, murder, and death. It left the sufferer feverish, restless, and wasting away, except for the eyes; according to one tradition, these showed signs through their brightness of infection through the optic nerve to the brain by the phantasmic image of the beloved. The unrequited lover became an obsessive with a ravaged body, emotionally and physically unstable, but with a ferocious capacity for enhanced sexual performance. An excess of erotic passion unbalanced the mind, distempered the soul, and maimed the entire bodily system before it finally killed the liver like slow poison.[8] The early modern synthesis of Jacques Ferrand perhaps best summarizes 2,000 years' worth of descriptions of the illness most often brought about by love:

> Love is little better then meere Madnesse: for they that are possest with it, are so humorsome, and Inconstant in their desires, that they know not themselves, what they would have: what they are perswaded to, that they cannot endure to heare of: and what they are disswaded from, that they make little choice of. What is denied them, that they earnestly desire: and when 'tis offered them, then they refuse it. &c. And the reason of this distemperature in the Mind of a Lover, is, saith *Aristotle*, because that he is wholy governed by his Passions, which stop and hinder all passage to his reason, which only is able to set him againe in the right way to Vertue, from which he is now gone astray.[9]

In later antiquity and ancient Greece, sufferers required purification, and the need for treatment often raised spectres of the shameful exploitation of the magic arts, bewitchment, and dark divine powers for sexual gain.[10] The catalogue of symptoms was already staggering and contradictory: manic, depressive, violent, sorrowful, or exalted, depending on the sufferer and describer. Although erotic illness was most often considered psychological or spiritual in origin, its symptomatology and progress were linked early on with the dark, brooding, yet occasionally inspired humoral imbalance of melancholy, caused principally by an excess of black blood.[11] To this basic set of pathologies and the later Galenic synthesis, the Middle Ages contributed much. The Christian tradition had insisted early on that the health of the soul take precedence over that of the body, rendering the cleric the highest earthly care-giver. God was accounted the ultimate 'Author of Physicke', but biblical authority also commanded adherents of the Judaeo-Christian tradition to 'honor yᵉ physicion with that honor that is due unto him … for the Lord hathe created him'.[12] By the thirteenth century, the Church had begun to acknowledge the secular physician as expert authority over specific problems, and the practice of medicine began to move toward greater autonomy. At the same time, the central texts of Graeco-Arabic medicine that had begun to circulate throughout Europe encouraged literate university-trained physicians to offer increasingly detailed explanations for psychological as well as physiological function. Indeed, the principal contribution of the Middle Ages to the history of Western medicine lay in the development of practical models for the overlap of mental and physical states based on a Christianized synthesis of earlier thought. Nowhere was this coalescence displayed with more detail or finesse than the study of the bodily passions, particularly love, in which external sense merged with the conscious and unconscious activities of the mind through the workings of intermediary agents.[13]

Lovesickness, *amor hereos*, *amor heroicus*, or 'heroic love' was most thoroughly delineated for subsequent eras during the thirteenth and early fourteenth centuries. Descriptions, diagnostics, and treatments were based most directly on the writings of Constantinus Africanus, and the Spanish doctor Arnald of Villanova was the first European to devote a separate treatise to the condition.[14] As outlined by European physicians, the disorder was ultimately one of cognitive failure. It remained closely related to the psycho-physical imbalances of melancholy, and, to a lesser extent, to frenzy. Perhaps because of the gender and educational status of its codifiers, the sufferer was most often assumed to be a man of the highest social status, not unlike his literary analogue in the era's most famous epics and love-poems.[15] The pathology of *amor hereos* began, like ordinary love, with simple sensory stimulation through which the sufferer felt pleasure at the perception of the beloved object. As 'the Morall Philosophers & Platonists' had taught since antiquity, the most direct causes of love were the five senses, which informed the innermost aspects of the human being of physical, and ultimately metaphysical, truths.[16] Upon seeing or hearing, but also touching, smelling, or tasting, the potential beloved, the subject's vital spirits, the intermediary messengers between perception and judgement, relayed the information to the interior faculties of heart, brain, imagination, and memory. If the estimative virtue in the median of the three ventricles of the brain judged the pleasure to be very great, the imaginative faculty and the memory, located respectively in the anterior and posterior ventricles, retained the full force of the sensory impressions, along with the intentions of the estimative virtue. If the latter judged that the pleasure

through all impediments, and hath nothing in Heaven but *God*, and desireth nothing on *Earth* in comparison of him.[20]

The channelling of erotic energy inward and upward in such a manner brought the sufferer closer to the non-medical traditions of courtly love and mystical devotion, both marked by paradoxically ecstatic longing for a perpetually lost object with which earthly union could never take place. Both forms of idealized love sought the eternal release that no medical recommendation, no temporary physical release, could provide. Sufferers of each yearned for rebirth through transfigurative death. The mystic in particular transcended the limitation and empty ache of mere desire through a clear vision of spiritual grace far beyond illness. This was eternal, sacred love, whose language was prayer, and whose end was the everlasting unity of soul with divine spouse. It was not within the purview of the physician, though the descriptive language of erotic suffering and longing for eternal union crossed boundaries between forms of healing. In the West, the end of all true love, no matter how physical at its outset, was the Godhead.[21]

The therapy most often prescribed for earthly lovesickness by the learned physicians traced much of its foundation to Ovid's ancient *Remedies of Love*. Short of consummation with the beloved or the extended suffering of transcendence, recommended relief came primarily from simple physical restoratives and distraction: baths, food, good wine, and sleep to restore vigour; and sports, games, music, travel, conversation with loving friends, and intercourse with substitute lovers on the grounds that 'many tymes it commeth to passe, that one love doth drive out another'.[22] There were also direct physical remedies to be found in diuretic, moistening agents, and occasionally cold ones, to provide relief to the desiccated brain and overheated systems.[23] It is in the former group that we find music, extending from Ovid through Constantinus, Arnald, and beyond. To the Western mind, practice of the art not only offered distraction for a fevered brain, but soothed and re-harmonized body and soul. 'Musica mortales recreat divosq[ue] beatos' ['Music refreshes mortals and the blessed gods'], proclaims an emblem published in Frankfurt in 1606, which visually links the sound of instruments and voices to unity and illumination.[24] In addition, music sometimes prepared body and soul for the interior impressions of true and lasting love, or worked the sympathetic magic of true harmony on the listener.

IV

The efficacy of music in matters of love gone wrong was based on therapeutic applications of esoteric ideas that connected the art to universal order and harmony, and which also assigned it psycho-physical affective capacities. Love and music were, in fact, accounted similar agents by numerous pre-modern thinkers. Both were paradoxi-cally insubstantial forces that produced evident physical effects, both spanned the distance between metaphor and matter, and both served as agents of divine promise and perfection. Both were easily abused by those with base sensual appetites, and were therefore subject to strict measures of social control.[25] By the early modern era, Western thought had debated the physical and metaphysical influence of music on all beings and things for as long as it had discussed the mecha-nisms and pathologies of love. The sixteenth and seventeenth centu-ries inherited from classical antiquity and from its medieval filters both an objective approach that positioned music within the sublime realm of numerical speculation, and a more subjective attitude that explained the capacities of music through its evident effects.[26] In keeping with such other dialectical considerations of the pre-modern West as those of love and wellness, early modern thinkers therefore found several massive bodies of work from which to select theories and reconcile seemingly contradictory information. The complicated discourse that ultimately circulated among sixteenth- and seventeenth-century theorists and practitioners concerning musical experience was a colourful web that incorporated the teachings of, among others, Plato, Aristotle, Aristoxenus, Galen, the Book of Ecclesiasticus, and the medieval and earlier Renaissance critics who had assimilated and recodified their often contradictory ideas.[27]

As West has shown, above, several strains of ancient Greek thought held that music could affect evident and arcane matter, and alter the disposition of its hearers. The art thus possessed extraordinary moral, educational and therapeutic qualities. Although music played no part in the prescriptions of learned physicians, popular medical practitioners and more esoteric philosophers accounted it a means to treat physical ailments and rebalance the psyche in numerous conditions, including love. Early Christian thinkers held sounding music with as much suspicion as any other art of embodied sensuality, but made exceptions for its powers to heal and inspire the highest love, especially in a sacred context. After all, the Old Testament David had demonstrated the mighty power of psalms to drain one of earthly cares, direct the mind upward, and calm troubled spirits. Saints Augustine and Basil, for instance, most famous for their suspicion of the dangerous erotic potential of music, praised the art's power to assuage the raging passions and direct the mind to higher things, especially spiritual refreshment and sacred love. The former in particular claimed in a sermon that 'to sing [wa]s the sign of the lover', and the latter found purgation and the balance of raging affections in the music that accompanied psalms.[28]

The sixth-century synthesis of Boethius retained its inestimable influence on musical thought well into the early modern era. Therefore, in the progress and passion of love – which involved the same junctures between the rational and irrational faculties as did *musica humana* – audible music, or *musica instrumentalis*, restored harmonious balance through its sympathetic action on body and soul. For the lone performer, sounding music was a means to encourage healing introspection and psycho-physical balance through the therapeutic descent into and beyond the self, and the consequent sympathetic vibration of the highest music of universal order. For the musician with an audience or performance-partner, the same effects that revitalized the self also promised affective reciprocity through a parallel form of sympathetic vibration beyond voice or instrument from body to body, and soul to soul. The body was simply an instrument on which the soul could play just as a musician coaxed harmony from a lower instrument, and one instrument caused another to vibrate to its own frequency across physical and metaphysical conceptual planes (Figure 10.2). It is these overlapping concepts of therapy, arising from the idea that music could manipulate mood and physical response with medical effect, that dominate writings about the use of music in lovesickness from the Middle Ages through to the early modern era.

10.2   Jacob Cats, *Proteus ofte Minnebeelden* (Amsterdam, 1627), p. 254.

By the time medicine evolved into something like a recognized profession in the Middle Ages, the scientific and philosophical study of the effects of music and its place in the cosmos was a necessary prerequisite for advanced university training. Would-be physicians, like future theologians and lawyers, studied the seven liberal arts, of which music was accounted one of the four mathematics, before admission into the higher university faculty in which they received their specialized education. Beyond this early training, some medieval medical curricula may have further endorsed Boethius' *De musica*.[29] The esoteric traditions of music, in which therapies were grounded, remained closely tied to philosophy and theology in and out of the universities. They were accounted, like medicine, to be arts of body, soul, and the natural world. As late as the seventeenth century, the lutenist–composer Thomas Robinson advertised his self-tutorial *School of Musicke* by reminding would-be purchasers that music relates to both Western traditions of healing, the theological and medical, and that it cures numerous maladies.[30] Evidence shows ample opportunity for musical performance and for private study of instrumental techniques in early modern universities, and the Elizabethan doctor Thomas Cogan recommends music for its psycho-physical restorative properties in his health handbook for students.[31] The sixteenth-century Oxford-trained physicians John Case and Mathew Gwinne, for example, certainly practised music on their own as members of the university community. Case not only wrote a learned Latin treatise defending music from its numerous detractors, but mentions musical instruments in his will.[32] Barber-surgeons of the same era, more popularly trained through an apprenticeship system, worked in shops that became associated with musical performance and also left musical instruments in their wills.[33] No surviving evidence records the personal musical tastes of either such learned physicians as Case or more popularly-trained barber-surgeons, nor their musical advice to patients.

The musical recommendations and descriptions made by premodern physicians, philosophers and music theorists regarding erotic illness generally reflect their esoteric book-learning rather than experience, perfectly consistent with the era's most elite medical training. Such writings also reinforce the complementary notions that

music could both purge troubling erotic affections and arouse
amorous feelings. According to one tradition at least as old as Virgil,
the great hero Orpheus, admired by medieval and early modern thinkers for his preternatural musical and rhetorical powers, was motivated
by lovesickness for his lost wife to sing his most otherworldly and
universally affective songs. This personal therapy moved rocks and
trees, tamed tigers, and finally aroused the Thracian women 'whose
beds he did despise' so completely that they 'scatter'd him peece-
meale ore the fields', perhaps a warning to future lovesick musicians
to consider their sympathetic effect on potential audiences.[34] Ovid's
much-cited *Remedio Amoris* recommends that the sufferer avoid the
public performance venue of the theatre, and use citharas, lotus-wood
flutes, lyres, and voice to enervate the mind.[35] The medieval prescription of music therapy for *amor hereos*, grounded on earlier Greek and
Arabic ideas in addition to the wisdom of Christian Europe, continued
to focus on music's capacity to alter moods and lift flagging spirits.
Music was part of a group of activities meant to draw sufferers out of
excessive brooding, which also included drinking wine, travelling,
visiting fragrant gardens with running water, reciting poetry, and
speaking with friends (compare Page, Chapter 5). Music worked best,
said some authorities, in synergy with wine or with warm baths,
because all of these things take away sadness, or because sound is like
the spirit and music like the body and therefore music and wine in
particular reinforce each other to effect complete psycho-physical
restoration.[36] These ideas were still current in Robert Burton's
comprehensive seventeenth-century synthesis, which considers lovesickness a form of melancholy (see Gouk, Chapter 8).

From the Middle Ages to the seventeenth century, such observations and recommendations invariably lack the specificity of more
substantive compounds made of herbs, minerals, and parts of animals.
Neither learned physicians nor music theorists who borrow their ideas
ever notate the music that chases away lovesickness. Nor do they suggest repertory. They simply explain that efficacious music in this case
should please or distract, should sympathize and harmonize with the
sufferer's constitution and goal of somatic restoration. Either there
was tacit cultural understanding of what sort of music accomplished
these effects, or the sufferer made selections based on individual

aesthetic taste. Arnald of Villanova, for instance, simply recommends pleasant music sung or played on instruments for the treatment of *amoris heroici*, not unlike the musical instruments and pleasant voices he recommends for the cerebral disorders of mania and melancholy, both of which, of course, produced symptoms similar to lovesickness. His love-curative music is typically listed between the equally healing properties of such aesthetically and physically restorative agents as flowers and sleep.[37]

Most famously from the days of Ovid through those of the most thorough seventeenth-century codifier of psycho-physical disorders, Robert Burton, music was considered an agent to arouse love. Music was the very 'food of love', sacred and profane, for a culture that heard in its sweet strains the hidden, healing harmonies of the body, soul, and divinely-created universe. For the fifteenth-century Franco-Flemish music theorist, Johannes Tinctoris, one of the most important effects of his art was to attract love. '*Musica amorem allicit*', he explains on classical authority, which is why Orpheus had provoked the love of women and of tender boys, and why Ovid recommends in his *De arte amandi* that girls should learn to sing.[38] The most famous and frequently imitated courtesy manual of the early modern era, Baldessare Castiglione's early sixteenth-century *Book of the Courtier*, likewise mentions the power of music to attract the love of women to the male courtier. In a phallic metaphor that draws on contemporary understanding of feminine cognition and also conjures images of love's flaming arrows, it points out that women's 'tender and soft breastes are soone perced with melody and fylled with swetenesse'.[39]

In matters of lovesickness, music was thus understood to be the flame to light the fire or to ignite the hope of reciprocal passion, as well as the cooling draught of purgation and distraction. Music sympathetically inspired love just as it drove off the harmful effects of superabundant erotic passion, as Virgil's retelling of Orphic legend demonstrates. Music literally represented the successful end of erotic passion even as it also harmonized a body and soul unbalanced by untoward affection. From antiquity through the Middle Ages and into the early modern era, the sound of voices and instruments played a distinct part in the rites of marriage, including epithalamia composed both to cover and to draw attention to ritual consummation.[40] The

same gardens with their soothing, flowing waters and fragrant flowers
that dispelled the ill effects of *Amor hereos* also stimulated love in the
era's writings and visual art.[41] The medieval musical medical heritage
likewise included auditory stimulation of erotic appetite in conjunction with banquets and communal baths, a reverse manifestation of the
same unities of sensation and self-care elsewhere meant to distract
from obsessive love.[42] Giovanni Bocaccio explains that songs and
musical instruments have the power to dispel the melancholy which is
stirred up by frigid humours and is strong against the effects of
Venus.[43] Close to three centuries later, Robert Burton, familiar with
the same literary, medical, and philosophical sources as the Italian
poet, still found music to be a powerful agent against the same
disease, as long as it did not originate in foolish, excessive love of
women.[44] He adds that:

> Amongst other good qualities an amorous fellow is endowed
> with, he must learn to play upon some instrument or other, as
> without all doubt he will, if he be truly touched with the Load-
> stone of Love. For as *Erasmus* hath it, *Musicam docet amor &*
> *Poesin*, love will make them Musitians ... 'Tis their chiefest
> study to sing, dance, and without question, so many Gentlemen
> and Gentlewomen would not be so well qualified in this kinde, if
> love did not incite them.[45]

This idea is given graphic reinforcement in a Dutch emblem designed
by P. C. Hoofts for international circulation (Figure 10.3). Here, the
magnificent goddess Venus, who holds her head high and does not
sink beneath the waves as do other vessels on the same tempestuous
sea, embraces all with the flame of love, represented as a burning
heart upon her outstretched left hand. As she passes, she has truly
rendered a lover musical. Behind her, bathed in light from high above,
a man plays a lute to a woman who leans through her window to listen
more closely. Like the proverbial music that refreshes and restores
gods and mortals, the lutenist's imagined strains become a source of
enlightenment that draws auditor and performer together. Will the
beloved's heartstrings vibrate in sympathy with his hidden instrument
like one lute tuned to another, or will he need to seek private solace
for the wounds of love? Either way, the viewers' culture would recognize in music relief for the lover's suffering.

10.3 P. C. Hoofts, *Minnezinnebeelden*, in *Werken* (Amsterdam, 1671), sig. Een.

V

Such images as this one indicate that the ancient traditions of musical therapy for love and lover's woes had become an indelible aspect of culture and the standard regimen for self-cure and basic health maintenance by the early modern era. Within a medical tradition that emphasized prevention and personal responsibility for self-care, such a simple remedy needed no prescription by learned physicians. Health of body and soul were primarily matters of following daily regimens to maintain balance. An extremely large number of artefacts from the sixteenth and seventeenth centuries, ranging from emblems and paintings to musical instruments and music-books, reinforce the paired ideas that music drove out pathological love and likewise encouraged mutual affection, and additionally suggest a flourishing market for related artefacts. Physicians knew well the powers of music, but it was not part of their surgeries or apothecary mixtures. Instruments, music-books, and narrative emblems and paintings became the pills to purge love's imbalances by providing distraction, systemic re-harmonization, a hope of reciprocity, or a focus for the strong drink and merry company that would augment music's potent effect. Sometimes these elements were cleverly combined in a single object, which might additionally suggest other standard remedies for love's misfortunes. The parallel tradition of spiritual healing, the yearning for true divine love, maintained its own store of similar artefacts in psalm-books, music for the sacred service, and holy images, beyond the scope of the present study, but omnipresent in early modern culture.

For a culture that stood at the boundary between orality and literacy, visual images often advertised and reinforced the learned lessons of elite tomes. In addition, even the most evidently iconoclastic pockets of the West at least subconsciously recognized the magical efficacy of the image, which could serve as a stand-in for the object depicted.[46] Thus, an image of musical therapy for love or a successful musical courtship could not only inspire the viewer, but serve as empathic narrative focus of triumphant outcome. The many loving players of stringed and keyboard instruments in the era's paintings and emblems functioned at once as metaphor, inspiration, and sympathetic objects, not to mention advertisements for the attainment of skill, or graphic warnings against deadly erotic excess.[47] As Castiglione suggests in his manual of courtly conduct, music, especially the lute, helped men gain sexual favours of the ladies.[48] Beyond Ayres's, Cats's, and Hoofts's visual exhortations of the great capacities for erotic relief or inspiration available to the male musician, many rendered his female equivalent an even more potent commodity in a society that generally emphasized female silence and invisibility. Normally the passive respondent to his action, keeper of the private domestic space in his world of statecraft and public profession, the woman sometimes reversed the equation in courtship. 'To heare a faire young Gentlewoman play upon the Virginals, Lute, Viall, and sing to it ... are *lascivientium delitiae*, the chiefe delights of lovers, [which] must needs be a great entisement', writes Burton during the century in which so much Dutch genre painting advertised just this quality.[49] Burton's words remind us of the great power assigned the female musician to render the heterosexual male listener sick with desire and then affect his cure, in a culture in which women's social and economic value was closely tied to their sexuality and potential as lifetime marriage partners. The manuscript Burwell lute tutor, compiled by a young gentlewoman toward the end of the seventeenth century, specifically explains the great value of the instrument in courtship and further commodifies the lutenist as a bargain in a marriage-market that emphasized a blend of sacred and secular attractive qualities:

> The Lute is a modest interpreter of our thoughts & passions[.] [T]o those that understand the language one may tell another by the helpe of it what he hath in his heart ... And [to] those that have the Grace to lift upp there mind to the Contemplation of heavenly things this Celestiall harmony contributes much to raise our Soules and make them melt in the Love of God. Nothing represents soe well the Consort of Angelicall Quires and give more foretaste of heavenly Joyes and of everlasting happiness ... Some have beleeved that they should possesse an Angell incarnate of they s[h]ould unite themselves by a Marriage to a person that injoyes this rare qualitye.[50]

Such statements presumably served as a powerful motivator for lute-lessons for the unmarried, particularly young women, who could use music to hide their own secret flame. For music never fully conquered love (Figure 10.4). Images like this one, with the eroticized shape of the lute and the performer's deft stroke of fingers over a rosette-covered hole in the belly of an instrument held close to her body, perhaps also suggest her potential for sexual skill and the masturbation held to make young virgins more chaste and wives more faithful.[51]

Musical instruments themselves, so beautifully depicted as sources of light and hope in many of the era's visual images, were linked to the inspiration of love and treatment of lovesickness. From no later than the fourteenth century to the end of the seventeenth, the plucked and bowed stringed instruments so closely associated with the musical lover in serenade and solitude were often decorated with images alluding to erotic desire and solace.[52] Merely to possess these extraordinary objects was to give the performer the positive power of love, for private self-regulation or to inflame a listener. Stringed keyboard instruments, decorative pieces of furniture which signalled wealth and status in homes and depictions of interior spaces from the fifteenth century onward, owed their rapid early development in large part to medical astrologers who knew the powers of music as well as the mechanical action of precision instruments.[53] What has gone previously unremarked is the prevalence of visual embellishment that reinforced their potential to alleviate or inspire love, as do the instruments under a performer's touch in the era's allegories and genre painting. The mottoes inscribed above the keyboards of many harpsichords, clavichords, and virginals of the sixteenth and seventeenth centuries refer to the healing powers of music, including healing in matters of love.[54] Perhaps more important are the fruits and flowers that decorate numerous soundboards and help to define the Flemish and Flemish-style instruments of the seventeenth century. Such exquisite little objects were sometimes directly inspired by the handiwork of the era's naturalists and increasing interest in cataloguing the works of nature, rendering the instruments into glorious objects that pleased all five senses by evoking the pleasures of taste, smell, and sight on artefacts primarily meant to be touched and heard.[55]

10.4 Jean 1er Le Blond after Pieter van Mol, *Omnia vincit amor nec mucica vincit amorem* ([Paris] n.d.).

We have already seen the efficacy of flowers and gardens combined with music in the healing and inspiration of erotic disorders in the Middle Ages, and here the same may be transferred into an unstated early modern recommendation to own and play keyboard instruments. The unruly elements of nature have been tamed and brought indoors, allowing the fingers to release the power of flora through the sound of music, the eye to become adjunct to the ear as the performer or auditor gazes past the keyboard to the source of sound. The sixteenth-century Italian neo-Platonist Tommaso Buoni explains that lovers delight in flowers

> *perhaps* because the colours, & names of flowers are apt to display those passio[n]s that they feele who are subject to this passio[n] of *love*... *Or Perhaps* because *Love* like a wanton, taketh delight in delicate things, and to rolle, and enwrappe it selfe in sweete odours, taking from thence some comforte in her passions. And this is the reason why we many times see *Love* painted in a plesant fielde, sitting upon a multitude of flowers mery, and jocund, crowned with garlands, lying upon a bed covered with a thousand roses and violets, fast by a fountaines side, compassed with many rich verdures and Beautifull plants.[56]

Here, the garden becomes part of the instrument of music, another of the lover's delights, each flower inspiring the memory of sweet odour and delicate colour.[57] From the days of Cato and Pliny onward, the glory of flowers was a delightful enrichment of sensual life, but yet, to the pre-modern era, most objects possessed additional symbolic value to those that sought it.[58] Natural histories, herbals, and other sources of flower-lore likewise teach that, for those who seek symbols and metaphysical significances, the species that dominate florid soundboards – the rose, the violet, the tulip, the carnation, the pink, the pansy, the lily, the strawberry, and the marigold among them – are cooling, moistening or sun-following agents often associated with sacred or secular love, suggestive of ancient remedies for erotic imbalance and increased delight in life.[59] For those devout souls who recognized the dangers of unbridled sensuality, or earthly pleasures taken at the expense of their heavenly equivalents, the same flowers offered a warning and a recollection that the instruments could be put to another purpose with a mere change of notes. Like the music whose sound decays in an instant, flowers fade, and remind one merely of earthly vanity, of the sorts of love that do not outlive the body and its deceptive senses.[60]

Lovely fruits, flowers, and exotic birds, which all suggest wealth, taste, sensory delight, and the verdant abode of Cupid described by Buoni were far from the only form of keyboard decoration. Perhaps most interesting are such instruments as a pentagonal virginal made in 1537 by Giovanni Francesco Antegnati[a], now owned by the Victoria and Albert Museum in London (Figure 10.5). Inside the lid, prominently displayed when the instrument sounds, is a painted device of clasped hands, scorpion perched harmlessly if dangerously between, to accompany the familiar Latin motto *Amoris vulnus idem qui sanat fecit*. The image tells us that the wounds of love pierce and poison like the scorpion, known to natural historians for its fatal venom that causes the sufferer to languish for days.[61] Cupid's arrows are here turned lethal, the darts to penetrate a lady's breast powerful indeed, a metaphorical conflation of many ideas of the pangs and fits of love and the powers of music. The original viewer or auditor would also have known that the terrible scorpion 'smiteth never nor hurteth the palme of the hand', here clasped on loving amity above strings that vibrate when other palms turn toward the keys that give the instrument its sound.[62] The same viewer would understand that music would not bring true death to the tender and soft lady listener, though it might lead her toward the 'little death' of sexual ecstasy, and would help to heal the stricken performer of either sex. In its subtle evocation of the power of music over venom, the image on the instrument perhaps further recalls the era's tradition of tarantism, musical cures for the melancholic symptoms induced from the bite of another poisonous creature, in yet another creative metaphor for the wounds of love and omnipotent power of music to rid the system of all toxins (see Gentilcore, Chapter 11).[63]

The era's madrigals, drinking-songs, courtly airs, and all other secular music from one end of Europe to the other pay extraordinary homage to the powers of love bright and dark. Likewise, sacred music for public and private devotion was often meant to rouse the heart to God even as its profane equivalent stirred the blood to lust or recalled the memory of lost loves. In this context, one must consider these innumerable manuscripts and printed collections as objects that could

10.5 Interior lid of Giovanni Francesco Antegnati[a], pentagonal virginal, 1537, Victoria and Albert Museum, London.

expel the pain of unrequited love; the compiler or purchaser came to own a varied repertoire determined by personal taste and training, which would help accomplish what learned physicians recommend through music. Given the prevalence of love-songs in all sorts of collections, the potential therapeutic market is staggering. Dutch artist Gabriel Metsu adds the efficacy of sheet music to several of the era's standard literal and metaphorical manifestations of music therapy for lovesickness (Figure 10.6). In his *Cello-Player*, the stricken man tunes the highest string on the title instrument, heart side of his body cast in darkness, as he looks upward toward the radiant figure of his beloved in a pose we have seen before. Clad in pale, glowing colours to his blackness, eyes cast down in modesty or in answer to his pleas, she literally and metaphorically holds the notes that he would play. She is his light, the goddess–mortal to be refreshed by the music that will also recreate him. Behind this tableau, between the would-be lovers, a second man leans out of a window as would a woman drawn by a serenade, attention riveted by the musician out of curiosity or desire of his own. To own such an instrument, to possess such a piece of music to play on it, is to relieve a similar condition as if the beloved held it in her hand, and to hold the attention of all as did Orpheus.

Perhaps the quintessential music-books for healing the wounds of love in the absence of the hand that inflicted them are the collections of rounds, catches, and canons that circulated as witty musical curiosities, particularly in England, during the early modern era. The stylistically-simple music was meant to be sung by men's voices. The texts most often refer to strong drink, to the pleasures of love, to games and pastimes – in short, the combined recommendations of centuries for the relief of lovesickness. The frontispiece of John Hilton's famous *Catch That Catch Can*, for instance, shows two images of three men each, singing from a book of catches spread on the table before them, with stringed instruments, lute and viol respectively, hung on the wall behind. Such content, images, and songs such as 'A Dialogue Catch Between Two Doctours, and Their Patients', suggest that this may have been the sort of collection kept in the homo-social environment of the barber-surgeon's shop, where men enjoyed music and each other's company, and traded sexual information in addition to receiving healthcare and grooming services. In case

10.6   Gabriel Metsu, *Cello Player*, Buckingham Palace, London.

the idea of healing was not foremost on the performer's or purchaser's mind, Hilton's dedication reminds the reader that music is 'the earthly solace of mans soule', provider of recreation and delight.[64] Henry Purcell's well-known and widely circulating catch, "'Tis Women', written in 1681 or 1685, perhaps summarizes the situation best. This brief piece, composed for four men to sing at four-bar intervals, follows the typical, simple one-note-per-syllable style clearly designed for amateurs, although, perhaps in deference to its topic, its vocal range is unusually wide. Its four lines of text are set to very clear musical phrases in C major, in a compound metre of 6/4. Its melodic motion is predominantly stepwise, but includes wider leaps of an octave or a fifth to illustrate the text and indicate the raging passions of the narrative voices.

> 'Tis women makes us love.
> 'Tis Love that makes us sad.
> 'Tis Sadness makes us drink.
> And drinking makes us mad.[65]

Here the singers have it all, as their medieval and earlier forbears would have recognized: mirth, strong drink, a merry company (of fellow sufferers) to join in a witty celebration of the purgation of the madness and sadness arising from heterosexual love.[66]

Notes

1.   T. Benedek, 'Beliefs About Human Sexual Function in the Middle Ages and Renaissance', in D. Radcliffe-Umstead (ed.), *Human Sexuality in the Middle Ages and Renaissance* (Pittsburgh, 1978), pp. 106–7; I. Couliano, *Eros and Magic in the Renaissance* (Chicago, 1987), pp. 50–51; J. Kristeva, *Tales of Love* (New York, 1987), pp. 269–73; D. de Rougement, *Love in the Western World*, revised edn (New York, 1956), pp. 22, 42–6; J. Dryden, *Sylvae: or, the Second Part of Poetical Miscellanies* (London, 1685), pp. 80–81; T. Gainesford, *The Rich Cabinet* (London, 1616), ff. 85–7; M. F. Wack, *Lovesickness in the Middle Ages: The Viaticum and its Commentaries* (Philadelphia, 1990), p. 5.

2.   K. J. Dover, *Greek Popular Morality in the Time of Plato and Aristotle* (Oxford, 1974), pp. 125–7, 208; B. S. Thornton, *Eros: The Myth of Ancient Greek Sexuality* (New York, 1997), pp. 17–23, 127, 213; Couliano, *Eros*, pp. 4, 38, 87; P. Lain Entralgo, *Mind and Body, Psychosomatic Pathology* (London, 1955), pp. 87–8; M. Foucault, *The Care of the Self, The History of Sexuality*, vol. 3 (New York, 1988), pp. 106–7, 133; A. Nygren, *Agape and Eros* (New York, 1969), pp. 30–34.

3. Thornton, *Eros*, pp. 130–31, 214; Wack, *Lovesickness*, pp. 22–3; A. Wear, 'Religious Beliefs and Medicine in Early Modern England', in H. Marland and M. Pelling (eds), *The Task of Healing: Medicine, Religion and Gender in England and the Netherlands 1450–1800* (Rotterdam, 1996), pp. 147, 151; M. Williams, 'Divine Image – Prison of Flesh', in M. Feher with R. Naddaff and N. Tazi (eds), *Fragments for a History of the Human Body* (New York, 1989), pt 1, pp. 137–40.

4. D. Beecher, 'The Essentials of Erotic Melancholy', in K. Bartlett, K. Eisenbichler and J. Liedl (eds), *Love and Death in the Renaissance* (Ottawa, 1991), p. 43; S. Peele, 'Fools for Love: the Romantic Ideal, Psychological Theory, and Addictive Love', in R. J. Sternberg and M. L. Barnes (eds), *The Psychology of Love* (New Haven and London, 1988), pp. 166–8.

5. J. Ferrand, *Erotomania* (Oxford, 1640), p. 7.

6. J. Spenser, *Things Old and New* (London, 1558), p. 49.

7. Ferrand, *Erotomania*, p. 7.

8. D. Beecher, 'L'amour et le corps: les maladies érotiques et la pathologie à la Renaissance', in J. Céard, M. M. Fontaine and J.-C. Margolin (eds), *Le corps à la Renaissance* (Paris, 1990), pp. 423–34; J. Cadden, *Meanings of Sex Difference in the Middle Ages: Medicine, Science, and Culture* (Cambridge, 1993), p. 140; Couliano, *Eros*, pp. 18–21; D. Jacquart and C. Thomasset, *Sexuality and Medicine in the Middle Ages* (Princeton, 1988), pp. 83–6; J. L. Lowes, '"The Loveres Maladye of Hereos"', *Modern Philology*, 11 (1913–14), pp. 491–546; Wack, *Lovesickness*, pp. xi–xiii.

9. Ferrand, *Erotomania*, p. 230.

10. R. Parker, *Miasma: Pollution and Purification in Early Greek Religion* (Oxford, 1983), pp. 221–3.

11. M. Ciavolella, 'Eros and the Phantasms of *Hereos*', in D. A. Beecher and M. Ciavolella (eds), *Eros and Anteros: The Medical Traditions of Love in the Renaissance* (Ottawa, 1992), pp. 75–6; M.-P. Duminil, 'La mélancholie amoureuse dans l'Antiquité', in J. Céard (ed.), *La folie et le corps* (Paris, 1985), pp. 91–110; S. W. Jackson, *Melancholia and Depression from Hippocratic Times to Modern Times* (New Haven and London, 1986), pp. 29–41; J. Kristeva, *Black Sun: Depression and Melancholia* (New York, 1989), pp. 5–7; P. Toohey, 'Trimalchio's Constipation: Periodizing Madness, Eros, and Time', in M. Gold and P. Toohey (eds), *Inventing Ancient Culture* (London and New York, 1997), pp. 60–62; Wack, *Lovesickness*, pp. 3–30.

12. *The Bible and Holy Scriptures* (Geneva), Ecclesiasticus 28.1, f. 438[v]; William Bullein, *The Government of Health* (London, 1595), p. 3. Also St Augustine, *Confessions*, trans. W. Watt (London, 1631), p. 572; A. Du Laurens, *A Discourse of the Preservation of the Sight*, trans. R. Surphlet (London, 1599); Lain Entralgo, *Mind and Body*, pp. 70–85; H. J. Cook, 'The New Philosophy and Medicine in Seventeenth-Century England', in D. C. Lindberg and R. S. Westmen (eds), *Reappraisals of the Scientific Revolution* (Cambridge, 1990), pp. 406–7.

13. Jacquart and Thomasset, *Sexuality*, pp. 82–4, 130–32; M. R. McVaugh, *Medicine Before the Plague* (Cambridge, 1993), pp. 200–201, 232; J. Starobinski, 'The Natural and Literary History of Bodily Sensation', in Feher et al., *Fragments*, pt 2, pp. 354–6; Wack, *Lovesickness*, pp. 90–93.

14. Arnaldi Villanovani, *De amore heroico*, in *Opera Omnia* (Basileae, 1585), pp. 1523–30; and in *Praxis Medicinalis* (Lugdini, 1586), pp. 197–200. Cadden, *Meanings of Sex Difference*, pp. 138–40; Couliano, *Eros and Magic*, pp. 18–21; D. Jacquart and C. Thomasset, 'L'amour "héroique" à travers le traité d'Arnaud de Villeneuve', in Céard, *La folie*, pp. 143–5; Wack, *Lovesickness*, pp. 31–108.

15. Bartholomeus Anglicus, *De Proprietibus Rerum*, trans. and ed. S. Batman (London, 1582), ff. 88ᵛ–89; Couliano, *Eros*, p. 38; W. F. Kümmel, *Musik und Medizin: Ihre Wechselbeziehungen in Theorie und Praxis von 800 bis 1800* (Freiburg and Munich, 1977), pp. 277–87, 307–10; Theophrastus von Hohenheim (Paracelsus), *The Diseases That Deprive Man of His Reason* (1567), trans. G. Zilboorg, in Paracelsus, *Four Treatises* (Baltimore, 1941; repr. 1996), pp. 156–7; J. Pigeaud, 'Reflections on Love-Melancholy in Robert Burton', in D. Beecher and M. Ciavolella (eds), *Eros and Anteros: The Medical Traditions of Love in the Renaissance* (Ottawa, 1992), p. 228.

16. T. Buoni, *Problems of Beawtie and All Humane Affections*, trans. S. L[ennard] (London, 1606), pp. 21 and 51; Du Laurens, *Discourse*, p. 118; R. Harvey, *The Inward Wits: Psychological Theory in the Middle Ages and Renaissance* (London, 1975), pp. 1–61; Thomas Hobbes, *Elements of Philosophy* (London, 1656), p. 299; L. Vinge, *The Five Senses: Studies in a Literary Tradition* (Lund, 1975), p. 74; T. Wright *The Passions of the Minde in Generall* (London, 1604), p. 168.

17. On the causes and progress of lovesickness, see D. A. Beecher, 'Quottrocento Views on the Eroticization of the Imagination', in Beecher and Ciavolella, *Eros and Anteros*, pp. 53–7; Cadden, *Meanings of Sex Difference*, pp. 139–40; Ciavolella, 'Eros and the Phantasms of *Hereos*', pp. 77–84; Jacquart and Thomasset, 'L'amour "héroique"', pp. 145–50; Wack, *Lovesickness*, pp. 90–98.

18. See, for example, M. F. Wack, 'From Mental Faculties to Magic Philters: The Entry of Magic into Academic Writings on Lovesickness, 13th–17th Centuries', and J. Céard, 'The Devil and Lovesickness: Views of 16th Century Physicians and Demonologists', both in Beecher and Ciavolella, *Eros and Anteros*, pp. 9–32 and 33–48; Ferrand, *Erotomania*, p. 192; Godfridus, *Booke of Astronomye* (London, n.d.), sig. F2; Ferrand, *Erotomania*, p. 192.

19. Ferrand, *Erotomania*, pp. 276–8. Also Couliano, *Eros*, pp. 18–21; Jacquart and Thomasset, *Sexuality*, pp. 85, 118. The motto, 'amoris vulnus ...', derives from Publilius Syrus, *Sententiae*, A31: 'amoris vulnus idem sanat qui facit'.

20. Spenser, *Things Old and New*, pp. 409–10; Jacquart and Thomasset, *Sexuality*, p. 150.

21. On the contrasting conditions of courtly love and ecstatic longing for God in the Middle Ages and early modern era, see P. R. Breggin, 'Sex and Love: Sexual Dysfunction as a Spiritual Disorder', in E. L. Shelp (ed.), *Sexuality and Medicine*, vol. 1 (Dordrecht, Boston, Lancaster and Tokyo, 1987), pp. 258–9; Couliano, *Eros*, pp. 18–19, 38–9, 50–51; Jacquart and Thomasset, *Sexuality*, p. 94; Kristeva, *Black Sun*, pp. 5–6, 8; T. A. Perry, *Erotic Spirituality: The Integrative Tradition from Leone Ebreo to John Donne* (University, AL, 1980), pp. 1–3; de Rougement, *Love*, pp. 50–55, 61–70, 168; Wack, *Lovesickness*, p. 21.

22. See L. Babb, *The Elizabethan Malady* (East Lansing, MI, 1951), pp. 131, 137–40; Du Laurens, *Discourse*, p. 123; Wack, *Lovesickness*, pp. xii, 27–30.

23. McVaugh, *Medicine Before the Plague*, p. 232.

24. Johann Theodor de Bry and Johann Israel de Bry, *Emblemata Saecularia* (Frankfurt, 1606).

25. L. P. Austern, '"Alluring the Auditorie to Effeminacy": Music and the Idea of the Feminine in Early Modern England', *Music and Letters*, 74 (1993), pp. 347–8; R. Monelle, 'Passion and Music', *Musical Praxis*, 1 (1994), pp. 9–12.

26. G. L. Finney, 'Music, Mirth and the Galenic Tradition in England', in J. A. Mazzeo (ed.), *Reason and the Imagination: Studies in the History of Ideas, 1600–1800* (London, 1962), p. 143; J. Hollander, *The Untuning of the Sky: Ideas of Music in English Poetry* (Princeton, 1961), pp. 20–161; S. K. Heninger, *Touches of Sweet Harmony: Pythagorean Cosmology and Renaissance Poetics* (San Marino, CA, 1974), pp. 46, 97–103; A. E. Moyer, *Musica Scientia: Musical Scholarship in the Italian Renaissance* (Ithaca, 1992), pp. 139–58. J. C. Kassler, *Inner Music: Hobbes, Hooke and North on Internal Character* (London, 1995), pp. 1–48. See also West, Chapter 2; and Jones, Chapter 6.

27. Kassler, 'Apollo and Dionysus: Music Theory and the Western Tradition of Epistemology', in E. Strainchamps and M. R. Maniates (eds), *Music and Civilization* (New York and London, 1984), p. 459; Kassler, 'Music as a Model in Early Science', *History of Science*, 20 (1982), pp. 126–7; S. McAdams, 'Music: A Science of the Mind?', *Contemporary Music Review*, 2 (1987), pp. 4–5; C. Palisca, *Humanism in Italian Renaissance Musical Thought* (New Haven, 1985), pp. 17–50.

28. St Augustine, *Preclarissima et inestimabilis doctrine atq[ue] utilitatis divi Aurelii Augustini sermonu[m] opera* (Paris, 1520), Sermon 256, f. 348. See also St Augustine, *Confessions*, trans. S. T. M. (Paris, 1638), bk 20, ch. 33, pp. 413–15; N. Breton, *A Solemne Passion of the Soules Love* (London, 1598), sigs B4–B4ᵛ; G. L. Finney, *Musical Backgrounds for English Literature, 1580–1650* (New Brunswick, NJ, 1962), pp. 47–75; Hollander, *Untuning*, pp. 250–65.

29. N. C. Carpenter, *Music in the Medieval and Renaissance Universities* (Norman, OK, 1958), pp. 115, 127; M. P. Cosman, 'Machaut's Medical Musical World', in M. P. Cosman and B. Chandler (eds), *Machaut's World: Science and Art in the Fourteenth Century*, Annals

of the New York Academy of Sciences, 314 (New York, 1978), p. 4; S. Howell, 'Medical Astrologers and the Invention of Stringed Keyboard Instruments', *The Journal of Musicological Research*, 10 (1990), p. 3.

30. T. Robinson, *The Schoole of Musicke* (London, 1603), sig. B.

31. See Carpenter, *Music in the ... Universities*, pp. 115–16, 313–17; T. Cogan, *The Haven of Health* (London, 1596), pp. 20–21; M. Pelling and C. Webster, 'Medical Practitioners', in C. Webster (ed.), *Health, Medicine and Mortality in the Sixteenth Century* (Cambridge, 1979), p. 193; D. C. Price, *Patrons and Musicians of the English Renaissance* (Cambridge, 1981), pp. 19–27.

32. See J. Case, *Apologia Musices* (Oxford, 1588); Price, *Patrons and Musicians*, pp. 25–6. The physician, poet, and composer Thomas Campion signs himself as 'T. Campion, Doctor in Physicke' at the end of his dedicatory verse 'to the worthy author' in A. Ferrabosco, *Ayres* (London, 1609).

33. M. Pelling, 'Occupational Diversity: Barbersurgeons and the Trades of Norwich, 1550–1640', *Bulletin of the History of Medicine*, 56 (1982), pp. 504–5.

34. Virgil, *Georgicks*, trans. T. May (London, 1628), bk 4, pp. 133, 135–6.

35. Ovid, *Libri de arte amandi et de remedio amoris* (Tusculani, 1526), Liber Secundus, f. 54.

36. See Arnald of Villanova, *De Amore Heroico*, in *Opera Omnia*, p. 1530; and *De Amoris Heroici* in *Praxis Medicinalis*, p. 200; N. Guidobaldi, 'Images of Music in Cesare Ripa's *Iconologia*', *Imago Musicae*, 7 (1990), p. 46; C. Burnett, 'European Knowledge of Arabic Texts Referring to Music: Some New Material', *Early Music History*, 12 (1993), pp. 3–5; Kümmel, *Musik und Medizin*, pp. 307–12; Wack, *Lovesickness*, pp. 45–6.

37. Arnald of Villanova, *Opera Omnia*, p. 1530; and *Praxis Medicinalis*, p. 200; McVaugh, *Medicine before the Plague*, p. 232.

38. E. Carleris and J. Tinctoris, *On the Dignity and the Effects of Music*, ed. and trans. R. Strohm and J. D. Cullington, Institute of Advanced Musical Studies, King's College London, Study texts no. 2 (1996), p. 59. See also Burton, *The Anatomy of Melancholy*, pt 3, sect. 2, mem. 2, subs. 4, pp. 488–9, which cites some of the same sources as Tinctoris, in addition to many others on the same theme; J. Gagné, 'L'Érotisme dans la musique médiévale', in B. Roy (ed.), *L'Érotisme au moyen age* (Montreal, 1977), p. 89; and Ovid, *De Arte Amandi or the Art of Love* (Amsterdam [c. 1625]), pp. 78–9.

39. B. Castiglione, *The Courtyer*, trans. T. Hoby (London, 1561), sig. J2.

40. See *The Arte of English Poesie* (London, 1589), pp. 40–43; Cosman, 'Machaut's ... World', p. 22; G. Sissa, 'Subtle Bodies', in Feher et al., *Fragments*, pt 3, pp. 143–4.

41. See R. D. Leppert, *The Theme of Music in Flemish Painting of the Seventeenth Century* (Munich and Salzburg, 1977), vol. 1, pp. 134–7; P. F. Watson, *The Garden of Love in Tuscan Art of the Early Renaissance* (Philadelphia and London, 1979), pp. 66–9.

42. Cosman, 'Machaut's ... World', pp. 13–16.

43. G. Boccaccio, *The Book of Theseus/Teseida delle nozze d'Emilia*, trans. B. M. McCoy (New York, 1974), p. 200.

44. Burton, *The Anatomy of Melancholy*, pt 2, sect. 2, mem. 6, subs. 3, pp. 296–7.

45. Burton, *The Anatomy of Melancholy*, pt 3, sect. 2, mem. 3, subs. 1, p. 540.

46. D. Freedberg, *The Power of Images* (Chicago and London, 1989) pp. 1–26, 429–40.

47. I. F. Finlay, 'Musical Instruments in Seventeenth-Century Dutch Paintings', *Galpin Society Journal*, 6 (1953), pp. 52–69; P. Fischer, *Music in Paintings of the Low Countries in the Sixteenth and Seventeenth Centuries*, Sonorum Speculum, 50/51 (Amsterdam, 1972), pp. 102–14; R. Goffen, *Titian's Women* (New Haven, 1997), pp. 159–69, 278–9; R. Leppert, 'Concert in a House: Musical Iconography and Musical Thought', *Early Music*, 7 (1979), pp. 6–8; A. P. de Mirimonde, 'La musique dans les allégories de l'Amour: I – Vénus', 'II – Eros', *Gazette des Beaux-Arts*, 68 (1966), pp. 265–90; 69 (1967), pp. 319–46; and 'Les sujets musicaux chez Vermeer de Delft', *Gazette des Beaux-Arts*, 57 (1961), pp. 41–4.

48. See Leppert, *The Theme of Music*, vol. 1, p. 80.

49. Burton, *The Anatomy of Melancholy*, pt 3, sect. 2, mem. 2, subs. 4, p. 488.

50. *The Burwell Lute Tutor*, intro. R. Spencer (Leeds, 1974), ff. 43ᵛ–44.

51. Jacquart and Thomasset, *Sexuality*, pp. 152–3. Early modern writers complained that young single women who learned music as an enhancement of desirability, at great cost to their parents, tended to put their instruments aside upon marriage: Austern, '"Sing Againe Syren": The Female Musician and Sexual Enchantment in Elizabethan Life and Literature', *Renaissance Quarterly*, 42 (1989), pp. 430–31.

52. G. Hellwig, *Joachim Tielke: Ein Hamburger Lauten- und Violenmacher der Barockzeit* (Frankfurt, 1980), pp. 100–117; L. Libin, 'A Musical Instrument from the Irwin Untermyer Collection', in J. Rasmussen (ed.), *Studien zum Europäischen Kunsthandwerk* (Munich, 1983), pp. 68–9; Watson, *The Garden of Love*, pp. 38–40.

53. E. De Johng, 'Erotica in Vogelperspectief', *Simiolus*, 3 (1968–69), pp. 41–3; Gagné, 'L'Érotisme dans la musique', pp. 89–102; also Howell, 'Medical Astrologers', pp. 4–13.

54. D. H. Boalch, *Makers of the Harpsichord and Clavichord 1440–1840*, 3rd edn, by C. Mould (Oxford, 1995), pp. 215–690; T. McGeary, 'Harpsichord Decoration: A Reflection of Renaissance Ideas about Music', *Explorations in Renaissance Culture*, 6 (1980), pp. 5–6; McGeary, 'Harpsichord Mottoes', *Journal of the American Musical Instrument Society*, 7 (1981), pp. 18–35.

55. *The Arte of English Poesie*, p. 70; G. O'Brien, *Ruckers: A Harpsichord and Virginal Building Tradition* (Cambridge, 1990), pp. 145–6.

56. Buoni, *Problems of Beawtie*, pp. 113–114.

57. Buoni, *Problems of Beawtie*, pp. 130–31.

58. See Pliny, *The Historie of the World*, trans. P. Holland (London, 1601), pp. 79–80; P. Taylor, *Dutch Flower Painting 1600–1720* (New Haven and London, 1995), p. 76.

59. See, for example, Bartholomeus, *De Proprietatibus rerum*, ff. 314^v–315, 331; J. Gerarde, *The Herball or Generall Historie of Plantes*, enlarged and amended by T. Johnson (London, 1633), pp. 590, 597, 741, 852–3, 855, 998–9, 1259, 1263–4; Pliny, *The Historie of the World*, pp. 102–3; Taylor, *Dutch Flower Painting*, pp. 56–8, 60–68, and 72.

60. Leppert, *The Theme of Music*, vol. 1, pp. 73–106; McGeary, 'Harpsichord Mottoes', pp. 18–35; Taylor, *Dutch Flower Painting*, pp. 43–55.

61. Bartholomeus, *De Proprietatibus rerum*, f. 380^v; Pliny, *The Historie of the World*, pp. 324–5; E. Topsell, *The Historie of Serpents* (London, 1608), p. 230.

62. Bartholomeus, *De Proprietatibus rerum*, f. 380^v.

63. See H. Grube, *On the Sting of the Tarantula, and its Cure by Music*, in E. Goldsmid (ed.), *Un-Natural History, or Myths of Natural Science* (Edinburgh, 1886), vol. 3, p. 72; C. Ripa, *Nova Iconologia* (Padua, 1618), pp. 287–8.

64. J. Hilton (ed.), *Catch that Catch Can* (London, 1652), frontispiece, sig. A3, and p. 25; Pelling, 'Occupational Diversity', pp. 504–5; Pelling, 'Compromised by Gender: The Role of the Male Medical Practitioner in Early Modern England', in Marland and Pelling, *The Task of Healing*, pp. 116–17.

65. *The Catch Club or Merry Companions* (London [1733]), p. 4; J. Playford (ed.), *Catch that Catch Can: or the Second Part of the Musical Companion* (London, 1685); F. B. Zimmerman, *Henry Purcell 1659–1695: An Analytical Catalogue of His Music* (New York, 1963), pp. 125, 484, 531.

66. I wish to thank the American Council of Learned Societies and the National Endowment for the Humanities, whose funding enabled the successful completion of this project; and Faye Getz, Paul Taylor, and Margaret Pelling for drawing my attention to relevant scholarly works.

PART IV

Tarantism

Commentary on Part IV,
with a Note on the Origins of Tarantism

Peregrine Horden

The cult of the tarantula spider in southern Italy, a cult that has involved music and dancing to cure the spider's bite, is the most superficially reassuring aspect of the history of music therapy because it has been so long-lasting. Few outline sketches of the subject fail to mention it. Not least because of Ernesto De Martino's magisterial ethnography (of which we shall learn much more below) it has a permanent place in the modern scholarship of the subject.[1] Between the music therapy of, say, Pythagoras and Juliette Alvin there falls a gulf (see Horden, Chapter 1). But between the seventeenth- and the twenty-first-century practitioners of this particular form of musical healing, there are demonstrable connections. Today's vestiges apparently reveal yesterday's full-blown activity.[2] A young man who was bitten by a spider in 1996, and who was urged to dance by older family members, seems to reanimate for us an otherwise obscure corner of the early modern world. Such continuity, visible across the last few centuries, moreover fosters the temptation to look for archaic origins, and to extend the continuity much further back into the past. This book sets out to examine all such presumed continuities critically. So it devotes as much space to tarantism – a decidedly regional and marginal phenomenon in terms of the overall profile of its topic – as to the major fields of the Middle Ages or the Renaissance.

Tarantism is a reassuring subject not only because of its longevity but because it seems so definite, so tangibly real.[3] This is what struck Renaissance commentators on it, from Ficino onwards. They invoked tarantism to demonstrate that, in their own time, there could be musical healing to rival antiquity's legendary feats.[4] It was their one 'modern' success story, and when they come to it in their texts after paragraphs of sub-Boethian cliché, their pleasure and enthusiasm are palpable. How can we blame them? After all, tarantula spiders exist, and some of them are extremely dangerous. This curative response to them is geographically definite – southern Italy is the centre, even though variants can be found elsewhere.[5] Still better, from within that area, historians of tarantism have actual case histories to study. Gentilcore adds for the first time, to the Italian dossier of indirectly reported cases, one that reaches us – with only a little help from the Inquisition – in the victim's own words; and, as we shall see, there are over fifty cases from eighteenth-century Spain. Nowadays, too, videos are available of Italian women dancing away their poison to the accompaniment of an equally real musical genre, the tarantella.

Alas, little of this 'reality' survives further analysis. First, as some Renaissance physicians sensed quite early on, the spider's symbolism is more potent than its bite (see Gentilcore, Chapter 11; and Lüdtke, Chapter 13). We are dealing with a culture-bound syndrome, or folk illness;[6] with social and psychological 'poisoning' rather than a biological threat; with a performance that is learnt rather than a cure that is administered. Nor is the geography of the subject as narrow as had often been thought. Here, for the first time in English, is a thorough discussion of the eighteenth-century Spanish material, astonishing for its quantity and clinical precision, both hitherto scarcely recognized. (Spanish evidence also offers a striking contrast with Italy: in Spain, the learned medical establishment seems on the whole to have accepted the spider's bite as the genuine cause of the affliction.) Also in what follows, for the first time anywhere, is a discussion that moves well beyond De Martino's classic ethnography and looks systematically at the multiple contemporary reinterpretations and recreations of the cult. Combining fieldwork and 'library work', Lüdtke shows that there can be no simple account of the decline and disappearance of the cult, or of the connections between *nuovi* and 'old' *tarantati*.

Quite generally, indeed, the continuities involved turn out to be have been far from straightforward. Obvious connections between periods and places may have as much to do with the literature of the subject as with local culture in the broader sense. Why does tarantism spread from Italy to Spain and take root there with such rapidity? Because of the translation of a book, it seems – a book by Giorgio Baglivi. Why, for that matter, is it possible to recover a well-documented, protracted, and in many respects classic case of tarantism from Rhode Island in the early 1800s? Because of the English translation of the same book, an article in the *New York Magazine* of 1797, and the physician's unwitting power of suggestion.[7] Why does modern neo-tarantism take the forms it does? Again, mainly, because of the indirect influence of De Martino. The very designation *nuovi tarantati* was coined by university professors.

Tarantism is an 'over-determined' phenomenon, a mutable complex of many different elements – literary, musical, medical, social, psychological. For each aspect of it numerous partial analogues can therefore be found.[8] Its possible sources in the past are equally numerous. That is why there have been so many conjectures as to its origin.[9] Yet these, in their sheer variety, coupled with their frequent compatibility with one another, show how improbable it is that the phenomenon actually had a discrete origin. Doubtless there is a later medieval background which needs to be uncovered. But is it any more than background? The earliest medical reference to something like tarantism reminds us that we do not necessarily have to look far for learned explanations of its musical component. Music therapy for a spider bite is no more improbable than a musical remedy for plague,[10] or for any serious disease upon which the passions of the soul, as moderated by music, can in theory have a beneficial effect.

In a treatise on poisons probably addressed to Pope Urban V (who reigned from 1362 to 1370), a Paduan physician called William of Marra asserts that the tarantula's venom engenders melancholy in the victim, and for this rejoicing is the best antidote. The vulgar and ignorant, he adds, say that the tarantula sings when it bites (which does not seem to be an explicit part of the insect's modern folklore) so that music similar to that singing helps relieve the patient. William rejects this account. He prefers to think that the joy inspired by the music attracts the noxious humours within the body to its periphery, thus preventing the poison from entering the vitals.[11] Of course there is no mention of dancing in his treatise, which is why students of tarantism have had to seek a precedent for that aspect elsewhere, for instance in the dancing epidemics associated with St Vitus that broke out sporadically in northern Europe of the thirteenth and fourteenth centuries. Yet these are somewhat remote in time and place from fifteenth-century Apulia and hardly explain the specific character of the Italian tarantula cult.[12]

Still bolder comparisons have often been essayed between tarantism and various cults of ancient Greece – Dionysiac, Corybantic, Orphic – as if some partial similarities, together with the fact that southern Italy was once part of Magna Graecia, were sufficient evidence of continuity.[13] Undeterred, the ethnographer Marius Schneider has offered a yet more extreme version of this approach. He apparently regards tarantism as a survival of a ritual dating from the time of the megaliths.[14]

To all such theories the blunt rejoinder is that ancient cults do not survive in this way for many centuries. Even if they have been forced 'underground' they should, if they exist, still break surface occasionally in the medieval evidence; and they do not. For example: when Norman troops invading Sicily in the 1060s were beset with an epidemic of tarantula bites outside Palermo, the chief symptom, according to their chronicler Gioffredo Malaterra, was not dance-like agitation but excessive flatulence; and the chief remedy, before the army simply decamped to a safer locale, was hot compresses, not musical exorcism.[15] All this, note, took place in former Magna Graecia, and the details are given by a monk who had lived in Apulia since adolescence. Yet he seemingly knows nothing of the 'vulgar' beliefs reported by William of Marra.

It is for its failure to reckon with such counter-examples, as well as for its inherent implausibility, that the 'survivalist' argument has, on the whole, rightly been consigned to the dustbin of historiography.[16] Not even its most sensible and scholarly exponent of recent decades, Carlo Ginzburg, could restore its credibility. His subject is the *benandanti*, members of a sixteenth-century agrarian fertility cult, which had a modest musical component,[17] and which was practised in the Friuli to the north-east of Venice. Not only has Ginzburg suggested that the cult members' out-of-body nocturnal battles against witches for the security of the harvest provided the actual popular counterpart of the fantasy of the Sabbath. He has also attempted to trace the history of such soul-journeys directly back to archaic Asian shamanism.[18] It is an attempt that inspires admiration and scepticism in equal measure: the parallels drawn are too loose, the purported channels of transmission too elusive. And if Ginzburg cannot carry conviction on this millennial scale, then it is tempting to suppose that no one can. Rather than search the mists of time, we should reckon with the possibility that new healing cults, tarantism included, can develop quickly; unconnected elements can quite suddenly coalesce. This has been shown convincingly with respect to a type of therapy that first flourished in the early modern period and is not so far removed from tarantism: that of the *pauliani*, healers of the victims of snakebite.[19] Tarantism may not have had a much of a prehistory before it emerges into the light of fourteenth-century evidence. Hence there is no chapter below on 'tarantism before the Renaissance'.

Notes

1. *La terra del rimorso: contributo a una storia religiosa del sud* (Milan, 1961). The classic historical essay has been H. E. Sigerist, 'The Story of Tarantism', in D. M. Schullian and M. Schoen (eds), *Music and Medicine* (New York, 1948), pp. 96–116, repr. from Sigerist, *Civilization and Disease* (Ithaca, NY, 1944), ch. 11. Tarantism is referred to in the present volume by Gouk, Austern and Howard, as well as by the authors in Part IV.

2. Thus G. Tomlinson uses De Martino extensively in *Music in Renaissance Magic: Toward a Historiography of Others* (Chicago and London, 1993), pp. 157–70.

3. It has also added to English the pleasing word 'tarantulated': Matthew Green, *The Spleen* (1737), ll. 141 ff.

4. Daniel Sennert, *Practica medicina* (1625), I.2.17, in *Opera Omnia* (Paris, 1641); Gioseffo Zarlino, *Istitutio harmoniche*, I.2, in O. Strunk (ed.) revised L. Treitler, *Source Readings in Music History* (New York and London, 1998).

5. De Martino, *La terra del rimorso*, p. 196.

6. For brief introduction see G. M. Foster and B. G. Anderson, *Medical Anthropology* (New York, 1978), pp. 96–100; B. J. Good, *Medicine, Rationality, and Experience* (Cambridge, 1994), pp. 174–5.

7. E. T. Carlson and M. B. Simpson, 'Tarantism or hysteria? An American case of 1801', *Journal of the History of Medicine and Allied Sciences*, 26 (1971), pp. 293–302.

8. P. Burke, *The Historical Anthropology of Early Modern Italy* (Cambridge, 1987), ch. 11, esp. pp. 213–16. Compare G. Levi, *Inheriting Power: The Story of an Exorcist* (Chicago and London, 1988), pp. 4, 6, 18, for a priest in 1690s Piedmont whose skill as a violinist provided a postlude to exorcism.

9. Surveyed in Lüdtke's forthcoming DPhil thesis, for a foretaste of which I am much indebted to her.

10. See Horden, Chapter 1; and Jones, Chapter 6.

11. L. Thorndike, *A History of Magic and Experimental Science*, 8 vols (New York, 1923–58), 3.526–7, 534, discussing *Sertum papale de venenis* [*Papal Garland Concerning Poisons*], Biblioteca Vaticana, MS Barberini 306, pp. 146–7.

12. De Martino, *La terra del rimorso*, pp. 228–41. C. W. Hughes, 'Rhythm and Health', in Schullian and Schoen, *Music and Medicine*, pp. 174–6. Contrast G. Mora, 'An Historical and Sociopsychiatric Appraisal of Tarantism and its Importance in the Tradition of Psychotherapy of Mental Disorders', *Bulletin of the History of Medicine*, 34 (1963), p. 420.

13. Sigerist, 'Story of Tarantism', pp. 113–14; Tomlinson, *Music in Renaissance Magic*, p. 162; G. Di Mitri, 'Le radici orfiche e l'innesto paolino sul tronco del tarantismo', in M. Paone (ed.), *Scritti di storia pugliese* (Galatina, 1996), pp. 11–28.

14. 'Tarantella', *Die Musik in Geschichte und Gegenwart: Allgemeine Enzyklopädie der Musik*, ed. F. Blume, vol. 13 (Kassel, 1966), cols 118–19; J. Godwin, *Harmonies of Heaven and Earth: The Spiritual Dimension of Music from Antiquity to the Avant-Garde* (London, 1987), p. 35.

15. *Historia sicula (De rebus gestis Rogerii Calabriae et Siciliae comitis ...)*, II.36, in L. A. Muratori (ed.), *Rerum Italicarum Scriptores*, vol. 5 (Milan, 1724), p. 570. De Martino, *La terra del rimorso*, p. 229.

16. See J. de Pina-Cabral, 'The gods of the Gentiles are demons: the problem of pagan survivals in European culture', in K. Hastrup (ed.), *Other Histories* (London and New York, 1992), pp. 45–61.

17. Tomlinson, *Music in Renaissance Magic*, p. 156.

18. *The Night Battles: Witchcraft and Agrarian Cults in the Sixteenth and Seventeenth Centuries* (London, 1983); *Ecstasies: Deciphering the Witches' Sabbath* (London, 1990).

19. I am indebted here to K. Park, 'Country Medicine in the Urban Piazza: Snakehandlers and Other Itinerants', paper delivered to the Wellcome Symposium for the History of Medicine, 'Medicine in the Renaissance City', London, 26 March 1999, publication forthcoming. See also D. Gentilcore, *Healers and Healing in Early Modern Italy* (Manchester, 1998), pp. 106–9.

CHAPTER ELEVEN

Ritualized Illness and Music Therapy: Views of Tarantism in the Kingdom of Naples

David Gentilcore

I

In March 1723 an eighteen-year-old farmhand named Francesco Malagnino appeared before the episcopal court of Oria to confess magical practices. Malagnino had sought the hand of a certain Apollonia, but when she turned him down for another man, he decided that only a love-philtre would bring her back. He went to a local *magaro* [cunning man] named Angelo, a guard at the Oria castle. Angelo told him to burn three bones of a dead man and tie the ash into a cloth which was to be thrown into a well, whilst pronouncing the following words:

> Diavolo io ti dò questa polve
> e tu dammi Apollonia per moglie
> E dammila proprio che ti voglio per compare
> E ti dò una coccia di sangue.
>
> [Devil, I give you this powder
> And you give me Apollinia as my wife
> And give me her truly, because I want you as godfather
> And I give you a drop of blood.][1]

The spell is more in the sphere of learned than popular magic; but, in any case, Malagnino was unable to perform it. He had been bitten by a tarantula spider in the meantime and, as he told the court, 'having done many dances to get better, I was ill for more than a month, during which time the said Apollonia got married'. But his problems were not over. While working at a local estate he confided in the steward, who said the magic was no good thing and persuaded Malagnino not to perform it. It is not clear whether this was before or after he performed the tarantism ritual. In any case, several days later, Malagnino was visited in the fields by a young woman he had never seen before. She asked him if he was married and if he knew about carnal pleasures 'and many other dirty things'. He replied that he was not married, but would not have anything to do with a woman who talked in such a way, and warned her that the other field-hands would have seen them. He took it as a vision of the devil.

The woman appeared a second time, several weeks later. The third time, during September, she appeared at night while he was sleeping at the estate. She began 'playing about with her hands' and he started touching her, with the result that he committed 'a sin of pollution' (without having carnal relations, he specifies). She visited him a fourth time and, while 'playing' with him, asked him if he 'wanted to know some woman carnally', since she could arrange it, if he gave his soul to the devil. He consented to this, so she pricked his little finger and wrote the pact with the devil in blood. She instructed him that when he took communion he should not swallow the host, but keep it. Then she disappeared. Not many days later he was on an errand when a young woman appeared before him and asked him if he wanted to know her carnally. But, despite his pact, he seems to have had enough, and he shouted, 'Madonna del Carmine, help me!' After which, he immediately heard a voice saying, 'leave him alone, he's a poor boy'.

This document is noteworthy because it provides us with the only first-hand account we have of tarantism during the early modern period. Admittedly it is only a brief reference and we need to refer to the abundant secondary literature of the period, and of more recent studies, to supply the socio-cultural context. Briefly, tarantism was – and, to a lesser extent, still is (see Lüdtke, Chapter 13) – a structured and ritualized response to deep psychological malaise, which included the evocation and discharge of the crisis by traditional forms of music and dance.[2] The typical case scenario is that of a man or woman falling into a deep depression, triggered by some social occurrence with which the individual cannot cope, but identified in this culture as being caused by the bite of the tarantula spider. Once the malady is thus identified, the sufferer proceeds to the only remedy regarded as efficacious: that of the dance, and the ritual paraphernalia associated with

it, which continues publicly for days on end, till the sufferer pronounces himself cured. The dances are repeated every year on the
anniversary of the 'bite'.

This study will examine the role of tarantism in the kingdom of
Naples during the early modern period, in particular at its historical
centre in the 'heel of the boot', then the province of Terra d'Otranto
(see Figure 11.1). Malagnino's testimony will be compared to the differing literary, medical and ecclesiastical descriptions of the phenomenon during the period. As we shall see, none of these approaches
was adequate to understand and account for a phenomenon existing
outside the medico-religious categories of the period. Medical anthropologists of the present use the expression 'culture-bound disorder' to
shed light on such maladies, but more on this below.

Although Malagnino tells us nothing in his testimony of the dance
itself, there is enough in the contemporary literature about tarantism to
fill in the gaps, much of it coming from witnesses of the phenomenon.
Nonetheless, we must beware of the factors which conditioned
Malagnino's testimony and, more generally, the limitations of trial
records as a source for ethnohistory. First of all, what made
Malagnino confess his crime – that of going to see the *magaro* Angelo
for a love-philtre – to the episcopal court? One possible response,
which however must remain hypothetical, was that he was troubled by
the erotic nature of his visions and feared that they were due to his
sinful request for a love-philtre. The link between his fears and his
appearance before the court was most likely his confessor, for absolution in confession was often dependent on the denunciation of illicit
magical practices. Such practices were widespread and had been repeatedly condemned by local bishops in their synodal decrees, while
preachers, missioners and confessors attempted to keep them in check.
Synods of the Oria diocese (to say nothing of the decrees included in
the pastoral visitations) beginning from 1641 stressed that all acts of
witchcraft, sorcery, incantations, and so on were to be denounced before the bishop or his vicar-general and that priests were to preach
this message frequently to their congregations. At the same time, penance for such crimes was light, when repentance was shown.[3]

There is thus the possibility that Malagnino's confession – and the
way he interpreted the events which had befallen him – had already

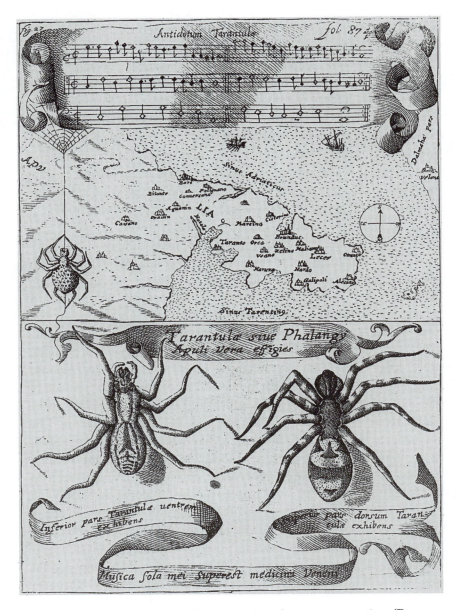

11.1   Athanasius Kircher, *Magnes sive de arte magnetica* (Rome, 1641), facing p. 874.

been conditioned before it reached the ears of the bishop. Despite these limitations, it is still useful to adopt Malagnino's confession as a starting point for a discussion of contemporary views about it, since it is the closest we can come to a direct, clinical example of tarantism. How does his case fit in with other descriptions? A late seventeenth-century study of tarantism offers a good description of the dance, picking up where Malagnino leaves off. The passage describes the moment after the bite, when the resulting melancholy and stupor is interrupted by the dance:

> Those who are bitten by the tarantula, shortly afterwards fall to the ground half dead, with a loss of their strength and senses, their breathing at times difficult, at times tormented; often [they are] immobile and lifeless. Once the music has started, little by little these symptoms diminish, and the patient begins to move his fingers, hands and then feet, followed by the other limbs. With the swift repetition of the musical rhythm the movement of the limbs increases by degrees. If the patient is lying on the ground, he gets to his feet, begins the dance, sighs and contorts himself in very strange ways. These first dances are prolonged for several hours, often two or three. After he has rested in bed for a bit to cleanse the sweat and restore his strength, he takes up the dance again with the same vigour, which happens a dozen times during the day ... These dances usually continue for four days, rarely for more than six. Their end is uncertain, since many [tarantati] continue dancing till they feel free of the symptoms, which usually takes place after the third or fourth day.[4]

The dancing was in fact part of an elaborate ritual that included a rope suspended from a tree, from which the tarantato (as the sufferer was called) imitated a spider hanging from its web. At times, the dancer would brandish a sword, perhaps symbolizing the bite; or, he or she would hold up a hand mirror, using it to direct their motions. Groups of tarantati would often assemble together, in town squares or in fields, undergoing the curative dance together. This would take place before an audience of musicians, concerned relatives, and townsfolk, including, according to one writer, 'gangs of youths in search of fun and laughs'.[5]

Descriptions of tarantism abound from the Renaissance onwards, as does the debate over the spider and its bite, and the precise role of the musical treatment. The Neapolitan humanist Giovanni Pontano highlighted the phenomenon's erotic content. In his satirical dialogue *Antonius* of 1491 one of his characters notes the opinion of the recently deceased Antonius (Antonio Beccadelli, alias Panormita), who believed that Apulians were the happiest of all mortals, favoured by God. He justifies the opinion thus:

> In truth, because other men, being all of them foolish [*stulti*], can barely advance a sufficiently convincing explanation to account for their foolishness. Whereas only the Apulians have a good and ready excuse to justify their insanity, attributing its cause to the spider they call the tarantula, the bite of which causes men to go mad. And this constitutes their greatest happiness, since, if someone wanted to, he could obtain – quite licitly – the desired fruit of his madness. There are, in fact, spiders of various poisons, even those capable of inciting lustfulness, which are called concubine keepers [*concubitarios*]. Women are wont very often to be bitten by this spider; and then, since the poison cannot be extinguished in any other way, it is licit for them to unite with men, freely and with impunity. In this way what for others would be a shameful act [*flagitium*], for Apulian women is a remedy. Does this not perhaps seem the greatest happiness to you?[6]

Although he speaks of the custom with apparent relish and envy, Pontano manages to bestow upon it an internal rationality and coherence. The sexual maliciousness of the humanist thinly cloaks the authentic role of tarantism in discharging crisis. What links Pontano with later writing on tarantism is the belief that the symptoms were the result of a real spider bite. It was this symbiotic relationship between tarantism and actual spider bites that formed the focus of debate, in the context of *de venenis* literature: writing on poisons, including the bites of venomous animals, and their antidotes. From this point on, cultural interest in tarantism moves in two essentially different directions, one after the other: musicological and medical.

II

Renaissance writers were the first to make the link between tarantism and the healing power of music. In Book 3 of Marsilio Ficino's treatise on medicine, *Three Books on Life*, first published in 1489 (see Voss, Chapter 7), the humanist physician and natural magician discusses the 'power of words and song for capturing celestial benefits'.

It is in this context of natural–celestial magic that he mentions tarantism, for the healing force of the music and dance associated with it is linked to the stars, particularly Jupiter and the sun.[7] Baldassare Castiglione's *The Book of the Courtier*, completed in 1516 and first published in 1528, brought readers down to earth. The book contains a reference to how music can bring health, by bringing the humour forth and initiating the all-important crisis:

> For, even as they say that in Apulia many musical instruments are used for those who are bitten by the tarantula, and various tunes are tried until the humour which is causing the malady is (through a certain affinity which it has with some one of those tunes) suddenly stirred by the sound of it and so agitates the sick man that he is restored to health by that agitation: so we, whenever we have detected some hidden trace of folly, have stimulated it so artfully and with such a variety of inducements and in so many different ways that finally we have understood what its tendency was; then, having recognized the humour, we agitated it so thoroughly that it was always brought to the perfection of an open folly.[8]

But the work which most fully explored the tarantula spider's bite and the musical 'antidote' was Athanasius Kircher's *Magnes sive de Arte Magnetica*. Kircher was a famed Jesuit collector, natural philosopher and teacher at the Jesuit College in Rome. He has been referred to as the embodiment of the 'exotic and speculative propensities of his age'.[9] The *Magnes* is an eclectic exploration of natural magic, the hidden magnetism of the universe, and the curative effects of music. Kircher devotes four chapters of Book 3 to tarantism, the sufferers' dancing and the music used. Based on the information provided by his two informants 'in the field', missionary priests at the Jesuit colleges of Lecce and Taranto, Kircher concluded that the music and dance of tarantism was the remedy for the real bite of the Apulian tarantula spider.

Like many of his time, Kircher believed in the therapeutic efficacy of music. The renewed interest in the classical world during the Renaissance had led to a revival of Pythagorean and Platonic ideas about music, culminating in the 'iatromusicology' [*iatros* = healer] of the baroque period. Macrocosm and microcosm were intimately interrelated. The four elements (earth, water, air, fire), bodily humours (blood, phlegm, yellow and black bile), and temperaments (sanguine, phlegmatic, choleric and melancholic) were mirrored by the four basic musical modes (Myxolydian, Dorian, Lydian and Phrygian). By virtue of these four modes, music could affect the balance of the humours, and therefore health and disease (see Gouk, Chapter 8). Kircher's iatromusical interpretation was in keeping with the symbolism of tarantism itself, given the centrality of music in the ritual. For this reason, Kircher maintains – and is one of the last to do so – the link between crisis, treatment and cure which tarantism displays to the twentieth-century ethnographer. Kircher provides us with the earliest music and texts of the ritual, as well as detailed descriptions of the dances. He informs us that the *tarantati* will not rise from their stupor and begin the dance until they have seen the colour, either in a cloth or ribbon, which corresponds to the colour of the tarantula believed to have bitten them. Some are attracted by the colour green, others by yellow or red. When the right colour is shown to them, they lunge forward as if to attack it, then they caress it, 'as if they were besieged by an amorous frenzy: mouth agape, arms spread open, eyes tearful, breast heaving. Lastly, they form an amorous embrace with the coloured cloth and seem to simulate a most ardent union, that is to say, an identification with it'.[10]

In the same way, the musical motif to which the *tarantato* chose to dance corresponded to the humour of the tarantula that bit him. As described by Kircher, the music was played using various wind and plucked-string instruments – bagpipes, lyre, guitar, dulcimer, hurdy-gurdy – accompanied by tambourines and drums. Musical motifs tended to contrast low- and high-pitched sounds, and made frequent use of semitones, thought to stimulate the nerves and muscles. As for mode, there was a clear preference for the Phrygian.

True to the context of writing on poisons, music was seen as the 'antidote' to the tarantula's bite. Once the tarantula bite was deemed to be the cause, the musicians were called. It was their responsibility to play a series of motifs and ask the *tarantato* the colour of his tarantula so that the corresponding musical motif could be found and the cure could begin. In the city of Taranto, according to Kircher, these musicians were public functionaries, paid a regular salary to help take the expense of hiring the musicians off the poor.[11]

The erotic content of the ritual is present in the songs, sung in chorus, that accompany the music, where the licentious tarantula bites the victim under her skirts:

> Deu ti muzzicau la tarantella?
> Sotto la pudìa de la vannella
>
> [Where did the tarantula bite you?
> Under the fringe of my dress.][12]

The songs supplied to Kircher by his two informants also contain references to unrequited love, with an erotic undercurrent. The following, in which the musical instrument and its parts are the body and soul of the troubled lover, also serves to demonstrate the importance of the music in tarantism:

> Stu pettu e fattu cimbalu d'amori
> Tasti i sensi mobili e accorti
> Cordi li chianti, suspiri e duluri
> Rosa è lu cori miu feritu a morti
> Strali è lu ferru, chiai sò li miei arduri
> Marteddu è lu pensieru, e la mia sorti
> Mastra e la donna mia, ch'a tutti l'huri
> Cantando canta leta la mia morti.
>
> [This breast has become a harpsichord of love
> Keys, the senses, feeling and ready
> Strings, the tears, sighs and pains
> Sound hole is my heart, mortally wounded
> Rod is a point, my ardours are wounds
> Hammer is my thought and my fate
> Conductor is my lady, who, singing without end
> Joyfully sings my death.][13]

III

A second interpretation of the phenomenon of tarantism, still within the writing on poisons, was more strictly physical, more medical, advanced essentially by practising physicians. Unlike the iatromusical interpretation represented by Kircher, the medical one was not consistent with popular tarantism's own mental orientation. Medical writers sought to reduce tarantism into some sort of simple ailment in order to fit it into the medical categories of the period. Their discussion of tarantism was based upon a clinical description of cases and on a search for the actual *taranta* – the tarantula spider – which for the peasant world seems to have been more mythical than zoological (see Lüdtke, Chapter 13). Since the cause was held to be either the toxic state resulting from a spider bite or a psychic disorder, the other aspects of tarantism, beginning with the musical treatment, became less and less relevant.

The first physician to write on the subject was a fervent supporter of the ritual dances, although he also advocated other more conventional poison antidotes, like theriac and orvietan. In 1621 Epifanio Ferdinando published his study of tarantism, based on the observation of *tarantati* in his home town of Mesagne. Much of his data comes from the case of a certain Pietro Simone, an adolescent who had been bitten while sleeping in the fields at night – reminiscent of our own Malagnino.[14] Ferdinando criticized those writers who did not believe that tarantism was caused by a real bite, ridiculing opinions which put it down to some chimerical malady, melancholy or dementia. Rather, melancholy and dementia were symptoms of the poisonous bite. Summer was the time of the 'first bite', according to Ferdinando, because the tarantula was then more dangerous, and its venom was such that an annual repetition of the symptoms could continue for as much as thirty years. It could affect anyone, although its victims were primarily adolescents. But Ferdinando's conclusions seem rather forced, as he seeks to make his data fit his hypothesis. Thus, with regard to the gender breakdown of the *tarantati*, he explains that female sufferers predominated over males in the Brindisi area because of the high numbers of gardens and orchards, where the picking was done by women; whereas in the Lecce area, where grain was cultivated, men were more exposed because they often slept in the fields during the harvest period. He asks whether those who have been bitten really need to undergo the dancing in order to be cured, proposing other medical antidotes, like the inevitable theriac.[15]

Whereas writers who had never witnessed tarantism directly were content to pass it off as a fraud,[16] those who experienced it at first-hand knew it to be quite real. But the dancing ritual, with its erotic undercurrent and precise melodies, was no longer convincing. The next development in medical interpretations of the phenomenon was

Giorgio Baglivi's 1696 study. Born in Ragusa (Dubrovnik), Baglivi was adopted, following the deaths of his parents, by Pietro Angelo Baglivi, a physician in Lecce. As a result, he may have observed the phenomenon at first-hand. But the exact source of Baglivi's information has not been determined, and his correspondence of the time contains only a few references to the his study of it.[17] He performed experiments on rabbits to test the poisons of various spiders, similar to the tests conducted by medical authorities on the poison antidotes that itinerant practitioners hoped to sell.[18] As a first-hand observer of the phenomenon, he could not help but notice that not all the *tarantati* had been bitten and poisoned by a spider bite. To account for this, Baglivi postulated two tarantisms: one real, caused by a tarantula bite, the other simulated, used by women as an excuse for merriment. The hours of intense dancing were still believed to help diffuse the poison, but the ritual ribbons, singing and group gatherings were no longer considered integral to the treatment. With Baglivi the musical ritual became part of the 'false' tarantism – fanatic and superstitious – practically overturning Kircher's interpretation.

Nevertheless, there was no clear separation between learned and popular culture – at least not yet. During this period the style of dance known as the tarantella became widespread throughout the south of Italy. The ritual dances of tarantism, which we could call 'liturgical', clearly lay behind this 'profane' tarantella.[19] In the mid-eighteenth century 'to dance like a *tarantata*' ['*ballare a tarantata*'] meant to dance the tarantella, referring to a kind of jig. This is the way the expression was used in a 1744 marriage trial, where the fiancée was accused of dancing with another man.[20]

These are the years of what was a very Neapolitan debate, over issues pertinent to the Enlightenment: reason versus superstition. The anti-Kircherian approach of Baglivi culminated in the series of lectures held by the Neapolitan physician Francesco Serao before the city's Academy of Sciences and Letters and published in 1742.[21] Serao had just written a widely-acclaimed study on a recent eruption of Mount Vesuvius and was keen to develop his reputation as an acute observer of natural phenomena. He directed his 'venom' against Kircher's gullibility in believing every word of his Jesuit informers, as well as the iatromusic of the ancients. Serao had searched in vain for a spider whose poison was capable of causing the reactions ascribed to it. For him, the cause of tarantism lay not in the tarantula itself, but in the inhabitants of Apulia, known to be excitable and melancholic. Tarantism was a myth or superstition of the ignorant, to which victims of chronic disease or extreme difficulties would have recourse in the false conviction that they were victims of a tarantula bite.[22] The supposed *tarantati* were in fact victims of melancholia, nothing else, Serao concluded. For this reason music could have brought some limited relief to the symptoms of melancholy.

For the rationally-minded Neapolitan, an absence of poisonous spiders meant a necessarily ineffective remedy. But by the same logic, why should the remedy not prove effective where poisonous spiders were found to exist? And it was this line of reasoning that led Spanish physicians actively to encourage the use of the remedy, as León Sanz demonstrates in her chapter below. It is certainly one of the ironies of history, demonstrating two things: first of all, the continued interaction between elite and popular culture, and, second, the power of the medical elites to set the 'health agenda' in times prior to our own.

Tarantism was thus marginalized in the kingdom of Naples and was fast on the way to becoming a quaint folkloric relic as far as many European intellectuals were concerned; but not before a last shot from the traditionalist side. Serao's treatise had been preceded, not coincidentally, by that of a fellow academician, the Lecce physician Nicola Caputo.[23] Although published only one year before Serao's lectures, Caputo's conclusions could not have been more different. Unlike Serao, Caputo was a frequent witness of the phenomenon. Indeed, included amongst the cases of the twenty-two *tarantati* he described, was that of his wife, Beatrice De Cesare.[24] On the basis of these cases, Caputo asserted the reality of the poisonous tarantula bite, as well as the efficacy of the ritual therapy. What is more, for the first time there is a detailed description of the miraculous intercession of St Paul in favour of *tarantati,* grafted on to tarantism as part of its Christianization at the hands of the ecclesiastical authorities. St Paul was proposed as patron and protector of *tarantati* in part because of the episode at Malta (described in Acts 28.3–5), where he harmlessly shook a viper off his hand. Caputo described the local belief according to which St Paul landed on the Otranto peninsula and went to the town of Galatina to visit some Christians there. Whilst there, he bestowed upon a local Christian and his descendants the power to heal those bitten by poisonous animals, by making the sign of the cross over the wound and having the victim drink water from his house's well. Caputo himself had seen *tarantati* come from all over to beseech St Paul's intercession and drink water from the well attached to the house known as the 'casa di S. Paolo'.[25]

The Church's role in all this was somewhat ambivalent. It is certainly no coincidence that both the well and the house of St Paul were part of a property owned by the church chapter of Galatina, which profited from the offerings left by *tarantati* who went there to drink the miraculous water. In 1752 the property was sold to a local landowner, though the chapter reserved the right to the offerings. The landowner's wish to build a chapel on the site in honour of St Paul was only met in 1793, after a long legal battle with the chapter.[26]

While learned ecclesiastics might approve of the healing role of tarantism, the local Church sought to tame what it considered tarantism's excesses. As we have seen, the Jesuit Athanasius Kircher had nothing but praise for the usefulness of the phenomenon. Because we do not possess the correspondence of his two informants (Paolo Nicolello and Giovan Battista Galliberto, missioners at the Taranto and Lecce Jesuit colleges, respectively) it is difficult to gauge just what they thought of tarantism.[27] What we do know is that in 1687 the bishop of Lecce, the Theatine Michele Pignatelli – and the rivalry between the Jesuits and Theatines is worth bearing in mind in this respect – threatened a ten-year imprisonment for clerics 'who danced or were otherwise seized by the *morbo tarantae*'.[28] By the mid-eighteenth century Jesuit missioners conducting parish missions in the Terra d'Otranto were themselves seeking to eradicate forms of what they referred to as 'choreatic dancing' from the towns they mis-sionized. They were especially scandalized by the fact that the dancers were of both sexes and were in various states of nakedness.[29] Opposition to tarantism had the result of driving the ritual under-ground; or, more precisely, of driving it indoors from its traditional outdoor setting.

In the years after Francesco Malagnino had performed the ritual dances, traditional tarantism started to become the object of scorn, by both intellectuals and local churchmen. Because it lay outside the mental categories of the time it was increasingly defined as a superstition of the ignorant. For intellectuals this meant a relegation to folklore; for the Church a threat to orthodox piety. As a result of such opposition and marginalization tarantism began to lose its cultural and ritual coherence. Even Malagnino attributed his erotic visions to diabolical temptation, linking them to his request for a love-philtre. The Counter-Reformation stress on the devil, believed to be behind all acts of magic and much more besides, was foreign to tarantism and popular culture. However, the erotic hallucinations described by Malagnino as part of his confession of 1723 were in fact an integral part of the malaise as observed by De Martino in the late 1950s (see Lüdtke, Chapter 13).

IV

How can *we* categorize tarantism? According to the ethnographic study of the phenomenon conducted by Ernesto De Martino in the late 1950s, tarantism's ritual content – from the initial phase of stupor and depression to the series of dances – allowed for the evocation, discharge and resolution of conflicts and crises resulting from societal pressures. The first of these was *eros*, subject to a rigid series of taboos and limitations in traditional Mediterranean society. This explains why women victims tended to outnumber men, even including members of the upper classes. Another contributing factor – at least in the 1950s – seems to have been that of poverty and low social condition. As the ritual's high erotic charge provided the *tarantati* with a means of discharging pent-up frustrations, so it also gave them a brief moment of importance and attention within the community.[30] Rather than actual cases of the toxic syndrome caused by the bites of certain spiders (quite rare, in any case), De Martino opted for a symbolic interpretation. He pointed to the fact that the town and surrounding countryside of Galatina, home of a chapel and well dedicated to St Paul (elected patron of tarantula bites), was held to be immune from such bites. Furthermore, there was the annual repetition of the ritual (known as the *rimorso),* the prevalence of women victims over men, the distribution of the victims within certain families, and the fact that the 'first bite' usually occurred during puberty or adolescence. The occasional occurrence of real tarantula bites and the symptoms thus caused shaped and influenced the ritual of tarantism. Indeed, the initial reactions of *tarantati* followed very closely those of a victim of a poisonous bite. But tarantism acquired a symbolic autonomy, utilising the toxic syndrome during times of existential crisis: harvest, adolescence, unhappy relationships, familial conflict, female dependence, death of someone dear, and so on.[31]

It would be a mistake to define tarantism as simply a psychological disorder. Terms like neurosis, hysteria or delirium do not tell us much about the phenomenon, for they say nothing of the cultural context.[32] As De Martino noted, 'in terms of cultural analysis, tarantism did not manifest itself as a psychic disorder, but as a culturally conditioned symbolic order (the exorcism of the music, dance and colours), in which a neurotic crisis, itself culturally modelled (behaviour of a victim of poison) found a solution'.[33] In addition, instead of individual crises without limit or focus, the seasonal symbolism anchored the crisis in a specific period of the year, providing for a suitable ceremonial setting.

The same difficulty which confronted the treatise-writers confronts the modern-day anthropologist: what to do with maladies and treatments that exist outside our own biomedical categories? It would be all too easy to marginalize the phenomenon, ascribing it to some sort of 'primitive mentality'. But this would bring us no closer to understanding tarantism than were its late eighteenth-century critics. Of course, tarantism is not the only malady to present medical anthropologists with a problem. The Spanish American malady known as *susto* ['fright' or 'shock'] is an analogous form of behavioural syndrome, by which its victims seek 'to correct trouble-some social relations or to call attention to their social or emotional needs'.[34] Amongst Hispanic Americans in the United States, *susto* means that symptoms of depression and anxiety are not only different from those of non-Hispanic groups, but that the whole illness experience is constructed in a distinct way, corresponding to the way *susto* sufferers are meant to feel and behave.

The Taiwanese culture-bound disorder known as *ching* (which also translates as 'fright') is another example. In the context of a study on *ching,* Arthur Kleinman defines culture-bound disorders as 'illnesses associated with culturally unique patterns of meaning superimposed on diseases that are universal'.[35] Such cultural patterning is particularly evident with depression, anxiety neurosis and other ubiquitous psychiatric diseases. As far as we are concerned, the healing of the illness within such a cultural system is often the management of the underlying disease, rather than its cure. Such would seem to be the case with tarantism, especially if we consider the *rimorso*: the annual repetition of the symptoms and dancing. For the society concerned, the important thing is that the ritual be perceived to treat the malady. Indeed, because indigenous healing is part of the same cultural system as the illness, it must heal; just as modern professional clinical care must fail to heal.[36] Thus only the ritual dance could heal a *tarantato,* labelled as such by the victim and those around him. As De Martino's *équipe* found, psychiatric treatment in hospital proved ineffective for those patients convinced that they were *tarantati.* In the same way, remedies proposed in the early modern period by the medical community (a prescription containing twenty-four herbs and spices), the Church (canonical exorcisms), and even local cunning folk, were destined to fail, preparing the way for the ritual dance.[37]

Whether or not tarantism provided Francesco Malagnino with sufficient treatment we shall never know. The fact that he confessed to the episcopal court suggests that there were other factors at work. As we have already had cause to note, the Counter-Reformation Church was at this time adding to the societal restrictions regarding *eros.* The message put forth with great urgency and insistence by missioners, preachers and confessors was part of an ongoing campaign against love magic, sexual relations before marriage, and sins of the flesh. This further contributed to the tensions and pressures already confronting members of this face-to-face society, sometimes leading to situations with which people could not cope: existential crises, interpreted and treated – in southern Apulia – as tarantism. In the case of Malagnino, this only added to his feelings of guilt, of which, he felt, only the episcopal court could absolve him.[38]

Notes

1. Archivio Diocesano, Oria, *Magia e stregoneria*, II, 'Contro Francesco Antonio Malagnino', 16 March 1723. All translations are my own, unless stated otherwise.

2. The standard, unsurpassed work on the subject is E. De Martino, *La terra del rimorso: contributo a una storia religiosa del sud* (Milan, 1961; though I shall be citing the 1994 edition). Several brief historical surveys are available in English: H. Sigerist, 'The Story of Tarantism', in D. M. Schullian and M. Schoen (eds) *Music and Medicine* (New York, 1948), pp. 96–116; D. Gentilcore, *From Bishop to Witch: the System of the Sacred in Early Modern Terra d'Otranto* (Manchester, 1992), pp. 149–55; and G. Tomlinson, *Music in Renaissance Magic: Toward a Historiography of Others* (Chicago, 1993), pp. 157–70.

3. *Synodus Dioecesana Ecclesiae Vritanae, a Reverendissimo Domino D. Marco Antonio Parisio* (Naples, 1646), pp. 11, 74.

4. G. Baglivi, 'Dissertatio de Anatome, Morsu et Affectibus Tarantulae' (1696), in his *Opera Omnia Medico-pratica et Anatomica* (Venice, 1754), p. 313.

5. Nicola Caputo, *De Tarantolae Anatome et Morsu: opusculum historicomechanicum inquo nonnullae demonstrantur insecti particulae ab alfis non ad huc inventae* (Lecce, 1741), p. 210.

6. Giovanni Pontano, *Antonius*, in *I Dialoghi*, ed. C. Previtera (Florence, 1943), p. 51.

7. Marsilio Ficino, *Libri de vita* [*Three Books on Life*], ed. C. Kaske and J. Clarke (Binghampton, NY, 1989), ch. 21.

8. Baldassare Castiglione, *Il libro del cortegiano* (Venice, 1528); *The Book of the Courtier*, trans. C. Singleton (New York, 1959), I.8.

9. P. Findlen, *Possessing Nature: Museums, Collecting and Scientific Culture in Early Modern Italy* (Berkeley, 1994), p. 80.

10. A. Kircher, *Magnes sive de Arte Magnetica Libri Tres* (Rome, 1641); I cite the Cologne 1643 edition: p. 758.

11. Kircher, *Magnes*, p. 770.

12. Kircher, *Magnes*, p. 758.

13. Kircher, *Magnes*, p. 762.

14. E. Ferdinando, *Centum historiae seu observationes et casus medici* (Venice, 1621), p. 248.

15. Ferdinando, *Centum historiae*, pp. 259–61.

16. Such was the case with Rafaele Frianoro, *Il vagabondo, ovvero sferza de bianti e vagabondi*, reprinted in P. Camporesi (ed.) *Il libro dei vagabondi* (Turin, 1973), p. 133.

17. D. Schullian (ed.), *The Baglivi Correspondence from the Library of Sir William Osler* (Ithaca, NY, 1974), letters 54, 57, 59.

18. Baglivi, 'De anatome'; D. Gentilcore, '"Charlatans, Mountebanks and Other Similar People": the Regulation and Role of Itinerant Practitioners in Early Modern Italy', *Social History*, 20 (1995), p. 302.

19. D. Carpitella, 'L'esorcismo coreutico-musicale del tarantismo', in De Martino, *La terra del rimorso*, p. 336.

20. Archivio della Guria Arcivescovile, Lecce, *Giudicati matrimoniali*, 'Tra Francesco Ardito e Catarina Russo', no. 891.

21. F. Serao, *Della Tarantola o sia Falangio di Puglia: lezioni accademiche* (Naples, 1742).

22. Serao, *Tarantola*, pp. 2–4.

23. Caputo, *Tarantolae*.

24. Caputo, *Tarantolae*, p. 111.

25. Caputo, *Tarantolae*, p. 228–9

26. De Martino, *La terra del rimorso*, pp. 108–9.

27. My thanks to Fr. Vincenzo Monachino, archivist at the Pontifical Gregorian University, for checking the Kircher correspondence held there.

28. Archivio della Curia Arcivesovile, Lecce, 'Prima Dioecesana Synodus', 1687, f. 59, in M. Semeraro, *Le Apostoliche Missioni: la Congregazione dei 'Padri Salesiani' o 'Preti Pietosi' nel sette-ottocento Leccese* (Rome, 1980), p. 16.

29. The reference offers no other details. Archivium Romanum Societatis Iesu, *Provincia Neapolitana*, 'Literae annuae' 1740–43, b. 76 II, f. 611.

30. De Martino, *La terra del rimorso*, pp. 169–70.

31. De Martino, *La terra del rimorso*, pp. 51–3.

32. G. Jervis, 'Considerazioni Neuropsichiatriche sul Tarantismo', in De Martino, *La terra del rimorso*, p. 301.

33. De Martino, *La terra del rimorso*, p. 57.

34. A. Rubel, C. O'Nell and R. Collado-Ardón, *Susto, a Folk Illness* (Berkeley, 1984), p. 113. The concept of fright, as an illness in its own right, also existed in early modern Europe, where it had classical origins. Only in the modern period were such beliefs abandoned by elite medicine, while remaining an important part of folk healing. See D. Gentilcore, 'The Fear of Disease and the Disease of Fear', in W. Naphy and P. Roberts (eds), *Fear in Early Modern Society* (Manchester, 1997), pp. 184–208.

35. A. Kleinman, *Patients and Healers in the Context of Culture: An Exploration of the Borderland between Anthropology, Medicine, and Psychiatry* (Berkeley, 1980), p. 77.

36. Kleinman, *Patients*, pp. 362–3.

37. For examples, see Caputo, *Tarantolae*, pp. 133, 218.

38. Which, we must conclude, it did, since the trial record comes to an end after Malagnino's confession.

CHAPTER TWELVE

Medical Theories of Tarantism in Eighteenth-Century Spain

Pilar León Sanz

I

The number of eighteenth-century Spanish physicians who developed theories of music therapy is striking. Between 1744 and 1793, a total of ten studies by medical practitioners appeared, and a further two were written by members of religious orders with an interest in medicine (Father Antonio José Rodríguez and Fray Vicente de la Asunción). To this corpus we must add a report, commissioned by the Supreme Council of Castile (the most important governmental body in the central area of Spain during this period), which records the cases of tarantism in the villages of La Mancha during the last thirty years of the eighteenth century. The large number of patients and, above all, the very existence of this document serve as evidence of the lively interest in this subject.

In general, the eighteenth-century doctors writing about music therapy were eminently practical men. Three of them held important positions in the healthcare hierarchy of the day: Francisco Xavier Cid was the official physician to the chapter of Toledo and the arch-diocese, member of the Real Academia Médica of Madrid, and of the Real Sociedad Vascongada de Amigos del País; Bartolomé Piñera y Siles was an official physician of the Hospital General y de la Pasión in Madrid, a practising physician of the Royal Chamber, chief doctor to the royal armies, president of the Junta Superior Gubernativa de Medicina, and so on; Bonifacio Ximénez de Lorite belonged to the faculty of professors of medicine at the University of Seville and was the first secretary of the Real Sociedad of Seville. The others, Félix Fermín Eguía y Arrieta, Manuel Irañeta y Jáuregui, Valentín González y Centeno, Bernardo Domínguez Rosains, Juan de Pereyra, Pedro

Francisco Domenech y Amaya and José Pascual, were practising doctors connected with various medical academies or societies, who also wrote and published other work of secondary importance.

Among all these studies devoted to music therapy, the work of Cid stands out because its focus is wider, and because it contains accounts of the greatest number of cases. The second place belongs to the official report by Miguel Cayetano Soler, the judge commissioned by the Supreme Council of Castile, because of the accuracy of its contents: the purpose of the document was to compile eyewitness reports of cases of tarantism in villages in La Mancha.[1]

There is no easy explanation for the large number of treatises on music therapy in general and tarantism in particular. The rise of the academies was doubtless influential. These institutions provided a vehicle for promoting the study of this phenomenon and publicising the results in scientific journals. But we now know that Athanasius Kircher and, especially, Giorgio Baglivi were the closest forerunners of Spanish writers' concepts of music therapy in the eighteenth century.[2] Baglivi's short work *De Anatome, morsu et effectibus tarantulae* is quoted and copied by all the writers listed above. The influence of this great Italian physician can be seen in the conception of medicine which underlies their writings.[3]

The Spanish writers are embedded in the medicine of their day: they discuss Hoffmann's therapeutics, Sauvages' dictionary, etc.[4] One of them, Piñera y Siles, translated William Cullen.[5] Perhaps the therapeutic utilitarianism characteristic of the era is another reason why writing on this issue proliferated. Prestigious doctors rejected the indiscriminate application of treatments and complex medication, preferring to return to natural resources: diet, tonics and music.[6]

The Enlightenment is clearly visible in all these writings. These authors rebel against assertions that cannot be demonstrated to be true, that lack prior grounding in experience. They take pains to put forward proofs and arguments for the usefulness and suitability of music as a therapeutic measure. Moreover, they are also committed to conveying to others every possible detail of the cases they have observed; data gathered by experience provide the basis for applying a more advanced methodology; they assess information recorded by the physicians of ancient Greece alongside the findings of their own contemporaries. These authors preserve the traditional explanation of the medicinal properties of music: disease, which is understood as a kind of dissonance or disharmony, can be overcome through the consonance or harmony of music. However, these ancient ideas are complemented by a tendency to seek the basis for the effects of music in the theories of modern physics: sound is a vibrating movement which obeys the laws of reflection and refraction.

These writers believe that music acts in the organism by means of three mechanisms: the vibrating movement of sound and the sound-bearing particles acts on the outside of all beings in a mechanical, and therefore involuntary, fashion (this is the mechanism by which music acts on things, animals and all people); the vibrating movement of music is transmitted from the eardrum to the brain centres, from which it is spread through the nerve fibres to the rest of the body (this type of action is also mechanical in origin); sound, and the psychological response which this causes – that is, its effect on the passions and the state of mind – has somatic repercussions.

Music acts above all on the mind. Hypnotic and analgesic effects are attributed to it. These writers concur in recommending music in all cases of sadness. They also believe that music in itself has diaphoretic and purging properties, and that its use is indicated in neurological disorders and tarantism. Rodríguez and Cid go as far as to state that music is a universal remedy that can be applied in all diseases.[7] They combine music therapy with other conventional treatments (diets, cordials, bleeding, and so on). But they insist on the advantages of music: it has no side effects, it is cheap and easy to administer, and in some cases, such as tarantism, its effectiveness is guaranteed.[8]

Let us take one example of the action of music therapy: tarantism. All the sources consulted refer to this disease. There are over fifty cases of tarantism reported directly by the doctors who witnessed them. Let us now analyse the concept of tarantism and knowledge of the tarantula and its venom in these works (see Figure 12.1 for the geographical distribution). We shall describe and tabulate the symptoms observed in these cases of tarantism by the physicians present, and compare the results of the music therapy that was applied.

These writers are innovatory, in that they present concrete observations as well as genuine clinical histories, which are sometimes

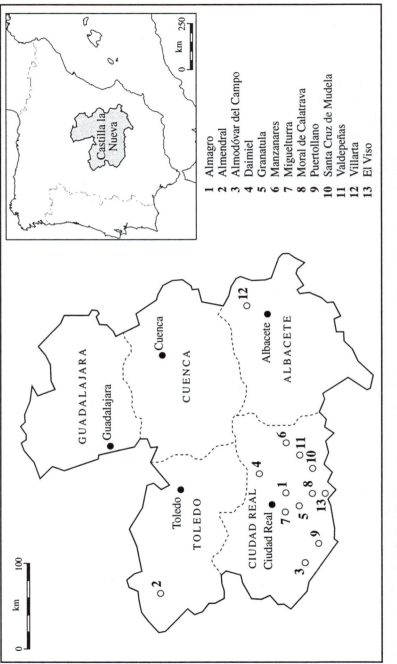

1   Almagro
2   Almendral
3   Almodóvar del Campo
4   Daimiel
5   Granatula
6   Manzanares
7   Miguelturra
8   Moral de Calatrava
9   Puertollano
10 Santa Cruz de Mudela
11 Valdepeñas
12 Villarta
13 El Viso

12.1   Geographical distribution of cases of tarantism discussed by eighteenth-century Spanish authors.

sketchy and have few details, but which on other occasions are written with some concern for accuracy. This can be seen from the fact that names of patients and doctors are given, as are the circumstances of the place (and, on occasions, the hospital), and that they also report the testimony of real people of the era, some of whom were people of note for reasons of learning or high birth.

II

The word 'tarantism' has, in Cid's opinion, two meanings which are used indiscriminately.[9] On the one hand, tarantism is the name of the malady caused by the bite of the tarantula, 'such that the set of diseased phenomena, such as prostration, debility, anxiety, heart palpitations, heaviness on the chest, etc., all of which are the effect of a powerful coagulating poison, is known as Tarantism'.[10] The other meaning refers to a curious symptom: 'this is the dance which music causes in the people bitten or stung by the tarantula'.[11] Later he states that this word is sometimes used analogously for every disease 'that manifests itself with jumping, prancing or any other movements, convulsive or not, that bear, or can be said to bear, any resemblance to dancing'.[12]

Domínguez Rosains says that 'in Italy, in the area of Apulia, there lies the ancient city of Taranto, which gave its name to Tarantalus'.[13] A jar containing tarantulas was sent with Miguel Cayetano Soler's report by way of appendix, but this container was no longer to be found by the time the report reached the Junta Gubernativa de Medicina in Madrid. Cid wanted to demonstrate that the same kind of tarantula was found in Spain as in Taranto, and, more particularly, that the bite of both creatures had the same effects. This is why he emphasizes the descriptions given by patients bitten by spiders; and he stresses that the sites in which they are found in Spain have climatic conditions that are very similar to those of the area of Puglia. The cases recorded by this author happened in various villages of La Mancha. It is from this region, too, that we have the first report of the use of the tarantella in Spain. The season in which most bites are said to occur is the summer: 81.8 per cent of bites are registered in July and August. This is directly related to the biological cycle of the tarantula, as Cid rightly observes (see Figure 12.2).[14]

All the treatise writers agree that the venom of the tarantula is of a coagulant kind.[15] Cid also emphasizes that the venom of different types of tarantula is the same, since 'a considerable number of observations confirm that the bite of all animals of this type, be they starred, horned or black, can be cured by the music of the Tarantella'.[16] The only thing that varies from one case to another is the amount of venom produced.

We studied fifty-one cases of tarantism described by these authors:

a) Juan de Pereyra: one case in 1767.[17]
b) Bonifacio Ximénez de Lorite: one case in 1776.[18]
c) Bartolomé Piñera y Siles: one case of tarantism in 1787.[19]
d) Pedro Francisco Domenech y Amaya: two cases which he witnessed in 1790.[20]
e) Francisco Xavier Cid: he compiled thirty-five case studies of 'tarantisms that happened in La Mancha, that were observed and reported by the doctors of the villages in which they occurred.'[21] These were written between December 1782 and March 1785.
f) Lastly, in the summer of 1782, Miguel Cayetano Soler travelled through various villages in La Mancha (Daimiel, Manzanares, Almagro, and Moral de Calatrava) where he was able to collect thirty-four eyewitness accounts, given under oath and in the presence of two witnesses, of the cases of tarantism that had occurred there. These concern a total of fourteen cases of tarantula bites that had arisen in the area over the previous sixteen years, all of which were treated with music. Three of these cases are also reported by Cid. The judge himself actually witnessed the phenomenon, as he happened to be present in Almagro when a person bitten by a tarantula was treated by music: 'the judge in charge of the report returned to his residence filled with wonder' at such an event.[22]

One aspect that is hard to explain is the way descriptions of cases of tarantula bites are concentrated in the last thirty years of the century. Some of the writers, such as Juan Marín Valdepeñas, reflect that in many years of general practice in villages of La Mancha they had

1.° Tarántula Hembra.
2.° Vista interior de los Obarios y Tarantulillas que sa-
len de ellos.
3.° Vista exterior de los Obarios.
4.° Tarántula Macho.
5.° Vista del Capullo ó nido que fabrican, de tres Obarios dentro del Capullo, y del Terrazo donde suelen
fabricar.

12.2   Representation of the biological cycle of the tarantula by F.
X. Cid, *Tarantismo observado en España* (Madrid, 1787), p.
19.

not seen a single bite, but that in these particular years they witnessed several cases.[23] It is my belief that, in addition to the suggestions made above as to the large amount written on music therapy, one explanation for the increase might be the fact that doctors were now more aware of this phenomenon. Along different lines, Martín Torrens Capellán attributes the increase in tarantism to the heat wave that had afflicted La Mancha in these particular years.[24] A further factor which should be borne in mind is the fact that this malady presents as a syndrome, which may be caused by a number of different disorders with similar clinical features (see Gentilcore, Chapter 11; and Lüdtke, Chapter 13).

All of the tarantula bites occurred in the countryside, and the victims were always unaware of the spider's presence, as the incidents took place when the labourers were sleeping after lunch or at night, lying in the hay. Most patients (thirty-one, or 79 per cent) were aged between eighteen and fifty. All but one were male and most worked in the fields in some capacity (though two were musicians and six were soldiers). The bite was most frequently found in the head or neck (39.6 per cent) or shoulder or hand (26 per cent).

The clinical features were similar in all cases, regardless of the location of the bite. The number of bites seems to have had no bearing on the symptoms.

Two kinds of symptom were recorded: local and general. The local symptoms went unnoticed unless the doctor asked about them or examined the patient carefully. In only three cases were local symptoms found to be absent. However, there were also two cases, recorded by Cid, in which only local symptoms were described. The manifestations listed are common to all bites and stings. For example, Francisco Ximénez explains that 'the bite looked like a flea bite with a straw-coloured ring'.[25]

The descriptions given by the various authors are not identical. Some report more symptoms than others. In seventeen cases, the writers describe the impression of having been stung. In another seventeen, they describe the formation of a haematoma or reddening of the skin. In fourteen they mention pain in the area, and in four this is described as a burning sensation. Swelling is mentioned in ten cases, and inflammation or papule in eight.

Systemic symptoms appear almost immediately after the patient is bitten.[26] They are described in forty-three of the fifty-one cases included by these authors:

Table 12.1
Main Systemic Signs and Symptoms

Symptoms (as given in records)	No.	Percentage of 43 cases
Panting/difficulty with breathing	30	69.7
Pressure on the heart	22	51.1
Alterations in pulse	21	48.7
Nausea/vomiting	18	41.8
Sensation of dying	17	39.5
Cold	15	34.8
Convulsions/trembling	13	30.2
Drowsiness	11	25.5
Paralysis/stiffness	11	25.5
Loss of strength	11	25.5
Clumsiness	11	25.5
Abdominal pain	10	23.2
Heart pain	10	23.2
'Facies hippocratica'	6	13.9
Sweating	6	13.9
Changes in state of mind	4	9.3
Difficulty with urination	4	9.3

The frequency of the symptoms is less noteworthy than the fact that they are described at all, since when one author reports several cases he usually takes knowledge of the symptoms for granted. Thus Irañeta, for example, when describing his fourth case, sums up the clinical features by saying that the victim was suffering 'the symptoms of acute pain, communicated immediately to the hypochondria, kidneys, accompanied by the other signs described in the previous observations'.[27]

The cases described in most detail are similar to each other, and there is a set order in the presentation of the symptoms. This uniformity is surprising, given that the reports are by different authors and are about tarantism in different places. They begin with panting or gasping for breath and the sensation that one is dying. They then move on to neurological symptoms: heaviness, convulsions, vertigo and relaxation of sphincters. Last come neuropsychiatric disorders such as sadness.

Convulsive movements of an involuntary nature were the reason why later authors thought that tarantism was a kind of chorea. In fact, as early as this period, Piñera first diagnosed Ambrosio Silván's condition as St Vitus's chorea.[28]

In general, the symptoms of the victims indicated that their condition was serious. Moreover, if no effective therapeutic measures were applied, the patients died.

The description of these cases of tarantism do not include the unlikely symptoms found in the earlier literature, such as nymphomania, immersion in water or attraction to vine leaves. These authors are sceptical about such manifestations: 'although we do not believe these extraordinary details, nor must we reject them completely because we can not understand these phenomena'.[29] There is just one remark concerning the reaction to colours. Piñera notes that Ambrosio Silván, on seeing the pharmacist's assistant dressed in red, 'was filled with extraordinary euphoria and jubilation, and his face seemed enchanted, as though enraptured; when García came forward, he rushed towards him, overwhelming him with exclamations'.[30] It was this event that made Piñera remember Baglivi's reference and diagnose the case as tarantism.[31]

III

A wide variety of therapeutic remedies were applied. It is possible that the number of measures employed was so large because the tarantula bite was thought to produce such a range of symptoms. Also, when the symptoms did not diminish after the first treatment (as was often the case), further medication was prescribed.

The forms of treatment given fall in to the following categories:

a) Diet: this is prescribed in half of the cases (twenty-six), and is a response to the idea that the inner balance of the body should be restored.

b) Bleeding: this was performed in a quarter of the cases of tarantism studied here; three patients were only bled once, but the others were all bled twice or three times. In Dr Irañeta's second observed case, the patient was bled five times. Most of the doctors who recommended this treatment concluded that bleeding did not improve the symptoms, and that it adversely affected the patients' condition because of the weakness it produced. They therefore did not recommend its use in tarantism.

c) Volatile alkali. Ammoniac: this was commonly used in cases of bites by vipers and other snakes. In this period it was the alternative to music therapy. Irañeta y Jáuregui administered it orally to the six cases he reports in his treatise on tarantism. The patients' symptoms gradually improved, they had a diaphoretic reaction and were cured.[32] The use of alkalis to treat this kind of complaint was widespread, and came to replace music therapy.[33]

d) Cordials: in some cases the use of a generic cordial drink was recommended, while in others the contents of the cordial were specified. Thus Dr Piñera gave Ambrosio Silván a cordial made of peony, orange leaves, lilac flowers and orgeat, and later a tisane of viper's grass.

e) Diaphoretic drink: this was used in ten cases (19.5 per cent) as an additional treatment. The main element in the treatment of these cases was music. Dr Irañeta also achieved a diaphoretic effect with a drink made of water germander, elder flowers with distilled vinegar, and a syrup of citron bark and chicken broth. It seems that these authors did not believe that the curing of the tarantism was related to the diaphoretic effect of these substances; however, we should point out that both Irañeta and the doctors who prescribed music observed profuse sweating in the patients before they made their recovery.

f) Laxatives and evacuants: these were used in six cases.

g) Topical local treatment: volatile alcohol, wine and lard compresses, emollient fomentations, saxifrage with onion, etc., were used in this way. The use of such remedies is normal in bites, which is why it is surprising that they are mentioned in only nine cases (15.6 per cent). The reason may be that the professionals involved emphasize treatment of the systemic features, and neglect the obvious local relief.

IV

For all the authors in this study except Irañeta, music is the only specific remedy for tarantism. It was used in forty-five of the tarantisms described in the eighteenth century. In fact, it was such use of music that inspired the writing of these treatises. On the basis of the application of music in tarantism, the authors suggested that this kind of therapy could be practised more generally. They state that the therapeutic use of the tarantella was not only typical of the Puglia region. It was also known in other regions of Italy (Sicily), other European countries and more distant lands (such as Africa).[34]

The music used was not the same in all cases. Domenech and Cid include in their reports the scores of several tunes. The best known are the tarantellas: 'this is the melody with which we waken the victims of the tarantula from their drowsiness and languor'.[35]

Cid explains that the tarantella can be played with the vihuela (a primitive guitar), the violin or other instruments. He also notes that in La Mancha three very similar kinds of tarantellas were used, and that their effectiveness varied according to the rhythm and liveliness with which they were played.

> The tarantelles written in solfa for the violin are: the first is that of Blind Recuero de Almagro, the second is from Puglia, and the others are used in different parts of Italy. On the vihuela they are played rapidly like the song of the canary.[36]

In the cases analysed here, the tarantella was mainly played on the guitar or the vihuela (see Figure 12.3).

Now let us look at the following aspects of the use of music: the duration of music therapy, the reaction to the music, and the result of using music.

The duration of music therapy

The duration of the music therapy was generally short. In 76 per cent of the cases in which the length of music therapy was reported, it was administered for one to four days, and in 39 per cent for only one or two days. In four cases music had to be provided for fifteen or more days.

When the music was not started soon enough, the patient might not be cured, or might make an incomplete recovery 'because some internal organ had been damaged'. In these cases, the symptoms that

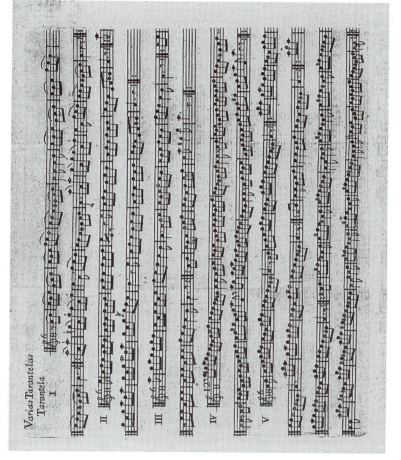

12.3   Music in F. X. Cid, *Tarantismo observado en España* (Madrid, 1787).

had appeared at the onset of the disease would return after a year had passed.[37]

The length of music therapy seems not to correlate with the swiftness with which treatment was initiated or the effects it produced (cure, chronic disease or death). The different durations of the therapy are not explained by these authors, nor do they credit the differences with much importance. The length of time is generally explained by the personal reaction of each victim.

Reaction to the music

Music produced several effects in the tarantula victims:
- it caused involuntary movements that only occurred while the music was being played; and which did not appear in the people around.
- when a full recovery took place, the patient ceased to react to the stimuli, although there were a few exceptional cases in which the patient remained sensitive to musical stimuli.
- not every kind of music worked as a stimulus, or caused these reactions. Only the tarantella or similar compositions could do so.
- it would seem that the movements were necessary to achieve the effect of the treatment.

In most cases, music therapy had immediate results. The first was the involuntary movement which followed the rhythm of the music. This occurred in thirty-nine cases (86.6 per cent). The type of movement varies and is described in different ways. Cid sums up the action of music therapy in tarantism by saying that:

> The patient who felt himself to be expiring, with faint and languid voice, if any, running with sweat, lacking in strength, sighing sadly and suffocating, begins to move his feet, fingers and hands, sensing joy and relief in his symptoms, and then in his other members. As the music goes on, the movement increases until he can stand up and begin to dance with such force, speed and rhythm that all around begin to wonder. Their wonder grows as they see this man, who a moment before lay prostrate on the earth, faint and lifeless, dance with such lightness, in such good time to the music, as though he were the most accomplished dancing master.[38]

In thirty cases (66.6 per cent) the tarantula's victim is 'thrown' into the dance. Ximénez de Lorite explains that 'in his movements the patient always kept time with the beat, and from one hour to another his symptoms were relieved'.[39] A third of these patients distinguished any dissonances or changes in tune introduced intentionally or unconsciously by the musician. When such a variation occurred, the patients started to wail, stopped moving or dancing, and the symptoms of tarantism that had been abating with the music would return. Piñera, Cid and Domenech all discuss the tests they performed on the tarantula victims to see whether this was the case.

As was to be expected, this form of treatment was greeted with great commotion and curiosity. Large numbers of keen spectators would congregate in the house where the music was being played for the tarantula victim. In the case of Piñera, the doctor himself called in other professionals and people of importance to witness the sessions of music therapy:

> the Marchioness of Mortara attended with her family doctor, Don Juan Soldevilla, the examiner of the Physicians appointed to His Majesty, who was left in no doubt that Ambrosio's dance was mechanical and involuntary; I was also present, and asked the worthy examiner to be so good as to perform any tests that he should deem opportune, and he replied that he was so deeply convinced that any further ascertainment would prove redundant.[40]

Other effects of the music were, in order of frequency:

– Profuse sweating: 60 per cent (twenty-seven cases). The treatise-writers place a great emphasis on this, and relate it to the cure. On the other hand, it is worth pointing out that in Irañeta's six cases, in which music therapy was not applied, there was also a reaction of intense perspiration before recovery.

– Cheerfulness, calmness, composure: these features were described in sixteen cases.

– Vomiting, relaxation of sphincters, fatigue, return to normal pulse, and so on are other symptoms described in a small number of tarantisms.

Cid classifies tarantism according to the speed with which the symptoms appear and the effectiveness of the music. Acute tarantism is that in which the music is most effective, and the symptoms most extreme. He subdivides this into the simple form (including only the symptoms caused by the venom) and the composite form, in which the effects of the venom and the music occur together.

In chronic tarantism the poison acts slowly; this form is harder to cure, and may often damage some organ.[41]

Result of applying music

A complete cure was reportedly achieved in over 80 per cent of cases. In 7 per cent, however, residual symptoms persisted: the patients started to dance again if they heard the same music. With time, this effect vanished. Thus Cid writes in his first case:

> It was observed that he had not so far recovered his former health and strength; he has a weak stomach and vomits in the evening and night, and if he happens to hear the sound that has been described, he has to distance himself quickly, or else he must throw himself uncontrolledly into the dance.

This incident occurred in 1778, and was reported in December 1782, which means that the case was followed for four years.[42]

The residual symptoms are attributed to the fact that a sufficient dose of music was not given at the necessary time. In the case of the patient who died, both Francisco Ximénez and Cid explain this by saying that, in addition to the fact that music was started late, the tarantula victim was suffering from quartan fevers.[43]

We can conclude that the tarantula victims' symptoms taken as a whole led physicians to think that this was a serious condition. They were convinced that if no treatment was given, the patients would inevitably die. As we have seen, they saw music as the specific therapy. As the tarantula victims listened to the music, their symptoms would abate and the sensation of imminent death would wane. In most cases, the music caused involuntary movements, which sometimes resembled real dancing, and which were followed by profuse sweating. Tarantism was later thought to be a kind of chorea, and perspiration was seen as being more directly related to cure: it was believed to be the way in which the tarantula's venom was exuded from the body.

In the nineteenth century, recourse to music therapy seems to have lost its impetus. Authors who mention this form of treatment confine themselves to quoting or discussing the writings of their predecessors.[44]

The reports studied maintain the traditional theory of the effects of music, but their real historical interest lies in the fact that they present concrete cases with precise clinical records, endorsed by the names of the patients and doctors involved, the place, and the circumstances of the incident.[45]

Notes

1. Analysis of the lives and work of these authors is to be found in P. León Sanz, 'Literatura médica española sobre musicoterapia en el siglo XVIII', *Nassarre*, 7.2 (Zaragoza, 1991), pp. 73–155.

2. G. Baglivi, *Opera Omnia. Dissertatio VI, De Praxis Medica. De Anatome, morsu, effectibus Tarantulae* (Venice, 1745). Compare Gentilcore, Chapter 11.

3. Thus, for example, Juan de Pereyra calls these authors 'trustworthy witnesses without exception' of the existence and reality of this phenomenon: J. Pereyra, 'Disertación médica del tarantismo, prodigiosos efectos del veneno de la Tarántula, y maravillosa utilidad de la música para curarlo', in *Memorias de la R. Sociedad de Sevilla*, vol. 2 (Seville, 1767), pp. 186–7; and Cid, at the beginning of his book, explains that 'he read, not without considerable interest, at the beginning of his medical practice, the treatise by George Baglivi, *Anatome, morsu, effectibus Tarantulae*. He wondered at the efficacy and special properties of the poison of this arachnid. He reflected on the strange and extraordinary effects it produced, and above all on music and the treatment given, which is specific to this poison, and which unfailingly cures it.' It was reading this that made him take an interest in the subject and study what others had written about it. F. X. Cid, *Tarantismo observado en España, con que se prueba el de la Pulla, dudado de algunos y tratado de otros de fabuloso: Y memorias para escribir la historia del insecto llamado tarantula, efecto de su veneno en el cuerpo humano y curación por la música, con el modo de obrar de ésta, y su aplicación como remedio a varias enfermedades ...* Imprenta de don Manuel González (Madrid, 1787), p. 1.

4. F. Hoffmann (1660–1742) was a professor in Halle and Friedrich I's physician. His best known work is *Medicina rationalis sistematica* (1718–40); F. B. de la Croix de Sauvages (1706–67) wrote a taxonomical classification of diseases (dividing them into 10 types, 295 genera and 2,400 species).

5. *Elementos de medicina práctica y materia médica* (Madrid, 1791). William Cullen (1712–90) was one of the leading figures in Scottish vitalist pathology. See also Commentary on Part V at n. 18.

6.   Castiglioni emphasizes Hippocratism, as the principal characteristic of therapeutics in the eighteenth century: 'the eighteenth century can be regarded as the Hippocratic century par excellence'. A. Castiglioni, *Historia de la Medicina* (Barcelona, 1941). Some consequences of this Hippocratism were the use of natural resources such as diet, hydrotherapy, and so on, the simplification of the composition of some drugs, a reduction in the number of remedies used, and the emergence of physical types of therapy. These features of the therapeutics of the eighteenth century are also described in P. Laín Entralgo, *Historia de la medicina moderna y contemporánea*, 2nd edn (Barcelona, 1963), pp. 121 ff.

7.   The way in which these authors consider that music acts is discussed in P. León Sanz, 'Teoría de la acción terapéutica de la música en la medicina del siglo XVIII', *Nassarre*, 9.1 (1993), pp. 79–117.

8.   'Who would think that the frequent effects of the poisons of these animals could be corrected by music? In the same way, would it not be possible to cure many other diseases? If this is attempted with the right degree of prudence, perhaps this remedy will become more universal than those which have passed as such until now?' Cid, *Tarantismo*, pp. 321–2.

9.   The way in which these authors consider tarantism is discussed in P. León Sanz, 'Musicoterapia y observación clínica en la España del siglo XVIII: el Tarantismo', *Nassarre*, 13.1–2 (1997), pp. 69–122.

10. Cid, *Tarantismo*, p. 11.

11. Cid, *Tarantismo*, p. 12.

12. Cid, *Tarantismo*, p. 12.

13. B. Domínguez Rosains, 'Disertación phísico-médico práctica en que se demuestra la música ser remedio de muchas enfermedades' (1766), MS, Archivo de la R. Academia de Medicina de Sevilla.

14. Cid, *Tarantismo*, pp. 40–46

15. 'Expediente de la tarantula', Legajo no. 11875, no. 1 in the section on 'Consejos suprimidos', f. 72^v (Archivo Histórico Nacional de España, Madrid). Compiled by Miguel Cayetano Soler in 1782.

16. Cid, *Tarantismo*, pp. 46–7.

17. Pereyra, 'Disertación médica', pp. 186–206, at 188 ff.

18. B. Ximénez de Lorite, 'Dissertación inaugural. Historia natural de la tarántula. Los prodigiosos phenomenos de su puntura, la espectacular idea de música con que se cura y el mecanismo con que obra' (1776), MS, Archivo de la R. Academia de Medicina de Sevilla, pp. 35 ff.

19. B. Piñera y Siles, *Descripción histórica de una nueva especie de Corea o baile de San Vito originaria de la picadura de un insecto que por los fenómenos seguidos a ella se ha creído ser la tarántula. Enfermedad de que ha adolecido y curado a beneficio de la música Ambrosio Silván: narración de los síntomas que ha presentado ...* (Madrid, 1787), p. 7.

20. P. F. Domenech y Amaya, 'Observación de un picado por tarántula', in *Memorias de la Real Academia Médico-práctica de Barcelona* (Madrid, 1798), pp. 132 ff., nn. I–VIII.

21. Cid, *Tarantismo*, pp. 103–230.

22. Cid, *Tarantismo*, p. 151.

23. Cid, *Tarantismo*, p. 26.

24. 'Because of the drought and intense heat in this village, a plague of terrible tarantulas arose in the bread'. 'Expediente de la Tarantula', f. 71ᵛ.

25. Cid, *Tarantismo*, p. 146.

26. Cid, *Tarantismo*, pp. 113–14.

27. M. Irañeta y Jáuregui, *Tratado del tarantismo o enfermedad originada del veneno de la tarántula, según las observaciones que hizo en los Reales Hospitales del Quartel General de San Roque* (Madrid, 1785), p. 19.

28. Piñera y Siles, *Descripción histórica*, pp. 8–9.

29. Cid, *Tarantismo*, p. 62.

30. Piñera y Siles, *Descripción histórica*, p. 10.

31. In fact, Baglivi states that 'the patients delight in certain colours, and are gravely afflicted by others, and according to the degree of depravation of the imagination, they can be revived by some colours and discouraged by others'. Baglivi, *Opera Omnia, Dissertatio VI*, p. 615.

32. Irañeta y Jáuregui, *Tratado del tarantismo*, p. 23.

33. There is a chemical basis for the use of this type of medication, as alkaline substances neutralize acids.

34. Cid, *Tarantismo*, pp. 26–7.

35. Cid, *Tarantismo*, p. 15.

36. Cid, *Tarantismo*, p. 17.

37. Cid, *Tarantismo*, pp. 100–101.

38. Cid, *Tarantismo*, pp. 98–9.

39. Ximénez de Lorite, 'Historia natural', p. 41.

40. Piñera y Siles, *Descripción histórica*, pp. 22–4.

41. Cid, *Tarantismo*, p. 112.

42. Cid, *Tarantismo*, pp. 105–6.

43. Cid, *Tarantismo*, p. 159.

44. In nineteenth-century Spain, Antonio Ballano wrote on music therapy. He published a *Diccionario de Medicina y Cirugía o Biblioteca manual médico-quirúrgica*, 7 vols (Madrid, 1804–1807). He quotes the description of the case of tarantism by Dr Piñera y Siles and is familiar with the contrasting views of Baglivi, Serao and Saint Gervais, vol. 7, p. 383. A. Chinchilla makes the point, in the context of tarantism, that

'from the mid-eighteenth century onwards, opinions on the poison of the tarantula and its effects in the human body were hotly debated': *Anales históricos de la Medicina ...* (Valencia, 1845), vol. 3, p. 151. The nineteenth-century author who reflects eighteenth-century writing on music therapy most fully is José Núñez, a homeopathic doctor who in 1864 published an *Estudio médico del veneno de la tarántula según el método de Hahnemann* (Madrid). In the first part of this book, he follows Cid; he mentions the volume by Bartolomé Piñera and that of M. Irañeta y Jáuregui, but he is not interested in music therapy itself. There is also a report in the *Boletín de Medicina, Cirugía y Farmacia* for March 1843 by Dr Mestre y Marzal, who states that the tarantula's sting can be cured by music. And there is the translation by Méndez Alvaro of *La patología externa y medicina operatoria* by the Italian Vidal (1846). He is aware of the cases of tarantism observed in Naples by De Renzi and published in the *Gazette medicale* for 1833.

45. My thanks are due to Professor Pedro Gil Sotres, for his comments on an earlier draft of this paper.

CHAPTER THIRTEEN

Tarantism in Contemporary Italy: The Tarantula's Dance Reviewed and Revived

Karen Lüdtke

I

In strong ritual doses the dance of the small tarantula – the tarantella – was for centuries prescribed in the southern Italian region of Salento. Symptoms of nausea, vomiting, dizziness, stomach and muscular pains, fever, feelings of anguish, physical agitation or inertia were alleviated through its impact.[1] Popular belief attributed these symptoms to the tarantula's bite, whilst biomedical diagnosis ascribed them to psychological disorders. Following the introduction of pesticides in the 1950s, the tarantula spider was largely eradicated from the fields of Salento. According to popular opinion this explains why tarantism has died out. Alternative perspectives view its extinction as based on the changing socio-economic context and the introduction of modern forms of mental health care.

In June 1996, a new case of spider poisoning was registered in the southern tip of Salento and newspaper headlines announced the tarantula's return. Elderly family members of the young patient prognosed that he would be forced to dance the following year, if he really had fallen prey to a tarantula. Laboratory tests confirmed the spider's culpability.[2]

The nature of the spider bite in question merges the real and the imaginary and raises the question of whether there are modern representations of tarantism. Few traces are left today of the arduous and extensive performances used for therapeutic purposes in the past. Many argue that tarantism has died out. Others insist that it persists in idiosyncratic forms, hidden from the public eye. The case of spider poisoning noted in 1996 reveals that the imagery of tarantism still colours the attitudes and experiences of a number of Salentines.

It is useful to follow two tracks in order to consider tarantism in its contemporary context: one concentrating on the academic interpretations of this phenomenon and one tracing its current and modified manifestations. This paper reviews and contextualizes De Martino's 'bible of tarantism studies', *La terra del rimorso,* and introduces further research published on this topic since the 1960s.[3] It discusses artistic performances, university workshops, music therapy sessions and academic conferences as well as the emergence of the *nuovi tarantati,* today's 'victims' of the tarantula's bite, illustrating the diverse levels of meaning the notion of tarantism has come to incorporate. The element of healing, originally at the base of this tradition, is considered throughout.

II

In the summer of 1959, Ernesto De Martino and his team of researchers undertook a first in-depth field study of tarantism.[4] Their research focused on detailed interviews with twenty-one *tarantati,* five men and sixteen women, between the ages of thirteen and seventy-six years. The research team observed a number of domestic dance rituals and participated at the festival of St Paul in Galatina (28 and 29 June) in order to witness the pilgrimage of the *tarantati* to the saint's chapel. Despite the limited period of fieldwork (20 June to 10 July), the success of this study partly depended on contacts established by De Martino in the early post-war period when posted to Bari and Lecce, Salento's capital, as commissioner of the Socialist Federation.[5]

In order to view this field trip within its intellectual context, it is useful to consider that De Martino falls amongst the founding figures of Italian ethnology, even though he saw himself as a historian of religion. The development of this discipline was influenced by both philosophical and political currents dominating the intellectual scene of post-war Italy.[6] De Martino's contribution was particularly innovative in respect to his studies on meridional Italy which emphasized that an alleviation of the enormous differences between southern and northern Italy required not only economic engagement, but also initiatives furthering a rebirth of the south on a cultural level.

Along these lines, *La terra del rimorso* proposes a new approach to southern Italy's situation. The magico-religious perspective of its protagonists is examined not as an evolutionary relic of primitive thinking, but as a culturally specific response to extremely harsh living conditions. De Martino discredits medical interpretations which perpetuate conceptions of tarantism as afflicting the psychologically susceptible and mentally ill.[7] Instead, he posits a historical and religious analysis identifying this tradition as a culturally determined phenomenon. Tarantism is defined as a form of musical, choreographic and chromatic exorcism, irreducible to any form of spider poisoning. The tarantula is conceived as a mythical spider, forming an ideological complex which is autonomous in its symbolism, in as far as it is used to explain the symptoms of the *tarantati*, even in the absence of an actual bite.

This symbolic spider is seen as a composite of the zoological and behavioural characteristics of the two main types of tarantula found in southern Italy. The visually impressive *Lycosa tarantula,* a large, black, hairy spider, living underground and equipped with threatening claws to hunt its prey, stands as a key contestant for the spirit spider, on the basis of its appearance and the striking local symptoms of its bite. Although its poison causes no discernible general effects, the *Lycosa*'s bite leaves a large, red, swollen mark on the skin surface. In contrast, the bite of the *Latrodectus tarantula*, a smaller, sluggish spider, awaiting its prey in its net, causes severe, although rarely lethal, general reactions afflicting the entire body. These are the symptoms according to which the acute crises of the *tarantati* are modelled.[8] The mythic tarantula consequently incorporates a dual ambivalence derived from the small but spiteful *Latrodectus* and the large and aggressive but harmless *Lycosa*.[9]

Through the injection of its poison, the mystic spider transfers its attributes to its victim. Many become melancholic, others aggressive or highly erotic in their behaviour. On average, three or four days of dancing to the rhythmic sounds of the *pizzica tarantata* (the Salentine version of the tarantella danced by the *tarantati*) provide the only way out.[10] The afflicted must submit themselves to the music and movements associated with their spider, identifying with it and fighting against it until a compromise is found, and the spider is pacified or killed. Only in the latter case is the cure final. For most the crisis returns annually. Once temporary relief has been granted, homage is paid to St Paul at his chapel in Galatina.

This shrine became the site of the *tarantati*'s annual pilgrimages and performances in the eighteenth century, following the attempts of the church to control the ritual practices of tarantism by blending the figure of St Paul into the tradition of tarantism.[11] Diverse accounts tell of St Paul's powers over poisonous creatures, justifying his position as patron of the *tarantati*.[12] It is said that he eradicated all snakes on the island of Malta and granted immunity against the tarantula's bite to the community of Galatina during his travels to Rome. Like the spirit spider, the nature of St Paul is highly ambivalent: he may both cure and curse his victims.

Few of De Martino's interviewees had suffered from a real bite. Amongst all, however, a 'crisis of presence', solicited primarily in the face of socio-economic and natural calamities, could be identified at the time of their initial affliction. This concept, underlying De Martino's studies on magico-religious traditions, refers to an individual's loss of referents in the surrounding world, provoking an experience of the self as unreal and unrelated to present circumstances. Corresponding to these individual cases, De Martino identifies a general 'crisis of presence' of the 'subaltern' group to which these individuals belong – as a result of the confrontation with subordinating forces imposed by other social classes.

La terra del rimorso proposes a psychoanalytically-tinged interpretation of tarantism viewed within a socio-economic framework. Tarantism is defined as a 'religion of remorse' allowing for a payment of debts contracted on the existential level. The tarantula is employed as a symbol for eliciting traumatic experiences of the past. It provides a means of reliving and healing individual crises which threaten to explode without control, and serves as a channel of expression and resolution according to a historically proven and socially acknowledged model.

Dramatic media such as dance, music, song and colour are integral elements of this model. De Martino argues that a certain rhythmic order of sounds not only releases tensions into movements, but also provides an 'acknowledged safety-net to confide in during times of existential crisis'.[13] Psychologically speaking, the dual nature of the *pizzica-tarantata*, characterized by a continuous rhythm providing the musical beat and by melodic variants constituting an interweaving off-beat, reflects two therapeutic aims: the crisis is both exacerbated through the impact of the musical off-beat and kept under control by the rhythmic beat.[14]

These two aims are also reflected in the prescribed phases of the dance cycle which are personally elaborated by each dancer. Initially, the tarantula's spirit is evoked and brought alive, as the dancer identifies with its shape and movements. Key actions of imitation include the performance of a 'bridge' with all four limbs stretched out insect-like from the body, the dancer's suspension from a rope in analogy to a spider in its net, or the miming of the round torso of the tarantula by dancing with a cushion held above the head. In the second phase, liberation from the spider is sought. The most common locations of the symbolic bite – the hands, feet and genitals – are referred to in the dance. The hands are armed with a knife or sword and elements of the *danza scherma* [knife or sword dance] may be performed to simulate a battle with the invisible spirit counterpart. The feet are engaged to trample and crush the spider, whilst the lyrics of particular songs provide sexually resolutive tools.[15]

In its ground work De Martino's thesis has not been challenged. Subsequent studies have built on his rich contribution. Nevertheless, some key critiques of his work are worth noting. *La terra del rimorso* has been censured for neglecting both an in-depth study of the socio-economic and political situation of southern Italy in the 1950s and an analysis of the relationship between those participating in the ideology of tarantism and those discounting it as a superstition, as well as an examination of the connection between tarantism and the dominant religious order in mid twentieth-century Salento.[16]

III

De Martino and his team were generally welcomed into the houses of the *tarantati*. Many participated in interviews hoping the medically qualified research members would find alternative forms of relief to their misery. The publication of *La terra del rimorso* brought on a crowd of curious visitors, annually flooding Galatina with film and photographic cameras at the festival of St Paul. For many journalists and amateur researchers Salento became an exotic location still harbouring pagan relics, which needed to be documented at all costs prior to extinction. Many condemned the *tarantati*'s performances as touristic events staged purely for the purpose of collecting money. At the same time, many benefited from the image Galatina gained through the *tarantati*, as every year masses of visitors spent their lire at local hostels and market stalls.[17]

Following De Martino, visits to Galatina continued to stimulate valuable insights for some visitors. The most significant of these contributions may be thematically subdivided according to their predominantly socio-economic, medical or anthropological focus.[18] In the wake of *La terra del rimorso*, research on tarantism tended to concentrate on the socio-economic context of this tradition, in order both to elaborate on aspects neglected by De Martino and to document and analyse tarantism's transformations in subsequent years.

Annabella Rossi's publication (1970) of her correspondence, from 1959 until 1965, with a *tarantata* initially encountered in company with De Martino, marked a first attempt to convey the perspective of a tarantula's victim in her own words.[19] These letters recurrently touch on the harshness of existing living conditions based on agricultural labour, the anxieties linked to gender and family relations, and the influence of the supernatural realm appealed to for well-being. Subjected to epileptic fits from an early age, the *tarantata* in question defines her physical unease as resulting from two maladies attributed to the Saints Donato and Paul, which are distinguished according to whether she feels the urge to dance or not. Despite a declining social consensus regarding the powers of these saints, the afflicted continues to seek relief from her personal misery with recourse to the interpretation elaborated in her letters to Rossi.[20]

With the work of Miriam Castiglione and Luciana Stocchi (1977) some of the key critiques of De Martino's work are addressed.[21] Their Marxist-inspired article excavates the roots of the *tarantati*'s symptoms from elements of the social fabric left unconsidered by De

Martino. The relationship between the *tarantati* and the diverse 'others', not partaking in the belief-system of tarantism, is analysed with reference to the ecclesiastical and socio-political context and the condition of women in Salento. The domestic exploitation of female labour is considered within the framework of capitalist development, rural depopulation and emigration. Many women were left to rely on limited family and neighbourhood contacts as well as the mass media to overcome situations of extreme social isolation. Castiglione and Stocchi argue that the religious ideology inherent in Pauline theology became inserted into tarantism rituals, thereby perpetuating the exploitation of woman as reproducers of the existing labour force and as substitutes for absent social services. The Christian influence on tarantism is unveiled as fostering the causes of the *tarantati*'s misery, despite the temporary relief conceded by pilgrimages to Galatina. This account provides an extremely valuable insight into the social strata within which tarantism was embedded in the late 1970s.

The documentary film, *Morso d'amore* (1981), throws into relief the changing socio-economic context and techniques of tarantism a few years later.[22] The filmmakers' encounter with a *tarantata* performing personalized rituals in her home enabled the documentation of a case of self-instigated therapy. Without the assistance of other participants, the tarantula's victim aims at overcoming her affliction by singing to herself and by rocking from side to side in time with the rhythmic beating of her hands. The protagonist had emigrated to Switzerland for several years. Following her return to Salento she was 'bitten' on her first day back at work in the fields. Accustomed to better working conditions as a factory labourer in the North, she had resisted going back to agricultural work but was forced to do so in the absence of other employment. According to the afflicted, her periods ceased from this day onwards and returned only when she finally received St Paul's grace, the very year she became the protagonist of *Morso d'amore*. These coincidences raise queries about the therapeutic role of the film team and the link between tarantism and its victims' sexuality.[23]

Medical perspectives on tarantism developed in parallel, refining psychologically reductive analyses opposed by De Martino.[24] Tarantism was inserted into a history of medicine and compared to

other therapeutic systems, challenging the incompatibility of biologic-
ally and socially determined interpretations.[25]

Angelo Turchini's extensive review of the existing medical literature on tarantism (1987) constitutes a useful complement to *La terra
del rimorso*.[26] A focus is placed on the use of therapeutic elements,
particularly music, songs and conjurations, and the role of healing
figures such as the *San Paolari*, descendants of St Paul said to have
healing qualities, and the *attarantati*, responsible for organising the
tarantula's rituals. On an interpretative level, Turchini's contribution
is less innovative. He concludes that tarantism's aim is to provide a
means of 'linguistic alchemy', a system of explanation facilitated
through the use of non-verbal media.

Vittorio Lanternari (1995) considers tarantism's alchemic capacities with reference to the realm of religious healing rituals, both
ancient and modern, directed at combating not so much clinically
definable states of psycho-physical illness, but experiences of
suffering linked to sensations of emptiness or to psychosomatic syn-
dromes.[27] Biomedicine has few criteria for defining these symptoms,
all of which may be provoked by the tarantula's bite. Drawing comparisons between tarantism and two charismatic healing cults,
Lanternari focuses on the performative use of the body, considering
physical enactments as a means of accessing a symbolic world and
activating the body's auto-therapeutic potential.

A comparative approach has also characterized anthropological
studies which developed De Martino's references to ethnographic,
folkloric and historic parallels of tarantism.[28] In particular, studies in
psychological anthropology, aimed at investigating psycho-
physiological states such as trance or illness within their cultural
contexts, have been central in weaving tarantism into a broader fabric
of healing rites revolving around spirit possession and altered states of
consciousness.

Bringing into play relations of power and gender, Ioan Lewis presents a somewhat reductionist perspective of tarantism as a form of
rebellion and possession determined by social marginality.[29] This
phenomenon is defined as 'a feminist subculture, with an ecstatic
religion restricted to women and protected from male attack through
its representation as a therapy for illness'.[30] It is presented as an

aggressive strategy for the politically impotent, predominantly women and occasionally men, constrained to live in socially oppressive cir- cumstances. Entry into this protest cult is achieved by succumbing to an illness for which the mythical tarantula is held responsible. Sub- scribing to cult membership becomes an integral part of the therapeu- tic process. Although personal situations may not be radically reme- died, relief is found in a 'religious idiom which men can condone as a divinely sanctioned therapy'.[31]

In 1980, Gilbert Rouget published his cross-cultural study on the role of music in triggering states of trance, in which he reprimands De Martino for his lack of consideration of the performers' movements during the tarantula's dance.[32] Therapy, according to Rouget, ensues from a form of possession involving corporeal identification with the mythic being and is facilitated through the rhythmic interaction between musicians and performers, allowing for an alteration of con- sciousness. Rouget's contribution calls for a study of the therapeutic role of dance and movement in the ritual process of tarantism (see Howard, Chapter 15).[33]

George Lapassade (1980, 1987, 1990, 1994) has elaborated on the comparative perspective, in his efforts to retrieve the meaning of trance rituals as a human resource for use in modern contexts.[34] Insert- ing tarantism into a historical study of manifestations of trance, Lapassade challenges the link between tarantism and Dionysiac rituals drawn by De Martino and others.[35] He argues that this tradition has a greater affinity to corybantian dances, based on a conception of the divine as multiple and diverse, as opposed to the understanding of Dionysus as reuniting diversity. The mythic tarantula, too, may embody a large spectrum of personalities. Always inherently ambigu- ous, it is held responsible for both the bite provoking illness and the healing process. This dual role leads Lapassade to affirm that tarantism constitutes not only a form of exorcism, aimed at the expul- sion of evil, but also elements of adorcism, involving an identification and reconciliation with the afflicting supernatural being. The plausi- bility of Lapassade's thoughts on the performer's experience of trance rituals, focused on the 'explosion' of an ordinary state of conscious- ness as a result of the rhythmic interaction between musicians and performers, is challenged by the difficulty of sustaining interpretations based on assumptions about others' subjectivity.

Experiences and accounts of the world of tarantism in the last few decades have been published in two recent books by Giorgio Di Lecce (1994) and Luigi Chiriatti (1995).[36] These studies document the persistence of tarantism on the margins of contemporary life and public healthcare, despite constant declarations of its extinction. This paradox is central to the multiple and changing manifestations of contemporary tarantism.

IV

With the advent of the 1990s the music of the *pizzica* experienced a new burst of popularity. The small number of groups playing its music multiplied as the tambourine drew more and more young people into its sphere and many learnt to dance to its rhythms. This revival was inevitably paralleled by a renewed curiosity in the tradition of tarantism, transforming and reinventing its significance. Spurred on by academic research, publications on this topic flourished. The notion of tarantism was charged with new meanings, locating it within commercial circuits benefiting from its links to the past. The contradictory and complex elements of this phenomenon may be roughly reduced to three dimensions.

Firstly, rare remnants of tarantism in its therapeutic sense described by De Martino persist in highly-mutated and idiosyncratic forms amongst the *anziani*, the old people.[37] For some who experienced the suffering and symbolism associated with the tarantula at first hand, its powers continue to live, as the 1996 case of spider poisoning reveals. Elderly family members of the patient had been bitten by the tarantula in the past and consequently advised him to visit St Paul's chapel at Galatina to thank the saint for his release from hospital.[38]

Nevertheless, my own impressions of a visit to St Paul's chapel in Galatina on 29 June 1997 and 1998 support the view that this phenomenon has become extinct as a public performance. No musical or dance performances took place inside or in front of the tiny church. Instead, visitors filtered through the chapel, stepping into its dark, cool space, circling the altar, throwing a glance at the closed-in well and the empty enclave, left without St Paul's statue since the desacralization of the chapel, before stepping out into the bright sunlight again. In 1997, a group of students carrying a video-camera, pen and paper and a copy of *La terra del rimorso*, wove through the crowd in front of the chapel interviewing bystanders. Some came to pay homage to the saint. Many crossed themselves in front of his picture above the altar. One old lady approached him on her knees, touching the altar's step with her forehead. Perhaps she had been a *tarantata*. Perhaps others were present, who had come to acknowledge the powers of the saint experienced previously.

Harassed by disrespectful crowds and by increasing restrictions imposed by the church, the *tarantati* have neglected their appointments with St Paul at Galatina.[39] Other sites in the territory of Salento, dedicated to the patron of venomous creatures, have been sought out in substitute.[40] Overall, however, a decline in religious faith, considerable progress in medical care and a profound mutation of the socioeconomic situation of the Salentine peninsula, have led to the disappearance of tarantism in its traditional, therapeutic sense.

On a second level, tarantism today has been revived by the emergence of the *nuovi tarantati*, the new 'disciples' of this tradition. Musicians, artists and dancers make up this highly heterogeneous group, expressing the need to experience the sounds, steps, colours and images of tarantism. Some see themselves as *nuovi tarantati* on the basis of an 'irresistible need to dance' when the *pizzica* is played, a key diagnostic clue identifying *tarantati* in the past. One young artist defined herself as possessed by the tarantula, during a period in which she obsessively sought out performances of the *pizzica* to inspire her paintings. Others explicitly play or perform the music and dance of the tarantula to create moments of intense engagement aimed at fostering sensations of unity and well-being.[41]

George Lapassade has posited the search for a local identity as another factor identifying the new *tarantati*. According to his diagnosis, tarantism's contemporary manifestations provide symbols of group identity and constitute a key to Salentine culture.[42] In particular, Lapassade and his academic colleague Piero Fumarola have identified the members of the music group *Sud Sound System* as today's curators of tarantism, on the basis of their musical productions, mixing

Jamaican reggae with southern Italy's musical heritage. It is interesting to note that initially the members of the *Sud Sound System* resisted being categorized as *nuovi tarantati*, objecting to any associations with the prejudices linked to the ancient tradition of tarantism. More recently, they have promoted this image for themselves, taking advantage of the new wave of interest in the modern forms of this phenomenon.

Potential points of contact between the performances of the *Sud Sound System* and the tarantula's dance were analysed by Lapassade and Fumarola. Firstly, in line with the traditional songs of tarantism, the young rap group insists on using the Leccese dialect, emphasizing its territorial origins. Secondly, the concerts of this group are viewed as ritualistic on the basis of their extensive involvement of the audience. A 'rotating microphone', passed between performers and spectators, allowing everyone to contribute a few improvised lines, marks these occasions. Thirdly, certain music pieces of the *Sud Sound System* explicitly contain *pizzica* rhythms.[43] Lastly, this rap music is seen as a means of accessing altered states of consciousness and is consequently compared to the *tarantati*'s use of ritual music.[44]

Lapassade argues that the obsessive rhythm characterising rave, rap or 'techno-pizzica' events, aided by drugs, flashing lights, smoke and extensive periods of dancing, facilitates an alteration of consciousness.[45] He considers these instances as tentatives of auto-therapy, in so far as a sense of collective cohesion and experiences of emotional solidarity are solicited amongst the groups dancing together. According to this perspective, these new forms of tarantism, although employed primarily for pleasure and entertainment, have not completely lost their therapeutic significance. These comparisons between old and 'new' *tarantati* must, however, be explored cautiously, since little information is available about the point of view of those labelled as *nuovi tarantati*.

Contemporary tarantism can be identified in a third dimension: on stage and on screen, at musical concerts, dance lessons, theatre and film productions or at academic conferences. Throughout the year and in particular during the summer, village festivals, fairs and holiday programs are marked by concerts circling around the *pizzica*. In 1998, these events culminated in 'the night of the tarantula' – *La notte della taranta* – a highly controversial concert, which brought together on stage diverse Salentine music groups and solicited a heated debate in the media on the role of the *pizzica* in Salento today. Controversies, both amongst the musicians themselves and with respect to the 'outsiders' involved – a Neopolitan musical director and two university professors – bought to the forefront the notions of identity embodied in these musical performances.[46] In yet another context, dance courses have been organized, at the University of Lecce and at diverse cultural associations, aimed at transmitting the *pizzica's* choreographic and musical elements.

Many of these performers gather annually to celebrate the festival of St Rocco in the small village of Torre Paduli. Until mass at dawn, tambourine players of all ages beat their instruments until their fingers bleed, standing in tight circles in which the *danza scherma* is performed. In the past, accumulated social grievances were fought out within this festive framework, as the dancing couple mimed a fight, using the middle and index fingers to simulate a knife. The *pizzica di cuore*, danced for entertainment, is increasingly replacing these confrontational dances. On such occasions, young and old perform together and the conceptual categories of contemporary tarantism posited so far – of the *anziani*, the *nuovi tarantati*, and the stage – merge into one another.

Through improvisation and experiment one music group has begun merging the musical elements of tarantism rituals with insights from psychology and alternative therapies, aiming to retrieve the therapeutic capacity of the tarantula's ritual during its concerts. Occasionally, for example, the band members descend from the stage and approach individuals on the dance floor in order to bombard them with their music at a closer range in the way that musicians in the past did for the *tarantati*. Professional music therapists based in Lecce, however, underline the limited validity of tarantism's idiom for contemporary use.[47] Although both tarantism and contemporary methods of music therapy rely on the principle of rhythmic interaction, there is a danger of imposing the symbolic order and techniques of tarantism on individuals already afflicted by a blurred sense of the self and of reality, thereby further encouraging the deterioration of existing symptoms.

Academic research has played a crucial role in the transformed persistence of tarantism.[48] Both in Salento and beyond its contours,
numerous conferences have given rise to abundant debates on this
topic.[49] For a consideration of the therapeutic aspect of tarantism a
conference held at Galatina on 29 June 1988, entitled 'Ritualized
madness and mythic memory', is of particular interest. Experts in the
fields of mnemodrama, psychodrama and theatre studies met to discuss the links between these disciplines and the rituals of tarantism.[50]
The techniques of mnemodrama were developed to enrich theatrical
practices by recuperating archaic human capacities, such as the ability
to enter into trance. Although not explicitly aimed at therapy, this
method presents key similarities with the tarantula's dance. Both
involve theatricalization, an altered state of consciousness and a focus
on the recovery of personal experiences. Similarly, the practice of
psychodrama, based on the principle that bodily experience through
physical enactment has a more direct therapeutic impact than verbal
expression, may be compared to more recent forms of highly idiosyncratic tarantism rituals. Clearly these considerations require care and
demand further research taking into account the respective social
contexts of these practices.[51]

Academic research on tarantism has been encouraged, moreover,
by the inauguration of the *Istituto Diego Carpitella*, located in
Melpignano and aimed at collecting, cataloguing and making publicly
accessible key aspects of Salentine culture. These include musical
recordings, and documents on oral, written and choreographic traditions as well as iconographic, photographic and cinematographic productions.[52]

The phenomenon of tarantism has also inspired diverse theatre
events.[53] The project *Il ragno del dio che danza*, the 'Dancing god's
spider', organized in 1981, was no doubt the most publicized and
polemical production.[54] At the outset, Euripide's *Bacchae* was chosen
as a foundation on which to elaborate the tradition of the *tarantati*.
Several renowned actors were engaged to direct the initial period of
seminars and workshops. The final goal was to create a high-class
theatrical production which would be able to tour both nationally and
internationally. Financial difficulties and internal misunderstandings
amongst the organizers led to an early collapse of this project.

The notion of tarantism has become entwined in a complex of associations, originally rooted or posthumously anchored in the past, to reinvent and adapt this concept for present use. It is engaged in to emphasize the distinctiveness of Salento, its territory and its people, to inspire artistic productions providing a source of income, to underline the touristic value of this region, and to create a highly politicized arena for academic discourse.[55] Moreover, the knowledge and experience of tarantism's therapeutic potential still simmers amongst the older generations and is being appropriated and developed today by those in search of alternatives to conventional medical and, perhaps, spiritual care.

IV

Whilst the tarantula's dance flourishes on village piazzas and under the spotlights of performance platforms, its image continues to mark the Salentine landscape, on tambourine skins, postcards and, next to a fresco of St Paul, on the walls of a dug-out roadside chapel. The significance of these manifestations remains subject to continual transformations, as a review of the literature produced on tarantism since the 1960s and an outline of its contemporary forms has revealed.

De Martino's historico-religious approach underlines the immense changes this tradition was subjected to over the past centuries. His study of tarantism as a culturally-specific and socially-acknowledged means of reliving and resolving individual traumas through music, movement and colour, continues to elicit respect as the most concise interpretation of this phenomenon. Research produced since has challenged and developed De Martino's ideas. Studies on the reciprocal and transforming relationship between tarantism and its socio-economic environment have highlighted the social nature of well-being. Medical and anthropological studies on tarantism, revealing the importance of rhythmic interaction for therapy in the field of mental health, have contested biomedicine's largely exclusive focus on the individual patient's body or mind.

Little research has been done on the most recent manifestations of the tarantula's dance. A survey of these raises numerous questions. How are 'crises of presence' confronted today? How does a search for identity or spiritual meaning correspond to well-being? Who are the *nuovi tarantati*? Future studies will require a sensitive consideration of the lives and worlds of the *pizzica*'s performers, who continue to raise dust, courting, competing and, perhaps, curing themselves.[56]

Notes

1. Although the use of dance, music and colours predominated during these ritual treatments, it is important to note that a great variety of ritual techniques (for example drinking sacred water, urinating or vomiting inside St Paul's chapel) and paraphernalia (such as images of St Paul, green twigs) were applied. Moreover, some of those bitten by the tarantula never resorted to any music or dance. See E. De Martino, *La terra del rimorso: contributo a una storia religiosa del sud* (Milan, 1961), p. 77. (Compare Gentilcore, above.)

2. L. Chiriatti, *Tarantismo: un saggio di Giuseppe De Masi, 1874* (Tricase, 1997). The appendix contains a medical report of this case as well as interviews with the doctors and patient involved.

3. De Martino, *La terra del rimorso*. This publication is reviewed by an unknown author in the *Times Literary Supplement*, 27 Apr. 1967, pp. 345–7, and by E. Cassin in *L'Homme*, 2 (1962), pp. 131–3. Visual records of this field trip include Franco Pinna's photographic collection partly inserted into *La terra del rimorso* and Diego Carpitella's film, *La terapia coreutico-musicale del tarantismo* (1960).

4. Team members: Giovanni Jervis (psychiatrist); Letizia Jervis-Comba (psychologist); Diego Carpitella (ethnomusicologist); Amalia Signor-elli D'Ayala (social anthropologist); Vittoria De Palma (social assistant).

5. F. Panico, *Il vestito bianco: ricerca etno-antropologica sul tarantismo pugliese* (Milan, 1983), p. 140.

6. For a summary of these intellectual currents, see C. Gallini, 'Ernesto De Martino: Vorläufer, Lebenswerk und Nachfolger', in H. Nixdorf and T. Hausehild (eds), *Europäische Ethnologie* (Berlin, 1982), pp. 221–41; R. Lorenzetti, 'Ernesto De Martino e le *tarantate* del Salento', *Sallentum*, 5.1 (1982), pp. 9–34.

7. For the psychologically determined view of tarantism see, for example, E. Giordano, 'Una particolare forma di psicosi colletiva: il tarantulis-mo', *Neuropsychiatria*, 13 (1957), fasc. 1.

8. De Martino, *La terra del rimorso*, pp. 59–80; I. Lewis, 'The Spirit Spider and the Pangolin', *Man*, 26.3 (1991), pp. 513–25 at 516–17; repr. in Lewis, *Religion in Context*, 2nd edn (Cambridge, 1996), ch. 2.

9. I owe this point to David Parkin.

10. Three types of *pizzica* may be identified; see G. Di Lecce (ed.), *Danza della piccola taranta* (Rome, 1994), p. 134: the *pizzica di cuore*, a dance of courtship and entertainment performed by couples on festive occasions and also danced in groups; the *pizzica scherma*, a knife or

sword dance originally enacted to settle disputes; and the *pizzica tarantata*, which may contain elements of the former two types, staged by the *tarantati* for therapeutic purposes. The term 'tarantula's dance' is used in this paper to include all three types of *pizzica*.

11. See G. Di Mitri, 'Le radici orfiche e l'innesto paolino sul tronco del tarantismo', in M. Paone (ed.), *Scritti di storia pugliese* (Galatina, 1996), pp. 11–28, for a refinement of this point. The author posits a pre-eighteenth-century link between St Paul and tarantism through the Orphic tradition. (Compare Commentary on Part IV.)

12. B. Montinario, *San Paolo dei serpenti: analisi di una tradizione* (Palermo, 1996).

13. De Martino, *La terra del rimorso*, p. 135.

14. De Martino, *La terra del rimorso*, p. 351.

15. D. Carpitella, 'L'esorcismo coreutico-musicale del tarantismo', in De Martino, *La terra del rimorso*, pp. 335–73.

16. Lorenzetti, 'Ernesto De Martino e le tarante', pp. 28–31.

17. Panico, *Il vestito bianco*, pp. 55–91.

18. This outline is limited to research in Salento. Related studies are not covered. E.g. C. Gallini, *I rituali dell'argia* (Padova, 1967); C. Gallini, *La ballerina variopinta: una festa di guarigione in Sardegna* (Napoli, 1988); A. Rossi, *E il mondo si fece giallo: il tarantismo in Campania* (Vibo Valentia, 1991).

19. A. Rossi, *Lettere da una tarantata* (Bari, 1970).

20. This case is analysed from a psychoanalytical perspective by Francesco Lazzari in his *Esperienze religiose e psicoanalisi* (Napoli, 1972), pp. 91–134.

21. M. Castiglione and L. Stocchi, 'Il tarantismo oggi: proposte per una verifica', *La critica sociologica*, 11.44 (1977), pp. 43–69.

22. A. Miscuglio, R. Daopoulos and A. M. Belmonti, *Morso d'amore*: *viaggio attraverso il tarantismo pugliese* (1981). See also C. Barbati, G. Mingozzi and A. Rossi, *Profondo Sud* (Milan, 1978), and the film by G. Mingozzi, *Sulla terra del rimorso* (1982).

23. For a consideration of the link between tarantism and sexuality see also: De Martino, *La terra del rimorso,* pp. 143–6; L. Chiriatti and G. Lapassade, 'Sessualità nella cultura Salentina', *Pensionate de 'Saraceni'*, 1 (1985), pp. 137–44; D. Caggia, 'Il ragno, la donna e il diavolo', *L'immaginale*, 2.3 (1984), pp. 163–74.

24. Medical perspectives on tarantism include G. Jervis, 'Il tarantolismo pugliese', *Il lavoro neuropsichiatrico*, 16 (1962), pp. 297–360; G. Jervis, 'Considerazioni neuropsichiatriche sul tarantismo', in De Martino, *La terra del rimorso*, pp. 287–306. The author denounces explanations couched in terms of individual psychological pre-dispositions, and defines tarantism as an 'ideology', a culturally-limited instrument of explanation, used to define and alleviate symptoms, irreducible to a single interpretative schema. Brizio Montinario discloses this 'ideology' as a rusty tool of the past, after

witnessing how a young man afflicted by a brain tumour is brought to the chapel of Galatina to ask for St Paul's grace. See B. Montinario, *Salento povero* (Ravenna, 1976).

25. For example Panico, *Il vestito bianco*. Panico concludes that tarantism is both a socio-culturally produced phenomenon embodied at the psychic level, as well as a culturally-modelled psychological malady.

26. A. Turchini, *Morso, morbo, morte: La tarantula fra cultura medica e terapia popolare* (Milan, 1987). For a brief summary of the medical history of tarantism see also J. F. Russell, 'Tarantism', *Medical History*, 23 (1979), pp. 404–25.

27. V. Lanternari, 'Tarantismo – dal medico neo-positivista all'antropologo, alla etnopsichiatria di oggi', *Storia, Antropologia e scienze del linguaggio*, 10.3 (Rome, 1995), pp. 67–92. Further valuable studies on tarantism and its relevance to contemporary mental health care include: R. E. Bartholomew, 'Tarantism, dancing mania and demonopathy: the anthro-political aspects of "mass psychogenic illness"', *Psychological Medicine*, 24 (1994), pp. 281–306; and G. Mora, 'An historical and socio-psychiatric appraisal of tarantism and its importance in the tradition of psychotherapy of mental disorders', *Bulletin of the History of Medicine*, 37 (1963), pp. 417–39.

28. De Martino refers to the *zar* (Ethiopia), *bori* (Nigeria), *voodoo* (Haiti), *argia* (Sardinia), the Greek Dionysiac rituals and the medieval dancing manias in Europe. *La terra del rimorso*, pp. 185–269.

29. I. Lewis, *Ecstatic Religion: an Anthropological Study of Spirit Possession and Shamanism* (Harmondsworth, 1971).

30. Lewis, *Ecstatic Religion*, p. 89.

31. Lewis, *Ecstatic Religion*, p. 92.

32. G. Rouget, *La Musique et la trance* (Paris, 1980).

33. For a comparative study on dance, trance and tarantism, see P. Vandenbroeck, *Vols d'âmes: traditions de transe afro-européennes* (Ghent, 1997), pp. 83–113.

34. G. Lapassade, *Saggio sulla transe* (Milan, 1980); G. Lapassade, *Les états modifiés de conscience* (Paris, 1987); G. Lapassade, *La transe* (Paris, 1990); G. Lapassade (ed.), *Intervista sul tarantismo* (Maglie, 1994).

35. For example G. Salvatore, *Isole sonanti: scenari archetipici della musica del Mediterraneo* (Rome, 1989), ch. 3.2, vol. 1, pp. 217–45.

36. L. Chiriatti, *Morso d'amore: Viaggio attraverso il tarantismo pugliese* (Lecce, 1995); Di Lecce, *Danza della piccola taranta*.

37. See M. Nocera, 'Nella cappella di San Paolo, suonando il tamburo rullante', pp. 255–66, and M. Almiento, 'E Maria continua a ballare', pp. 178–86, in Di Lecce, *Danza della piccola taranta*. The authors tell of dance rituals experienced inside the chapel of Galatina in the 1990s.

38. Chiriatti, *Tarantismo*, Appendix.

39. See Panico, *Il vestito bianco*, pp. 53–93, for a description of the church's influence.

40. L. A. Santoro, 'Macare e tarantate', *Quaderni di Teatro*, 5.18 (1982), p. 75.

41. These points have emerged during my DPhil research commenced in June 1997. This project in medical and performance anthropology focuses on tarantism in its past and contemporary forms with reference to the use of music and movement therapies in Salento today. See also M. A. Epifani, *Ematoritmi – la donna nella tradizione e nei canti dell'area messapica* (Lecce, 1998), p. 169. The author makes reference to her own liberating experience of the *pizzica*.

42. Lapassade, *Intervista sul tarantismo*; C. Ardillo, 'Tarantismo, tarantella, etnorap: metamorfosi e sincretismi nella cultura del Salento' (Tesi di laurea, University of Bologna, 1997).

43. For example the piece 'Afro ragga taranta jazz' on the LP *Comu Na Petra* (1996).

44. S. Maggiorelli, 'Dalla tarantula alla tecno – stati alterati di coscienza', *Liberazione*, 4 Dec. 1996, p. 25.

45. G. Lapassade, 'Notti Rituali 2', in I. C. Cingolani and S. Barisio (eds), *L'ombra di Dioniso sulle discoteche* (Bologna, 1996), pp. 106–28; P. Fumarola and G. Zappatore, 'Carnevale, immediato estetico – Pizzica e techno, oltrepassando tradizione e metropoli', *Leccesera* (24–25 February 1998), p. 11. The authors describe two initiatives bringing together musicians playing the *pizzica* and a DJ specializing in techno music.

46. For example P. Fumarola, 'La techno-pizzica impazza purché sia salva la qualità', *Quotidiano di Lecce*, 27 Aug. 1998, p. 8; and R. Raheli, 'E così tornammo a parlare di notti e di tarante', *Quotidiano di Lecce*, 29 Aug. 1998, p. 16.

47. The association *Music'arte* uses the method *Globalità dei linguaggi* developed by the Italian music therapist Stefania Guerra-Lisi. See S. Guerra-Lisi, *Il metodo della globalità dei linguaggi* (Rome, 1987).

48. See L. A. Santoro, 'Il paese dove il ragno canta', *Hyphos*, 1.1 (1987), pp. 62–70.

49. This includes a conference with participants from diverse European universities and institutions held at Galatina on 24–25 October 1998 entitled *Il tarantismo quarant'anni dopo De Martino*.

50. L. A. Santoro, 'L'attore nella tela del ragno', *Quotidiano di Lecce*, 29 June 1988, p. 9; M. Almiento, 'Per una visione estetico-antropologica del tarantismo pugliese' (Tesi di laurea, University of Lecce, 1990), pp. 85–168.

51. See also K. Lüdtke, 'Theatre as Therapy with a Special Reference to Tarantism in Southern Italy' (MPhil thesis, University of Oxford, 1997).

52. C. Petrachi, 'Il Salento, l'identità, la memoria', *Leccesera*, 2.21 (27–28 Jan. 1998), p. 15. Filmography: D. Carpitella, *La terapia coreutico-musicale del tarantismo* (1960); A. Miscuglio, R. Daopoulos and A. M. Belmonti, *Morso d'amore: viaggio attraverso il tarantismo pugliese* (1981); G. Mingozzi, *Sulla terra del rimorso* (1982); R. Durante, *La*

Sposa di San Paolo (1989); E. Winspeare, *San Paolo e la tarantula* (1989); R. Stegmueller and R. Koeplin, *Der Tanz der kleinen Spinne: Tarantella* (1992); L. A. Santoro, *Viaggio a Galatina* (1993); E. Winspeare, *La Pizzicata* (1994); F. Bevilaqua, *Stretti nello spazio senza tempo: viaggio nel tarantismo salentino* (1995).

53.   See M. Mangiafico, 'Il tarantismo nel teatro' (Tesi di laurea, University of Lecce, 1984).

54.   C. Colazzo, 'La questione del "Ragno del dio che danza"', in Lapassade, *Intervista sul tarantismo*, pp. 34–77; L. A. Santoro, 'Macare e tarante', *Quaderni di Teatro*, 5.18 (1982) pp. 71–82.

55.   See: http://www.medea.clio.it/nardo/tradi.htm
http://www.worldnetwork.it/galatina/tradizio.htm.

56.   My thanks go to David Parkin, David Gentilcore, Hannes Pichler and Stefano Boni, and to all those who have welcomed me to Salento and generously shared their knowledge and experiences with me. This research was made possible through grants from the Economic and Social Research Council and the European Commission.

PART V

Modern Currents

Commentary on Part V, with Notes on Nineteenth-Century America and on Mesmerism and Theosophy

Peregrine Horden

I

The subject of this book is a history that embraces some 2,500 years. In most projects of such broad scope, the section dealing with recent centuries might reasonably be the longest. As we approach our own time, evidence and expertise multiply exponentially; interest and sense of relevance quicken. In this volume, however, the last two centuries bulk less large than the early modern period. And they do not get much more space than the decidedly marginal phenomenon of tarantism (although Lüdtke of course deals with recent decades, and so belongs in this final part as much as in the previous one).

This allocation is not mere perversity. First, the modern age is not to be seen as the focus of the book, the reason for compiling it. Contemporary music therapy was introduced in the first chapter in order to gain some preliminary empirical notion of music's therapeutic potential. And the modern music therapy profession is the subject of the final chapter (Tyler) because its establishment is the most notable recent event in a long, complicated, and continuing story. But, overall, we are not offering a teleological account in which early phases of that story are of importance only in so far as they reveal the taproots of contemporary practice. Differences between remote periods and our own are as significant here as continuities. Second, as was emphasized in the Commentaries on Parts III and IV, there are particular grounds for focusing at length on their periods and topics. Third, the modern period – let us say, since 1800 – is paradoxically the least well explored of all the phases of music therapy's varied history.[1]

One reason for that comparative neglect is contingent. Neither musicology nor medical historiography has, until recent decades, adopted the broad cultural (postmodern) remit which would allow such a seemingly peripheral topic more than a brief airing. There is, however, another reason that goes deeper. It is that the very terms of reference of a history of music therapy in the modern period are uncertain, the contours of the subject are fundamentally obscure. Unlike antiquity, the later Middle Ages, or the Renaissance, this phase has no one clearly dominant paradigm: rather, it falls between two paradigms. The first of these is the humoral system of medicine. By the beginning of the nineteenth century it had more or less collapsed. Some treatments derived from it still flourish today, of course; but in European learned medicine it has been defunct for around two centuries. The legacy of classical antiquity, particularly of Hippocrates and Galen, it had been under assault since the time of the Scientific Revolution; yet as Gouk demonstrated above, it long continued to provide a broad framework which could accommodate even new medical philosophies. In the eighteenth century, Browne, Brocklesby or Roger are intent on providing contemporary ways of approaching old problems, problems with which Ficino was familiar. The second paradigm is constituted by the professionalization that has taken place since the Second World War. This supplies a basis for global comparisons, of the sort briefly attempted in Chapter 1, even though it brings with it the danger that 'first-world' music therapy will be privileged over 'traditional' forms of musical healing. Much remains to be explored, but here at least, in the post-war decades, we have some bearings.

And between the two paradigms? It is still not clear where we should look – not clear which figure or idea should be connected with which other; what the important currents of thought are, what the subsidiary. The three chapters that make up this final part of the book are, then, mere soundings in a large and inadequately-charted ocean. In the next section, I shall anticipate each of them briefly (in the reverse order), noting parallels and contrasts with what has come before. I shall then (sections III–IV) try to take a larger view, of at least some other waters within that ocean, sketching two related topics which a much larger collection of essays would ideally embrace.

II

The third and last author is the one whose presence here is presumably the least controversial. No history of music therapy written in English could ignore the modern British profession. Clearly the second paradigm had to be explored, and not only its very recent history – which can reasonably be seen as culminating in the state registration of music therapists – but also its perceptible origins. So Tyler begins with Canon Frederick Kill Harford, an obscure yet unusually interesting late-Victorian figure whose plans to 'pipe' music via the telephone to patients' bedsides seem forward-looking. Harford is apparently an isolated figure; and Tyler's principal concern must, inevitably, be the post-war years in Britain – the period of those great figures such as Juliette Alvin who were among the first both to set out music therapy's past in a reasonably scholarly manner (see Chapter 1) and also to establish its professional credentials.

In this post-war period, we at last find the type of music therapy used earlier on by Page as the yardstick with which to estimate the thirteenth century: a music therapy that is systematically empirical and has the requisite technology to make itself a regular part of treatment. We find joint music-making by both therapist and patient such as we have not, I believe, encountered in earlier periods. And that is because we have also moved into a musical culture which makes such prolonged and, in many respects, intimate transactions possible. This is all new. Tyler's point, anticipated in Chapter 1, bears repetition for emphasis: the sorts of wholly unskilled improvisation which may be elicited from the 'client' in a contemporary music therapy session are virtually unprecedented in the prior histories we have been uncovering. For many of the sounds that clients nowadays make would not have been classified as music. We may accept them as a vulgarization of Cage or Stockhausen. To almost anyone in Europe before, say, 1950 they would have been taken as the symptom, not the cure, of disease or disability. (In the nineteenth century, perhaps only German asylums of the kind described by Kramer found ways of 'musicalizing' the musically unskilled or incapacitated.)[2] Elsewhere, and in earlier centuries, basic technical accomplishment was a prerequisite – whether in the auto-therapy of the singing or playing patient, such as

Ficino, or in the more usual performance to which the patient listened. There is a major discontinuity here. The professional music therapy with which we are becoming familiar is, strictly speaking, a very recent phenomenon indeed.

Differences between present and past obtrude again in Howard's chapter. That is why his topic, shamanism, is represented here, in the historical collection rather than in its ethnographic companion.[3] Those who heal in ways that have something to do with trance, ecstasy, and the world of the spirits have appeared at several points above: in my introductory survey (Chapter 1), as well in the opening section of Shiloah's chapter and in Lüdtke's account of neo-tarantism. On each occasion, some connection has, reasonably, been drawn between present and past. But the historical role often accorded to the shaman has been of a different order. The shaman's contacts with the spirit world have been seen as age-old, reaching back into Siberian pre-history. These are, as in the title of Eliade's celebrated study cited by Howard, 'archaic techniques of ecstasy'. By the same token, West can find traces of aboriginal shamanism in early Greek literature. In the background to many of the therapists discussed in this book stands Orpheus,[4] and behind Orpheus, on West's conjecture, stands the shaman. Some historians have posited a direct historical line of descent from prehistoric shamanism to much more recent rituals (see Commentary on Part IV). Overall, then, the shaman has been a figure of key cultural significance to Western musical therapeutics. But what is a shaman? Historians need to know – in the first instance, from ethnographers.[5] Howard offers us an unusual perspective: the view from Korea, where shamans are female. Moreover, he uses his field-work as a point of departure for a 'deconstruction' of a category that historians – and ethnographers – have used too unthinkingly. Both will have to be more careful in future.

Though Howard by implication looks back, and Tyler begins with Harford at the beginning of the twentieth century, both are also focused very much on our own time: theirs is above all 'contemporary history'. How, then, to represent the nineteenth century? The lesson of previous chapters is that not much of relevance is to be expected of the history of general medical practice. Neither West for antiquity, nor Jones, Gouk and Austern for the period *c*. 1350–1800, have found any evidence that music was often recommended by the run of practitioners, however profound its artistic and philosophical resonances. The period 1800–1900 does not, in the present state of research, appear obviously different. Where we might look for music therapy is, rather, in the two of the great new phenomena of the time – phenomena not unconnected – Romanticism and institutional psychiatry.

Romanticism is exceedingly hard to characterize, in music or any other domain, and virtually impossible to characterize briefly. At least it can be said that Romantic musical thought substitutes an emphasis on the power of individual expression for the aesthetics of the eighteenth century, which dwelt mostly on imitation or which held out the possibility of a rational codification of musical effects.[6] Romantic music supposedly arises from deep in the composer's psyche and dives deep into that of its listener. Composing it might seem to require something akin to Platonic divine madness.[7] Hearing it could be comparably deranging. The arch-Romantic Wagner envisaged that his *Tristan and Isolde*, unless too badly performed to have any real effect, would drive its audiences mad.[8] Romantic music also, metaphysically speaking, reaches 'higher' or 'further' than ever before – beyond the *musica mundana* of ancient and Renaissance Platonism. For its greatest philosopher, Schopenhauer, music was the only art form that went beyond 'representations' to the very Will itself, that force underlying all apprehensible reality.[9]

In Romantic hands, therefore, music ought to be potent. Yet it is an ambivalent potency. As in the baroque age with lovesickness (Chapter 10), so in the early Romantic era (Chapter 14), music can be either cause or cure of a disorder. And that disorder, which in a sense the age invented, is insanity: a psychological breakdown which does not necessarily have an organic component and which is treatable by means of psychiatry, the other medical 'invention' of the late eighteenth century. Even before Wagner began to derange his audiences, Liszt the recital pianist could already be found inspiring hysteria in his (especially female) listeners – hysteria of the kind which we associate with Beatles concerts. But, as we shall see, Liszt also visited a Paris asylum to play to an inmate.

In many asylums music apparently became, if not a regular feature, then at least a surprisingly common one from the last decades of the eighteenth century onwards.[10] It might seem as if this represented a continuation of the Galenic emphasis on 'diet', the daily regimen which included among its objectives the moderation of the 'passions of the soul' through entertainment. But the context is different, and there is as much discontinuity as continuity. Galenic medicine sees mental illness as essentially somatic, though the passions of the soul may have a part to play in its onset. There had been a 'therapy of the word', a 'talking cure', in Western medicine since antiquity, but it was always limited in scope.[11] The eighteenth-century treatment of insanity, at least to begin with, is a treatment of a disorderly body. That century may not have been quite the 'disaster for the insane' once discerned in it;[12] there was no 'great confinement' in asylums, nor the over-reliance on whips and chains that some historians have supposed. Nevertheless, humanitarian treatment in the private mad-houses which began to flourish in the eighteenth century was still based on an essentially somatic understanding of mental health. The 'moral management' (or 'moral therapy') that characterized avant-garde asylums of the latter part of the eighteenth century and the first half of the nineteenth derived from the axioms that psychology was preferable to restraint and that mental illness was precisely that, a failure of reason to be countered by rational means.

Now music for explicitly curative rather than liturgical purposes had not been heard in hospitals (apart from some monastic ones) or in institutions for the insane since the early Middle Ages in the Near East.[13] But with the advent of 'moral' treatment towards 1800,[14] it took its place in the asylum under new theoretical auspices. Its presence may also have had much to do with the commercialization of leisure and of social life generally. Moral managers were not necessarily medically trained. They were trying to restore their mentally abnormal patients to 'bourgeois' normality, within which music, both heard and performed, held an increasingly important place.

It is against this background that we must read Kramer's chapter. She looks at asylum music in several countries, but her main example is from the land that gave us the term *Psychiatrie*. Drawing on her detailed work on the Illenau asylum, Kramer shows just how far music could determine the ethos of an entire community – ethos in a sense both like and unlike the ancient Greek conception, just as the asylum's notion of *Gemüth*, the rhythm of the soul, is both like and unlike the medieval *musica humana*.

III

Modern music therapy (in Britain), shamanism (mainly in Korea), Romantic insanity (mainly in Germany): three chapters – four, if we include Lüdtke's – for our two most recent centuries. What else should ideally be said?

First, most obviously, there is a chapter to be written on the USA to set alongside the European material that has dominated this collection since Part II. Tyler's contribution shows how closely intertwined were the histories of American and British music therapists in the earlier twentieth century. To grasp the American background to that, the nineteenth-century background, we must turn, on one hand, to secondary works which provide the likely context but say nothing about music and, on the other hand, to basic studies of the specific literature of music therapy which say little about the context.[15] What follows, then, is a preliminary attempt to bring the two sides together.

The earliest known North American publications on music therapy date from the late eighteenth century; they sound conventional, even old-fashioned.[16] An article in the *Columbian Magazine* for February 1789, entitled 'Music Physically Considered', seems to reassert the Galenic axiom of the interdependence of mind and body and the force of the 'passions of the mind' on bodily health; and it does so expressly in the face of Cartesian dualism[17] and the 'hydraulic' and 'neurological' physiologies of Boerhaave and Cullen, which left little scope for music therapy.[18] The article also cites a case of music's being used to cure extreme depression in a dancer. A few years later, in 1796, a short notice appeared in the *New York Weekly Magazine* for 10 August, recounting the case of an unnamed music teacher (first a dancer, now a musician, as if only the musical were receptive to music therapy) whose fever had been abated and eventually, after a fortnight, dispelled by command performances of music – 'without any other assistance than once bleeding the foot ...'.

Such is the *ancien régime* in North American music therapy: somewhat flimsy, unoriginal productions. Medical dissertations written in the early 1800s show a transition to a different phase of thinking, even if they do not represent a huge advance in scholarship.[19] In a nineteen-page tract of 1804, *An Inaugural Essay on the Influence of Music in the Cure of Diseases*, Edwin Atlee paid homage to the Galenic notion that excessive grief could lead to physical illness, and once more included fevers among the conditions susceptible to musical treatment. Yet he also asserted, in keeping with European 'moral' therapy, that music alone could attack the causes of mania, which he regarded as 'the consequences of a delirious or mistaken idea', not a physiological aberration. And he concluded by relating three cases known to him personally in which hearing music had relieved mental distress: those of a melancholic, a hysteric and a maniac.

In 1806 there appeared another, equally compact work in the same vein. Samuel Mathews's *On the Effects of Music in Curing and Palliating Diseases* is steeped in much earlier authors such as Baglivi (see Part IV) and is still invoking David's playing to Saul. Although he takes his historical anecdotes from Burney's *History of Music*,[20] Mathews also appears forward-looking in his suggestions. He excites modern music therapists by his anticipation of what they call the 'iso' principle ('we should be particular in having the notes accommodated to the patient's mind').[21] And he was the first to recommend in print that music therapy should become part of clinical practice in institutions.

The brevity of these two pieces, and the fact that they give as much space to classic texts as to actual case histories, does not suggest that their subject was a particularly lively one in early nineteenth-century America. The dissertations were published in Philadelphia, and had been produced in partial fulfilment of the graduation requirements of the medical faculty of the University of Pennsylvania. Mathews admitted to having written his piece in a mere ten days;[22] and both authors were perhaps casting around for an untried topic. Like Joseph Comstock, who in 1801 treated an apparent case of tarantism with music (see Commentary on Part IV),[23] they were, however, pupils of Benjamin Rush. Both Atlee and Mathews cited Rush extensively in their works and Mathews credited Rush with a plan – thwarted by practical difficulties – to introduce music therapy into the Pennsylvania Hospital.[24]

Benjamin Rush (1746–1813), pupil of William Cullen in Edinburgh, signatory of the Declaration of Independence, father of American psychiatry, is often taken as the chief American proponent of moral therapy.[25] And moral therapy, as has already been suggested and will be documented more fully in Kramer's chapter below, is likely to include music. Rush enjoyed exclusive charge of the insane in the Pennsylvania Hospital from 1787. Yet it seems he had not, by 1806, managed to include music in his therapies. The truth is that Rush was not quite the great advocate of musical healing that his pupils, and some of his later historians, would wish us to see in him. What he did introduce to the Pennsylvania Hospital, in 1810, 'to assist in curing madness', was his celebrated 'tranquillizing chair':

> It binds and confines every part of the body ... Its effects have been truly delightful to me. It acts as a sedative to the tongue and temper as well as to the blood vessels. In 24, 12, six, and in some cases four hours, the most refractory patients have been composed.[26]

That is from a letter by Rush to his son. Nowhere in his published correspondence does he discuss the possibilities of music therapy. His enthusiasm is all for treatments at the somatic rather than the psychological end of the spectrum: 'warm and cold baths', 'copious bleeding', 'low diet', and the like.[27] In keeping with that preference, Rush's last medical book, *Medical Inquiries and Observations upon Diseases of the Mind*, published in the year before his death, while admittedly mentioning music therapy several times, is each time very brief and often somewhat abstract. Where individual patients do merit mention, it is not Rush's prescriptions that they are following. For example: 'I attend a citizen of Philadelphia, occasionally, in paroxysms of [hypochondriasis], who informed me that he was cured of one of them by hearing the old hundred psalm tune sung in a country church.' Or again: 'music has been much commended in this state of madness [mania] ... Dr. Cox mentions a striking instance of its power over the mind of a madman'.[28] It is always someone else who describes or prescribes the music. And Joseph Mason Cox, though claimed by historians as a 'moral' therapist, was also the first to develop a working model of yet another mechanical device for subduing the insane, the 'swinging machine'.[29] He was no more a friend of music therapy than was Rush, whose tone in the *Inquiries* perceptibly brightens when he turns from music back to more congenial strategies for the management of lunatics – such as the use of terror, or even of torture.[30]

If this is moral treatment, then its arrival in America might be thought a mixed blessing. One begins to understand why early writers on music therapy such as Atlee and Mathews seem to have had little practical experience to go on, and look back to Baglivi. Perhaps music was never very prominent in the American version of moral treatment. The York Retreat, the British exemplar of a musical asylum, was widely imitated in the USA, starting with the Friends' Asylum near Philadelphia in 1817. Yet Rush's work remained the primary textbook on the treatment of insanity and was hardly the best advertisement for music's cause.[31]

That may be why the first clearly documented institutional use of music in the USA apparently occurred not in a hospital or asylum, but in a school for the blind – the Perkins School established in south Boston in 1832 by Samuel Gridley Howe. His wife Julia composed children's songs and wrote the words for the 'Battle Hymn of the Republic'. Hers was probably the influence that determined the addition of music to the curriculum. In the Perkins School, as later in other schools for the blind and indeed for the deaf, the music was not particularly therapeutic in intent; it was more to offer the handicapped 'intellectual gratification'.[32] The point (then as now) was presumably to communicate with the handicapped, to integrate them, to compensate for their physical deficiency with modest artistic success.

Meanwhile, after the brief flurry of the early 1800s, medical periodicals and dissertations seem to have been silent on the subject of music therapy for some time. A clutch of articles in the *Musical Magazine* for 1840–41 rehashed anecdotes from antiquity to the time of Farinelli (see Chapter 1), once more drawn overwhelmingly from Burney's *General History of Music*, and registering none of the practical applications recorded or envisaged in the earlier publications.[33] Little is detectable thereafter until the 1870s (see Chapter 16). In 1874, James Whittaker published in the *Cincinnati Clinic* a renewed assertion of the possibilities of music therapy in the treatment of, above all, mild mental disturbance. Then, in 1878, *The World*, a New York newspaper, reported a set of experiments on the reactions to professional music-making that were evinced by pauper 'lunatics' in the Blackwell's Island (now Roosevelt Island) asylum. This was the first time that government-sponsored music therapy had been seen in the United States.[34] After some further published rehashes of Burney, a paper of 1892 by G. A. Blumer, Chief Executive Officer of the Utica State Hospital in New York, once more explicitly aligned the use of music therapy with moral treatment – long after it had passed out of fashion in asylums. Blumer also hired immigrant musicians to perform to the patients in his hospital.[35] Finally, as the century closed, a prominent neurologist, James L. Corning, published in the *Medical Record* an article reporting the first controlled attempt to treat disease with music. Combining the auditory and visual stimulation of patients who were presomnolent, Corning hoped that the music would bypass the cognitive faculties that were becoming (literally) dormant and would penetrate the unconscious. Appropriate music – which for Corning meant Wagner and other Romantics – was to facilitate the transfer of pleasant emotions from presomnolency into waking hours, thus lifting his patients' depression.[36]

At this point the present note begins to dovetail with Tyler's chapter below. Early twentieth-century American developments are tabulated by her and more detail of them is also conveniently available elsewhere.[37] So it will be enough here to conclude by signalling the major contribution that women were then making, for the first time, it would seem, in the entire history of music therapy: women such as Eva Vescelius, who treated insomnia, fever and other ailments with 'musicotherapy' in New York during the early 1900s, Margaret Anderton, who believed that particular pieces could be assigned to specific ailments (Schubert for insomnia, Brahms waltzes and, improbably, Sousa marches for the terminally ill), Harriet Ayer Seymour, Esther Gatewood, and indeed others. It is a remarkable list, only partly to be explained by women's role in caring for veterans of the First World War.

IV

The other missing chapter which I now want briefly to delineate is harder to characterize. 'Music therapy and occultism', or 'Music therapy and the esoteric' (or 'the para-scientific'), might serve as a heading but immediately engenders prejudice; and it is at once vulnerable to the charge of lumping together a diversity of ideologies. Occultism might be defined as the belief that nature has properties not amenable to the senses, properties beyond, or contrary to, those postulated by science – which the adept can learn to manipulate.[38] Such a definition does small justice to the complex connections between occult and mainstream scientific thought, either during the Renaissance, in which most modern occult traditions originated, or during the nineteenth to early twentieth centuries, when occultism achieved almost as large a cultural significance. Rather than try to disentangle that complexity, however, I shall simply illustrate it, by describing two types of music therapy very much a part of the wider picture, and without which no broad survey of the subject could be complete: the Mesmeric and the Theosophical.

First, Mesmerism. A caption to an early representation of a Mesmerist seance provides a useful introduction:[39]

> M. Mesmer, doctor of medicine in the faculty of Vienna in Austria, is the sole inventor of animal magnetism. That method of curing a multitude of ills (among others, dropsy, paralysis, gout, scurvy, blindness, accidental deafness) consists in the application of a fluid or agent that M. Mesmer directs, at times with one of his fingers, at times with an iron rod that another applies at will, on those who have recourse to him ... The sick, especially women, experience convulsions or crises that bring about their cure ... In the ante-chamber, musicians play tunes to make the sick cheerful.

The techniques and associated apparatus (including a tub of 'magnetized' water) would evolve. But the essentials are all there in that early description. Franz Anton Mesmer (1734–1815) studied medicine in Vienna and was an accomplished amateur musician. Friend of Gluck, Haydn and the Mozart family (the infant prodigy's *Singspiel*, *Bastien and Bastienne*, was supposedly first performed in Mesmer's garden theatre) Mesmer was also skilful on the glass harmonica. The method of treatment which he elaborated may seem like a forerunner of hypnotism and psychoanalysis (brainchild of another Viennese physician);[40] but it is actually best understood against a background of both Renaissance cosmology and Enlightenment science. Mesmer's thesis of 1766, 'De planetarum influxu', was on the familiar Renaissance topic of the influence of the stars on the human body. From Renaissance sources such as Paracelsus and Fludd (his many critics were quick to puncture claims to originality) but also from the some of the physics of his own age, Mesmer derived the notion of a single universal fluid, visible (like its subspecies, ferromagnetism and electricity) only in its effects. This animal fluid (from *anima*, soul) was the medium for the interaction of heavenly bodies with the earth and with animate objects – or to put it in older terminology, of *musica mundana* with *musica humana*. Just as there was in Mesmer's scheme of things only one humour rather than four, so there was only one illness: not a humoral imbalance but a disorderly configuration of magnetic forces within an individual body. This disorder could be counteracted by passing a magnet, or later just a capable hand, over the patient's initially entranced and then convulsed body.

Magnetic fluid could, moreover, supposedly be directed and strengthened by sound.[41] No specifically Mesmeric music survives, at least from the circle of Mesmer himself.[42] And Mesmer never fully articulated its role in his curative sessions. Yet music – sung, or played on the glass harmonica by Mesmer himself or on the piano by an assistant – seems to have been a regular and more than ancillary part of the whole elaborate ritual. So much is clear from the recollections of disciples, among them the poet–physician Justinus Kerner (1786–1862), who himself played the Jew's harp as part of his magnetizing of a famous nineteenth-century 'case', that of the woman whom he immortalized in print as the seeress of Prevorst.[43] The enormous scholarly literature that Mesmerism has generated says relatively little about its musical aspect. Yet that literature has shown what a potent, popular force Mesmerism became in late eighteenth- and nineteenth-century Europe, despite the denunciations of various medical authorities. So there is a type of music therapy here, the possible diffusion of which has been too little noticed. And it is perhaps different from most other European types in that it seeks to induce rather than to end abnormal functioning – to provoke a crisis.

Whether musical or not, a Mesmeric seance was a performance. That does not make it wholly remote from contemporary medical or scientific orthodoxy. We should remember that the ancient postulate of an invisible universal substance held an essential place in Newton's mechanics (see Gouk, above), and that it was not finally banished from physics until the Michelson–Morley experiment of 1887, or indeed until the debates of the early 1900s surrounding Einsteinian relativity.[44] Nor was Mesmeric therapy obviously a failure – by the standards of either the humoral medicine of its time or of its obvious later comparandum, psychoanalysis. The effects may have owed everything to psychodynamics and nothing to magnetism; but they were palpable enough, and in the case of at least some female patients, palpably sexual.[45] Mesmerism has been seen as marking the end of the Enlightenment. In the present context, it might equally be called the revival of the Renaissance or the beginnings of Romantic occultism. But under neither heading should it be thought of as culturally marginal.[46]

Much of its resonance can be detected in the musical world. The most famous example is of course Mozart's comic portrayal of Mesmerism in the first act finale of *Così fan tutte*, in which Despina magnetizes the supposedly arsenic-poisoned suitors.[47] Less well known is Schubert's attendance at a Mesmerist session in 1825. The treatment was directed by the painter Ludwig Schnorr von Carolsfeld, and Schubert participated in it by playing some of his newly-composed dances so that their effect on the patient, Louise Mora, could be observed while she was in a trance.[48] In Kramer's chapter, below, we shall find Liszt being described as mesmerizing his listeners. Wagner too, as composer–conductor, was credited in some quarters with similar powers. A caricature of 1868 shows notes raining down from his baton into the eyes and mouths of a stupefied audience. Another, which appeared in the *Revue trimestrielle* during 1864, explicitly portrays him and Berlioz as engaged in a battle of mutual mesmerizing, score in one hand, baton in the other. Berlioz is the loser: his eyes are closed and he slumps forward in his chair.[49]

Magnetism runs through nineteenth-century esotericism like the powerful unifying force it was claimed to be. It provides the context within which to approach a range of figures who continued the eighteenth-century tradition of conjecturing the physiology of musical healing – a tradition represented, for Britain, by Browne and Brocklesby, and for France by Roger (see Gouk, Chapter 8).[50] In 1874 Antoine Joseph ('Hector') Chomet published the revised text of a lecture that he had been invited to give in Paris in 1846, *Effets et influences de la musique sur la santé et sur la maladie*. In this he postulated a quasi-Mesmerist 'sonorous fluid', to set beside those which respectively conducted heat, light and electricity, and which would explain the physical and psychological effects of music far more satisfactorily than could the already available theories. Two years later, in 1868, Louis Adolphe Le Doulcet, the self-styled Marquis de Pontécoulant, published a tract which bears even more deeply the stamp of 'occultized' Mesmerism, *Les Phénomènes de la musique, ou l'influence du son sur les êtres animés*. This author also conjectured a sonorous fluid to link performer and patient. He had for example 'seen a subject put to sleep by simply touching a guitar that had previously been magnetized, the sonorous fluid being propagated by the vibration of the strings'.[51] Whether or not such figures occupy 'a watershed in the history of music therapy', as their most sympathetic yet scholarly modern commentator has it,[52] they here provide a transition from the Mesmeric world to that of modern organized occultism.

In 1875, Madame Blavatsky, along with Henry Steel Olcott, founded the Theosophical Society in New York.[53] In true Pythagorean style she averred that

> sound may be produced of such a nature that the Pyramid of Cheops would be raised in the air, or that a dying man, nay, one at his last breath, would be revived and filled with new energy and vigour.[54]

Yet musical therapeutics were never very prominent in her thinking. It was rather among second-generation Theosophists that such matters came to the fore. In 1909, for example, Edmond Bailly started publishing *La magie du son* in his own journal, and this was the first part of a project for a book to be entitled *Du merveilleux dans la musique et de la thérapeutique musicale.*[55] Far more influential among this generation, however, was Rudolf Steiner (1861–1925). In 1913, Steiner had founded Anthroposophy (or Spiritual Science), a 'break-away movement' from Theosophy that, unlike its progenitor, has had a lasting educational, medical and musicological impact in Steiner schools and hospitals.[56] Music imbues Steiner's whole mode of expression. There is 'eurhythmy', a conception of movement as visible song.[57] And there is a thoroughly musical conception of the inner life: Steiner looked forward to 'a time when a diseased condition of the soul will … be spoken of in musical terms, as one would speak, for instance, of a piano that was out of tune'.[58] This is reminiscent of Novalis (Chapter 1, above). But Steiner's pronouncements on 'the astral body, which is a musician in every human being, and imitates the music of the cosmos' are more thoroughly neo-Platonic, and seem to be a restatement of the analogy between *musica mundana* and *musica humana* in terms of Victorian spiritualism.[59] Steiner also believed that each musical interval of the chromatic scale expresses a distinctive kind of experience – the minor second, one of movement and activity within the self, extraversion with the perfect fifth, and so on.[60] And it is through the manipulation of such features, presumably, that a therapist can alter the astral body and realign it with the cosmic harmony. The ambition is treat the whole person in artistic and spiritual terms, seeing illness as an opportunity for positive change rather than a setback that should be reversed.

Steinerian practice overlaps with the modern Western music therapy adumbrated in Chapter 1, its development chronicled by Tyler below.[61] It does so, first, through influencing the practice of Nordoff and Robbins, itself extremely influential; second, through Steiner institutions such as the Herdecke Hospital of the University of Wittenberg, where the music of 'natural instruments' such as lyre and recorder is piped to patients in an otherwise 'high-tech' hospital.[62] David Aldridge, whose conception of human life as a musical composition we encountered above (in Chapter 1), writes of the music therapy practised at Herdecke as not of the Anthroposophical type. Yet he reproduces a Steinerian table of the emotions with which specific intervals may be linked.[63] Pervasive connections between Steiner therapists and mainstream professionals have clearly endured.

A final question: what place should be given to composers in the recent history of music therapy? Are there modern equivalents to Schubert, Liszt or Wagner as quasi-Mesmerists? Alexander Scriabin and Arnold Schoenberg were, to differing extents, Theosophical adepts. Schoenberg's esotericism emerges in such works as the incomplete oratorio, *Die Jakobsleiter*, but he does not seem to have conceived his music with therapeutic intent.[64] Scriabin, by contrast, thought of himself as another Orpheus, and planned the ultimate therapy of total dissolution. His final work was to be the *Mysterium*, of which – mercifully – only a 'Prefatory Act' was sketched (and has been posthumously reconstructed, and recorded). The whole would have been performed over seven days. (Seven was the number of human races according to Madame Blavatsky.) Even the 'Prefatory Act' by itself – to which, with unwonted pragmatism, Scriabin eventually confined himself – was to take place in a specially built temple in India, with spectators seated in tiers according to their degree of spiritual advancement. There were to be costumed speakers, processions, parades; dancers as well as musicians would take part, each in their thousands. Pillars of incense would form part of the scenery. And all this was merely the prelude to the final mystery, in which everyone would be dissolved in ecstasy. 'A brand-new race of purified, purged, clarified and spiritually advanced men is born ... to repeat this monster act all over again, but on a higher plane.'[65]

Other composers, since Scriabin, have also seen themselves as therapists of a sort. Answering Hölderlin's question, 'what are poets for in a barren age?', Michael Tippett for instance portrayed the composer as virtually healing society – and as doing so very traditionally by contraries: restoring harmony and balance in a way that would not have surprised the Renaissance figures who populate Part III.[66] A related theme of Tippett's work, derived from Jung, was the need to know both one's 'shadow', or dark side of the personality, and one's 'light', so as to achieve wholeness. It was a theme that Tippett dramatized in almost all his operas, from *The Midsummer Marriage* to *New Year*, and, pre-eminently, in the oratorio *A Child of Our Time*; and by dramatizing it he could be said to have attempted to induce it in his audiences. This is not, however, a particularly esoteric project, for all Jung's interest in the occult. Cyril Scott (1879–1970), by contrast, professed himself inspired by the Mahatma Koot Hoomi, a 'Master' described by him as a reincarnation of Pythagoras and over 150 years old.[67] Scott was a neo-Platonist and occultist with decided views on how music has surreptitiously influenced the whole history of mankind. He wrote books on medicine, health, and cancer, and looked forward to a 'type of music calculated to heal'.[68]

The main inheritor of the mantle of Wagner and Scriabin – his *magnum opus* also a gargantuan seven-day multi-media work, the opera cycle *Licht* – is, however, Karlheinz Stockhausen. Stockhausen believes himself to have come from another world, the star Sirius, and his thought has for decades been deeply coloured by that of Sri Aurobindo and by that of *The Urantia Book* of the Urantia Brotherhood of Chicago, as well as by Jakob Böhme, Nostradamus, Madame Blavatsky and Jakob Lorber. Of all major contemporary composers, it is Stockhausen who has shown the greatest interest in professional music therapy, while all the time relating it to his occult cosmological concerns.[69] Clearly he sees all his compositions as potentially therapeutic. One excerpt from a characteristic discourse can serve as conclusion here, and indeed (in anticipation) as conclusion to the whole volume.

> Music should above all be a *means* of maintaining the soul's link with the beyond [Stockhausen said in an interview of 1973] ... Nowadays there is something new, music therapy, which is becoming more and more popular ... We have no idea about what music therapy can do. Only now are we slowly starting to rediscover that ... Rather strangely, therapists only start helping people with music when they are already afflicted. My music is often used for therapy. Unfortunately that only happens when people are hospitalised and already completely unbalanced. Only very few people *know* that *every single one of us* basically needs music as a means of self-healing.[70]

Notes

1.   Carl Gregor, Herzog zu Mecklenburg, *Bibliographie einiger Grenzgebiete der Musikwissenschaft* (Baden-Baden, 1962), contains over 120 entries on music therapy and cognate topics published since 1800 and I would guess that few of them have been explored by historians.

2.   See C. Kramer, 'Soul Music as Exemplified in Nineteenth-Century German Psychiatry', in P. Gouk (ed.), *Musical Healing in Cultural Contexts* (Aldershot, 2000), p. 137.

3.   Gouk, *Musical Healing*.

4.   See Voss, Chapter 7; and Heather, Chapter 9.

5.   See, for example, from a vast literature, C. Humphrey, *Shamans and Elders: Experience, Knowledge, and Power among the Daur Mongols* (Oxford, 1996).

6.   For some primary texts see P. Le Huray and J. Day, *Music and Aesthetics in the Eighteenth and Early-Nineteenth Centuries* (Cambridge, 1981).

7.   Voss and Gouk, above; R. Klibansky, E. Panofsky and F. Saxl, *Saturn and Melancholy* (London, 1964), ch. 1.

8.   *Richard Wagner an Mathilde Wesendonk: Tagebuchblätter und Briefe 1853–1871*, 5th edn (Berlin, 1904), no. 66 (1859), p. 123.

9.   A. Schopenhauer, *Die Welt als Wille und Vorstellung* [*The World as Will and Idea*] (Leipzig, 1819), and many subsequent editions and translations.

10. For this and what follows, among a large literature see J. Goldstein, 'Psychiatry', in W. Bynum and R. Porter (eds), *Companion Encyclopedia of the History of Medicine*, 2 vols (London, 1993), vol. 2, pp. 1350–72, with good general bibliography. For Britain see further: R. Porter, *Mind-Forg'd Manacles: A History of Madness in England from the Restoration to the Regency* (London, 1987); Porter, 'Madness and its Institutions', in A. Wear (ed.), *Medicine in Society* (Cambridge, 1992), pp. 227–301; A. Scull, *The Most Solitary of Afflictions: Madness and Society in Britain 1700–1900* (New Haven and London, 1993); C. MacKenzie, *Psychiatry for the Rich: A History of Ticehurst Private Asylum, 1792–1917* (London and New York, 1992), ch. 1. On the contrasting world of pauper asylums see J. Melling and B. Forsythe (eds), *Insanity, Institutions and Society, 1800–1914* (London, 1999).

11. P. Lain Entralgo, *The Therapy of the Word in Classical Antiquity* (New Haven and London, 1970).

12. M. McDonald, *Mystical Bedlam: Madness, Anxiety, and Healing in Seventeenth-Century England* (Cambridge, 1981), p. 230; see also his 'Lunatics and the State in Georgian England', *Social History of Medicine*, 2 (1989), pp. 299–300.

13. Shiloah, Chapter 3; though compare Page on monastic infirmaries. W. F. Kümmel, *Musik und Medizin: Ihre Wechselbeziehungen in Theorie und Praxis von 800 bis 1800* (Freiburg and Munich, 1977), pp. 260–63, notes the apparent exception of the hospital of S. Spirito in Sassia, not far from St Peter's, the most elaborate hospital in early modern Rome, but music there was played as an accompaniment to eating, an aid to digestion.

14. See Goldstein, 'Psychiatry', pp. 1352–7, for a helpful outline sketch. Compare A. Scull, *Social Order/Mental Disorder: Anglo-American*

Psychiatry in Historical Perspective (Berkeley and Los Angeles, 1989), ch. 4.

15. Remarkably, no chapter of synthesis on the nineteenth century is to be found in D. M. Schullian and M. Schoen (eds), *Music and Medicine* (New York, 1948).

16. For detail on what follows see G. N. Heller, 'Ideas, Initiatives, and Implementations: Music Therapy in America, 1789–1848', *Journal of Music Therapy*, 24.1 (1987), pp. 35–46 at 35–8.

17. While also drawing on Descartes' *Les passions de l'âme* [*The Passions of the Soul*] (1649).

18. On Herman Boerhaave (1668–1738) see G. A. Lindeboom, *Herman Boerhaave: The Man and His Work* (London, 1968); Boerhaave's very occasional interest in music therapy is noted by Kümmel, *Musik und Medizin*, pp. 300, 356. For William Cullen (1710–90), see A. Doig, J. P. S. Ferguson, I. A. Milne and R. Passmore (eds), *William Cullen and the Eighteenth Century Medical World* (Edinburgh, 1993). For Cullen's treatment of insanity see his *First Lines of the Practice of Physic*, 4 vols, new edn (Edinburgh, 1786), vol. 3, pp. 266 ff. Cullen's translation into Spanish was noted by León Sanz, Chapter 12.

19. W. B. Davis, K. E. Gfeller and M. H. Traut, *An Introduction to Music Therapy: Theory and Practice* (Dubuque, IA, 1992), p. 22; Heller, 'Ideas', pp. 38–9; W. B. Davis, 'Music Therapy in 19th Century America', *Journal of Music Therapy*, 24.2 (1987), pp. 76–87 at 77; E. T. Carlson and M. B. Simpson, 'Tarantism or Hysteria? An American Case of 1801', *Journal of the History of Medicine and Allied Sciences*, 26 (1971), p. 301.

20. C. Burney, *A General History of Music*, 2nd edn (London, 1789, repr. New York, 1957), 'Dissertation on the Music of the Ancients', section 10.

21. Mathews, *On the Effects of Music*, p. 14, cited from Heller, 'Ideas', p. 40.

22. Davis, 'Music Therapy', p. 78.

23. Carlson and Simpson, 'Tarantism', p. 302.

24. Heller, 'Ideas', p. 40; Davis, 'Music Therapy', p. 78.

25. Goldstein, 'Psychiatry', p. 1357. Biographies of Rush include those by N. G. Goodman (Philadelphia, 1934), C. Binger (New York, 1966), D. F. Hawke (Indianapolis, 1971).

26. *The Letters of Benjamin Rush*, ed. L. H. Butterfield, 2 vols (Princeton, NJ, 1951), p. 1052.

27. *Letters*, pp. 443, 763, 766–7, 769.

28. *Medical Inquiries and Observations upon Diseases of the Mind* (Philadelphia, 1812, facsimile edn, New York, 1962), pp. 122–3, 211, 228, 329, 355; quotations from pp. 123, 211.

29. J. M. Cox, *Practical Observations on Insanity* (London, 1806), pp. 140 ff., with Scull, *Social Order / Mental Disorder*, pp. 71–3.

30. *Medical Inquiries and Observations*, pp. 11, 229. Contrast D. Ramsay, *An Eulogium upon Benjamin Rush MD* (Philadelphia, 1813), p. 47, who writes approvingly of Rush's never having needed to use chains or whips.

31. G. N. Grob, *The Mad Among Us: A History of the Care of America's Mentally Ill* (New York, 1994), ch. 2, and pp. 66–70; Scull, *Social Order / Mental Disorder*, ch. 5 ('The Discovery of the Asylum Revisited: Lunacy Reform in the New American Republic'); N. Dain, *Concepts of Insanity in the United States* (New Brunswick, NJ, 1964). For a Canadian instance of music therapy in the asylum see S. E. D. Shortt, *Victorian Lunacy: Richard M. Bucke and the Practice of Late Nineteenth-Century Psychiatry* (Cambridge, 1986), pp. 133–4.

32. W. W. Turner and D. E. Bartlett, 'Music among the Deaf and Dumb', *American Annals of the Deaf and Dumb*, 2 (October, 1848), p. 6, cited by Heller, 'Ideas', pp. 41–2.

33. Heller, 'Ideas', pp. 43–4.

34. Davis, 'Music Therapy', pp. 79–81.

35. Blumer, 'Music in its Relation to Insanity', *American Journal of Insanity*, 50 (1891–92), pp. 350–64, cited by Davis, 'Music Therapy', pp. 81–94.

36. J. L. Corning, 'The Use of Musical Vibrations Before and During Sleep ...', *Medical Record*, 14 (1899), pp. 79–86, cited by Davis, 'Music Therapy', pp. 85–6.

37. Davis et al., *An Introduction to Music Therapy*, pp. 26–30.

38. R. Galbraith, 'Explaining Modern Occultism', in H. Kerr and C. L. Crow (eds), *The Occult in America: New Historical Perspectives* (Urbana and Chicago, 1983), pp. 15–19.

39. R. Darnton, *Mesmerism and the End of the Enlightenment in France* (Cambridge, MA, and London, 1968), pp. 6–7.

40. See H. Ellenberger's classic *The Discovery of the Unconscious: The History and Evolution of Dynamic Psychiatry* (London, 1970), pp. 57 ff., where Mesmer's work is presented as a turning point in the evolution of dynamic psychotherapy. Note also A. Crabtree, *From Mesmer to Freud* (New Haven and London, 1993). For Mesmer's career, conflicts with the medical establishment, and larger impact, among a substantial recent literature see F. A. Pattie, *Mesmer and Animal Magnetism* (Hamilton, NY, 1994); A. Gauld, *A History of Hypnotism* (Cambridge, 1992).

41. E. Völkel, *Die spekulative Musiktherapie zur Zeit der Romantik: Ihre Traditionen und ihr Fortwirken* (Düsseldorf, 1979), pp. 118–34. L. Brockliss and C. Jones, *The Medical World of Early Modern France* (Oxford, 1997), p. 792.

42. Robert Darnton, personal communication.

43. *Die Seherin von Prevorst*, 2 vols (Stuttgart and Tübingen, 1829). See the abbreviated English translation by Mrs Crowe, *The Seeress of Prevorst* (London, 1845), p. 73. Völkel, *Die spekulative Musiktherapie*,

pp. 126, 128–31; for Kerner, pp. 135–9. Ellenberger, *Discovery of the Unconscious*, pp. 79–81.

44. G. N. Cantor and M. J. S. Hodge (eds), *Conceptions of Ether: Studies in the History of Ether Theories, 1740–1900* (Cambridge, 1981).

45. Brockliss and Jones, *The Medical World of Early Modern France*, p. 789.

46. See T. James, *Dreams, Creativity, and Madness in Nineteenth-Century France* (Oxford, 1995), ch. 3. For the USA, see R. C. Fuller, *Mesmerism and the American Cure of Souls* (Philadelphia, 1982).

47. Compare the portrayal of moral therapy in Paisiello's *Nina*: S. Castelvecchi, 'From *Nina* to *Nina*: Psychodrama, Absorption and Sentiment in the 1780s', *Cambridge Opera Journal*, 8.2 (1996), pp. 91–112 at 94.

48. L. Feurzeig, 'Heroines in Perversity: Marie Schmith, Animal Magnetism, and the Schubert Circle', *19th-Century Music*, 21.2 (1997), pp. 223–43. Compare H. Goldschmidt, 'Schubert und kein Ende', *Beiträge zur Musik Wissenschaft*, 25 (1983), p. 290. Feurzeig tries, unconvincingly, to show that Mesmerism permeated some of Schubert's songs: pp. 240–43.

49. A. Winter, *Mesmerized: Powers of Mind in Victorian Britain* (Chicago and London, 1998), pp. 314–15.

50. For what follows see J. Godwin, *Music and the Occult: French Musical Philosophies 1750–1950* (Rochester, NY, 1995), pp. 141–2.

51. Paris, 1868, p. 21.

52. Godwin, *Music and the Occult*, p. 142.

53. See P. Washington, *Madame Blavatsky's Baboon: Theosophy and the Emergence of the Western Guru* (London, 1993).

54. H. P. Blavatsky, *The Secret Doctrine*, 2 vols (London, 1888, and many subsequent editions), vol. 1, p. 555 (addenda to bk 1, no. 10).

55. Godwin, *Music and the Occult*, p. 157.

56. R. Steiner, *Anthroposophy: An Introduction* (1950, trans. London, 1983), *The Nature of Anthroposophy* (New York, 1964), *The Essential Steiner*, ed. R. McDermot (San Francisco, CA, 1984).

57. Steiner, *Eurhythmy as Visible Music* (London, 1977).

58. *Essential Steiner*, p. 349.

59. *Essential Steiner*, p. 348. Compare D. P. Walker, 'The Astral Body in Renaissance Medicine', *Journal of the Warburg and Courtauld Institutes*, 21 (1958), pp. 119–33.

60. A. von Lange, *Man, Music and Cosmos* (London, 1992).

61. See also K. E. Bruscia, *Improvisational Models of Music Therapy* (Springfield, IL, 1987), pp. 30–32.

62. Gary Ansdell, personal communication.

63. *Music Therapy Research and Practice in Medicine: From Out of the Silence* (London and Bristol, PA, 1996), pp. 8, 152.

64. I have not yet seen C. Cross, *Political and Religious Ideas in the Works of Arnold Schoenberg* (New York and London, 1999).

65. F. Bowers, *Scriabin*, 2nd revised edn, 2 vols (New York, 1996), vol. 2, p. 254. See also B. de Schloezer, *Scriabin: Artist and Mystic* (Oxford, 1987), pp. 236 ff., 260 ff.

66. *Moving into Aquarius*, new edn (St Albans, 1974), p. 156 (and p. 100).

67. M. Trend, *The Musik Makers: The English Musical Renaissance from Elgar to Britten* (London, 1985), pp. 144–7 at 146.

68. C. Scott, *Doctors, Disease and Health* (London, 1938), *Medicine, Rational and Irrational* (London, 1946), *An Outline of Modern Occultism* (London, 1935), *Music: Its Secret Influence throughout the Ages* (London, 1958), quotation from p. 200.

69. M. Kurtz, *Stockhausen: A Biography* (London and Boston, 1992), pp. 185, 188, 190, 196, 207.

70. *Towards a Cosmic Music: Texts by Karlheinz Stockhausen*, ed. T. Nevill (Shaftesbury, Boston, MA, and Melbourne, 1989), p. 58. See also J. Cott, *Stockhausen: Conversations with the Composer* (London, 1974), pp. 113–114, a discussion of the music therapy of chickens.

CHAPTER FOURTEEN

Music as Cause and Cure of Illness in Nineteenth-Century Europe

Cheryce Kramer

I

Long before music therapy had consolidated into the specialist discipline that it has become today, physicians, musicians, priests and philosophers throughout Europe had, as we have seen, imagined ways in which music might be used for curative purposes. In the nineteenth century these speculations acquired an increasingly mechanical bent as medical contrivances exhibiting a fantastic, even sinister, inventiveness were conceived for harnessing the so-called power of music.

So, for example, at the very beginning of the nineteenth century, a prominent German physician, Johann Christian Reil, urged the 'cat-piano' for the treatment of mental illnesses. As implied by its name this instrument consisted of a series of cats selected by pitch and placed with their tails pointing backwards towards a keyboard of sharp nails. According to Reil, a fugue played upon such an instrument would be able to cure most any condition, 'especially if the patient be placed so as to witness the physiognomic reactions and gestures of the animals in question'.[1] Though peculiar, Reil's piano was not peculiarly impractical. This was not the wild ratiocination of a crank working on the fringe of educated society. Reil enjoyed considerable public esteem in his day, and was one of the preferred physicians of, among others, Goethe and Schelling.[2] What is most striking, however, is not Reil's faith in medical contrivance but his assumption that musical sensation has medicinal qualities. He believed the effects of music to be primarily psychological, not physical, and consequently promoted its use for the treatment of mental disorders, not somatic ones.

Reil belongs firmly to the world of musical Romanticism. From Mendelssohn in Germany to Berlioz in France and Elgar in Britain, Romantic music presumed the musical experience to be an essentially psychological phenomenon. This conception represented a profound shift from the reigning sensationalist philosophy of the eighteenth century in which musical experience had been associated primarily with physical states and employed for the treatment of what were seen as somatic disorders.[3] It will not be possible to trace the epistemological foundations of this shift in the space of the present article. Nor is it necessary for illustrating what concerns us here: namely, the historical ramification of this shift, which was the association of music therapy with mental medicine in the nineteenth century.

This association was as much a cultural artefact as an intrinsic quality of Romantic music. Psychiatry and music therapy were not only employed by the same groups of physicians for the same therapeutic purposes but were linked in the public perception where, as reflected in Romantic literature, music and madness regularly figured as twin concepts. Moreover, with the 'psychologization' of musical experience, music became subject to a nineteenth-century commonplace which held that, in the realm of psychological causation, the very factors that can provoke a psychological disorder can also serve to cure it. Thus music was perceived as alternately pathogenic and salutary. A few evocative examples from the realms of fiction, history and philosophy will illustrate the perceived therapeutic ambiguity of music and its intimate association with psychiatric practice in nineteenth-century Europe.

II

First, Romantic music as toxin. A compelling portrayal of its deleterious effects is to be found in a satirical German short story published in 1807 by Clemens Brentano and Johann Joseph von Görres: Romantic poets, literary collaborators and close friends. Together they composed an absurd, surreal and ironic account of musically-induced madness. The intricate humour of this account is anticipated in its title, elaborate even by the standards of German syntax: *Either the Fantastic Tale of BOGS, the Clockmaker, and How after Having Left*

*His Earthly Form He Did Eventually Have Hope of Being Accepted
into the Respected Citizen's Society of Archers but Only After
Prolonged Musical Adventures over Water and Land, Or the Concert
Advertisement which Moved Beyond the Borders of the Baden Weekly
as a Supplement.*[4]

Bogs, the protagonist, seeks admission to a closed society, the
Respected Citizen's Society of Archers, whose condition of membership is that applicants renounce every last vestige of their humanity.
As proof of readiness, applicants must submit a psychological self-
assessment form which, in Bogs's case, reveals several suspiciously
human traits. The society challenges him to a trial by fire, or rather
by music. Bogs is required to sit through 'a concert of the new music'
– that is, Romantic music – without losing his mind. The implication
is that no human being can resist the power of this music. And,
indeed, Bogs succumbs immediately upon hearing the opening lines
of the concert. He lapses into a precarious mental state with a patently
erotic component, the sexual innuendo providing conclusive evidence
of Bogs's residual humanity:

> I resembled the charged column of a Galvanic machine, the hall
> and I spun around, a hurricane of sound broke forth from every
> instrument, I pressed my eyes shut, my knees together, both of
> my hands into my pockets and fondled my watches. Adieu
> world! The storm of a Haydn-like symphony took hold of my
> hair, then my brain, from there to escape by my ears with all of
> my cognitive functions, which opened up like two sails billowing
> in the wind and carried me through heaven and earth, water and
> fire and occasionally even threw me against a rock, ouch my
> watches, oh my, oh my.[5]

This quotation is just the beginning of a detailed, sixteen-page
account of Bogs's reaction to the concert, virtually beat by beat, as he
gradually loses the struggle to keep his swelling and surging emotions
from overwhelming his reason. In the course of this struggle,
Cartesian dualism, Kantian rationalism, and Romantic idealism are,
by turns, implicated. Bogs dies at the end of a concert and the society
commissions a dissection report to examine his susceptibility to musical influence. The report identifies a number of contributing factors,
including the fact that Bogs is anatomically comprised of bad music,
his internal organs consisting almost entirely of 'rather unpleasant

musical repetitions', 'isolated notes', 'stray melodies' and 'scales from the previous night's concert'.[6]

In chronicling the progressive stages of the concert ordeal, Brentano and Görres draw the reader into the vortex of Bogs's sensory world; his musical hallucinations conjure a corresponding aural sensation in the reader, who can hear the concert that Bogs is hearing from the description of the visions he is said to be having. This is not only a literary trick but a psychological experiment suggestive of William James's applied introspective method. It explores the power of musical suggestion by means of the synaesthetic connection between different forms of sensory arousal: fiction can equal a visual image, can equal an aural sensation. By arousing in their readers the experience of a fictitious concert, the authors locate the apprehension of Romantic music in the realm of the psychological.

While poking fun at the excesses of the Romantic posture in music, Brentano and Görres actually wrote the satirical piece as a vindication of the Romantic sensibility in general. Their humour is directed more against those who fear the psychological effects of Romantic music, and Romantic art in general, than against those who revel in its transformative effects. Bogs, whose name derives from the first and last letters of 'Brentano' and 'Görres', is a Romantic hero. Yet what makes the Bogs story suitable for our interpretative purposes is that Görres was also a practising physician. His medical experience permeates both the narrative structure and the thematic content of the story.

Implausible as Bogs's fate may seem, its psychological veracity is corroborated by contemporary historical events – for example, the reception of Franz Liszt in Europe during the 1820s and 1830s. According to the Romantic author Alexander Sternberg, an 'insane stupor' overcame the female population of the city when Liszt performed in Berlin. Sternberg, who witnessed this stupor with his own eyes, places the event in 'the annals of medical history rather than the history of music'. He consistently refers to Liszt devotees, who were primarily women, as 'the mesmerized ones' ['die Electrisierten'], comparing the effects of Liszt's musical performances to a Mesmeric seance.[7] As he remembers, 'the galvanized ones' would collapse into a state of either manic excitation or deep melancholy. The manic

would have no other desire than 'to draw attention to themselves ...
They would bribe waiters, stand behind doors and wait by the carriage
until the concert ended in order to drink the dregs of tea remaining in
the cup of their beloved'.[8] The melancholic would 'waste away, stare
fixedly at one point and turn inwards for days on end' after having
been 'helped home' from the concert on the arm of a friend. The
passions stirred by a Liszt recital are confirmed by the music historian, Percy Scholes, who writes that 'so fervid was feminine admiration that if [Liszt] dropped his handkerchief it was torn to pieces as
"souvenirs"'.[9]

Romantic music was potentially pathogenic. It could produce such
a powerful psychological response that it robbed the subject of all reason. The same fate that befell Bogs at his trial concert also befell
many a hapless listener at a Liszt concert – confirming, for anyone in
need of such confirmation, that real life will tend to surpass even the
most satirical literary accounts.

III

Romantic music was also tonic as well as toxin. In 1840 the Czech
physician, Leopold Raudnitz, published a popular book on music
therapy summarizing the views of his French and German counterparts and presenting his own findings as director of the Prague insane
asylum.[10] Raudnitz claimed to have witnessed delirious patients
'cease to babble', melancholy ones 'find comfort and calm', maniacs
'relax their tense posture', idiots 'become relatively animated' and
even delusional patients 'show marked improvement' under the influence of restorative music. Raudnitz dedicated this book to Liszt, the
very man whose music allegedly produced those same mental disorders. Yet this was not as paradoxical a gesture as it might seem.
Besides driving his listeners out of their minds, the young Liszt also
dabbled in some amateur music therapy. Around 1830, he seems to
have started visiting the hospitals of Paris. A newspaper cutting that
survives from the Paris journal *Variété*, datable to 1831–32, reveals
the headline 'L'idiote mélomane'. As Liszt's biographer, Alan
Walker, reports, the cutting

tells the strange story of a sixty-year-old woman who had been a patient in the Salpêtrière hospital for the insane from childhood. She was incapable of understanding anything, of dressing herself, of working, and even of speaking ... It was noticed, however, that she responded at once to music. She was able to sing back melodies that were sung to her, and she could even recall them after a lapse of time.[11]

Liszt was invited to visit the hospital and play to her, a piano having been set up in her cell.

The moment Liszt's fingers touched the keyboard, the old woman's eyes became fixated on them. Gnawing her fists, she appeared to enter a highly charged state, and she vibrated to every cord struck by the young musician. The passage he played produced a visible effect on her similar to that of an electrical discharge.

The outcome is not recorded; but the description suggests that Liszt's music had a restorative effective on this patient.

Music was perceived as a means of adjusting and calibrating psychological states and, hence, as a tool for psychiatric intervention. In the nineteenth century, psychiatry emerged as a specialist discipline with its own taxonomy of illnesses and treatment methods, including music therapy. The natural place to administer musical cures to patients was the newly-founded curative insane asylum.[12] The German medical historian, Werner Friedrich Kümmel, credits Etienne Esquirol, director of the Charenton asylum in France, with introducing a new sophistication into the application of music to the treatment of mental illness.[13] But Kümmel's study ends in 1800, giving the reader little sense of the diversity of psychiatric approaches and musical therapies in the asylum after that point. This diversity has, however, been captured by Rudolf Schumacher, who describes asylum music from Naples to Berlin and St Remy to Dorpat.[14] His examples demonstrate that the uses of music in the asylum were at least as culturally specific as were musical practices outside it. Unfortunately, Schumacher's historical analysis does not present a systematic differentiation of these national traditions. In the absence of a general overview, the following discussion of asylum music will focus on a single country while adducing examples from other countries for illustrative contrast. Germany recommends itself for our purposes because it was the centre not only of Romantic music but also of 'speculative' music therapy in Europe at the time.

In 1807 Peter Lichtenthal published a popular book entitled *Der musikalische Arzt* [*The Musical Physician*], advocating a musical therapeutics in which each note of the scale was believed to have a distinct psychological effect.[15] C-sharp correlated with 'innocence, naiveté' and 'baby-talk' while B-flat is 'somewhat cranky and unhappy'.[16] Although Lichtenthal held that mental disorders could be treated by means of a suitable musical composition, he never specified the psychological mechanism underlying this musical transference. He did, however, emphasize that receptivity to music depended upon the patient's frame of mind when the musical cure was being administered. Listening, he maintained, is an event which requires careful psychological preparation:

> When listening to fine music we should not be distracted by any foreign interferences; rather, we must listen attentively with our general perception, with clear awareness, in order to pick up all that is in our power to pick up. For example: what is the theme? what is the tempo? what is the key, what harmonic relations have been used, what embellishments, transitions, phrases? How has the composer planned the piece: that is, how does the theme unfold, how much does it resemble the object it is supposed to reflect? and, most importantly, what is the instrumentation? the answers to all of these [questions] will enable us to see whether the composer has created a meaningful achievement or not. Once we have inspected this *what* and *how*, we will have heard the music.[17]

For Lichtenthal, musical cures were associated with pleasure. Really hearing the music entailed conscious listening to the music; unconscious hearing, that is to say hearing with one's body alone, was insufficient for purposes of medical treatment. Presumably Lichtenthal would have been appalled by the notion of forcing patients to make music. But this is precisely what Esquirol did to a patient who was refusing to practise the violin; after being threatened with the 'douche' the patient finally capitulated and played the *Marseillaise*.[18]

A more comprehensive and influential work on music therapy was Peter Joseph Schneider's three-volume compendium, *System einer medizinischen Musik* [*A System of Medical Music*], published in 1835.[19] Unlike Lichtenthal, who assumed that music would form part of a physician's general medical training, Schneider envisaged the creation of a specialist medical discipline in music therapy. This difference is reflected in their choice of titles: Lichtenthal's echoed Weikard's popular book, *Der Philosophische Arzt*, a metaphysical study of healing, while Schneider's title echoed Frank's *System einer Medicinischen Polizey*, suggesting that music therapy could form part of a state-sponsored program of mental hygiene.

But Schneider, like Lichtenthal, construed music therapy and psychiatry as complementary activities best pursued in the context of asylum medicine:

> Every insane asylum should, alongside its collection of surgical instruments, also keep a collection of musical instruments for the treatment of mental illness; these musical instruments should, however, be employed by specially-trained physicians for the sake of patients.[20]

Schneider argued that, because psychiatry was based on an unsound medical taxonomy – in his words 'the thin skeleton of a dry nomenclature' – resources currently being directed towards developing psychological medicine would produce better results if directed towards musical medicine.[21] Moreover, he warned, psychiatrists administer musical cures to their patients without having received a proper musical education. Schneider's critique of psychiatry, combined with his efforts to obtain some of the professional resources controlled by his psychiatric counterparts, reveals the disciplinary proximity of music therapy and mental medicine at this time.

Both Lichtenthal and Schneider agreed that soul states could be modified and adjusted through music. Schneider cited as evidence the case of a woman whom he had personally cured of menstrual constipation. I shall quote the passage in full because it is such a vivid portrayal of asylum-based music therapy, blending together one patient's subjective reactions and the modulations of the music itself:

> She sat there mute, mute as a fish, and without motion. Then I began to play my fantasy in a pitch appropriate to the spiritual tone of one sunk deep in melancholy, E-flat. Quietly, then crescendo-ing into the strongest fortissimo and from there to a

moderate piano; emphatic at times, at times restrained, prolonging the chord and then continuing through the full range of harmonic changes and variations. After the third crescendo ... the
patient exhaled a deep sigh. But still she remained mute and
otherwise still. I preludized on G-sharp and gave the key-note for
the chorus to begin. Its first words could still be heard, swelling,
then leading to a murmur and back. They had not as yet subsided
and one could hear the leading tenor clearly, discernibly and
quietly supported by the choir – when suddenly the patient cried
out: 'O! Antonio, Antonio!' [the tenor's name]. Thereupon she
cried so much that the singing had to desist. The unhappy patient,
deeply shaken, had to be brought to bed. Once her room was
illuminated we made the pleasing discovery that with the utterance of 'Oh! Antonio, Antonio!' her flow of monthly bleeding
had been released: and it had thickly, very thickly covered the
entire floor.[22]

This scene of musical healing is curiously reminiscent of Bogs's
musical experience, except that, instead of death from Romantic over-
stimulation, the patient's menstrual fluids are released by the strains
of curative music. Schneider notes that within less than a year the
patient had been entirely restored.

Various aspects of the music therapy proposed by Lichtenthal and
Schneider were taken up and promoted in German asylum practice.
The Illenau asylum in Baden (1842–1940), for example, prided itself
in excelling 'all other asylums' in the use of music for treatment.
According to an article published by Illenau officials in 1886:

> Music and singing have become indispensable components of the
> Illenau way of life. These arts are perceived as restorative thera-
> peutic instruments; and former members of our asylum cannot
> look back upon their Illenau years without remembering the
> musical performances that took place in the large central court or
> assembly hall, in the day rooms of the wards or in the region
> around the asylum.[23]

And indeed this claim was corroborated by the accounts of Illenau
patient of their treatment at the asylum. In a letter written to the
asylum in 1867, for instance, a patient requested copies of her three
favourite Illenau songs because she associated these songs with her
restored sanity which she revealingly described as a sense of 'feeling
all singing-like'.[24]

Illenau boasted its own choir, in-house brass band and full-time music instructor. The asylum also published a hymn-book which became the standard text for asylums throughout Germany.[25] In 1879 alone, Illenau staged 140 separate musical events drawing on the talents of doctors, patients and visitors and featuring primarily Romantic pieces inspired by folk-songs and children's ditties. One Illenau concert announcement documents the musical virtuosity of Illenau trainee Richard von Krafft-Ebing, more famous today for inventing the terms 'masochism' and 'sadism', but appreciated by fellow members of the asylum community for his inspired piano-playing.[26] Nor was composing the prerogative of Illenau's medical staff: patients were also encouraged to write music, as is documented in the file of a female patient containing several musical compositions.

Illenau doctors held the soul to be a rhythmic entity, the so-called *Gemüth*, whose mode of apprehension they likened to a form of musical phenomenology. This soul concept was informed by idealist philosophy and accounts for the particular role of music in German psychiatric practice.[27] German psychiatrists equated mental disorders with a state of 'arrhythmia' which could be combated by means of music (broadly construed to embrace gymnastics and the daily routine).[28] Again life surpasses literature as Bogs's musical anatomy was here effectively elevated to a serious and respectable medical theory about the structure of the soul.

Yet Illenau's musical cures were not entirely as Schneider envisaged in that music therapy was decidedly subordinate to the psychiatric objectives of the asylum. Musical selections had 'in every instance to be approved by the medical director' and compositions deemed emotionally or intellectually too demanding had to be rescored by him.[29] The preferred composer at Illenau was Mendelssohn, presumably because of the exemplary harmonic balance achieved in his pieces. As Charles Rosen has argued, Mendelssohn's *Songs Without Words* have

> a Mozartean grace without Mozart's dramatic power, a Schubertean lyricism without Schubert's intensity. If we could be satisfied today with a simple beauty that raises no questions and does not attempt to puzzle us, the short pieces would resume

their old place in the concert repertoire. They charm, but they neither provoke nor astonish. It is not true that they are insipid, but they might as well be.[30]

This moderate musical style appears to have been just what the doctor ordered at Illenau.

According to the American psychiatrist Pliny Earle, who toured European asylums in the 1850s, 'music was one of the principal sources of entertainment' in most German asylums.[31] The truth is that few of them could compete with the musical facilities at Illenau.

Outside Germany, too, the configuration of musical therapeutics differed not only from country to country but from institution to institution. Music functioned variously as medication, entertainment and an alternative form of restraint, and, most often, as some combination of all of the above. So, for example, a letter written to Hector Berlioz by one of his friends in 1848 likened the introduction of music therapy in the asylum at Auxerre to a form of aestheticized restraint which facilitated the running of the asylum:

> Last year when I had visited I found the asylum to be well-appointed but full of grated and oppressive spaces in which a large number of inmates suffered frequent fits of rage and were forcibly confined like animals. So you can well imagine my astonishment when Girard of Cailleux, the asylum director, showed me open rooms which had been transformed into halls containing not a single piece of furniture out of place. The rooms were filled with unrestrained, calm people occupied with a variety of tasks. Stunned by this extraordinary improvement I asked the director by what method he had produced this result. 'Through gentle persuasion, activity and *music* which I use to reward the lunatics for good behaviour.'[32]

By contrast the German psychiatrist Wilhelm Horn reported on another French asylum in 1831 where music and bathing had been combined to form a peculiar style of shock-therapy. According to Horn, the bath house, which had eight stone bath tubs, showers and a sauna, also contained a very loud organ, large drum and cymbals; as soon as a patient began to undergo treatment 'an awesome spectacle was unleashed which gave me fright even though I had been prepared for it'.[33]

The preferred manner of performing and witnessing a musical event was also culturally specific. Esquirol, for example, insisted that asylum music should involve only a small number of instruments, that the musicians should be hidden from the patients, and that there should be no outsiders present.[34] This was quite unlike Illenau, where patients and medical staff collaborated in the production of music and gathered together in large concert assemblies.

In Britain the role of asylum music appears to have been different yet again. If it did not quite encompass the range of 'sensual delights' attributed to British asylums by a German journal of 1857,[35] it should not be thought of as restricted to the popular 'lunatics' ball'.[36] In the York Retreat, where William Tuke pioneered the institutional use of non-coercive, 'moral treatment', 'music played an increasingly important role: individual patients played the piano, violin, harmonium or accordion and in the 1850s musical soirées and concerts were begun'.[37] At the Ticehurst Private Asylum, playing the harpsichord and violin were among the permitted recreations, along with spinning and sewing, drawing and writing; and fortnightly concerts were given by a brass band comprising the male attendants.[38] At Bethlem, once notorious for making entertainment out of, rather than for, its inmates, the governors of around 1840 felt that

> music might be introduced with advantage into the house, and that a musical clock or self-acting piano-forte would be a source of gratification and enjoyment, melancholy and mopish patients being frequently greatly revived by the sound of music.[39]

The standard of musicianship in British asylums was sometimes surprisingly high. For example, at the Worcester City and County Lunatic Asylum near Powick, Edward Elgar, the English Romantic composer *par excellence*, worked as an asylum conductor for five years, from 1879 to 1884.[40] Although not amongst his most celebrated works, Elgar composed a number of pieces for Powick patients based upon 'the most popular types of dances of the period, Polkas and Quadrilles'. Thanks to the Rutland Sinfonia, Elgar's asylum music can be relished outside the asylum today.[41] Moreover, the asylum's records reveal that many patients responded extremely well to musical evenings. Physicians occasionally even used a patient's reactions to the music as a means of assessing his or her mental health.[42]

IV

In the Romantic period musical experience was construed as a psychological event and thus associated with psychiatry. It acquired the ambiguity of all psychological events, that is, it came to be perceived as both cause and cure of mental disorders. The mechanism by which music was able to exercise this psychological influence was never fully explained in the medical literature. But one feature upon which most nineteenth-century authors appear to have agreed is that the propagation of musical influence, though psychological, occurred in the manner of a physical propulsion. Musical relations were imprinted directly upon the listener's soul, thus altering its state. Whether this alteration was permanent or temporary depended upon a large number of factors, including the prior condition of the listener, the quality of the composition and, perhaps most of all, the virtuosity of the performance.

The cultural proximity of music and madness is reflected in Kleist's short story, 'The Holy St Cecilia', whose four characters end up in an insane asylum after prolonged exposure to a requiem of truly fantastic powers. Examining the phenomenon of musical projection in all its Romantic ambiguity, Kleist's plot balances every palliative effect of music with a corresponding destructive effect. This projection of emotional states by means of music is given an interesting twist by Berlioz, another Romantic composer with a medical bent. Berlioz originally studied medicine, and he dedicated his *Symphonie fantastique* to the study of a mental disorder, the *idée fixe*. In his *Soirées de l'orchestre* he republished a literary sketch of 1850 which conceived of a musical composition so powerful that even inanimate objects would succumb to its internal logic. In the story, the piano upon which this piece is played repeatedly (because it is the set piece in a conservatoire competition) first starts to play the music by itself and then literally goes mad.[43] Ironically, the piece that Berlioz claimed to have produced this effect was Mendelssohn's concerto in G-minor – Illenau music.

Notes

1.   Johann Christian Reil, *Rhapsodieen über die Anwendung der psychischen Curmethode auf Geisteszerrüttungen* (1803), Amsterdam

(1968) edn, p. 205. The cultural significance of the cat-piano as a symbol of Romanticism has been examined by R. Richards, 'Rhapsodies on a Cat-Piano, or Johann Christian Reil and the Foundations of Romantic Psychiatry', *Critical Inquiry*, 24 (1998), pp. 700–737.

2.   R. Mocek, *Johann Christian Reil (1759–1813)* (Frankfurt am Main, 1995).

3.   W. F. Kümmel, *Musik und Medizin: Ihre Wechselbeziehungen in Theorie und Praxis von 800 bis 1800* (Freiburg and Munich, 1977), pp. 410–14. R. Leppert, *The Sight of Sound: Music, Representation and the History of the Body* (Berkeley and Los Angeles, 1993), p. 153. See Gouk, above.

4.   All translations from the German are my own unless otherwise indicated.

5.   *Clemens Brentano's Gesammelte Schriften* (Frankfurt am Main, 1852), pp. 329–69, quotation at pp. 339–40.

6.   *Clemens Brentano's Gesammelte Schriften*, pp. 361–2.

7.   On Mesmerism see Commentary on Part V.

8.   A. von Sternberg, *Erinnerungsblätter* (Berlin, 1856), pp. 146–7.

9.   P. A. Scholes, *A Listener's History of Music*, 3 vols (Oxford, 1944), vol. 2, p. 122.

10.   O. Rock, 'Geschichte und Grundlagen der Musik-therapie' (dissertation, University of Cologne, 1971), p. 22.

11.   A. Walker, *Franz Liszt*, vol. 1: *The Virtuoso Years 1811–1847* (London, 1983, revised edn 1989), pp. 151–2.

12.   For survey of these institutions from a comparative perspective, see D. Jetter, *Grundzüge der Geschichte des Irrenhauses* (Darmstadt, 1981).

13.   Kümmel, *Musik und Medizin*, p. 409.

14.   R. Schumacher, *Die Musik in der Psychiatrie des 19. Jahrhunderts* (Frankfurt am Main, 1982).

15.   Lichtenthal's classification is borrowed from Schubart's *Ästhetik der Tonkunst*. See S. Baraddasran-Chassemi, 'Der Musikalische Arzt' (dissertation, University of Düsseldorf, 1965), p. 17. For Hanslick's view of Lichtenthal, later in the century, see Horden, Chapter 1.

16.   E. Völkel, *Die spekulative Musiktherapie zur Zeit der Romantik: Ihre Traditionen und ihr Fortwirken* (Düsseldorf, 1979), p. 61.

17.   Völkel, *Spekulative Musiktherapie*, p. 42.

18.   Schumacher, *Musik in der Psychiatrie*, p. 32.

19.   Völkel, *Spekulative Musiktherapie*, p. 77.

20.   Völkel, *Spekulative Musiktherapie*, p. 103.

21.   Völkel, *Spekulative Musiktherapie*, p. 102.

22.   Völkel, *Spekulative Musiktherapie*, p. 97.

23.   *Illenau Weekly*, Nr. 19, 1886.

24. *Illenau Weekly*, Nr. 4, 1867.

25. Petition of 5 June 1880, in Staatsarchiv Freiburg, Illenau Employee Records, Fidel Ehinger, B 821/1, Nr. 514.

26. *Illenau Photoalbum*, Generallandesarchiv Karlsruhe, 65/11731, B.24.

27. C. Kramer, 'A Fool's Paradise: The Psychiatry of Gemüth in a Biedermeier Asylum' (PhD thesis, University of Chicago, 1998), ch. 2.

28. Kramer, 'Fool's Paradise', ch. 3.

29. C. F. Roller, *Die Irrenanstalt nach allen ihren Beziehungen dargestellt* (Karlsruhe, 1831), p. 202.

30. C. Rosen, *The Romantic Generation* (London, 1995), p. 581.

31. P. Earle, *Institutions for the Insane in Prussia, Austria, and Germany* (New York, 1854), p. 183.

32. Letter from Marquis de Louvais to Hector Berlioz about the asylum in Auxerre, in *Allgemeine Zeitschrift für Psychiatrie*, 5 (1848), pp. 495 ff.

33. Cited from Schumacher, *Musik in der Psychiatrie*, p. 31.

34. Kümmel, *Musik und Medizin*, p. 409.

35. *Europa: Chronik der gebildeten Welt* (Leipzig, 1857), p. 162.

36. Pace E. Showalter, *The Female Malady: Women, Madness, and English Culture, 1830–1980* (New York, 1985), pp. 39–40.

37. A. Digby, *Madness, Morality and Medicine: A Study of the York Retreat* (Cambridge, 1985), p. 45.

38. C. MacKenzie, *Psychiatry for the Rich: A History of Ticehurst Private Asylum, 1792–1917* (London and New York, 1992), pp. 43, 147, 182.

39. J. Andrews, A. Briggs, R. Porter, P. Tucker and K. Waddington, *The History of Bethlem* (London and New York, 1997), p. 449.

40. J. Northrop Moore, *Edward Elgar: A Creative Life* (Oxford, 1984), pp. 71, 82, 87.

41. *Elgar, Powick Asylum Music*, Rutland Sinfonia, cond. Barry Collett, ENS 161, Forties Recording Company: Whitetower Records (Milton Keynes, 1989).

42. Frank Crompton of University College, Worcester, has kindly searched his database of pauper patients at the Powick Asylum for references to music-making.

43. H. Berlioz, *Soirées de l'orchestre* (Paris, 1852), 'eighteenth evening', trans. J. Barzun, *Evenings with the Orchestra* (Chicago and London, 1956), pp. 215–19. For publication history see D. K. Holomon, *Catalogue of the Works of Hector Berlioz* (Kassel and London, 1987), no. C683.

CHAPTER FIFTEEN

Shamanism, Music, and the Soul Train

Keith Howard

I

Shamanism, in Siberia and elsewhere, is a holistic system for cathartic healing. Shaman rituals address – often simultaneously – personal afflictions, malaise within the spirit realm, and communal disharmony, utilizing oracles, narration, secret systems of knowledge, altered states of consciousness, music, and dance. The ritual gestalt does not readily allow any single component to be separated out, but music, to extend David Riches' description of shamanism itself, is 'fundamental in the social'.[1]

In Korea, to which, as the culture with which I am most familiar, I will frequently return, a shaman still narrates in recitative the exploits of admirable ancestors. She – for in contrast to Siberia, the majority of Korean shamans are female – sings melodiously to entertain the spirits she invokes. She chants invocations and prayers. She dances to percussion music. She constantly reacts to comments from her instrumental accompanists. Whenever she pauses, her accompanists take over, improvising around folksong melodies, or singing settings of well-known folk stories. No Korean ritual can take place without music, and I have observed occasions where a single musician played both the gong and the oboe, one with each hand, complaining to me in an aside that nobody could these days afford to pay enough musicians to provide 'proper' rituals.

Although music is vital, it is difficult to demonstrate specific affective musical stimuli valid beyond a single culture. To John Blacking, challenging the concept of universality, musical meaning is determined by a complex of symbolically ordered sounds, social institutions, and cognitive or sensory motor capabilities of the body.[2] In contrast, in Western neo-shamanism, music is typically separated out, and

rhythm comes to the fore. A typical justification runs: 'Rhythms –
flowing, staccato, chaos, lyric, stillness – constitute the fluid structure,
the DNA, of our physical lives.'[3]

In 1993, at a conference of the International Society for
Shamanistic Research in Budapest, I mentioned that I was an ethnomusicologist. 'Ah,' said a new colleague, 'you must study shaman
drumming'. She had in mind the recordings designed to accompany
soul recovery exercises such as Michael Harner's *Drumming for the
Shamanic Journey (The Primary Tape)*.[4] Harner employs an incessant
drumbeat sequenced in fast, slow, and faster sections. There is little in
the drumming to explore, but the sections on the tape are designed to
assist the user to stabilize his or her breathing, concentrate on introspection, and then be led back to the everyday world. The purpose of
such exercises is to heal modern Western man in a Jungian sense; by
bringing the user into contact with his or her soul, and his or her protecting forces, the mental, physical, and spiritual damage caused by
life in the contemporary world is repaired.

In this chapter, I explore how music is used, and has been considered to be used, within shaman rituals. The term 'shamanism' presents
me with an initial hurdle, since it is widely employed to signify a
variety of diverse practices; writing as we approach a new millennium, and as I have already indicated by citing Harner, it would be
disingenuous to ignore the many contemporary practices which can be
labelled as 'neo-shamanism'. First, then, I consider definitions. I
argue that any description of shamanism needs to be more flexible
than the classic 'archaic technique of ecstasy' proposed by Mircea
Eliade.[5] I then look at how musicologists have sought to capture
'shamanistic' music. Next, I explore relationships between music and
trance and, in a final section, I look at the use of drums and other
instruments in rituals.

II

No single consensus definition of shamanism exists. 'Shamanism'
was coined more than 200 years ago to characterize religious activities amongst the peoples of Siberia, taking as its base the Tungus
word *saman*. *Saman* is typically taken to indicate ritual practitioners

who act as intermediaries with the spirit world, but Roberte Hamayon argues that the etymology should be extended to include 'play', or jumping in dance.[6] The normative definition, extracted largely from pre-Soviet ethnographies and crystallized by Eliade, has it that the shaman journeys in flight to the realm of the spirits, seeking help as a healer or seer and conducting or guiding the soul of a newly-deceased. The other world is reached through trance, in which the shaman acts out stages on the journey.[7] Shamans typically also bind society together through the ritual enshrining of historical origins in what have been called 'diagnostic events'.[8]

Theories of diffusion and cultural survival allow for shamans or records of shamanistic activities to be found beyond Arctic and Ural-Altaic groups, amongst Lapps, Inuit, American Indians, the Ainu of Japan, the Koreans, in many parts of south-east Asia such as Vietnam, Thailand and Indonesia, and elsewhere. As a phenomenon associated with an altered state of consciousness, the provenance could be extended to include Africa, ancient Israel, the Pacific, and parts of Europe. Such a broad stage threatens any single, unitary definition. A marked divergence in practice and spirit canon between distinct social groups, different concepts of journeys and the need for them, and various descriptions of ecstasy and trance have been noted. To Spencer, the whole shindig should be thrown into the 'ethnographic dustbin',[9] and to Michael Taussig shamanism is:

> a made-up, modern, Western category, an artful reification of disparate practices, snatches of folklore and overarching folk-lorizations, residues of long-established myths intermingled with the politics of academic departments, curricula, conferences.[10]

In 1959, Raymond Firth distinguished spirit possession and spirit mediumship from spirit shamanism. The former was to be used to classify behaviour or actions of a person interpreted as evidence of control by a spirit, and possession in which a person is considered to serve as an intermediary with the spirit world, respectively.[11] Both were widely encountered in Africa, but the latter, according to Firth, was restricted largely to Asia, where the shaman was the 'master of spirits'. The distinction is to a great extent reliant on Eliade, who saw the shaman's control over spirits as vital, and ecstasy, as opposed to trance, as the defining feature. Such a narrow definition of shamanism, however, fails to tackle the coexisting diversity of religious practices in many societies.[12] At one extreme, anthropologists have, since Levi-Strauss's analysis of Franz Boas's account of the Kwakiutl Indian Quesalid from Vancouver, emphasized that ecstasy and trance are expressions of social idioms.[13] At the same time, scholars following Eliade continue to see the charismatic shaman as archetypal, and differentiate priestly activities where no trance or ecstasy is involved as a later or corrupted development.[14]

Korean shamanism highlights the problems of definition. The ascription of 'shamanism' to indigenous religion began amongst Western missionaries conversant with ethnographies on Siberia.[15] By the 1920s, the Siberian association was widely accepted by local writers, supported by known migrations of people several thousand years before and supposed links between Korean and Ural-Altaic languages. Indigenous 'shamanism', however, does not entirely satisfy Eliade's definition. First, no Korean shaman goes on a journey or experiences flight. Second, four distinct practitioners are differentiated. Two are ecstatic, *mudang* and *myŏngdu* (together with cognates), and experience the descent of the gods. *Mudang* are found in central and northern Korea, and suffer an initial illness, known as *shinbyŏng*, interpreted as the call of spirits. *Myŏngdu* are typically found further south and claim possession by the spirits of children, spirits who usually have some claim to kinship. The other two types know no ecstasy, the widespread hereditary *tan'gol* of Korea's southern coast, and *shimbang* on the southern island of Cheju.

Shamanism is still a part of contemporary Korea. Many Koreans believe non-agnatic spirits ensure peace in the world beyond, and call on direct ancestors for support and assistance. The large pantheistic canon, which in detail differs from area to area, attributes various identities and roles to spirits, from goblins through ancestors to legendary figures and mighty gods of nature and disease.[16] Shamans, of whichever type, are grouped together, and the largest organization today, until recently known as the Korean Federation of Associations for Victory over Communism and Respect of Beliefs [*Taehan sŭnggong kyŏngshin yŏnhaphoe*] – the name reflected widespread persecution in the recent past and the fact that many of its members are refugees from what is now North Korean territory[17] – in the early

1980s claimed a membership of over 40,000 spread between 215 branches. The belief system has adapted to recent change, perhaps assisting its survival, and rituals now placate, for example, the spirits who arrive with white goods and who run the amazing internal combustion engine.

III

One persistent idea encountered in the literature is that shamanism marks a certain moment in the development of religion.[18] Within a pre-Socratean frame, shamanism becomes the key to unlock religion itself, defined in terms of three aspects: trance, a capricious and all-encompassing spirit pantheon, and ritual specialists – shamans – who have the knowledge and ability to access the spirit world. Shamanism is typically seen as part of, or a leftover from, pre-modern systems. This idea has been seized by musicologists, and Gilbert Rouget thus looks at relations between music and trance amongst the ancient Greeks and the Arabs,[19] while Curt Sachs couples sacred Dervish dancing at the central compound of the founding poet in Konya, Turkey, to a primitive past:

> These old men with outspread arms spun like tops for a full half hour – an astonishing, inconceivable performance. Here the dance severs the natural bonds of human posture and motion. In dizziness the dancer loses the feeling of body and of self; released from his body he conquers dizziness ... There is no doubt that it is something primitive, preserved from a period thousands of years before Islam, inherited from the shamanism of central Asia.[20]

Since Sachs wrote these words, Sufism has taken its place as a world religion, part of a construct within which the World Music bins of record shops accommodate not just the Whirling Dervishes and similar sect groups, but South Asian *qawwali* from the Sabri Brothers to Nusrat Fateh Ali Khan, Javanese *gamelan*, and Persian classical music.[21]

A further example would be the Balinese *ketjak* [*kecak*] which, according to David Lewiston:

> is a creation of this century, but descended from something much more ancient – the trance dance, dance of exorcism called

> *sanghyang* ... Most of the movements are exorcistic in origin and
> contribute together to produce a tremendous unity of mood ... to
> drive out evil by an incantation.[22]

To Indonesians, the ritual still involves a communal exorcism to avoid
or expel pestilence, and is reported to continue in the south-central
districts of Gianyar and Badung. The exorcism itself is done by
performers in trance, incessantly hocketing while rocking in
movement, gradually accelerating until they move frantically forward
and back in a tightly packed space. The resultant dissociation parallels
Sach's Dervishes. But, as Eliade notes, specialist practitioners need to
retain consciousness if they are to exercise control. Chanting is done
by others, who do not enter trance. This begins to challenge the
validity of the pre-modern notion of shamanism, and the distinction
between charismatic shamans and non-ecstatic priests, for two
chanters sit within the group of *ketjak* chanters, the *juru tarek* chorus
leader who signals starts, stops and transitions, and the *juru gending*
melodic leader, singing repetitive melodies. These are joined by the
juru klempung, shouting out regular punctuation, and in effect acting
as a drumless percussionist.[23] Similarly, senior leaders guide the
Dervish dancers from the periphery of the circle. Healing, though,
differs in the two traditions. In the *ketjak* it is the community, all the
men who take part, who are made whole, whereas among the
Dervishes, it is the individual dancer who seeks to move close to the
Deity.

   A further element in definitions of shamanism, and one which
would not alarm Eliade, is that it is characteristic of non-descent ori-
ented and non-hierarchical societies, specifically hunter-gatherer
groups. There are rich data to consider here. The supposedly egalitar-
ian nature of hunter-gatherers lends itself to rituals characterized by
reciprocity. Thus, Hamayon argues that the act of killing animals for
food must be balanced by a ritual dying and rebirth performed by a
group's shaman.[24] This leads to the identification of spirits with animals. Four examples of ritual music can serve to illustrate. First, the
Çukç musician Slava Egroviç Kemlil (b. 1963), in a recording made
in Çerskij above the Arctic circle near the mouth of the Kolyma river
in 1992, juxtaposes the imitation of dogs, ravens, and reindeer with a
suggestion of entering trance through a rasped rapid in–out breathing.

He accompanies himself on a frame drum, playing rapidly for the animals and slower and more regularly when trance is sought. Kemlil attempts to recreate a shaman's ritual heard in his youth, before singing about his prized animal:

> My beloved reindeer has great antlers
> and when he arrives behind the hill
> one sees his antlers before seeing him.
> When he comes down the hill, full of strength and beauty,
> I admire him, I love him very much, I yoke him to the sledge ...
>   and praise my reindeer.[25]

Second, on a very different recording, the Tuvan shaman Alexander Tavakay is heard to call his animal helpers to heal a child, imitating a cuckoo to calm the child, a raven to scare evil away, and an owl to calm cattle. Tavakay considers his songs to be sacred, and his basic percussion battery – rattles, rings, metal strips and bells attached to the back of his costume – to frighten any evil spirits that threaten his patient. As he beats his large frame drum, the *dungur*, the spirits congregate in it, only to be sent away to the other world. The ritual procedure is used to treat specific illnesses, but many of these are seen to have their root in psychological problems related to deceased relatives.[26]

Third, Marina Roseman recalls a Temiar tiger song from Malaysia; protection rather than direct healing is invoked. The song is preceded by the call of the bird considered the tiger's companion, the chequer-throated woodpecker:

> Late at night, in the darkness of a tiger ceremony, I've often looked over my shoulder with a shudder, sensing the tiger's presence in the singer's gravelly vocal timbre and low-pitched song. Hitam Tamboh received this song from his father. In dreams, the tiger appears as an old man. Its connection is ... through the heart-soul. When a member of the community has received songs of the Tiger genre, real tigers are less likely to prowl around that community or bother its members.[27]

Fourth, in 1992, above the Arctic circle at Ust'-Avam on the Ienisseï river in Siberia, Delsjumjaku Demnimeevic Kosterkin sang and played excerpts from a ritual that originally protected from diseases but which, today, aims to prevent the young from committing suicide. He wore a cloak with bronze and iron pendants representing a bear's skeleton, and accompanied himself on a frame drum with metal rings attached to cross-members behind. A bearskin was placed on the ground, which the shaman caressed with his drum stick before throwing it in the air and divining from the way it fell. The bear is invoked as the helping spirit, protecting the vulnerable:

> A shaman and his helpers call the spirits, benefactor animals from earth, water and sky. When they meet, the shaman starts singing. Now it is night, it is December. One can hear [the bear's] steps. It is really dark ...
> In December, three days, [the bear's] steps. We do [this ritual] against diseases and also so the young ones will not kill themselves anymore. When I plunge the knife in, I divert suicide.
> When they get up, they start to make the road to be able to leave when warmer days come. For the moment, the bear is sleeping. His fur is the shaman's friend, his spirit. He helps build the road. The mallet of the drum is the tongue of the shaman. The mallet fell on its side: It's good ... Everything the shaman says comes to him from the nape of his neck. In my nape I have a hole through which I hear everything I then transmit to others.[28]

In Siberia, Shamanism was forced underground during the Soviet period. Komsomol followers burnt drums and ritual implements, and Stalin initiated a pogrom to destroy supposedly primitive rituals. Hunters collected the scalps of shamans and many of those who remained after 1945 were incarcerated as schizophrenics in mental institutions. On one level, this makes it difficult to return to much of Eliade's ethnographic data, but it also explains the relative paucity of the surviving ritual music. A story recounted to Marjorie Mandelstam Balzer by Marfa Mikhailovna Zamorshikova in the Siberian village of Tekhtiur in today's Sakha Republic reflects the effect of the Soviet policies:

> My brother became ill ... In the emergency, my mother invited an old woman to come. We did not call her a shaman, but she was known for doing things that the [outlawed] shamans had done. She came, looked at my brother, and took down a frying pan ... She took up the pan and beat it with a wooden spoon.

The pan was a substitute for the frame drum. It would have become the drum to the shaman, despite its metallic sound, and the drum, in turn, would have metamorphosed into a horse on which to journey to the spirit world. Balzer notes, however, that this would only have been the case if the old woman was a genuine shaman; if not, the pan would just have been played 'for musical resonance'.[29]

By the early 1990s, Balzer calculates that only seven individuals survived with reputations as shamans in Sakha; Piers Vitebsky suggests there were eight.[30] A revival has begun, sponsored by largely urban societies whose members include teachers, doctors, folklorists and historians, to promote shamanism as the ancient knowledge of local people. Support comes from abroad. The resulting ambiguities blur any distinctions between sacred and secular in the music. A ritual song with frame drum recorded by Henri Lecomte in the Amur basin to the east of Sakha, sung by the Nanaj shaman Njura Sergeevna Kile (born between 1906 and 1910) is suggestive of the problem:

> People coming from afar have come to me, and I address you my spirits. I touch no one, I aggress no one. What can I sing? What can I say? In the old days I had much power, but now I live like this. I am so weak. If anything comes out of me, out of my mouth, it will come from my ancestors, my spirits. Do not feel hurt [my spirits], even if I don't always talk like I should.[31]

What shaman music actually survives? The question has no simple answer. Some would argue that revival is now widespread, stimulated by the seminal writings of Carlos Castaneda, Harner and others, but equally reflecting the reawakening of nationalism, and creating a new shamanism.[32] None the less, any notion that the sacred must be separated from the secular seems out of step with modern performance situations throughout the world. Dervishes perform on Western stages. Similarly, alongside the communal exorcism of the *ketjak*, a second, popular, secular and dramatic form coexists. Performed for Indonesian and foreign tourists, and an integral part of the alliance between government and media to promote a national identity, the vocal complexity is offered for entertainment alone. No trance is expected or needed. Ritual is downplayed, by describing *ketjak* in terms of a story, the re-enactment of the battle from the Ramayana epic in which monkey hordes come to the aid of Prince Rama against the evil King Ravana.[33]

Since the 1970s, Korean shamanism has been considered worthy of protection and preservation, a marker of national identity against the onslaught of Westernization. Scholars and ritualists have duly encouraged the government to designate exemplary rituals as Intangible Cultural Assets [*Muhyŏng munhwajae*], and to pay shamans as 'holders' [*poyuja*], or, in common parlance, Human Cultural Assets [*In'gan munhwajae*].³⁴ Preserved, shaman rituals have been put on urban stages, where no spirits are required to attend. The best ritualists have become media stars. Kim Kŭmhwa (b. 1929), a migrant from North Korea living in Seoul who is today a 'holder' of Asset no. 82, a west-coast ritual known as *Taedong kut*, is a prime example, while Kim Suk Chul [Kim Sŏkch'ul] (b. 1922), a holder of a ritual from the south-eastern seaboard, *Tonghaean pyŏlshin kut*, again part of Asset no. 82, and Park Byung Chon [Pak Pyŏngch'ŏn] (b. 1933) and Kim Taerye (b. 1935), both 'holders' of the south-western *Chindo Ssikkim kut*, Asset no. 72, are famed ritual musicians.³⁵ Park is a *tan'gol*, a hereditary shaman who has no need of ecstasy or trance, but who considers his knowledge of ritual texts and music gives him the right to address both spirits and men:

> To some families, shamanism is integral to life. I was born into a family where my grandfather had been a very famous shaman. We controlled the largest *tan'gol pan* [an area in which they had exclusive rights to give rituals] on Chindo ... In my house, we knew shamanism really well. I left Chindo to get an education, and studied sufficiently so that I could restore the local ritual to its original form. Because of my background, I was able to tell other ritualists what words or music should be corrected. I knew so many words, I knew how to do things, and I knew my lineage.³⁶

Korean musicologists, in a search for origins common throughout East Asian scholarship, consider shamanism to provide the archetypes of Korean music. Hahn Man-young has written the seminal article.³⁷ Shamanistic fertility rites are identified on archaeological finds connected with music, notably 1,500-year-old pottery remains depicting the twelve-string half-tube zither [*kayagŭm*]. Iconography is supportive, particularly a well-known eighteenth century painting by Shin Yunbok (1758–?) which shows a shaman supported by two musicians. One particularly common dance rhythm, *kutkŏri*, has a name which employs two Korean words allied to shamanism: *kut*, the normative term for ritual, and *kŏri*, a term for ritual scenes.[38]

IV

Trance and/or ecstasy remain key features in most accounts of shamanism, even though, as I hope I have demonstrated above, it is clear that charisma often coexists with more priestly behaviour. Outwardly, two distinct states are usually distinguished, one associated with noise and hyperactivity, loss of knowledge, dissociation, and lack of control, and the other with silence, solitude, hypoactivity, increased gain of control, intuitive knowledge, and heightened awareness. There is, surely, an infinite number of degrees from one to the other. And, in the process of a neophyte shaman's becoming Eliade's 'master of spirits', there is a shift over time from one to the other. Classic descriptions of the shaman's call are typically tied to an unknown illness or involuntary behaviour; the call is considered to be from specific spirits, who in time become the initiate's helping spirits. To give one example from Niger, Erlmann reports serious illness that proves incurable by conventional methods, such as paralysis or sterility, is taken as evidence of 'an offence against one of the more than 400 spirits of the Hausa pantheon'. The affected person must be initiated into the *bòorii* cult to be healed, a process that lasts seven days; the adept 'is then considered to be the spirit's "mare" whom the spirit may "ride" during particular rites'.[39]

Explanations of trance differ quite considerably. Erlmann, for example, medicalizes the states as an expressive outlet for hysteria, psychological illness and mental disorder, but also notes they can be seen as part of a conditioned reflex to cultural stimuli. To Rouget, trance is a state 'composed of two components, one psychophysiological, the other cultural'.[40] Other interpretations describe the effects of a plethora of hyperventilation and hypoventilation techniques, and heightened awareness or bodily disorientation brought on by diverse agents ranging from drugs, tobacco, alcohol, smoke, and food, to music, dance, noise, silence, and repetitive action. Some commentators frame a shaman's trance as a particular form of an altered state of consciousness,[41] some find little to differentiate

European magicians from African witches and Asian shamans,[42] and others identify a specific and unitary 'shamanic state of conscious-ness'.[43] Chemical changes are involved, beta-endorphins released by the anterior pituitary, enkephalin, linked to states of 'parasympathetic dominance in which the frontal cortex is dominated by slow [alpha] wave patterns originating in the limbic system and related projections into the frontal parts of the brain'.[44]

Music, then, is but one potential stimulus to generate such an altered state. From an anthropological perspective, it has an effect because of the social coding of meaning. Music, as the most plastic of the arts, is the most open to interpretation and the most needy of interpretation. Blacking, in a consideration of the Venda 'drums of the ancestors' [*ngoma dza midzumi*] from Transvaal, thus writes:

> No music has power in itself. Music has no effect on the body or consequences for social action, unless its sounds and circum-stance can be related to a coherent set of ideas about self and other and bodily feelings. There can surely be no direct connec-tion between the sounds of music and people's emotional responses to them.[45]

To the Venda, it is ancestors, not music, that cause an altered state of consciousness. It is, none the less, commonplace to suggest that music itself is the stimulant. Music can block out physical surround-ings and errant thoughts. Music can be used to regularize body activ-ity or to destabilize, to focus concentration or to blunt awareness. Neurophysiologists describe a shared potential to experience a com-mon set of somatic states, and in his discussion of sentic cycles Manfred Clynes argues that there are musical analogies for such states. But, since hearing is linked to other sensory experiences, the aural cannot be entirely separated from other stimuli. Rouget seems to have this in mind when he says:

> Music has often been thought of as endowed with the mysterious power of triggering [trance] ... there is no truth whatsoever in this assumption.[46]

Such a comment needs careful elaboration, which Rouget provides:

> Although ... music does play a part in triggering and maintaining the trance state [trance] does not owe its effect to the properties

of its musical structure, or if it does, it does so only to a very small degree.[47]

Both Rouget and Blacking had revisited the writings of Jean-Jacques Rousseau, to whom music had a moral action, but little power 'over the affections'.[48] Rouget quotes Rousseau's discussion of tarantism to emphasize that affect is tied to social meaning:

> Neither absolute sounds nor the same tunes are required to cure all those stung by [the Tarantula], for each needs the airs of a melody known to him and phrases that he understands ... Each is only affected by accents familiar to him; one's nerves will respond only to the degree to which one's mind prepares him for it.[49]

Andrew Neher, in contrast, has argued that sound waves have a neurological impact, and identifies rhythm as the trigger of what he calls 'auditory driving'. In effect, he rejects Rousseau. To Neher, pulses which match alpha brainwaves, at between 8 Hz and 13 Hz per second, will lead to 'sensory bombardment and convulsions'.[50] From here, Rodney Needham, returning to African ethnographic accounts, has suggested that percussion instruments have the greatest sensory affect.[51] No, says Rouget, for Neher's experiments indicate quite implausibly that any beating at between 240 and 720 times per minute will induce trance, and if this were so, then much of sub-Saharan Africa would be in a constant state of trance.[52]

Rhythm does, however, seem to play an important role in inducing trance in many cultures, most commonly through irregularity and by sustained increases in tempo and intensity. For example, Frances Densmore, in a study of North American Indians, notes that healing songs are characterized by rhythm, specifically by changes of stress and rhythmic regularity. Liu Gui Teng, describing Manchurian rituals in the Heilongjiang river delta, distinguishes two drums, the *zhuagu* and *dangu*, the former struck in sequences of odd-numbered patterns and the latter struck in sets of irregular patterns (much Chinese percussion music, and in particular the repertory of *Shifan luogu*, is based on regular mathematical formulae). On a broader stage, Daniélou talks of the importance of irregular 5-, 7-, or 11-beat patterns and violent and complex, accelerating, rhythmic sequences.[53] In Korea, pounding rhythmic regularity characterizes shaman activity: a neophyte in her initiation ritual is told to dance 'like a metronome', and wanting to tap and dance to the drum is considered to make one vulnerable to attention from the spirits.[54]

V

Drums are closely identified with shaman rituals (see West, Chapter 2), and today, one influential journal is called *Shaman's Drum: A Journal of Experiential Shamanism*. In respect to neo-shamanism, recent work claims to demonstrate that drumming assists 'journeying' by increasing affective, cognitive and physical well-being, and ameliorating anxiety, anger, confusion, depression, fatigue, and stress.[55] Frame drums are the most widely-reported instrument in central-Asian and Arctic shamanism, but, and in keeping with Blacking and Rouget, it is as much the symbolism enshrined in them as their sound that lends them significance.[56] Among the Transbaikalian Tungus the frame drum is a canoe for crossing the sea. Among Mongols it represents a horse. Among the Siberian Evenki and Oroquen it is the receptacle through which different spirits come to the shaman. By singing directly into the skin, the shaman pleads with the spirit world, in effect marking the skin as the entrance to the other realm. In Siberia, the drum is often shaped like an egg, symbolising birth; in Scandinavia, the shape takes on a more feminine, motherly, figure-of-eight. The frame often has a cross-stave that symbolizes fertility, a theme echoed in paintings on the drum skin. It may be round, like the sun. It may have feathers or bones attached to the frame, metal ringlets may be attached to symbolize bones, or the drum skin itself may be considered to harness the spirit of the donor animal: the drum, energized, becomes the shaman's spirit helper.

If music can be the trigger for a conditioned reflex, a reflex which can be instantaneous or gradual, the picture which emerges is complex. In Tibet, for example, the use of pellet drums in rituals assists with dislocation, creating increases in tempo and intensification,[57] but displaces much of the symbolism of frame drums. African case studies abound with examples: Nketia tells us that in Ghana individuals are known to get possessed outside the contexts of drumming and dancing, while a number of commentators note that adepts and priests may enter trance when music is heard, but also when no music is played.[58] Amongst the Yoruba, the drums fall silent at a certain point on the first day of the annual feast for Shango, the god of lightning, at which time, and as an officiant chants to the god, an adept goes into trance and rushes forwards. In the Hausa *bòorii* cult, drums are used to encourage women in trance to dance, to help them emerge from the trance and to counteract the effects of the betel hallucinogen.[59] Violent drumming in rituals for initiates among the Wolof and Thonga force the possessed to dance until they reach a state of nervous exhaustion, at which point they reveal the names of the possessing spirits.[60] Further and similar examples have been documented amongst the Segeju of Tanzania and the Fon, and there is a widespread use of rhythmic (and melodic) motifs to identify particular spirits.[61]

In Korea, the symbolism of the frame drum has, of necessity, disappeared in the ubiquitous drum, the double-headed hourglass-shaped *changgo or changgu*. The two drumheads create a sealed body that lacks any opening; the practitioner cannot sing into the instrument, it cannot be metamorphosed into a boat or a horse, and it cannot function as a channel between the worlds of spirits and men. In the southwest, it gains greater symbolic significance when a branch of bamboo encased in a knotted piece of paper, the *sŏndae*, is threaded through the drum's thongs to become a temporary resting place for the deceased's soul. Upended, the drum is beaten by the shaman as she welcomes the spirit of pox: the danger inherent in addressing this spirit means she and the deceased must stand (hence, she turns the drum on end, and strikes just one drumhead).

On the southern Cheju island there were no *changgo* until after 1945, and a pottery or gourd water vessel, the *hŏbŏk*, sufficed.[62] This was partially filled with water and struck with the palms of the hands or with a small stick. A similar instrument known as the *mul pagaji* or *mul changgu* was sometimes used in parts of the south-western Chŏlla province. This was a gourd placed upside down in a bowl of water, which resonated when struck. Early in the twentieth century it is reported to have been common in rites of passage for childbirth and marriage conducted by a shaman.[63] A colloquial term, *toshin*, combines the idea of prayer with an onomatopoeic representation of the sound. A further instrument was noted by the Japanese ethnographer

Murayama in the 1930s, the *koritchak*. This was a wicker basket used for intimate Korean rituals which, although considered effective in calling the spirits of the dead, might indicate a reaction to persecution, since the limited sound potential would have kept rituals from public view.[64] A plethora of metal instruments are also used, from rice-bowl lids and finger cymbals (collectively described after terms for Buddhist cymbals as *para*, *chabara*, and *chegŭm*) to bell trees [*pangul*] in the centre and north, small gongs [*kkwaenggwari*] and upturned prayer bowls in the south-east, and a brass clapperless bell [*chŏngju*] struck with a small deer antler in the south-west. Throughout Korea, it is the large gong [*ching*] that functions more like central Asian frame drums. Vestiges of its role as the residence of a helping spirit remain. 'The spirit of the gong is angry', said the shaman Yi Wansun one rainy night in 1984 when nothing seemed to be going right in a ritual conducted after a man had broken his leg in a fall. She leaned the gong against the wall, assembled a small altar table in front of it, replete with food and drink, and prayed. Park Byung Chon routinely raises the gong to his chest and holds it not with a cord (as is normal in secular contexts), but with his right hand behind and inside. He sings into it, intently concentrating on the sound, addressing the spirits.

Percussion instruments are not the only instruments of rituals. In Korea today, the melodic line-up varies, often including flute [*taegŭm*], bowed zither [*ajaeng*], and fiddle [*haegŭm*]. Variety reflects availability and the fickle vagaries of musicians, but the oboe, with an oversize double reed lending itself to considerable pitch and embouchure adjustment, is always a core instrument. The oboe, shamans have explained to me, is the instrument closest to the human voice. It can, virtually alone amongst instruments, offer portamenti, rapid and large melodic leaps, and wide and sudden dynamic fluctuations. It can plead, full of emotion, and as a consequence is considered the instrument spirits most readily respond to.[65]

In the rituals of different African groups, different instruments are used, from the fiddle amongst the Songhai, through fiddles and occasionally flutes amongst the Hausa, the harp accompanied by water drums amongst the Kotoko of Chad, spherical whistles amongst the Gula Iro, the gourd trumpet amongst the Mundang and Mussey, the xylophone amongst the Ngbaka-Mangja of the Central African Republic, and the accordion among the Vezo in Madagascar.[66] A particularly well-known instrument is the Shona *mbira*, a lamellaphone resonated in a large gourd with rows of hand-forged, tuned metal keys bound to a wooden soundboard. This is the lynchpin of Zimbabwean all-night family ceremonies to communicate with ancestors, *bira*, and indeed, the phrase *mbira dza vadzimu* in the Zezuru dialect means 'notes of the ancestors'. Spirits are considered to have favourite tunes, and performance involves experimenting with melodies to encourage ancestors to attend and to identify them as they possess people in trance. Ceremonies may be given to heal an individual, but the overall effect is one of catharsis, cementing a social group together.[67]

In conclusion, then, music is clearly an integral, universal part of shaman rituals. Rituals heal, by addressing spiritual problems that exist either within the domain of an individual's psyche or within the spirit realm. But it remains difficult to separate musical stimuli from the other elements of a ritual, or to relate music to specific affect. I close with a statement about the power of music, the power of voice and drum, words and rhythm, combined but not separable into constituent parts. The speaker, a contemporary American Indian, the Anishnabe (Chippewa) Kanucas Littlefish, relates how after he sang one man regained his hearing and another had a broken leg cured. Music heals:

> When I sing I use vocables and words in my native language. Lines of power exist all around us. What I try to do is tap into that power through sound and vibration using my voice and a drum. I also use a rattle, a gourd or a deer-horn shaker. When the lines of power are met, it is said a healing can occur.[68]

Notes

1. D. Riches, 'Shamanism: the Key to Religion', *Man*, 29 (1994), pp. 382–3.

2. J. Blacking, *Music, Culture, and Experience* (Chicago, 1995), pp. 304–5.

3. G. Roth, *Teachings of an Urban Shaman* (London, 1990), p. 28.

4. Norwalk, 1991. See also M. Harner, *The Way of the Shaman: A Guide to Power and Healing* (San Fransisco, 1980).

5.   M. Eliade, *Shamanism: Archaic Techniques of Ecstasy* (Princeton, NJ, 1964), originally published Paris, 1951.

6.   R. Hamayon, 'Why do ritual games please shamanic spirits and displease transcendent gods?', unpublished paper given at the School of Oriental and African Studies (London, 1995). See also R. Hamayon, *La chasse à l'âme: esquisse d'une théorie du chamanisme sibérien* (Nanterre, 1990).

7.   The definition of 'trance' is contentious. See G. Rouget, *Music and Trance: A Theory of the Relations between Music and Possession* (Chicago, 1985), pp. 3–4. 'Possession' is also used for a similar 'altered state of consciousness', except for the implicit acceptance of the presence of an invasive spirit. Both, like 'ecstasy', are in reality Western categories, variously applied for a wide range of indigenous practices, for which see R. Hamayon, 'Are "Trance", "Ecstasy" and Similar Concepts appropriate to the Study of Shamanism?', *Shaman*, 1.2 (1993), pp. 3–23.

8.   S. F. Moore, 'Explaining the Present: Theoretical Dilemmas in Processual Ethnography', *American Ethnologist*, 14.4 (1987), pp. 727–36.

9.   R. F. Spencer, 'Review of Studies in Shamanism', *American Anthropologist*, 70.2 (1968), pp. 396–7.

10. M. Taussig, *Shamanism, Colonialism, and the Wild Man: A Study in Terror and Healing* (Chicago, 1987).

11. R. Firth, 'Problems and Assumptions in an Anthropological Study of Religion', *Journal of the Royal Anthropological Institute*, 89.2 (1959), pp. 129–48.

12. J. G. Campbell, 'Approaches to the Study of Shamanism', *Wiener Völkerkundliche Mitteilungen*, 17–18 (1976), pp. 61–93, and J. M. Atkinson, 'Shamanisms Today', *Annual Review of Anthropology*, 21 (1992), pp. 307–30.

13. See, for example, C. Lévi-Strauss, *Structural Anthropology* (New York, 1963), pp. 175–8; V. Crapanzano, 'Introduction', in V. Crapanzano and V. Garrison (eds), *Case Studies in Spirit Possession* (New York, 1977), pp. 1–40; G. Oboyesekere, *Medusa's Hair: An Essay on Personal Symbols and Religious Experience* (Chicago, 1981); A. Hultkrantz, 'Ecological and Phenomenological Aspects of Shamanism', in V. Diószegi and M. Hoppál (eds), *Shamanism in Siberia* (Budapest, 1978), pp. 27–58.

14. W. Lebra, *Okinawan Religion: Belief, Ritual, and Social Structure* (Honolulu, 1966), pp. 74–83.

15. B. C. A. Walraven, 'Shamans in Popular Religion around 1900', in H. H. Sørensen (ed.), *Religions in Traditional Korea* (Copenhagen, 1995), pp. 107–30; and 'Interpretations and Reinterpretations of Popular Religion in the Last Decades of the Chosŏn Dynasty', in K. Howard (ed.), *Korean Shamanism: Revivals, Survivals, and Change* (Seoul, 1998), pp. 55–72.

16. L. Kendall, *Shamans, Housewives, and Other Restless Spirits: Women in Korean Ritual Life* (Honolulu, 1985); Ha Hyogil, '*Kwishin*', in

Han'guk minsok taegye, 3 (Seoul, 1982), pp. 401–46; Tae-gon Kim, 'Regional Characteristics of Korean Shamanism', in Chai-shin Yu and R. W. I. Guisso (eds), *Shamanism: The Spirit World of Korea* (Berkeley, 1988), pp. 124–5.

17. Cho Hung-youn, 'Problems in the Study of Korean Shamanism', *Korea Journal*, 25.5 (1985), pp. 18–30 (see, particularly, p. 25), and Youngsook Kim Harvey, *Six Korean Women: The Socialization of Shamans* (St Paul, 1979), p. 11.

18. Riches, 'Shamanism', pp. 381–405.

19. Rouget, *Music and Trance*, pp. 187–226 and 255–314.

20. C. Sachs, *World History of the Dance* (New York, 1963; first published 1937), pp. 41–2.

21. See R. Qureshi, *Sufi Music of India and Pakistan: Sound, Context and Meaning in Qawwali* (Chicago, 1995; first published Cambridge, 1986); J. Becker, 'Tantrism, *Rasa*, and Javanese Gamelan Music', and P. Bohlman, 'World Music and World Religions: Whose World?', both in L. Sullivan (ed.), *Enchanting Powers: Music in the World's Religions* (Cambridge, MA, 1997), pp. 15–60, 61–8.

22. D. Lewiston, sleeve notes to *Music from the Morning of the World* (Elektra Nonesuch 9-79196-2, New York, 1988; first released in 1967).

23. Description taken from I. Wayan Dibia, *Kecak: The Vocal Chant of Bali* (Denpasar, 1996).

24. Hamayon, *La chasse à l'âme*, and 'Shamanism in Siberia: From Partnership in Supernature to Counter-Power in Society', in N. Thomas and C. Humphrey (eds), *Shamanism, History, and the State* (Ann Arbor, 1994), pp. 76–89.

25. Tracks 11–12 on *Kolyma: chants de nature et d'animaux* (Musique du Monde 92566-2, Paris, n.d.). Text cited from p. 22 of the CD booklet. Recordings and texts by Henri Lecomte.

26. Track 9 on *Shaman, Jhankri and Néle* (Ellipsis Arts CD3550, Roslyn, New York, 1997). Recording made in 1991 by Tom Anderson and Tamia Marg-Anderson. Commentary extracted from sleeve notes by B. Kleikamp to *Tuva: Echoes from the Spirit World* (PAN 2013CD, Leiden, 1994).

27. Track 17 on *Dream Songs and Healing Sounds: In the Rainforests of Malaysia* (Smithsonian Folkways CD 40417, Washington, 1995). Text cited from p. 19 of the CD booklet. Recordings and texts by Marina Roseman. For descriptions of tiger ceremonies, see also S. Jennings, *Theatre, Ritual and Transformation: The Senoi Temiars* (London, 1995), pp. 139–86.

28. Track 12 on *Chants chamaniques et narratifs de l'Arctique Sibérien* (Musique du Monde 92564-2, Paris, n.d.). Text cited from pp. 23–4 in the CD booklet (grammar corrected). Recordings and notes by Henri Lecomte.

29. M. M. Balzer, 'Changing Images of the Shaman: Folklore and Politics in the Sakha Republic (Yakutia)', *Shaman*, 4.1 and 2 (1996), pp. 5–8.

30. Balzer, 'Changing Images', p. 12; P. Vitebsky, 'From Cosmology to Environmentalism: Shamanism as Local Knowledge in a Global Setting', in R. Fardon (ed.), *Counterworks: Managing the Diversity of Knowledge* (Routledge, 1995), p. 188.

31. Track 7 on *Chants chamaniques et quotidiens du bassin de l'amour* (Musique du Monde 92671-2, Paris, n.d.). Text cited from p. 25 in the CD booklet (grammar corrected). Recordings and notes by Henri Lecomte.

32. See, for example, M Hoppál, 'Shamanism in a Post-Modern Age', *Shaman*, 4.1 and 2 (1996), pp. 99–107.

33. I. Wayan Dibia, *Kecak*, pp. 25–9 and 54–7.

34. See K. Howard, *Bands, Songs, and Shamanistic Rituals: Folk Music in Korean Society* (Seoul, 1989), chs 7, 9; and 'Preserving the Spirits? Rituals, State Sponsorship, and Performance', in K. Howard (ed.), *Korean Shamanism: Revivals, Survivals, and Change* (Seoul, 1998), pp. 187–215.

35. A. Guillemoz, 'Seoul, la veuve et la *mudang*: les transformations d'un chamanisme urbain', *Diogène*, 158 (1992), pp. 104–15. The shaman musicians appear on a number of CDs with secular musicians, including *Nopsae param* [*East Wind*] (Nices SCO-023CSS, Seoul, 1994), *Kyŏljŏngp'an* [*Final Say*] (Samsung SCO-121CSS, Seoul, 1997), *Ch'ŏnmyŏng* [*Supreme*] (Nices SCO-055CSS, Seoul, 1995), *Eurasian Echoes* (Nices SCO-070CSS, Seoul, 1996), and *West End* (Samsung, SCO-105CSS, 1996).

36. Park, interviewed in August 1990.

37. Hahn Man-young, *Kugak: Studies in Korean Traditional Music* (Seoul, 1991), ch. 2.

38. See K. Howard, 'Sacred and Profane: Searching for the "Shamanistic" *Kutkŏri* and Kindred Rhythmic Cycles', *Han'guk ŭmaksa hangnon* [*Journal of the Society for Korean Historico-Musicology*], 11 (1993), pp. 601–42.

39. V. Erlmann, 'Trance and Music in the Hausa *Bòorii* Spirit Possession Cult in Niger', *Ethnomusicology*, 26.1 (1982), p. 49.

40. Rouget, *Music and Trance*, p. 3.

41. R.-I. Heinze, *Shamans of the Twentieth Century* (New York, 1991).

42. N. Drury, *The Shaman and the Magician: Journeys Between the Worlds* (London, 1982).

43. Harner, *The Way*.

44. R.-I. Heinze, *Trance and Healing in South-East Asia Today* (Berkeley and Bangkok, 1988), p. 85; also 'Shamanic States of Consciousness: Access to Different Realities', in M. Hoppál and K. Howard (eds), *Shamans and Cultures* (Budapest and Los Angeles, 1993), pp. 169–78.

45. J. Blacking, *Music, Culture and Experience* (Chicago, 1995), p. 176.

46. Rouget, *Music and Trance*, p. 325.

47. Rouget, *Music and Trance*, p. 96.

48. J.-J. Rousseau, *Dictionnaire de la musique* (Paris, 1768), p. 312.

49. J.-J. Rousseau, *Essai sur l'origine des langues, où il est parlé de la mélodie et de l'imitation musicale*, ch. 15, cited in Rouget, *Music and Trance*, pp. 167–8. Compare Gentilcore, Léon Sanz, Lüdtke, above.

50. A. Neher, 'A Physiological Explanation of Unusual Behavior in Ceremonies Involving Drums', *Human Biology*, 4 (1962), pp. 151–60.

51. R. Needham, 'Percussion and Transition', *Man*, n.s. 2 (1967), pp. 606–14.

52. Rouget, *Music and Trance*, pp. 172–6.

53. A. Daniélou, *Sémantique musicale: essai de psychophysiologie auditive* (Paris, 1967), p. 72.

54. Kendall, *Shamans, Housewives*, p. 63; and *The Life and Hard Times of a Korean Shaman: of Tales and the Telling of Tales* (Honolulu, 1988), pp. 80–81; B. C. A. Walraven, 'For Gods and Man: Music in Korean Shaman Rituals', in W. Van Zanten (ed.), *Oideion: The Performing Arts Worldwide*, 1 (Leiden, 1993), pp. 44–5; and Howard, 'Why Should Korean Shamans be Women?', *Papers of the British Association for Korean Studies*, 1 (1991), pp. 75–95.

55. Notably, S. Harner and W. W. Tryon, 'Effects of Shamanic Drumming on Salivary Immunoglobulin A, Salivary Immunoglobulin M, Anxiety, and Well-Being', in J. Pentikäinen and M. Hoppál (eds), *Proceedings of the International Association of Historians of Religion, May 1990* (Helsinki, 1992); S. Harner and W. W. Tryon, 'Psychological and Immunological Responses to Shamanic Journeying with Drumming', *Shaman*, 4.1 and 2 (1996), pp. 89–97.

56. Hamayon, *La chasse à l'âme*, pp. 459–73, and Lisha Li, 'The Symbolization Process of the Shamanic Drums used by the Manchu and Other Peoples in North Asia', *Yearbook for Traditional Music*, 24 (1992), pp. 52–80.

57. The Tibetan shaman–oracle Phawo Nyidhon plays the *damaru* pellet drum, rotating it back and forth so that cloth pellets hung from above strike both heads, on track 18 of *Shaman, Jhankri and Néle*.

58. J. H. Nketia, 'Possession Dances in African Societies', *Journal of the International Folk Music Council*, 9 (1957), pp. 4–9.

59. J. Monfouga-Nicolas, *Ambivalence et culte de possession* (Paris, 1972), p. 200.

60. Rouget, *Music and Trance*, p. 69.

61. R. F. Gray, 'The Shetani Cult among the Segeju of Tanzania', in J. Beattie and J. Middleton (eds), *Spirit Mediumship and Society in Africa* (1969), p. 178; M. J. Herskovits, *Dahomey, an Ancient West African Kingdom* (Evanston, 1938), vol. 2, pp. 186–7; and Erlmann, 'Trance and Music', pp. 54–5.

62. An Sain, personal communication, July 1983. An, who has since died, was the 'holder' of Intangible Cultural Asset no. 71, *Cheju ch'ilmŏri tang kut*.

63. Ch'oe Kilsŏng, *Chosŏn musok ŭi hyŏnji yŏn'gu* (Taegu, 1987), esp. pp. 153–4.

64. Walraven, 'For Gods and Man', p. 41.

65. Likewise, in *Piri*, a composition of 1971 by Isang Yun (1917–95), the Western oboe is metamorphosed to represent the pleas of souls unjustly imprisoned.

66. J. Rouch, *La religion et la magie Songhay* (Paris, 1960; 2nd rev. edn, Brussels, 1989); Rouget, *Music and Trance*, pp. 73–8.

67. P. Berliner, *The Soul of Mbira: Music and Traditions of the Shona People of Zimbabwe* (Chicago, 1993), particularly pp. 186–206, and Chartwell Dutiro, personal communication.

68. Cited in P. M. Cook, text for *Shaman, Jhankri and Néle*, p. 33.

CHAPTER SIXTEEN

The Music Therapy Profession in Modern Britain

Helen M. Tyler

St Cecilia, known now as the patron saint of music, was a Christian mystic and martyr who met her death by beheading *c*. 176 AD. Her association with music seems to date from the thirteenth century, when a cult developed from the various legends which had grown up around her,[1] most of which came to include some reference to her musical gifts. In Renaissance works of art, she is depicted playing the organ and singing, although her legend says that she sang 'in her heart to the Lord alone'. The liturgy of St Cecilia includes the phrase 'singing in the heart' and associates this inner music with transformation or conversion. In this bare outline of the story of St Cecilia, we can see some of the universal attributes of music – emotional expressiveness, connection to the inner life, and the power to bring about change. All these elements may have been present in the thinking of Canon Frederick Kill Harford (1832–1906) when he conceived his plan to form a group of 'musician healers' which he named the Guild of St Cecilia.[2] This guild is the starting point from which I shall explore the development of music therapy in Britain, from the 1890s to the 1990s. I shall look at some of the influences which have facilitated this development – the scientific, medical and physiological and the aesthetic, philosophical and psychological – and at how these have come together at the end of the twentieth century in the modern profession of music therapy.

As earlier chapters have shown, the link between music and healing has been recognized over the centuries and across many cultures. Alongside the countless references in history, myth, legend, literature and anecdote, there have also been serious attempts to evaluate the use of music as a form of medical treatment. In modern times, much of the research was by physicians such as Louis Roger[3] and Hector

Chomet,[4] who were fascinated by the idea of using music as an adjunct to healing. Only since music therapy became a recognized profession in the last part of the twentieth century has it been possible, however, to begin to build up a body of research based on clinical practice. It may be that today's researchers will merely corroborate the speculations and theories of the past, but this is a necessary process for a new profession to undergo, no matter how ancient its roots.

The late nineteenth century in Britain was a period of rapid scientific development, particularly in medicine. Alongside advances in medical techniques, there was also a growing awareness of the need to treat the social and psychological aspects of illness. Attention was directed to the poor quality of the conditions that people had to endure in hospitals, and connections were made between improvements in the patients' surroundings and the speed of their recovery. Harford, an accomplished musician, composer, hymn-writer and Minor Canon at Westminster Abbey, had a conviction that music could be an effective form of treatment for certain medical conditions. He devised and carried out some experiments on his own and then set about publicizing and promoting his ideas. He used both the medical and the musical press, his first articles appearing in *The Lancet*[5] and *The Magazine of Music*.[6] In these, he described an occasion where he had successfully used soothing music and a sacred text to induce sleep in an elderly sick woman. His hypothesis was that music could alleviate pain and relieve anxiety, thus having a sedative effect. He appealed to professional musicians to make themselves available to perform for patients and to doctors to take part in some trials in order to test his theories.

In response to these articles, sufficient musicians came to the first rehearsal in 1891 to enable Harford to form the Guild of St Cecilia, which consisted of a group of violinists and female singers. His plan was that, after rehearsing music composed or arranged by him, the Guild would be available to travel to any hospital in London when requested by a doctor. The musicians would be paid for their work, with double fees after midnight. Harford considered it to be essential that the patients should not see the musicians or have any contact with them, so the music would be played from behind a screen or in an adjacent room. Furthermore, he planned to use the newly-invented telephone system as a means of relaying live music to more than one hospital at a time and, eventually, to extend the service to the whole country. A series of experiments was then carried out in which selected patients were treated with music, under the supervision of a doctor, and then interviewed by Harford. He wrote up the results in the medical press.[7] Patients told him that they felt better or were soothed, and one depressed patient reportedly spoke for the first time in two weeks after hearing the music. After the appearance of this article, there came the following sceptical response in the press:

> We have not the slightest wish to throw cold water on any enter-prise, especially one with so laudable an object as attempting to alleviate the pain of the sick or soothe the crucial and critical hour of the moribund. But we have not much faith in Canon Harford's plan of sending music through the telephone to people in the condition mentioned above ... As to the dying, let us hope Nature is kind, letting us down gently so to speak, and removing from our senses, stage by stage, the desire for any sensuous pleasure, music included.[8]

Undaunted, Harford continued with his experiments, extending his repertoire to include lively 'stimulative' music as well as calming 'sedative' music. He again questioned the patients to see which treatment was most effective and wrote up the findings.[9] The results were mixed and Harford admitted that he did not have enough information to draw any firm conclusions. The first patients to receive the treatment were those with 'nervous' conditions; a further development was to treat victims of a scarlet fever epidemic in 1892, using specially trained medical personnel to supply the music so as to avoid infecting the musicians. Again, responses varied. One doctor claimed that music had reduced the patients' fevers,[10] while an editorial in *The Musical Times* ridiculed the idea.

The Guild continued for several more years, but the increasing costs of providing the service and the poor health of its founder prevented it from developing further and, when Harford died in 1906, it soon faded away. An editorial in the *British Medical Journal* acknowledged that the Guild had been useful in some areas, particularly in reducing fever and calming patients, but doubted that music could ever become a recognized form of treatment. It concluded: 'The

St Cecilia Guild – excellent as their intentions were – worked somewhat fitfully and aimed too high.'[11]

After the death of Canon Harford no more was heard of the Guild
of St Cecilia and it might have seemed that his hopes and aspirations
for music in medicine had died with him. Looking back, however, on
the main precepts of his work, it can now be seen that similar ideas
have formed the basis of subsequent developments in music therapy.
The precepts which can be inferred from Harford's venture may be
summarized as follows:

1. That music has the power to affect patients in physical or emo-
    tional distress.
2. That music is effective as a form of treatment, alongside medical
    intervention.
3. That there needs to be co-operation between the medical and
    musical professionals.
4. That training is essential before undertaking the work.
5. That the efficacy of the work must be established by systematic
    evaluation and the publication of research findings.

All these precepts can be found in current definitions and descriptions of music therapy, nearly a century after the demise of the Guild.

Harford had seen the potential of the new invention, the telephone,
for extending his work. In the USA at around the same time, the
phonograph, invented in 1877, opened up further possibilities.[12] With
the aid of gramophone records, music was regularly being used as an
entertainment or distraction by day and as a sedative by night. It was
also played in the operating theatre to calm patients and to help in the
administration of anaesthetics. In a letter to a medical journal, Dr
Evan O'Neil reports using a phonograph in his operating room for
'calming and distracting patients from the horror of the situation',
before and during general anaesthesia.[13] O'Neil and others of his time
were struck by the physiological effectiveness of music applied in this
way, increasing the efficiency of anaesthetics and enhancing post-
operative recovery. It soon came to be used in dentistry, obstetrics,
gynaecology and children's operations, such as tonsillectomies, with
similar results.

Two theoretical stances underpinned these developments. The first was the scientific principle that the sensory stimulus of music entering the nervous system neutralized other stimuli such as pain and fear, thus facilitating medical procedures.[14] The second was the observable influence of music on the mood of the patients in bringing comfort and pleasure while counteracting anxiety, boredom and tension.

Such was the interest in music in American hospitals that several organizations were set up to promote its use, and this eventually led to professional training. The main developments can be tabulated as follows:[15]

1919   Course in Musicotherapy taught at Columbia University by British musician, Margaret Anderton, specializing in treating orthopaedic and paralysis cases.

1926   National Association for Music in Hospitals formed by Isa Maud Ilsen.

1944   Michigan State University – first academic curriculum in music therapy designed.

1945   National Music Council formed a music therapy committee.

1946   Kansas University, Texas, first full academic course taught.

1950   National Association of Music Therapy (NAMT) formed.

In the first half of the twentieth century, in both the USA and Great Britain, we can see the emergence of two distinct applications of music as therapy in medicine. On the one hand, the gramophone and live music provided a therapeutic form of entertainment, and, on the other, music was used as part of a specific medical treatment. These could be described as the 'recreational model' and the 'medical model'. Although following different paths, they were both acknowledging the power of music to bring about change, whether emotional or physical, and both were seen increasingly as contributing to the patient's return to health.

The recreational model in Britain, as in the USA, developed rapidly. It found expression in hospitals through the provision of recorded music, the setting up of choirs, bands and orchestras, and the introduction of professional musicians to perform to the patients. The nineteenth century had seen the burgeoning of music groups and municipal societies, as music-making became available to a far wider section of society than previously. Brass bands, amateur orchestras and choral societies flourished in the wider community but also permeated the hospitals. (In 1879, for example, as we have seen in the preceding chapter, Edward Elgar was appointed Bandmaster of the Worcester County Lunatic Asylum Band, a post which he took seriously as a professional commitment, composing some music especially for the band.) It was particularly in the large mental hospitals, as they were then called, that this kind of activity was encouraged. Patients often stayed there for most of their lifetimes, and the hospital community mirrored the outside world with its provision of recreational activities. Active participation of patients in singing and playing in organized groups was also developing in the first part of the twentieth century, and the therapeutic value of this was increasingly recognized.

During the Second World War, the work of ENSA (Entertainments National Services Association) in taking music to British servicemen, whether active or wounded, was seen as vital to the morale of the troops. When the war ended, a new organization, the Council for Music in Hospitals, was set up by Sylvia Lindsay[16] and from modest beginnings became a well-established charity which now arranges nearly 4,000 concert performances annually throughout Britain.

Children, too, benefited from the growth of music within hospitals. Before the Education (Handicapped Children) Act, 1970, children who were born with disabilities or who developed illnesses like poliomyelitis, often spent many years in hospital. Because of their disabilities, they were deemed inappropriate for normal schooling or, in the terminology of the day, 'ineducable'. Musicians and music teachers working within hospitals found enormous potential within the children, no matter how serious their condition. A report entitled *Music in the Wards*[17] summarizes the teaching of music in Queen Mary's Hospital for Children, Carshalton. Here the emphasis was as much on taking part in musical activities as in listening to music or in using it in a remedial capacity (such as exercising to it). The following is a description of music lessons in a muscular dystrophy ward:

> Muscular dystrophy is not yet curable. Little by little the patient loses the use of his muscles, cannot walk or use his limbs any more. But the physical deterioration itself leaves his mind unim-

paired. In this ward I found 8 boys sitting in wheelchairs round a large table. Their teacher uses music as a creative and intelligent activity which can be kept on for a long time in spite of worsening physical conditions. The boys are taught to read music well and some of them can even follow an orchestral score. They learn singing, and if able to move their fingers, play the bamboo pipe. Thus they are able to express themselves with a musical sound, however small ... [The teacher] seems to be enlarging as much as possible the musical horizon of these boys whose activity of life is relentlessly shrinking.

Later in the same report, Alvin describes music teaching in the cerebral palsy unit for young children:

The teacher of spastic children faces an arduous task. The nature of the illness puts severe limitations to the physical and mental development of the patient. This makes normal contacts and communication difficult. But music reaches these children and can give many of them various emotional and mental experiences that they could not get in any other way ... This music lesson in the ward was an active experience in which each of them could participate. Once more, I was convinced of the power of music to reach the deprived mind and body ...

Here we see two examples of music being used educationally but also therapeutically, with the two complementing each other. We could term this an educational model of music therapy.

The author of that report, Juliette Alvin (1897–1982), was born in France and began her musical career as a professional cellist. On marrying an Englishman, she settled in England and became involved in performing in hospitals, institutions and special schools. Her experience in playing to, and with, people suffering a variety of illnesses and disabilities, led her to organize meetings and information groups for interested doctors and musicians. By 1958, she had attracted sufficient support to form the first music therapy organization in Britain, the Society for Music Therapy and Remedial Music (which in 1967 was renamed the British Society for Music Therapy). The inaugural meeting was attended by musicians, doctors, educationalists, teachers, therapists and students, with the opening address being given by Frank Howes, music critic of *The Times*, on the subject 'The Affects of Music'. The Society flourished, producing a bi-annual news *Bulletin* out of which grew a professional journal, the *Journal of*

British Music Therapy, which was renamed the *British Journal of Music Therapy* in 1995. These events took the newly-emerging discipline of music therapy out of the closed world of the hospital, and placed it in the wider arena, to be open to a broader range of influences. Juliette Alvin was to become one of the most significant figures in these developments, which eventually led to her setting up the first music therapy training course, in 1968, at the Guildhall School of Music in London. Before that took place, however, there was another significant influence to be absorbed, alongside the medical, recreational and educational models, that of analytical psychiatry, or psychoanalysis.

Freud's innovative approach to his patients had several distinct features. The first was the use of free association, in which the patient was asked to relate all his thoughts as they spontaneously occurred. This technique was based on the assumption that the free following of a line of thought would lead the patient to talking about what was most significant. The second feature was the importance Freud attached to the unconscious part of the self or mind, differentiating it from the conscious self. Thirdly, Freud used interpretation to bring the meaning of dreams, thoughts and actions to the patient's consciousness. These techniques were contained within the therapeutic relationship between analyst and patient.

Freud and his followers concentrated mainly on analytic work with individual patients who lay on the couch in the privacy of the consulting room. It was two British analysts, S. H. Foulkes and W. R. Bion, who developed this work in the very different milieu of the military hospital. Many soldiers returning from the war in the 1940s had psychological scars as well as physical injuries. Foulkes and Bion, working separately with groups of soldiers in different hospitals, both found ways of using psychoanalytic techniques to enable their patients to work at their difficulties in groups, facilitated by the analyst. Foulkes called himself the group conductor, using the musical analogy to indicate the principle that everyone should work at their individual parts (or problems) but be held together by their leader.[18] These groups were known as psychotherapy groups, 'psychoanalytic' having a more specific meaning, involving a long-term process of daily analytic sessions.

Psychotherapy groups spread to civilian psychiatric hospitals and became an accepted form of treatment, alongside drugs and other forms of medical intervention. The significance of this for the development of music therapy was that musicians working in psychiatric hospitals in the 1950s were becoming aware of current psychological approaches to treatment. They were making connections between these and their own work, which was experienced as psychological in impact because of the perceived connection between music and the psyche. These musicians began to call themselves music therapists, and became founder members of the Society for Music Therapy and Remedial Music, attending meetings to share ideas, give lectures, and run short training courses (which were precursors of the first professional training). At this time, however, many doctors, while recognizing the general value of music therapy, could not accept it as being a viable form of specific treatment. At a meeting of the Society for Music Therapy and Remedial Music, Dr Henry Rollins, superintendent of Horton Hospital, Epsom, gave a lecture entitled 'Music in a Mental Hospital' which was summarized in the Society's *Bulletin*.[19] Dr Rollins gave a description of the wide range of musical activities in the hospital at that time, where patients put on concerts of classical and popular music, even performing musicals and operettas. He attributed some of these achievements to the fact that there were many trained musicians in the hospital after the war, particularly from central Europe. In his opinion, activity was the key to success in music therapy, while he dismissed recorded music as mere background noise. He praised the efforts of the part-time music therapists in bringing music to all parts of the hospital and contributing to the improvement of the condition of some patients. He warned, however, against too-high expectations:

> Let it be emphasized that at no time was it considered possible that music could replace established methods of treatment such as electro-convulsive treatment, deep insulin therapy, leucotomy, psychotherapy or chemical agents. Music could only be rated as an ancillary form of treatment, or perhaps as a catalyst, facilitating other therapeutic procedures. Music therapy must still be regarded as an experimental project.

Here Dr Rollins uses 'music' and 'music therapy' interchangeably
– common practice at that time when the profession was not yet
established. He also raises the pertinent issue of the function of music
therapy in the hospital: 'It was difficult to specify when this activity
was entertainment or of therapeutic value. Often it was a mixture of
the two and to distinguish between them was futile.' It was difficult,
too, for the pioneer music therapists, who in the course of one day
could be required to change from singing old-time songs with elderly
patients, to accompanying a patient who was an accomplished musician, and then to running a group of the severely mentally ill. Mary
Priestley, a professional violinist who trained as a music therapist with
Alvin, and worked at St Bernard's psychiatric hospital in Southall in
the 1960s and 1970s, describes this period vividly. Answering the
question, 'What is music therapy?', she writes:

> It is rejection and relegation to the file of 'Quackery and
> Witchcraft' in some circles. It is a warm welcome into the multi-
> disciplinary medical team in others. It is toiling round institution
> wards with baskets of percussion instruments and bags of music
> ... It is exploration and astonishment. Frustration and delight.
> But it is always music and people.[20]

One of Priestley's music therapy colleagues at St Bernard's, Gillian
Lovett, describes sing-songs with percussion accompaniment, hymn-
singing, relaxation sessions to music, and monthly classical recitals as
part of the music therapy programme. She continues:

> One of the greatest encouragements to the therapist is when a
> doctor refers a patient for individual help ... There is one young
> woman who has spent all her life either in a Special School or a
> Mental Hospital. She is often aggressive and deluded but is very
> intelligent and artistic ... This patient will go to the piano and
> improvise on a series of chords whose sounds she likes. These
> chords are generally dissonant yet meaningful, and I have known
> her sit for twenty minutes, repeating her strange harmonies again
> and again, appearing at the end to be satisfied in some way. My
> hope is that these sessions may give her the chance to express
> herself and also offer some solace to this very unhappy young
> person.[21]

This more exploratory and individual approach was fostered by the
training course at the Guildhall School of Music, which included

lessons in improvisation. Here the music therapy students were encouraged to forget their formal training and to work with the musical equivalent of free association, improvising atonally, avoiding conventional harmonies and clichés. In this kind of free improvisation, the process of creating the music was of more significance than the finished performance. When such improvisation was encouraged in the hospital setting, the patients' musical skill or aptitude became irrelevant; improvising on accessible percussion instruments they were freed from the necessity or pressure to perform. In an article entitled 'The Identity of a Music Therapy Group – A Developmental Process', Juliette Alvin writes:

> Singing or playing instruments together creates interpersonal musical relationships throughout the session. Drums or percussion instruments can speak to one another and express unlimited kinds of feelings through rhythm, tone and intensity.[22]

She then goes on to describe her method of working, which had moved away from the structured performances of earlier groups:

> I try to make the group work 'the modern way', namely without a conductor, never giving a beat to begin with ... We usually begin with a complete silence of about 30 seconds before the first sound is heard; then anyone can begin as they like.

Here two new ingredients are added to the basic precepts which I drew from the work of the Guild of St Cecilia. The first is improvisation, which would have had no place in the rehearsed performances in nineteenth-century hospitals. The second was the concept of relationship, which had been totally absent from the work of the Guild, where the musicians were hidden from the patients. The relationship between patient and therapist and the shared improvised music were now seen as integral parts of the therapeutic process. Throughout this period of change, the musical framework remained constant, but as in medicine, music itself had gone through far-reaching changes in the early years of the twentieth century. The progression from the harmonic language of Wagner and Richard Strauss, to the atonality of Berg, Webern and Schoenberg, leading to the music of Messiaen, Boulez, Stockhausen, Reich and, especially, Cage, was influential on all musicians, whether or not they consciously espoused the new techniques of composition. Alvin writes of this 'new' music:

> Music therapy benefits from the fact that musical means are becoming richer and available to all ... Contemporary composers of the avant-garde act as explorers in a world of sounds and often provide us with strange experiences.[23]

Rachel Darnley-Smith agrees that the ability of music therapists to improvise in a free and atonal way is in part due to developments in music in the twentieth century.

> Twentieth century musicians have a concept of music and the ears to comprehend such musical sounds ... ranging on a continuum from a recognized harmonic/tonal formula, to sounds whose dissonance may not include resolution and whose musical language and form may not be easily recognizable or logical ... Music therapists work with musical sounds that have not necessarily been crafted into compositions and are at their best raw and spontaneous.[24]

A colleague of Alvin, Julienne Brown, describes the effect of using such music in the clinical setting of a hospital group for people with psychiatric problems:

> Experiments carried out at St George's psychiatric club using rhythmic and atonal improvisation did highlight some of the most important problems met in treating neurotic disorders ... the diagnostic possibilities are enormous and no musical technique on the part of the patients is required.[25]

Thus, we can begin to see a synthesis emerging between the medical, recreational, educational, psychological and musical influences on the developing profession.

At the same time as Alvin was developing her approach to music therapy and to training music therapists, two other pioneers were beginning to create an impact, both in Britain and in America. They were Paul Nordoff and Clive Robbins. They began their collaboration in 1959, when they met by chance in a school where Robbins (b. 1925) was a teacher of children with special needs. Nordoff (1909–76), an American composer, pianist and gifted improviser, was visiting the school to give a recital to the staff. The school, at Sunfield Children's Home in Worcestershire, England, was run on the principles laid down by the philosopher Rudolf Steiner, according to which great emphasis was put on the importance and relevance of music and the other arts in the lives of all people, even the most severely damaged. Nordoff was persuaded by Dr Herbert Geuter, a psychologist running a research programme at the school, to stay on and work experimentally with the children, using improvisation to draw them into a relationship and assessing what improvements could be brought about in their conditions. Robbins, who had a particular interest in using music with his pupils, became his partner in the ensuing research project.

In the period from 1959 to 1960, Nordoff and Robbins worked with both individuals and groups of children with a wide range of needs, disabilities and impairments. In the initial sessions, each child was brought to the music room and was given simple percussion instruments to play such as drum, cymbal, tambourine and bells. While Robbins facilitated or encouraged the child's participation, Nordoff improvised at the piano and with his voice, reflecting and responding to whatever sounds and reactions the child made, whether it was playing, dancing and singing or screaming, crying and rocking. The sessions were all audio-recorded and the results analysed, so that the development of the relationship through the musical participation could be monitored. After this early work Nordoff and Robbins wrote:

> The children were making musical self-portraits of themselves in the way they were reacting. Each was different and it was becoming obvious that there must be a connection between the individual's pathology, personality, psychological condition and the musical self-portrait he or she revealed.[26]

Their approach was based on the premise that there is an innate responsiveness to music that remains unimpaired despite even the most profound handicaps. Nordoff and Robbins eventually came to call this concept 'the music child':

> The Music Child is the individualized musicality inborn in each child ... the universality of musical sensitivity ... and also the distinctly personal significance of each child's musical responsiveness.[27]

The theories of the Anthroposophical movement, as propounded by Steiner, were influential on the thinking of Nordoff and Robbins at this time. The Music Child can be related to Steiner's concept of the 'astral body', which has clear roots in the classical analogy between *musica humana* and *musica mundana*. Writing about the universality of music, Steiner said: 'this is the work of the astral body which is a musician in every human being, and imitates the music of the cosmos'.[28] Although the work of Nordoff and Robbins was undoubtedly influenced by Steiner's philosophy and incorporated some of his musical concepts, such as the theory of intervals, they did not embrace the Anthroposophical school of music therapy. This acquired a small following, particularly in Germany, and had a unique approach. Steiner's insistence on natural materials and his abhorrence of mechanical products led to the use of wooden lyres, recorders and pipes and the banning of the piano or other 'mechanical' instruments from the music therapy sessions.

Nordoff and Robbins left Britain and continued their research as part of a team in a day-care unit for autistic children, funded by the University of Pennsylvania in Philadelphia, USA. Here they were able to progress beyond their early diagnostic work into showing how the use of improvisational music therapy could bring about change, first in the musical relationship with the therapist and then in daily life generally. Their work was meticulously recorded on tape, and afterwards analysed and evaluated according to rating scales which they had devised. This material then formed the basis of their joint books which contain many descriptions of children's therapy sessions. In one case, a five-year-old boy, described as psychotic and autistic, unable to speak and with disturbed, volatile behaviour, found in his music therapy sessions an outlet for his distressed and frustrated feelings. Through matching his screams and body movements with music of equal intensity, Nordoff and Robbins were able to build a relationship of trust with the child. Gradually, his screaming turned to crying–singing, and his singing developed into speech, thus improving his ability to make relationships, communicate and fulfil his potential.[29]

A second case study describes in detail the progress of therapy with an emotionally-disturbed girl, Audrey, who had been sent to live in a residential school because of her uncontrollable behaviour. The central part of her therapy was the musical re-enactment of the fairy-tale of Cinderella, in which Audrey and the therapists improvised the story and the music. Through shared improvisation, a rich and powerful musicality emerged from the troubled child, and for the first time in her life she could express her deepest fears and feelings. Aigen writes:

> [Nordoff and Robbins] did not merely tell the story to Audrey but rather *lived* it with her. It was their ability to approach the story seriously and as a myth and with an important inherent psychological experience which allowed her to use the story as the vehicle for the resolution of an inner crisis leading to a dawning self-awareness.[30]

This experience enabled her to find the strength to overcome many of her difficulties, and eventually she went home to live with her family.

Nordoff and Robbins returned to Britain in 1974 to set up the first Nordoff–Robbins training course, based on their approach to improvisational music therapy. The course was specifically designed for musicians with a high level of skill at the piano to become therapists, working with children with special needs. Later, the remit of the course expanded to include the music therapy of adults.

By 1976 there were two professional training courses in music therapy, one at the Guildhall and the other run by Nordoff and Robbins, both giving a postgraduate diploma as a qualification. Music therapists who had completed the training were employed by the National Health Service, the Department of Education, and the social services. At this point pay and conditions were quite haphazard and there was still no official recognition of the qualification. The next stage was to create a career and pay structure that would recognize the growth and development of the profession. In 1976 the Association of Professional Music Therapists (APMT) was formed and this became the governing and representative body of the profession, with membership open only to fully trained and qualified music therapists. As a result of the APMT's campaigning work, in 1982 the Department of Health and Social Security awarded music therapists a career and grading structure, comparable with that of other paramedical professions. The APMT has remained the official body of the profession, while the pioneering organization, the BSMT, has taken on the role of publicizing the profession through meetings, workshops and publications, with its membership open to lay people as well as professionals. As the profession became more firmly established, further training courses were developed and the number of music therapists increased. The following is a summary of the significant dates in the recent history of music therapy:

1958   Society for Music Therapy and Remedial Music formed, renamed The British Society for Music Therapy (BSMT) in 1967.

1968   Guildhall School of Music and Drama, London. First training course.

1974   Goldie Leigh Hospital, Surrey, first training course taught by Paul Nordoff and Clive Robbins (now at the Nordoff–Robbins Music Therapy Centre in North London).

1976   Association of Professional Music Therapists (APMT) formed.

1980   Research Fellowship set up at the City University, London. Southlands College (now Roehampton Institute), new course.

1982   Award of pay and grading structure for music and art therapists by the Department of Health and Social Security.

1991   Bristol University, first part-time course.

1994   Anglia Polytechnic University, first MA course.

1996   State Registration of music therapy achieved.

1997   Welsh College of Music and Drama, new course.

The development of new courses increased the number of practising music therapists in Britain from a few dozen to nearly 400 (in 1998). This can be compared with the growth of the profession in the USA where there are over seventy training courses available and over 3,000 music therapists (1998). In the USA many of the courses are at undergraduate level, followed by a period of internship. In Britain all training is postgraduate, with applicants already having a first degree or the equivalent in music. A high standard of musicianship and competence on an instrument is essential and auditions include performance of repertoire and improvisation as well as an intensive interview to assess personal qualities. Successful completion of the training after one or two years leads either to a diploma in music therapy or to a Master's degree, depending on the length and intensity of the course. Following initial qualification, there is a mandatory period of work under supervision before full membership of the APMT is given. The curriculum and theoretical orientation of each course varies slightly, but there is a basic module of training and a list of core competencies which the courses have all agreed. All trainings give the students experience of working under supervision with adults and children with various special needs, disabilities or illnesses and lectures give a background to the medical and psychological conditions of clients. Improvisational skills are taught and the trainings also include voice and movement classes. Increasingly, students are being introduced to research methodology and are required to present dissertations. With the demand from employers for evidence of clinical effectiveness, research has become of even greater importance.

As the training and research have developed, so too has the range of places in which music therapy is accepted. The work in general and psychiatric hospitals has been extended to include hospices, units for people with cancer or AIDS, and specialist areas such as neurology, eating disorders, addiction or Alzheimer's disease. As in the USA during the early years of the century, music therapy is making a contribution to pain relief and to reducing the quantities of anaesthetic needed in operations. In the wider community, forensic psychiatry has been a recent area of expansion with music therapy being given to offenders in secure units.[31] There has also been a specialization by some music therapists in the field of child protection, working with children who have suffered emotional, physical or sexual abuse.

Despite all these positive advances, the sceptical attitude of Canon Harford's detractors remains evident in many quarters and music therapy continues to fight to be taken seriously as a profession. In theory, the profession has never been safer – it enjoys official state recognition, validated training courses and a well-organized professional body. In reality, it is the success of recent years which is bringing new problems, for a highly-skilled and trained therapist needs financial recognition alongside professional status. When resources are scarce all sections of the arts become vulnerable, and are required to justify their existence in measurable financial terms. Just as classical music is under pressure to become increasingly 'popular' to make money, so music therapy still struggles to be accepted as a serious intervention for people in need, precisely because it will not necessarily be 'cost-effective'.

One of the causes of the eventual demise of the Guild of St Cecilia was lack of funding. The 'obituary' of the Guild stated that it 'aimed too high'. It is vital that today's music therapists continue to aim as high, but, at the same time, they must ensure that the profession in modern Britain does not meet the same fate.

Notes

1.   T. Connolly, *Mourning into Joy: Music, Raphael, and Saint Cecilia* (New Haven and London, 1995), pp. 219–21.

2.   W. B. Davis, 'Music Therapy in Victorian England', *Journal of British Music Therapy*, 2 (1988), pp. 10–17.

3.   See Gouk, Chapter 8.

4.   See Commentary on Part V.

5.   F. K. Harford, 'Music in Illness' (Letter to the Editor), *The Lancet* (4 July 1891), p. 43.

6.   Harford, 'Music in Illness' (Letter to the Editor), *Magazine of Music* (August 1891), p. 159.

7.   Harford, 'The Guild of St Cecilia' (Letter to the Editor), *The British Medical Journal* (26 Sept. 1891), p. 714.

8.   Editorial, *Musical Opinion and Trade Review* (Oct. 1891), p. 4.

9.   Harford, 'Is Exhilarating or Soft Music Best for Invalids?' (Letter to the Editor), *The British Medical Journal* (October 1891), p. 770.

10.   J. E. Hunter, 'Is Music a Calmative in Case of Fever?' (Letter to the Editor), *The British Medical Journal* (October 1892), p. 923.

11.   'Music as a Hypnotic' (Editorial), *The British Medical Journal* (March 1896), p. 679.

12.   D. B. Taylor, 'Music in General Hospital Treatment', *The Journal of Music Therapy*, 18 (1981), pp. 62–73. Harford had also envisaged using the phonograph: Davis, 'Music Therapy in Victorian England', p. 13.

13.   E. O. Kane, 'Phonograph in the Operating Room', *Journal of the American Medical Association*, 62 (1914), p. 1829.

14.   E. Gatewood, cited from Taylor, 'Music in General Hospital Treatment', pp. 64–5.

15.   L. Bunt, *Music Therapy: An Art beyond Words* (London, 1994), p. 4.

16.   S. Lindsay, *A Songbird for the Heart: The Story of the Council for Music in Hospitals* (Durham, 1995).

17.   J. Alvin, *Music in the Wards: Queen Mary's Hospital for Children, Carshalton, and Surrey* (London, 1958), pp. 4–5, 8.

18. S. H. Foulkes, *Group Analytic Psychotherapy: Method and Principles* (London, 1975).

19. H. Rollins, 'Music in Mental Hospitals', *Bulletin of the Society for Music Therapy and Remedial Music*, 10 (1962), p. 2.

20. M. Priestley, *Music Therapy in Action* (London, 1975), p. 15.

21. G. Lovett, 'Pioneers of Music Therapy', *British Journal of Music Therapy*, 2.1 (1969), p. 16.

22. J. Alvin, 'The Identity of a Music Therapy Group', *British Journal of Music Therapy*, 6.3 (1975), p. 14.

23. J. Alvin, *Music Therapy* (London, 1975), pp. 104–5.

24. R. Darnley-Smith, 'What do Music Therapists Hear?', unpublished paper presented at the 'Music and the Psyche' Conference, City University, London (1996), p. 2.

25. J. Brown, cited from Alvin, *Music Therapy*, p. 105.

26. P. Nordoff and C. Robbins, *Therapy in Music for Handicapped Children* (London, 1973), p. 34.

27. P. Nordoff and C. Robbins, *Creative Music Therapy* (New York, 1977), p. 1.

28. R. Steiner, cited from K. Bruscia, *Improvisational Models of Music Therapy* (Springfield, 1987), p. 31.

29. Nordoff and Robbins, *Creative Music Therapy*, pp. 23–36.

30. K. Aigen, *Paths of Development in Nordoff–Robbins Music Therapy* (Gilsum, 1998), pp. 33–4.

31. C. Teasdale (ed.), *Guidelines for Arts Therapists Working in Prisons: Art Therapy, Dance Movement Therapy, Drama Therapy, Music Therapy* (Croydon, 1997).

Index

accidents of the soul, *see* non-
  naturals
AC/DC 6
Agrippa, Heinrich Cornelius 174
AIDS 13
Aldobrandino of Siena 135–6, 139
Aldridge, David 11, 330
allopathic medicine 8, 21
Alvin, Juliette 19–20, 249, 317, 381–
  2, 384–6
Alzheimer's disease 13
Anastenarides (Greek Macedonia) 18
anthropology, *see* social
  anthropology *under* music
  therapy
Anthroposophy, *see* Steiner, Rudolf
Arabic medicine
  medieval 26–7, 28, 45–6, 105
  translation into Latin 105, 133,
    147
Arabic, translation from Greek into
  76–7
Aristides Quintilianus 65
Aristotle 64, 104, 106, 112, 147–8,
  216
Arnald of Villanova 136, 139, 219,
  221, 227
Asclepiades of Bithynia 61–2
Association of Professional Music
  Therapists 389, 390
astrology 80, 87, 105, 147, 156, 161,
  167, 180, 220
attunement 15, 58, 64,
Augustine, St 164, 223
aulos (reed instrument) 59–60
Avicenna 137
Awakenings, *see* Sacks, Oliver
Ayres, Philip 213
Ayurveda 6–7, 44, 47, 85–6

Baglivi, Giorgio 250, 265, 274, 282,
  322, 324
Bartholomaeus Anglicus 28, 129,
  133
Berlioz, Hector 328, 348, 350
biblical commentary 123
Black Death, *see* plague
Blacking, John 17–18, 353, 364–5
Blavatsky, Helena Petrovna 329
Boethius 29, 61, 66, 103, 124, 223,
  225
Bogs, Fantastic Tale of 339–41
Brethren of Purity 73, 79, 80, 81
British Society for Music Therapy
  381, 389
Brocklesby, Richard 20, 178, 189,
  316, 329
Browne, Richard 178, 316, 329
Buchan, William 183
Bunt, Leslie 15, 19–20
Burney, Charles 322, 324–5
Burton, Robert 9, 20, 28, 149, 174–
  5, 179–83, 187, 226, 227, 228,
  231

Cage, John 32, 317, 385
Campion, Thomas 181
Canterbury, religious houses in 109–
  11
Cantigas de Santa Maria 9
Caputo, Nicola 266–7
Cardano, Girolamo 31
Castiglione, Baldessare 227, 231,
  261
Cecilia, St 350, 375
  Guild of 375–8, 385
cell cultures, response *in vitro* to
  music 5–7
chain of being 198

Cheyne, George 188–9
China, *see* music therapy, history
Chomet, 'Hector' 329, 375–6
Christianity, early, and medicine 104
Cid, Francisco Xavier 273–4, 275,
      277, 278, 284, 287–8
classical tradition 2, 7, 44, 112
*Companion Encyclopedia of the
      History of Medicine* 22
composition, human being as 11, 12
confession as medical process 116,
      118
conjuring spirits 16–18, 52–3, 318;
      see also magic
consilia (letters of medical advice)
      25
Constantine the African
      (Constantinus Africanus) 28,
      127, 133, 219
contra-naturals 27, 134
Cosman, Madeleine Pelner 106
cosmic harmony, *see musica
      mundana*
culture-bound syndrome 250, 269–70

Damon 57
dancing
      epidemic 181, 251–2
      therapy 61, 137, 138
Darnley-Smith, Rachel 386
David and Saul 20, 29, 70, 104, 106,
      121, 123–4, 127, 129, 183, 197,
      200–202, 205–8, 223
David's harp as symbolic cross 104,
      127, 128
De Martino, Ernesto 249, 268–9,
      294–302, 307
      criticism of 298–301
Dols, Michael 74
Du Bartas, Guillaume 149, 195–6,
      200–211
Dunstan, St 109

Eadmer 109
Earl, Pliny 348
Eden, Garden of 203–5
Elgar, Sir Edward 349, 380
emblem literature 150, 213, 215,
      221, 228, 230
ENSA 380
entrainment, *see* attunement
epilepsy 61, 63, 180
Esquirol, Etienne 343–4
ethos 26, 45, 47, 57–8, 147, 168
exorcism 104, 117, 124; *see also*
      David and Saul

al-Farabi 74, 113
Farinelli 20, 29
Ferdinando, Epifanio 264
Ferrant, Jacques 218, 220
fever 162
Ficino, Marsilio 148, 154–71, 174,
      175, 178, 179, 182, 184, 239,
      260, 316, 318
      'Fitting One's Life to the
      Heavens' 159, 164–7, 190
flowers 234
Fludd, Robert 175, 327
Fourth Lateran Council 115
Freud, Sigmund 382
Friedson, Steven M. 18

Galen 26, 44, 46, 134, 185, 218
Gemisthos Pletho 160
Gemüth 321; *see also* Illenau asylum
Ginzburg, Carlo 252–3
Gnawa 70–71
Gouk, Penelope 3, 18, 22
Gregorian chant 9
Grocheio, Johannes de 112, 118

Hamadisha 70
Hanslick, Eduard 29–30
Harford, Frederick Kill 317, 375–8

Harmony of the Spheres, *see musica mundana*
Hebrews 7; *see also* David and Saul
Hermeticism 154–5, 156; *see also* occult philosophy
Hildegard of Bingen 31
Hippocrates 26
Homer, *Odyssey* 54
Homeric hymns 52
hospitals, music therapy in 73–5, 320, 382–4
  Islamic 47
  modern 379–80
  monastic infirmaries 107, 110–11
humoral medicine 26, 29, 32
  decline of 29, 316
  early medieval 105
Hunain ibn Ishaq (Johannitius) 27, 78, 133–4

Iamblichus 160
iatrogenic disease 14
iatromusicology 261
Ibn Butlan 135
Ibn Hindu 46, 80
Illenau asylum 320, 346–8, 350
incantation, *see* magic
India, *see* music therapy, history
infirmary, *see* hospitals

Jackson, Stanley 28
Janzen, John 17, 18
Jenty, Charles Nicholas 189–90
John of Erfurt 114
Jubal Cain 200, 206
Jung, Carl Gustav 331
Justin II, Byzantine emperor 62, 104

Kabbalah 148
katharsis 96
Kerner, Justinus 327
keyboard instruments, decoration of 232–5

al-Kindi 80
Kircher, Athanasius 175, 183, 261–3, 274
Korea, *see* shamanism
Krafft-Ebing, Richard von 347
Kümmel, Werner 23–32, 106, 343

Lambert, Constant 4
lambda formula 197–8
Langer, Susanne 15
Lanternari, Vittorio 300
Lapassade, George 301–2, 303
Lemba cult 17
Lewis, Ioan 300–301
Lichtenthal, Peter 30, 344
Liszt, Franz 319, 328, 341–3
little vein 131–2
liturgy, therapy of 31
love
  cultural history of 215–17
  imagery in treatment of 230, 232–5
  pathology of 217–21
lovesickness 62, 112–13, 135, 150, 213–39, 319
lute 79, 231
lyre 53–5, 56, 57, 58, 59–60, 70, 161, 163, 169, 197, 200

madness, divine, inspired, creative 162, 182
magic 43, 47, 54, 60, 76, 85, 148, 158, 255
  and music therapy 31
  see also natural magic; occult philosophy
Mahler, Gustav 53
Maier, Michael 31
Maimonides 72
Malaysia 17
Malleus maleficarum 124
mania 129–30
mantra 85, 87

Martianus Capella 59, 61
Mead, Roger 180
Medici, Cosimo de' 155
Medici, Lorenzo de Pierfrancesco de'
        170–71
medicine
    ancient 28, 43, 52–66; see also
        Galen; Rufus of Ephesus
    Chinese 43
    early modern 173, 178–9, 184–5;
        see also Renaissance
    Indian 85–7
    medieval European 28, 218–19
    monastic 9
    practical in Middle Ages 134–5,
        136
    see also Arabic medicine;
        Ayurveda; Christianity;
        humoral medicine
'Medicine of the Prophet' 46
melancholy (melancholia) 24, 28,
        124, 129–30, 137, 162, 173,
        174, 182, 186, 187, 228; see
        also Burton, Robert
Mesmer, Franz Anton 326–7
Mesmerism 326–9, 341
Metsu, Gabriel 237
Middle Ages, definition of 147
Molière 149
monochord 10
moral management, therapy,
        treatment 320, 349
Mozart, Wolfgang Amadeus 326,
        328
Mozart effect 13
Music and Medicine, ed. Schullian
        and Schoen 21–2
'Music and the Mind', TV series 11
Music Thanatology, School of 9
music, omnipresence of 4–5
music theory
    Arabic 79
    early modern 222; see also neo-.

Platonism
    Indian 84–8, 89, 91–2
    Platonic 58–9, 63–4, 103, 106,
        147, 261–2; see also Plato;
        neo-Platonism
music therapy 1
    appeal to history 7
    definition of 2, 14, 384
    scope 12–13, 135, 185, 391
    social anthropology 16–19
music therapy, contemporary 315
    criteria of success 14
    effectiveness of 13–15
    effects of 14
    and the family 12
    as form of diagnosis 16
    illustration of 14–15
    in operating theatre 12–13
    in prisons 13
music therapy, history
    ancient 44, 52–66; see also ethos;
        Pythagoras
    asylums 320, 325, 343, 346–9
    Chinese 44, 47–8
    continuity in 21, 316–17
    cosmology 27, 55–6, 109–11,
        147–9, 150, 165–8, 196–8
    early medieval 105
    early modern English 225
    esoteric traditions 8; see also
        Mesmerism; occultism;
        Theosophy
    Indian 44, 47, 84–96
    Islamic 70–82, 147
    Jewish 69–70, 72–3, 76
    medical profession 138
    medieval 23
    narrative literature 29, 118
    nineteenth-century German 338,
        342–8
    Paracelsian 151–2
    phonograph 378
    physical disorder 60–62, 103

pre-classical 43, 51–2
psychological disorder 26, 55, 56, 59, 61, 62, 73, 103, 114, 135, 320; *see also* scope *under* music therapy
recreation 115, 121, 123
relationship of theory to practice 2, 25, 45, 121, 136–9, 170–71, 317, 319
repertory 226–7, 325
role of women 325
scepticism about metaphysics 107, 110–12, 113–14, 317
USA 321–5
see also under individual diseases; hospitals; liturgy; love-sickness; magic; pulse
music therapy, modern profession 316
  Britain 375–92
  Europe and America 8, 13, 379, 386–9
  and social anthropology 17–18, 70–71
  training courses 13, 382, 384–5, 389–91
musica humana 25, 27, 103, 159, 207, 208, 223, 330, 388
musica instrumentalis 27, 103, 159, 209, 223, 327, 330
musica mundana 27, 64–5, 80, 103, 109, 157, 159, 175, 198, 203, 327, 388; *see also* attunement
muzak 5

Napier, Richard 31
natural magic 173–4; *see also* occult philosophy
naturals 27, 79, 133–4; *see also* contra-naturals; non-naturals
neo-Platonism 148–50, 156–8, 160, 166–9, 175, 179, 196–8, 209–10, 261–2, 319

New Age 8–9
New Grove Dictionary 22
Newton, Isaac 174, 188
Niceta, bishop of Remesiana 104
non-naturals 27, 28, 29, 105, 107, 134–5, 148, 173, 183, 185, 188, 226
Nordoff, Paul 330, 386–9, 390
Novalis 3, 23
nuovi tarantati 251, 303–5

occult philosophy 148, 173; *see also* Hermeticism
occultism 326, 329–30
Ofhuys, Gaspar 120–33, 139
Orpheus 19, 54, 148, 149, 154, 197, 198, 200, 201, 202, 204–6, 210, 226–7, 318
Orphic poems 56, 155, 161, 163, 169, 170
Ovid 220, 226

Paracelsus 151–2, 181, 327
Pargeter, William 183
Parkinsonism 11
passions of the soul, *see* non-naturals
Paul, St, as patron of *tarantati* 266–7, 268, 296, 298, 299–300, 302–3
pauliani 253
Perkins School for the Blind 324
Persia 7, 46
phrenitis 128–30, 181
plague 27, 54
Plato 57–8, 60, 157, 216
Plotinus 157–60, 175
Poliziano 169
Pontano, Giovanni 259–60
primordial sounds 6
psychiatry 320
Ptolemy 65, 168–9
pulse, music of 24, 63, 134, 185
Purcell, Henry 239

Pythagoras 20, 45, 55, 147, 197, 249
Pythagoreans 56–7, 63–4
    and music therapy 60, 103

rāga 89–90, 92–3, 96
Ramos de Pereja 168
rasa 92
Raudnitz, Leopold 342
al-Razi (Rhazes) 46
Red Cloister 122
regimen 135–6
Reil, Johann Christian 338
Renaissance 147; *see also* early
    modern *under* medicine
rhythm, in music and neuro-
    physiology 12
Richard of Middleton 117–18
Robbins, Clive 330, 386–9, 390
Robertson, Paul 11
Rodericus a Castro 23–4
Roger, Louis 178, 316, 329, 375
Romantic music
    harmful effects of 319, 339–42
    psychiatry and 339
Romanticism 319, 339
Roseman, Marina 17–18, 359
Rossi, Annabella 298
Rouget, Gilbert 301, 357, 363, 365
Rufus of Ephesus 46, 62, 150
Rush, Benjamin 322–4

Sacks, Oliver 10–11
Salernitan questions 113
Sāmaveda 89–90
śānti 87
sciatica 61
Schneider, Peter Joseph 344–6
Schoenberg, Arnold 331
Schopenhauer, Arthur 319
Schubert, Franz 328
Scientific Revolution 149
Scott, Cyril 331–2
Scriabin, Alexander 331

Sekeles, Chava 69
Serao, Francesco 265–6
shamanism 3, 19, 44, 52, 252, 353–
    69
    definition of 354–6, 358–9
    discontinuity in history of 318
    drums 52, 354, 360, 365–7
    female 318, 353
    instruments 368–9
    Korean 318, 353, 356–7, 362–3,
        367–8
    Siberian 359–61
Sigerist, Henry 22
Smashing Pumpkins 9
snakebite 61, 86
social anthropology, *see* music
    therapy
Society for Music Therapy and
    Remedial Music 381, 383, 390
Sophocles 53
soul
    actions of 187
    therapy 29, 116–17
Spintge, Ralph 11
Steiner, George 5
Steiner, Rudolf 330, 387–8
Stockhausen, Karlheinz 32, 317,
    332, 385
St Vitus's chorea 282; *see also*
    dancing, epidemic
Sud Sound System 303–4
Sufism 357, 361
syphilis 24

al-Tabari 78
tarantella 265, 277–8, 284, 286, 293
tarantism 20, 22, 178, 181, 183–4,
    249, 365
    analysis of 256–7, 268–9, 277–8,
        293–4, 295
    contemporary Italy 293–308
    early modern Italy 250, 255–70
    medieval 251–2

North American 251
Spanish 250, 273–89
    case histories 275, 278–88
    and music theory 275
    music therapy 283–8
    non-musical therapies 282–6
    symptoms 280–82
    supposed ancient origins 252
    see also nuovi tarantati
Theosophy 329–30
Timotheus 208
Tinctoris, Johannes 23, 29, 227
Tippett, Sir Michael 331
trance 318, 357–8, 363–6
Turchini, Angelo 300
Turner, Victor 18

university medicine 185
    and music 29, 103, 139

van der Goes, Hugo 106, 120–23,
    127–9, 139–40
vibro-acoustic bed 13
vimbuza (northern Malawi) 16

Wagner, Richard 319, 328, 385
William of Auvergne 113, 115
Witten Herdecke, University of 11,
    330
World Federation of Music Therapy
    13, 14
Wright, Thomas 183, 187

Xenocrates of Chalcedon 59

Yoga 94
York Retreat 324, 349

Zarlino, Gioseffo 148